Business Politics and the State in Twentieth-Century Latin America

Despite the new prominence of business in the political economy of postreform Latin America, business politics remains a relatively neglected area of research. This book is the first systematically comparative and historical analysis of the incorporation of business into politics in Latin America. It examines business organizing and political activity over the past century in five of the largest, most developed countries of the region to construct an explanation for why business ended up better organized in Chile, Colombia, and Mexico than in Argentina and Brazil. The explanation for the surprising cross-national variations lies in neither economic characteristics of business nor broader political parameters, but rather in the cumulative effect of actions of state officials. The book also considers the consequences of these differences in organization and finds that stronger encompassing associations offer government officials opportunities for concerted policy making with business that can enhance policy implementation. The strong hand of the state in organizing business has important implications not only for theories of collective action, but also for our understanding of civil society and its potential to promote democratization.

Ben Ross Schneider is Professor of Political Science at Northwestern University. Schneider's articles and other publications focus on a range of issues in Latin American politics and development including privatization, democratization, regional integration, corporate organization, and market-oriented reforms. He is the author of *Politics within the State* (1991) and coeditor of *Business and the State in Developing Countries* (1997) and *Reinventing Leviathan* (2003). He has received fellowships and research funding from the Tinker Foundation, the Searle Foundation, the Heinz Foundation, and the Fulbright Program.

Business Politics and the State in Twentieth-Century Latin America

BEN ROSS SCHNEIDER

Northwestern University

CAMBRIDGE
UNIVERSITY PRESS

PUBLISHED BY THE PRESS SYNDICATE OF THE UNIVERSITY OF CAMBRIDGE
The Pitt Building, Trumpington Street, Cambridge, United Kingdom

CAMBRIDGE UNIVERSITY PRESS
The Edinburgh Building, Cambridge CB2 2RU, UK
40 West 20th Street, New York, NY 10011-4211, USA
477 Williamstown Road, Port Melbourne, VIC 3207, Australia
Ruiz de Alarcón 13, 28014 Madrid, Spain
Dock House, The Waterfront, Cape Town 8001, South Africa

http://www.cambridge.org

First published 2004

Printed in the United States of America

Typeface Sabon 10/13 pt.   *System* LATEX 2$_\varepsilon$ [TB]

A catalog record for this book is available from the British Library.

Library of Congress Cataloging in Publication Data

Schneider, Ben Ross.
Business politics and the State in twentieth-century Latin America / Ben Ross Schneider.
    p. cm.
Includes bibliographical references (p.) and index.
ISBN 0-521-83651-4 (hardback) – ISBN 0-521-54500-5 (pbk.)
    1. Business and politics – Latin America – History – 20th century.   2. Industrial
policy – Latin America – History – 20th century.   3. Latin America – Politics and
government – 20th century.   I. Title.
JL964.P7S36   2004
322'.3'098–dc22   2004040684

ISBN 0 521 83651 4 hardback
ISBN 0 521 54500 5 paperback

For Kate

Contents

List of Tables

List of Abbreviations

Note: To keep clutter out of the text, English translations are included only here. Longer acronyms are sometimes given as capitalized nouns, largely in keeping with common usage in the literature of the respective countries. Most others are all in capital letters.

AAPIC   Asociación Argentina de la Producción, la Industria y el Comercio (Argentine Association of Production, Industry, and Commerce)

ABA   Asociación de Bancos de la Argentina (Association of Banks of Argentina)

ABDIB   Associação Brasileira para o Desenvolvimento das Indústrias de Base (Brazilian Association for the Development of Basic Industries)

ABIF   Asociación de Bancos e Instituciones Financieras, Chile (Association of Banks and Financial Institutions)

ABIMAQ   Associação Brasileira da Indústria de Máquinas e Equipamentos (Brazilian Association for the Machinery and Equipment Industry)

ABINEE   Associação Brasileira da Indústria Elétrica e Eletrônica (Brazilian Association for the Electrical and Electronic Industry)

ABIQUIM   Associação Brasileira da Indústria Química (Brazilian Association for the Chemical Industry)

ABM	Asociación de Banqueros de México (Association of Bankers of Mexico)
ABRA	Asociación de Bancos de la República Argentina (Association of Banks of the Republic of Argentina)
ACIEL	Acción Coordinadora de las Instituciones Empresariales Libres, Argentina (Coordinating Action of Free Enterprise Institutions)
Acopi	Asociación Colombiana de Medianas y Pequeñas Industrias (Colombian Association of Medium and Small Industries, originally Asociación Colombiana Popular de Industriales)
ADEBA	Asociación de Bancos Argentinos (Association of Argentine Banks)
AMCB	Asociación Mexicana de Casas de Bolsa (Mexican Association of Stock Brokers)
AMIS	Asociación Mexicana de Instituciones de Seguros (Mexican Association of Insurance Institutions)
ANAC	Asamblea Nacional Constituyente, Colombia (National Constituent Assembly)
ANDI	Asociación Nacional de Industriales, Colombia (National Association of Industrialists)
Anfavea	Associação Nacional dos Fabricantes de Veículos Automotores, Brazil (National Association of Manufacturers of Automotive Vehicles)
ANIF	Asociación Nacional de Instituciones Financieras, Colombia (National Association of Financial Institutions)
ANIQ	Asociación Nacional de la Industria Química
ANTAD	Asociación Nacional de Tiendas de Autoservicio y Departamentales, Mexico (National Association of Self-Service and Department Stores)
APEGE	Asamblea Permanente de Entidades Gremiales Empresarias, Argentina (Permanent Assembly of Business Associations)
Asexma	Asociación de Exportadores de Manufacturas, Chile (Association of Manufacturing Exporters)
Asobancaria	Asociación Bancaria de Colombia (Banking Association of Colombia)
Asocaña	Asociación de Cultivadores de Caña de Azúcar, Colombia (Association of Sugar Cane Growers)

Asocoflores	Asociación Colombiana de Productores de Flores (Colombian Association of Flower Producers)
ATI	Association of Thai Industries
BDI	Bundesverband der Deutschen Industrie (Association of German Industry)
CAC	Cámara Argentina de Comercio (Argentine Chamber of Commerce)
CACIP	Confederación Argentina del Comercio, la Industria y la Producción (Argentine Confederation of Commerce, Industry, and Production)
Camacol	Cámara Colombiana de la Construcción (Colombian Chamber of Construction)
Canacintra	Cámara Nacional de la Industria de Transformación, Mexico (National Chamber for the Manufacturing Industry)
Canaco-DF	Cámara Nacional de Comercio, Mexico City (National Chamber of Commerce)
CAPIC	Confederación Argentina de la Producción, la Industria y el Comercio (Argentine Confederation of Production, Industry, and Commerce)
CARBAP	Confederación de Asociaciones Rurales de Buenos Aires y La Pampa (Confederation of Rural Associations of Buenos Aires and La Pampa)
CBI	Confederation of British Industry
CCAP	Consejo de Cámaras y Asociaciones de la Producción, Ecuador (Council of Chambers and Associations of Production)
CCE	Consejo Coordinador Empresarial, Mexico (Business Coordinating Council)
CDE	Conselho de Desenvolvimento Econômico, Brazil (Economic Development Council)
CDES	Conselho de Desenvolvimento Econômico e Social, Brazil (Council for Economic and Social Development, 2003–)
CDI	Conselho de Desenvolvimento Industrial, Brazil (Industrial Development Council)
CEA	Congreso Empresario Argentino, 1948–9 (Argentine Business Congress)
CEA	Consejo Empresario Argentino, 1967– (Argentine Business Council)

CEESP	Centro de Estudios Económicos del Sector Privado, Mexico (Center for Economic Studies of the Private Sector)
CEPB	Confederación de Empresarios Privados de Bolivia (Bolivian Confederation of Private Business)
CEN	Conselho de Economia Nacional, Brazil (Council for the National Economy)
CES	Consejo Económico y Social, Chile (Economic and Social Council)
CFCE	Conselho Federal de Comércio Exterior, Brazil (also CFCEX, Federal Council for International Trade)
CG	Consejo Gremial, Colombia (Business Association Council)
CGE	Confederación General Económica, Argentina (General Economic Confederation)
CGE	Câmara de Gestão da Crise de Energia Elétrica, Brazil (Chamber for Managing the Crisis of Electric Energy)
CGI	Confederación General de la Industria, Argentina (General Confederation of Industry)
CIB	Centro Industrial do Brasil (through 1931, when it became FIRJ) (Industrial Center of Brazil)
CIB	Confederação Industrial do Brasil (after 1933) (Industrial Confederation of Brazil)
CIESP	Centro de Indústrias do Estado de São Paulo (Center of Industries of the State of São Paulo)
CIM	Consejo Industrial Mercosur (Mercosur Industrial Council)
CINA	Confederación Industrial Argentina (Argentine Industrial Confederation)
CIP	Conselho Interministerial de Preços, Brazil (Interministerial Council on Prices)
CLT	Consolidação das Leis do Trabalho, Brazil (Consolidation of Labor Laws)
CMHN	Consejo Mexicano de Hombres de Negocios (Mexican Council of Businessmen)
CMN	Conselho Monetário Nacional, Brazil (National Monetary Council)
CNA	Confederação Nacional de Agricultura, Brazil (National Confederation of Agriculture)

CNA	Consejo Nacional Agropecuario, Mexico (National Agricultural Council)
CNC	Confederação Nacional do Comércio, Brazil (National Confederation of Commerce)
CNI	Confederação Nacional de Indústria, Brazil (National Confederation of Industry)
CNPF	Conseil national du patronat français (National Council of French Employers)
CNPIC	Conselho Nacional de Política Industrial e Comercial, Brazil (National Council for Industrial and Commercial Policy)
Codelco	Corporación Nacional del Cobre de Chile (National Copper Corporation of Chile)
Coece	Coordinadora Empresarial de Comercio Exterior, Mexico (Business Coordinator for International Trade)
Concamin	Confederación de Cámaras Industriales, Mexico (Confederation of Industrial Chambers)
Concanaco	Confederación de Cámaras Nacionales de Comercio, Mexico (Confederation of National Chambers of Commerce)
Conclap	Conferência das Classes Produtoras, Brazil (Conference of the Producing Classes)
CONEP	Comissão Nacional de Estímulo à Estabilização dos Preços, Brazil (National Commission for the Promotion of Price Stabilization)
CONFIEP	Confederación Nacional de Instituciones Empresariales Privadas, Peru (National Confederation of Private Enterprise Institutions)
Conindustria	Confederación Venezolana de Industriales (Venezuelan Confederation of Industrialists)
CONPES	Consejo de Política Económica y Social, Colombia (Council for Economic and Social Policy)
Coparmex	Confederación Patronal de la República Mexicana (Employers Confederation of the Mexican Republic)
Corfo	Corporación de Fomento de la Producción, Chile (Corporation for Promoting Production)
CPC	Confederación de la Producción y del Comercio, Chile (also know as Coproco) (Confederation for Production and Commerce)

CPE	Comissão de Planejamento Econômico, Brazil (Economic Planning Commission)
CT	Congreso de Trabajo, Mexico (Labor Council)
CTEF	Conselho Técnico de Economia e Finanças, Brazil (Technical Council for Economy and Finances)
CTM	Confederación de Trabajadores de México (Confederation of Workers of Mexico)
CUT	Central Única dos Trabalhadores, Brazil (Single Workers' Central)
CVF	Corporación Venezolana de Fomento (Venezuelan Development Corporation)
DIAP	Departmento Intersindical de Assessoria Parlamentar (Inter-union Department for Legislative Analysis)
FAA	Federación Agraria Argentina (Argentine Agrarian Federation)
FCES	Foro Consultivo Económico–Social, Mercosur (Consultative Economic–Social Forum)
Febraban	Federação Brasileira de Associações de Bancos (Brazilian Federation of Bank Associations)
Fedearroz	Federación Nacional de Arroceros, Colombia (National Federation of Rice Growers)
Fedecamaras	Federación Venezolana de Cámaras y Asociaciones de Comercio y Producción (Venezuelan Federation of Chambers and Associations of Commerce and Production)
Fedemetal	Federación Colombiana de Industrias Metalúrgicas (Colombian Federation of Metalworking Industries)
Federacafe	Federación Nacional de Cafeteros de Colombia (also known as FNC and Fedecafé) (National Federation of Coffee Growers)
Federalgodón	Federación Nacional de Algodoneros, Colombia (Federation of Cotton Growers)
Fenalco	Federación Nacional de Comerciantes, Colombia (National Federation of Merchants)
FIERGS	Federação das Indústrias do Estado do Rio Grande do Sul (Federation of Industry of the State of Rio Grande do Sul)
FIESP	Federação das Indústrias do Estado de São Paulo (Federation of Industry of the State of São Paulo)

FIRJ	Federação das Indústrias do Rio de Janeiro (also Firjan) (Federation of Industry of the State of Rio de Janeiro)
FKI	Federation of Korean Industry
FONAC	Fondo Nacional del Café, Colombia (National Coffee Fund)
Fonacot	Fondo de Fomento y Garantía para el Consumo de los Trabajadores, Mexico (Fund for Promoting and Guaranteeing Workers' Consumption)
FTAA	Free Trade Area of the Americas
FTI	Federation of Thai Industries
GATT	General Agreement on Tariffs and Trade
GDP	gross domestic product
IBAD	Instituto Brasileiro de Ação Democrática (Brazilian Institute for Democratic Action)
IBC	Instituto Brasileiro do Café (Brazilian Coffee Institute)
IBS	Instituto Brasileiro de Siderurgia (Brazilian Steel Institute)
IEDI	Instituto de Estudos de Desenvolvimento Industrial, Brazil (Institute for the Study of Industrial Development)
Infonavit	Instituto del Fondo Nacional de Vivienda para los Trabajadores, Mexico (Institute for the National Fund for Workers' Housing)
IPES	Instituto de Pesquisas e Estudos Sociais, Brazil (Institute for Research and Social Studies)
ISI	import-substituting industrialization
JPPCC	Joint Public and Private Sector Consultative Committee, Thailand
Mercosur	Mercado Común del Sur; known in Brazil as Mercosul, Mercado Comum do Sul (Common Market of the South)
MIA	Movimiento Industrial Argentino (Argentine Industrial Movement)
MIN	Movimiento Industrial Nacional, Argentina (National Industrial Movement)
MNC	multinational corporation
Nafinsa	Nacional Financiera, Mexico (also known as NAFIN) (National Development Bank)

Nafta	North American Free Trade Agreement
PAN	Partido de Acción Nacional, Mexico (National Action Party)
Pemex	Petróleos Mexicanos (Mexican Petroleum)
PICE	Programa de Integración y Cooperación Económica, Brazil and Argentina (Program of Economic Integration and Cooperation)
PNBE	Pensamento Nacional das Bases Empresariais, Brazil (National Thinking of the Business Bases)
PRI	Partido Revolucionario Institucional (Institutional Revolutionary Party)
PT	Partido dos Trabalhadores, Brazil (Workers' Party)
SAC	Sociedad de Agricultores de Colombia (Society of Farmers of Colombia)
Secofi	Secretaría de Comercio y Fomento Industrial, Mexico (Secretariat of Commerce and Industrial Promotion)
SENA	Servicio Nacional de Aprendizaje, Colombia (National Training Service)
Senai	Serviço Nacional de Aprendizagem Industrial, Brazil (National Service of Industrial Training)
Sesi	Serviço Social da Indústria, Brazil (Social Service of Industry)
Simesp	Sindicato da Indústria de Máquinas do Estado de São Paulo (Syndicate of the Machinery Industry of the State of São Paulo)
Sindipeças	Sindicato Nacional da Indústria de Componentes para Veículos Automotores, Brazil (National Syndicate for Manufacturers of Components for Automotive Vehicles)
SNA	Sociedad Nacional Agraria, Peru (National Agrarian Society)
SNA	Sociedad Nacional de Agricultura, Chile (National Agricultural Society)
SNI	Sociedad Nacional de Industrias, Peru (National Industries Society)
Sofofa or SFF	Sociedad de Fomento Fabril, Chile (Society for Manufacturing Promotion)
Sonami	Sociedad Nacional de Minería, Chile (National Mining Society)
SRA	Sociedad Rural Argentina (Argentine Rural Society)

TBA	Thai Bankers Association
TCC	Thai Chamber of Commerce
UBE	União Brasileira de Empresários (Brazilian Union of Businessmen)
UCR	Unión Cívica Radical, Argentina (Radical Civic Union)
UDR	União Democrática Ruralista, Brazil (Democratic Ruralist Union)
UIA	Unión Industrial Argentina (Argentine Industrial Union)
UTICA	Union Tunisienne de l'Industrie, du Commerce et de l'Artisanat (Tunisian Union of Industry, Commerce, and Artisans)

Acknowledgments

It is always revealing at the end of a long project to look back and re-member how certain offhand remarks or coincidental events posed key puzzles to work through or renewed hopes that the puzzles were worth investigating. At the beginning of this project I was talking with Elio Gáspari, an *eminence grise* of Brazilian journalism and an early professor of mine at Columbia University, and I told him some of my hypotheses on business politics in Brazil. As I recall the conversation, Elio responded that the problem was fairly simple: the Brazilian bourgeoisie did not have a telephone. At the time, I was not sure of his meaning. This sentence, though, became one that I mulled over from time to time as I worked further on my hypotheses, got into the field research, and expanded the scope of the project to include first Mexico and then Argentina, Chile, and Colombia. In the end, I think I understand Elio's diagnosis of the organizational weakness of Brazilian business and I have collected a lot of comparative evidence to support his assessment.

As this book evolved, several colleagues made passing remarks on the need for a companion volume on the political incorporation of business to complement the comprehensive opus of Ruth and David Collier on labor incorporation. Over the course of this project, I have often been struck by the lack of sustained comparative analysis of business politics in Latin America, especially compared to the more extensive and sophis-ticated research on labor. This relative neglect seems even less warranted in recent years, when freer markets and politics have granted business an ever more central role in the political economy of Latin America. Al-though not designed as an extension of the Colliers' work, I do hope this book helps to balance somewhat the scholarly attention devoted to the political incorporation of various social groups in Latin America.

As I was finishing the manuscript, reports leaked out of a meeting in May 2003 of Latin American billionaires in Mexico City (followed by golf in Ixtapa). Carlos Slim, the wealthiest man in Latin America, organized the event, invited a few dozen prominent businessmen from each of the major countries to attend, and reportedly bore the full cost of the three-day meeting. (*Reforma*, 23 May 2003, electronic version). The meeting may not have any lasting effect, like many meetings of top businesspeople. And international or inter-American business organizations of any sort have always been particularly diaphanous. However, it was of little surprise that the meeting took place in Mexico, where the business community has long been better organized and more accustomed to acting collectively than business in other large countries of the region.

This often-interrupted project accumulated debts for years. On the financial side, I am grateful for support from the Fulbright program, the Searle Foundation, the University Research Grants Committee at Northwestern University, and the Center for International and Comparative Studies at Northwestern University. At various stages, the Centro de Investigación y Docencia Económicas (CIDE), the Lateinamerika Institut at the Free University in Berlin, and the Wissenschaftskolleg zu Berlin were generous in providing office space and logistical support.

The success of a comparative project like this one depends heavily on the good will of scholars who really know the politics of each of the countries involved. Among Brazilian scholars who greatly helped in my research, I thank Renato Boschi, Luiz Carlos Bresser-Pereira, Eli Diniz, Maria D'Alva Kinzo, Edson Nunes, and Gesner Oliveira. Marilene Lara de Oliveira provided indispensable logistical support. In Mexico, Marcela Briz, Denise Dresser, Blanca Heredia, Matilde Luna, Yemile Mizrahi, Juan Manuel Ortega, Alicia Ortiz, Cristina Puga, Ricardo Tirado, and David Zúñiga provided both logistical assistance and substantive feedback. Alicia Ortiz was especially gracious in taking time to comb through her files and send me the cover photograph. Roderic Camp, Edward Gibson, and Blanca Heredia made remarkable gestures of scholarly solidarity by giving me copies of their interviews with Mexican business leaders. In Argentina Juan Carlos Torre, José Maria Ghio, and Ernesto Calvo helped guide my research, as did Alfredo Rehren, Eduardo Silva, and Manuel Garretón in Chile and Angelika Rettberg and Eduardo Sáenz in Colombia. I also owe a debt to the many businesspeople and government officials listed in Appendix B and others who preferred anonymity.

These interviewees were generous with their time and willing to engage my many questions.

I was fortunate to have the opportunity to present work in progress at seminars at Harvard University, the Kellogg Institute at the University of Notre Dame, Northwestern University, the Institute of Latin American Studies at the University of London, the Lateinamerika-Institut of the Free University, MIT, the Center for Brazilian Studies at the University of Oxford, and the University of Miami. I am grateful for the feedback from participants at these seminars. I am also greatly indebted to many colleagues for comments on various drafts: Nancy Bermeo, James Brennan, Luiz Carlos Bresser-Pereira, Ernesto Calvo, Dennis Chong, Forrest Colburn, Richard Doner, Omar Encarnación, Tulia Falleti, Elizabeth Jay Friedman, Edward Gibson, Mauro Guillén, Frances Hagopian, Evelyne Huber, Wagner Iglecias, Peter Kingstone, Atul Kohli, Jonathan Krieckhaus, Harry Makler, Cathie Jo Martin, Sylvia Maxfield, Kenneth Shadlen, Eduardo Silva, David Soskice, Peter Swenson, Judith Tendler, Kurt Weyland, and Laurence Whitehead.

Kathleen Thelen worked over more of this manuscript, more often, and longer than anyone else. Her contribution to this book was enormous, overshadowed only by everything else she did along the way.

Berlin, August 2003

PART I

INTRODUCTION AND ARGUMENTS

I

Patterns of Business Politics in Latin America

> A landed interest, a manufacturing interest, a mercantile interest, a moneyed interest with many lesser interests grow up of necessity in civilised nations and divide themselves into different classes actuated by different sentiments and views. The regulation of these various and interfering interests forms the principal task of modern legislation and involves the spirit of party and faction in the necessary and ordinary operations of government.
>
> James Madison, 1788[1]

Variations in Business Organization

Patterns of business organization and relations between business and government varied widely across Latin America in the twentieth century. Coffee provides an early and illustrative example. By the middle of the twentieth century, Brazil and Colombia were the largest coffee producers in Latin America and coffee generated most of their export revenues, yet the economic and political organization of coffee growers in the two countries differed remarkably. The Colombian coffee sector had by the 1960s been thriving for decades and pulling much of the rest of the economy along with it. The association of coffee growers, Federacafe (Federación Nacional de Cafeteros de Colombia), had firmly established Colombian coffees in the high-quality, high-price segments of the world market, and coffee overall accounted for over two-thirds of Colombian exports.[2] The political power of the coffee elite and their association matched their economic clout. Federacafe was influential in a wide range of economic

---

[1] *The Federalist Papers*, no. 10, cited in Wilson (1981, 2).
[2] See the List of Abbreviations for English translations.

policies, and the head of Federacafe was viewed as the second most powerful man in the country after the president (Urrutia 1983, 116).

By comparison, the marginal situation of coffee growers in Brazil, the
world's largest producer, would probably have dismayed the Colombian
elite. Brazilian coffee exports had also grown dramatically and by 1960
represented about half of Brazil's exports.[3] Brazilian coffee, though, filled
the lower end of the market, and politically the organized, collective
power of coffee growers was rarely mentioned. Of course, coffee was
not economically as dominant in the larger and more diversified Brazilian
economy, and the geography of coffee cultivation varied notably between
the two countries. However, the major differences in the political economy of the two coffee sectors derived largely from the institutional and
organizational legacies of the 1920s and 1930s. In 1924 state officials in
Brazil created the Coffee Institute, which took over many functions of sectoral governance without the organized participation of coffee growers.[4]
In Colombia in 1928, state actors delegated these governance functions
(such as marketing, infrastructure, and credit), as well as control over an
earmarked tax, to a new association of growers, Federacafe, that subsequently became a major institutional actor. Any general book on Colombian politics or development in the second half of the twentieth century
devotes substantial attention to Federacafe; similar books on Brazil make
no mention of a national organization of coffee growers.[5]

In the 1990s, to take a more recent example, quite different patterns of business–government relations emerged in the large countries
of Latin America in their respective negotiations over regional economic
integration. Strong business associations in Mexico and Chile collaborated closely with government negotiators in devising the terms of regional integration. In Mexico representatives of government and business
associations met literally thousands of times to exchange information,
reconcile conflicting preferences, and work to reach consensus positions
for Mexican officials to take into the negotiations over Nafta (North

---

[3] Coffee accounted for 59 percent of Brazilian exports in 1955 and 56 percent in 1960, then
dropped to less than a quarter in the 1970s (Baer 1983, 162).

[4] Font (1990, Chapter 3) provides the full story. Overall, Font concludes, "Big Coffee elites
sought, considered vital, and largely failed to get, direct control of a regulatory mechanism
not subservient to other policy objectives. This amounts to one of the most interesting
cases on record of the failure of private corporativism in Latin America" (271).

[5] Contrast, for example, Skidmore (1967, 1988) on Brazil with Thorp (1991) on Colombia.
See Bates (1997) for an extended comparison of the political economy of coffee in the two
countries.

American Free Trade Agreement). In Brazil and Argentina, in contrast, government officials negotiated largely in isolation the terms of integration into their common market, Mercosur (Mercado Común del Sur). Other political factors influenced business–government relations in these trade negotiations, but policy options for negotiators in Brazil and Argentina were generally constrained by the fact that business associations, especially in industry, were weak and unrepresentative.

The cases of coffee and regional integration are only two examples of many wide variations in the organization of business and in business–government relations in Latin America. These variations have profound consequences for the kinds of issues business brings to policy making, what political channels they use to push their preferences, and what, if any, contributions they can bring to policy making and governance overall. These issues have become ever more important in recent decades as states have relinquished economic controls, greatly extending the realm of business discretion in the economy, and as democratization has generated new opportunities for open, organized participation by business in politics.

Why does the organization of business vary so dramatically across the large countries of Latin America? In this book I argue that most major variations in patterns of business organization – weak versus strong, rich versus poor, encompassing versus narrow, politicized versus neutral – can be traced back to actions of state actors and the cumulative effect of these actions over the twentieth century. In other words, states organized or disorganized business. This argument holds not only for the obvious cases where government decrees forced business to belong (state corporatism) but also for a range of formally voluntary associations. Especially in the case of voluntary associations, existing theory is poorly equipped to explain variation over time and space since much of it neglects the state and focuses instead on economic characteristics of the firms involved or, sometimes, on political factors like development strategies or regime type. A good deal of mythology, derived in part from overly simple economic models, sustains the mistaken impression that collective action is mostly the spontaneous, short-run result of individual calculations largely in isolation. In Latin America, capitalists did seem to weigh rationally the costs and benefits of investing in associations, but when they invested or disinvested, it was usually in response to prior actions by state officials and after evaluating other opportunities for political investment. State actions ranged from direct decrees outlawing some associations or obliging firms to join new state-chartered organizations to more indirect measures such as granting associations public resources or special access to policy makers. A core theoretical challenge is to explain how various types of state incentives for business to act collectively generate diverse organizational responses and how these responses cumulate over time into institutional capacity within associations.

An additional theoretical challenge is to specify when and why state actors are likely to want to organize business.[6] Historically in Latin America, as traced out in Part II, state actors sought to organize business in periods of economic and political crisis. The exact timing and nature of these crises varied country by country, but crises clustered across the region in the 1930s and 1940s and later in the 1980s and 1990s. In periods of crisis, state officials sought ways to reduce their vulnerabilities and bolster political and administrative support. So, for example, economic ministers caught in the middle of deep economic crises were likely, other things being equal, to solicit business support and to help business organize in order to manage the crisis. Other things were, of course, not always equal, especially over time, and successive teams of economic officials confronted evolving sets of associations. In the crisis years of the Depression and World War II, business associations were generally weak, if they existed at all, and state actors across all the major countries of Latin America intervened strongly to shape the organization of business. By the time of the crisis decade of the 1980s, the incentives for state officials to intervene in business organization were again strong, but state officials were constrained by variations in how the organizational space for business had in the intervening half century become more crowded and less malleable.

A cursory glance at the full range of business associations in the major countries of Latin America reveals a bewildering array of hundreds of associations, and larger businesses belong to several of them. The vast majority of these associations are similar across Latin America: they are small and narrow, and often consist of little more than a letterhead and a telephone. Where the differences are more striking and more relevant for policy and politics, as well as theory building, is in the voluntary associations that organized broad segments, or all, of the private sector. Table 1.1 lists major voluntary, encompassing associations in five countries of Latin America and divides them between countries with strong

---

[6] As specified further in Chapter 2, state actors are top officials in the executive branch. Generally I subscribe to Stepan's definition of the state as "the continuous administrative, legal, bureaucratic, and coercive system" and to his three-way distinction among the state, civil society, and political society (that includes parties, electoral rules, and legislatures) (2001, 100–1).

TABLE 1.1 *Voluntary Encompassing Associations in Five Countries of Latin America*

	Association	Scope	Staff
Strong Encompassing Associations			
Mexico	Coparmex (1929–)	Economy-wide	30
	CMHN (1962–)	Economy-wide	0
	CCE (1975–)	Economy-wide	80
Chile	CPC (1933–)	Economy-wide	8
	Sofofa (1883–)	Industry	50
Colombia	Federacafe (1927–)	Coffee	3,500
	ANDI (1944–)	Industry	150
	CG (1991–)	Economy-wide	3
Weak Encompassing Associations			
Argentina	ACIEL (1958–73)	Economy-wide	0
	APEGE (1975–6)	Economy-wide	0
	CGE (1952–)	Economy-wide	10?
	UIA (1886–)	Industry	50
	CEA (1967–)	Economy-wide	2
Brazil	UBE (1987–8)	Economy-wide	Few to none
	IEDI (1989–)	Industry	8

Note: See appendixes for sources and further basic information. Figures for staff are rough estimates for average total employment in the last quarter of the twentieth century.

encompassing associations – Mexico, Colombia, and Chile – and countries with weak associations – Brazil and Argentina (where several of the ephemeral associations listed in the table survived for only a few years).

The mere existence of voluntary encompassing associations is one good indicator of the amounts of money and time that prominent capitalists invest in collective action. The rough estimates of staff are a further proxy useful for comparing across countries the material investments members make in their associations. Other indicators of organizational strength include the time capitalists invest in associations and the quality of internal representation (indicators considered further in Chapters 3 to 7). Although they cannot be summarized in a table, historical instances of organizational capacity to aggregate or reconcile members' interests were more common in the histories of encompassing associations in Mexico, Chile, and Colombia than in Argentina and Brazil. "Institutional" or "organizational strength," in my usage, refers always to these internal characteristics – material resources and internal intermediation – not to the amount of power or influence of the association in the political system.

This book focuses largely on economy-wide associations (that organize most of industry, commerce, agriculture, and finance) and encompassing industry associations representing most subsectors of industry.[7] These associations were generally most prominent after the 1940s and eclipsed associations in other sectors. The analysis sometimes also incorporates agricultural, commercial, and financial associations when they developed significant institutional capacity, as for example the coffee association in Colombia, or when they help generally to fill out the arguments. Absent from Table 1.1 are the state-chartered, nonvoluntary associations in Brazil and Mexico that were major political players in the mid-twentieth century and that receive more attention in later chapters. The primary focus of the book is on voluntary associations because they raise so many theoretical and comparative questions. Theoretically, voluntary, encompassing associations, with many members with diverse interests, are anomalous. Prevailing theories predict that they should be rare, weak, and short-lived. This was sometimes true but often not, and the analytic challenge is to explain why.

Of the large countries of Latin America listed in Table 1.1, big business in Mexico was the best organized, mostly through two voluntary, encompassing, and interlinked associations, CMHN (Consejo Mexicano de Hombres de Negocios) and CCE (Consejo Coordinador Empresarial). Formed in the 1960s, the CMHN was an exclusive club of 40 or so of the most prominent capitalists who collectively had business interests in all major sectors of the economy. The CCE is an economy-wide peak association established by seven member associations that formally represented nearly a million firms from all sectors of the economy. By the 1980s the CCE had a large staff of about 80 people and a budget of $2 million. In Chile and Colombia economy-wide associations were not as institutionally developed; however, industry associations were strong and over time became even more encompassing by attracting members from outside industry. In addition, Federacafe, Colombia's powerful coffee federation, acted more like an encompassing association because its leadership had diversified business interests.

At the other end of the spectrum, in Brazil and Argentina, voluntary encompassing associations were weak or nonexistent, but for different

---

[7] By my definition, in encompassing or multisectoral associations, member firms do not have common market or technological relationships with one another. So, for example, an association that represents both paper and auto parts firms is encompassing. My focus is primarily big business. "Encompassing" refers to multisectoral, not inclusive, associations, and most small firms did not belong to voluntary encompassing associations.

reasons. Brazil had no lasting economy-wide peak association, and the appearance of strength in other associations was deceptive. In industry, the compulsory associations were among the largest and best funded in the region, but corporatist statutes severely distorted internal representation. For example, voting in the national association for industry was by state, so that federations of industry of tiny rural states had the same vote as the industry federation of São Paulo, whose members generated half or more of total industrial output. The problem for business in Argentina was less the absence of encompassing associations or the distortions of corporatist regulation and more the multiplicity, rivalry, and politicization of the numerous fleeting associations that have existed. For example, UIA (Unión Industrial Argentina) was a voluntary, encompassing association for industry that had grown quite strong by the 1940s. However, President Juan Perón outlawed the UIA and created rival associations in the 1950s. For the rest of the twentieth century business representation was divided along multiple cleavages, and one set of associations or the other was periodically repressed by alternating governments.[8]

Explaining Collective Action by Business

The analysis of business politics and organization intersects with three broad literatures on civil society, corporatism, and collective action. Chapter 2 provides further coverage of these contending approaches, but it is useful to introduce them briefly here and summarize their differing explanations for the emergence of strong associations in order to set up and distinguish my own statist argument. The explanatory power of each approach is limited on its own, but particular conceptual tools of each can be reconfigured to use in building my arguments on how and why state actors help organize business. Let me start with the limitations.

---

[8] For making shorthand distinctions and comparisons, I sometimes revive Schmitter's original categories of pluralism, state corporatism, and societal corporatism (1974, 103–5). Where voluntary associations were strong – in Mexico, Chile, and Colombia – corporatism was more societal. In Brazil business organization was dominated by state corporatism. Lastly, Argentina had neither form of corporatism (outside of a few years of state corporatist experimentation in the early 1950s), but rather a polarized, politicized kind of pluralism. Although Schmitter devised his concepts to categorize countries, the distinctions are also useful for comparing associations within the same country (Mexico's voluntary, societal associations versus compulsory, state-chartered associations, for example) or for comparing periods in particular countries: Brazil and Argentina, for example, started in the 1930s and 1940s with something closer to societal corporatism that subsequently degenerated.

In the diffuse literature on civil society, and on the related concept of social capital, there is little agreement on just what civil society is and where
it comes from. Despite this conceptual dispersion, nearly all definitions
include business associations as a part of civil society. On the theoretical
challenge of explaining variation, many scholars, Robert Putnam (1993)
prominent among them, view strong civil societies as the result of centuries
of evolution that are embedded in broader social, political, and cultural
transformations. Change in civil society, if it happens at all, is glacial and
part of overall systemic change. Government policy, or human agency of
any sort, has little impact.[9] Jonah Levy sums up the literature: "civil society is inherited, not constructed" (1999, 4). On the whole, this perspective
offers little in the task of explaining shorter-term variations in business
associations, primarily in the second half of the twentieth century in my
case, in societies that share a common heritage and broadly similar political and economic challenges. Finally, in contrast to my statist argument,
scholars of civil society consider the state as essentially a threat and argue
that the best thing the state can do to promote civil society "is to get out
of the way" (Levy 1999, 6).

The somewhat faded literature on corporatism does not have much
more to offer to general causal explanations for the emergence of various forms of business organization in Latin America. Both literatures,
on corporatism and on civil society, focus in fact more on the consequences of variations in organizational strength than on the origins of
variation. Although organizations are not as immutable as some analyses
of civil society, change in the corporatist literature is slow and constrained.
Most analyses are thus historical and contextualized; explanations for
collective action by one group, say business, are related to other groups,
political actors, and institutional constraints. Most corporatist analyses
also weave the state back in but usually only as structure and monolith.
The state was central to Philippe Schmitter's (1974) foundational analysis
of corporatism, even societal corporatism, though the distinctions were
more descriptive than causal. In another influential review, Schmitter and
Wolfgang Streeck (1999) identified over a dozen hypotheses on characteristics of states that affect business organization, yet most of these features
are relatively constant, such as the level of government centralization or
the degree of professionalization of the state bureaucracy, and are not

---

[9] There are, of course, some exceptions in the diverse literature on civil society. See, for
example, Evans (1996), Friedman and Hochstetler (2002), Encarnación (in press), and
others considered in Chapter 2.

subject to strategic manipulation by political actors who might want to change business organization. Overall these literatures on civil society and corporatism have, to borrow a phrase used in Latin America, "too much architecture and not enough engineering."

The emphasis is reversed in the literature on collective action, where scholars are first (and often exclusively) interested in engineering: namely, the causal dynamics that lead individuals to create and contribute to organizations like business associations. For Mancur Olson (1965), collective action is likely when the numbers are small and the members homogeneous, or when the association offers selective benefits to members. For most Olsonian analyses, the calculus of collective action is immediate and largely unaffected by past investment in collective action (and the resulting constellation of civic organizations) or by much of the general context. For example, Jeffry Frieden's analysis of collective action by business in Latin America focuses primarily on the economic characteristics of business and rarely mentions pre-existing associations.[10] The neglect of context often includes an explicit rejection of the state. Frieden specifies: "I downplay the possibility that a significant set of pressures may have emanated from the bureaucratic or political institutions of the government itself." The economic bureaucracy may have interests of its own, but it is "essentially a reactor to private demands" (Frieden 1991, 39).

My argument is the opposite of Frieden's: when it organizes, the private sector is essentially a reactor to government actions. Historically state actors were, of course, the proximate cause of corporatist associations they created by fiat, but state actors were also the central protagonists in encouraging the formation of voluntary, encompassing associations, sometimes unintentionally (as when they threatened business with reformist policies) and, more importantly, intentionally by offering associations selective benefits such as representation in policy forums or authority over public functions or funds. Moments of conflict between business and government over reformist policies were often important in the initial creation of encompassing associations, but these associations became strong institutions only if they received further encouragement and benefits from the government. From my perspective, business associations in Latin America

---

[10] Frieden does sometimes bring in contextual factors, such as levels of class conflict, but his point of departure is that the organization and lobbying activities of business depend primarily on the economic characteristics of their sectors: "individuals or firms tend to come together with others holding similar assets" (1991, 23). Using economic criteria, Frieden further claims that "the more concentrated the industry, the easier we would expect it to be able to exert political pressure" (24).

were neither the outcome of some centuries'-old traditions in civil society nor the immediate result of some back-of-the-envelope Olsonian calculus; nor were they shaped merely by interactions with particular state structures.

Despite the general limitations of the literatures on civil society, corporatism, and collective action, I borrow and develop some conceptual components from each. Specifically, I rework Olson's concept of selective incentives, re-introduce a more proactive state (peopled by strategic officials rather than passive structures), and in the end embed the analysis in broader trends in the economy, society, and politics. My focus on "unnatural" encompassing associations takes me, following an Olsonian line of reasoning, to selective benefits, which do in fact exist in most instances of voluntary, encompassing associations. Yet these selective benefits typically originate not in associations but in the state, about which the Olsonian literature on collective action has relatively little to say. Other scholars, especially those in the corporatist tradition, acknowledge the role of the state in shaping business organization, but they rarely take the next step to examine when and why state actors would want to organize business. State actors have strategies of their own, and in pursuing them they sometimes have a lasting impact on business associations. Chapter 2 attempts to "endogenize" state officials and examine the conditions under which they would have stronger incentives to promote collective action by business, as well as the longer-term implications of various forms of promotion on institutionalizing channels of business representation. Thus, state actors, reacting to exogenous political and economic conditions, are the agents of change. However, they do not make their histories out of whole cloth. The institutional sediment left from the actions of previous state actors populated the associational universe, more so late in the twentieth century than earlier, so each successive group of state actors had to deal with existing associations of varying strength.

Lastly, although the primary influence on business organization was the dynamic interaction and exchange between state officials and business leaders, the political strategies of business were also influenced by the broader context of political contention and the full range of existing political opportunities. Analyzing decisions by business to invest in collective action requires a wider examination of the other political alternatives – such as parties, elections, or personal networks – available to business people. Political strategies pursued by business are in part a function of this *portfolio* of options, and understanding business associations thus requires attention to the broader context of business politics.

To reiterate, in my argument state actors, usually top officials in the economic bureaucracy, were the pivotal causal agents. Over the course of the twentieth century in Latin America these state actors adopted policies, in response to changing political and economic crises, that helped business to organize or in other cases undermined business organization. Sometimes these policies were threatening to business and had the unintended consequence of promoting short-term defensive organization. Over the longer term, the positive selective benefits that held most encompassing associations together came from the state, either material resources or, more commonly, privileged access. These selective benefits were more valuable if, in the portfolio of political investments, other options for participating in politics were less effective. These arguments, and the central role of state actors, explain both the static variation across countries and the dynamic changes over time within individual countries. In the dynamic argument the benefits or threats from the state in one period may diminish, for example, in subsequent governments, with negative consequences for collective action by business.

Unpacking Civil Society, Democracy, and State Capacity

The primary empirical and theoretical goals of this book are to explain variations in business organization and, by extension, in business–government relations. A secondary goal, taken up in the final two chapters, is to begin an assessment of the consequences of this variation. Contending positions in debates on these consequences are often maniquean. On the negative side, authors who analyze rent seeking and "distributional coalitions" fear mostly harmful consequences from organized business. On the positive side, scholars of social capital, civil society, and corporatism emphasize the benefits organized social groups, including business associations, can confer on their societies.

Olson argued that "when special-interest groups become more important and distributional issues accordingly more significant, political life tends to be more divisive." In the extreme, divisive politics can "encourage intransitive or irrational and cyclical political choices. The divisiveness of distributional issues, and the fact that they may make relatively lasting or stable political choices less likely, can even make societies ungovernable" (1982, 47). Olson's view of associations grew even dimmer with time: "a society dense with narrow special-interest organizations is like a china shop filled with wrestlers battling over its contents, and breaking far more than they carry away" (Olson 1986, 173). Olson (1982) argued that "distributional coalitions," made up of associations of labor, business, and other groups that shared sectoral interests, choked off growth in those rich countries that did not lose World War II. The historical trend, Olson concluded, was for democratic societies to spawn increasing numbers of distributional coalitions with negative consequences for general welfare. Olson did admit the possibility that all-encompassing associations might have a "less parochial view than the narrow associations of which they are composed" (1982, 50). In principle, more encompassing organizations have an interest in increasing the total national income, whereas narrow organizations seek to increase their share, regardless of the impact of their actions on the size of the whole pie. However, Olson (1986) thought encompassing associations were likely to be few and short-lived, and he rarely considered them in later work.

In contrast, scholars of civil society and social capital are mostly optimistic about the contributions civil society – including business associations – can make to democracy and development. Larry Diamond (1996) lists 10 contributions that civil society can make to democracy, including limiting arbitrary state power, providing alternative channels of representation, and schooling citizens in the practices and attitudes of democratic governance.[11] Beyond contestation, the adequate representation of business is also a core concern of several major theories of democratic consolidation. For instance, Dietrich Rueschemeyer, Evelyne Stephens, and John Stephens concluded that in Latin America "democracy could only be consolidated where elites' interests were effectively protected either through direct influence of elite groups on the state apparatus or through electorally strong political parties" (1992, 156).[12] For other scholars, strong civil societies do not just limit states through contestation but in fact, sometimes simultaneously, strengthen them. Tocqueville concluded that freedom of association may "after having agitated society for some time,... strengthen the state in the end" (cited in Diamond 1996, 234). Putnam offers a more axiomatic formulation: "strong society, strong economy; strong society, strong state" (1993, 176).

Although sometimes more ambivalent, the literature on corporatism, or organized capitalism more generally, also makes a positive case for

---

[11] Several years later, Diamond's list of positive functions had grown to 13 (1999, 239–49). See also Cohen and Rogers (1995a), Rueschemeyer, Stephens, and Stephens (1992), and Zakarias (1997).

[12] They further specify that democratic survival depended "on the availability to elites of political institutions for control within a constitutional context (elite political parties or state corporatist institutions)" (1992, 163).

business associations. Focusing largely on Japan and Europe, scholars credit societal corporatism, neo-corporatism, or "coordinated market economies" with superior macroeconomic management and sectoral governance.[13] On the political side, associations can unburden the political system and enhance the quality of democracy (Katzenstein 1985; Schmitter 1992). Compared to periodic elections and party mobilization, associations provide avenues for the continuous and disaggregated intermediation of interests (Schmitter 1995b, 285). Citizens may interact more with associations of all sorts than with the formal institutions of electoral democracy, and may therefore base more of their evaluation of the political system on these associations.

In sum, these theories, as well as the sharp discrepancies among them, all direct us to the intermediation of business interests as a privileged locus for understanding the quality, capacity, and resiliency of new democracies and more market-oriented economies. In other words, these theories suggest that business associations are key institutional dimensions for distinguishing among "varieties of capitalism" in Latin America (Hall and Soskice 2001). However, both dim and rosy visions are too sweeping. What is needed is a more fine-grained, contextualized analysis, attempted in Part III, that considers the precise functions of business associations that affect specific dimensions of development and democracy.

The Plan and Methods

Chapter 2 develops the core arguments: (1) that state actions best explain variation in business organization in Latin America; (2) that state actors help organize business in order to reduce their own vulnerabilities and advance their policy agendas; and (3) that the diverse kinds of selective incentives states provide to business have significantly different effects on business organization. State actors meddle in business organization to generate support (or reduce opposition), get information, seek cooperation for policy implementation, and force contending interests to compromise. In addition, state intervention in labor markets and property rights often had the unintended consequence of provoking defensive mobilization by business. This chapter also assesses the limitations of alternative hypotheses that rely on other economic or political factors to understand variation in the organization of business. Specifically, factors

---

[13] For recent overviews, see Hall and Soskice (2001), Hollingsworth and Boyer (1997), Traxler and Unger (1994), Baccaro (in press), and Schmitter (1992).

relating to geography (country size and regional concentration), corporate ownership (economic concentration, foreign investment, and conglomeration), and macropolitical parameters (regime type and party systems) add further nuance to a full analysis but cannot explain major variations in business organization.

Part II turns to the empirical, comparative, and historical examination of business politics over the course of the twentieth century. In Mexico (Chapter 3) government support fostered several strong, encompassing associations. The core explanation for the greater organization of big business was its love–hate relation with the Mexican state. The "hate" factor revolves around the abiding distrust business had of state actions and the periodic threatening actions by state actors that promoted collective action. Specifically, state threats in the late 1920s, late 1950s, early 1970s, and early 1980s all led big business to create or strengthen voluntary, encompassing associations. The "love" factor emerged in postconflict periods when state actors sought to assuage business fears and court their support. In the process they often favored the business associations created in conflictual periods, especially by giving them privileged access to policy makers.

In Brazil (Chapter 4) the main question is not just why business never managed to create an economy-wide peak association but also why the vibrant industry associations founded in the 1940s subsequently became marginal and unrepresentative. State actors helped business establish strong, well-funded industry associations in the 1930s and 1940s, but over time corporatist statutes undermined the ability of these associations to intermediate member interests. After the 1950s, state actors excluded these corporatist associations from policy making and gave capitalists incentives to invest in narrow sectoral associations or personal networks. By the late 1980s industrialists began investing in other types of voluntary, encompassing associations, but none emerged as central interlocutors in Brazilian politics or developed institutional capacity, largely for lack of support from the state.

Colombia (Chapter 5) had some of the most robust and influential associations in the region, associations that were created or indirectly strengthened by sustained government action. From the 1920s on, state actors supported institutionally strong, relatively encompassing associations in coffee, industry, and other sectors. State actors often had quite explicit motives. They created or bolstered associations in order to get aggregated information, to gain support for policies, and to depoliticize policy making. An economy-wide association did not emerge until the

1990s (when the minister of development asked business to form one) in part because prior reformist threats were relatively mild.

In Chile (Chapter 6) the evolution of business–government relations and business organization resembled the pattern in Mexico of alternating periods of conflict and harmony that strengthened business associations over time. In the 1940s and again in the 1960s and 1970s, conflicts between reformist governments and business reinforced encompassing organization. In other periods, especially the 1950s and 1980s, institutionalized access through policy councils and other forms of close business–government consultation consolidated these associations.

In Argentina (Chapter 7), in contrast, polarized politics never allowed institutionally strong, or even stable, business associations to emerge. Industrial and agricultural associations were vibrant in the early twentieth century, but in the 1940s Perón politicized them and created rival associations. Thereafter alternating governments favored one set of associations and repressed the other, and none achieved lasting access to policy forums. After concluding the Argentine story, this chapter closes with some further comparisons to business–state relations in other developing countries. Much evidence in the secondary literature suggests that the state is the place to start in analyzing variations in the organization of business in other countries of Latin America, Africa, and Asia. The broader comparisons also help situate business–government relations in the five large countries of Latin America on a spectrum between the extremes, found in other regions, of coercive state corporatism and pervasive, predatory clientelism.

Part III returns to the question "What do associations do?" with two concluding chapters, the first economic and the second political. Chapter 8 analyzes some contributions that associations made to evolving market economies and provides empirical illustrations from the five cases. Institutionally strong associations contributed in some instances to macroeconomic stabilization, coordinated policy reform, trade negotiations, and other aspects of economic governance. Where associations were strong, they opened up the option of developing a more negotiated, coordinated, and concerted "variety of capitalism." The concluding section of Chapter 8 returns to conceptual issues raised in Chapter 2 to reexamine foundations of microeconomic theorizing on preference formation, free riding, rent seeking, and encompassing collective action. Many of the anomalies for these theories uncovered in this research derive from the problems of extrapolating theories based on individuals – methodological individualism – to interpret the behavior of organizations.

On the political side, Chapter 9 assesses some of the contributions business associations offered, or can offer, to democracy. For example, associations provided more continuous, targeted, and transparent representation for business than elections or informal influence peddling. Associations also have a record in some countries of effectively opposing authoritarian rule, supporting democracy, and checking arbitrary state power. The political record, of course, was not all positive, and when it was, associations were only part of the solution. In order to understand the peculiar contributions of business associations, they need to be carefully distinguished from other groups in civil society. The book closes with a consideration of the dilemmas of state-dependent civil societies for democratic consolidation.

The rationales for selecting my cases were several.[14] The cases vary along a range of independent and dependent variables, and allow for comparisons using a variety of qualitative methods and multiple assessments of competing arguments. The primary method of comparison is to assess the strength of state incentives in the cases of strong organization – Mexico, Chile, and Colombia – versus the weakness of these incentives in the disorganized cases – Brazil and Argentina. Variation within the categories of strong and weak organization extends the comparative dimension and adds nuance to the overall argument. So, for example, state actors promoted economy-wide associations in Mexico, while in Chile they gave greater encouragement to industry associations, and business in both countries shifted their investment in institutional capacity according to these incentives. Lastly, the study deals with a small number of country cases, but the historical analysis of each country's evolution over most of the twentieth century allows for the close examination of causal factors over time, and adds numerous within-case comparisons across discrete periods of interactions between business and government.

By the 1990s these five countries accounted for 70 percent of the population and 80 percent of the gross national product (GNP) of Latin America and the Caribbean (World Bank 1997, 215, 237). They comprise

---

[14] There are few genuinely comparative studies of business politics in Latin America. Important comparisons of two countries include Cardoso (1978) and Story (1986, Chapter 5). Several edited volumes include contributions on many countries, but the analysis is not always systematically comparative: see Garrido (1988), Bartell and Payne (1995), Tirado (1994), and Durand and Silva (1998). Excellent but brief comparative articles include Boschi (1993), Boschi (1994), Silva (2002), and Durand (1994). Comparative work on labor is more abundant and theoretically developed. See, for example, Collier and Collier (1991) and Buchanan (1995).

the major large, middle-income countries in Latin America. With enough time and space this book would also have covered Peru and Venezuela, the remaining medium-sized countries of the region, and later chapters incorporate occasional comparisons to these and other countries. Initial research suggests that a lot of business investment in encompassing associations came in response to state actions and overall that my arguments work fairly well in both countries. My case selection holds relatively constant variables of region, country size, and level of development. Chapter 7 returns to the question of extending my arguments to other countries and regions, but my point of departure is that my approach should be most applicable to larger, middle-income countries.

2

States and Collective Action

> The immense majority of the merchants of our Republic flee, as from the plague, from whatever action that might cause them to aggregate their interests.... They refuse to join the chambers. We have heard merchants say: Why should I join, if when the chamber gains a benefit for commerce, it is for all of us, and on the other hand when the same chamber has difficulties with the government or town council its members are exposed to reprisals.
>
> Letter from the National Mining Chamber of Chihuahua to the
> Minister of Industry, Commerce, and Labor, 1927[1]

Olson's Uneven Legacy

Some four decades later, Mancur Olson (1965) formalized the lament of the Chihuahua Mining Chamber into his microeconomic theory of collective action. For Olson, potential members of associations have incentives to free-ride, to let others do the work of organizing and then enjoy the benefits of, say, successful lobbying. These incentives to free-ride discourage spontaneous collective action unless the numbers involved are small or an association provides selective benefits, available to members only, that effectively compensate members for their efforts and dues. And, some three decades after Olson published his *Logic of Collective Action* in 1965, his theories were hegemonic in several subfields of political science.[2] However, not all components of Olson's original book have

---

[1] The letter goes on to request legislation to provide sanctions against firms that refused to join. It is cited in Shafer (1973, 32).

[2] One review claimed that Olson's *Logic* was "one of the half-dozen books by economists that have had the greatest impact on the political science discipline" (Miller 1997, 1177).

had the same impact or have benefited from equally intense theoretical development.

One large literature inspired by Olson's *Logic* essentially applies and elaborates the core microeconomics of small numbers and homogeneous interests. These applications were central to much of Olson's own subsequent work (especially Olson 1982) and to important works on international political economy and rent seeking.[3] Since this microeconomic approach is so strong in scholarship outside Latin America, later sections of this chapter review a series of geographic and economic factors that might be expected, according to this perspective, to affect collective action by business, and assess why these factors do not, as it turns out, have much impact on business politics in Latin America.

Another large literature spawned by Olson starts with the question, similar to mine, of why people act collectively more often than Olson's theory would predict. Surveying this large literature, Lichbach identified a dozen market or economic "solutions" to the problems of free riding and collective action (1996, chapter 3). Other "solutions" focus on expanded notions of self-interest and sociological factors like peer pressure and reputation to explain "excessive" collective action.[4] Most of these studies work to add nuance to Olson's brute calculations of self-interest and free riding. However, these nuanced approaches and expanded notions of self-interest are in fact less relevant for the study of business, the group for whom quite limiting assumptions about rationality and self-interest probably hold best.

Another set of insights from the second half of *Logic* about selective benefits and "by-products" received less attention and development, even from Olson himself. In this part of *Logic* Olson addressed the question of why many large, heterogeneous groups do manage, despite the obstacles,

---

[3] See Sandler (1992) for a full review of elaborations on Olson's work. See Manzetti (1993) for a direct application of Olson's theory of distributional coalitions to Argentine political economy. Frieden (1991) and Shafer (1994) used core Olsonian logic to generate sophisticated sectoral models of politics and development.

[4] Knoke (1990), for example, argues that individuals join associations not only for instrumental but also for affective and sociological (peer pressure) reasons. Hardin (1982) uses game theory to make the analysis of collective action more dynamic and embedded. When individuals interact over time and have overlapping types of interaction, then in ways reminiscent of Knoke's diverse incentives, they have more good reasons to engage in collective action. Similarly Chong (1991) explains collective action in the civil rights movement in the United States with reference to a range of contextual factors such as reputation, peer pressure, and assessment of the likelihood of success. Hardin (1995) explores further norms, identities, and collective action, especially in contexts of ethnic conflict.

to organize. His answer was selective incentives provided often, as in the case of labor and agriculture in the United States, by the state. Furthermore, institutionally strong and politically powerful associations are not necessarily the primary goals of members drawn by selective benefits but rather are the by-product of their contributions. However, there has been relatively little development of these arguments in terms of how and why states provide selective benefits or how different kinds of selective incentives have different effects on organizational development.

After considering briefly some partial theories of states and collective action, this chapter elaborates at greater length my argument that political variables best explain why business is better organized in Mexico, Chile, and Colombia than in Brazil and Argentina. This chapter develops an analysis of the "micro foundations" of state incentives and examines the political logics that lead state actors to seek, for example, to mobilize political support from business or to solicit business assistance to implement policies and enhance economic governance. The analysis then elaborates how state actors dissolve obstacles to collective action (primarily through selective benefits like delegated resources or access to policy forums) or in other cases promote defensive organization accidentally as they push reformist policies.

Subsequent sections of this chapter return to examine in greater detail some rejected hypotheses on the potential explanatory power of more static or structural variables such as geography, ownership patterns, regime type, and party systems. Overall these potential independent variables do not explain much of the variation discussed in Chapter 1, either because the variables have ambivalent impacts on incentives for collective action or because they do not vary enough or in the right direction to explain the remarkable differences in business organization over time or across the five cases. However, these factors sometimes add further nuance to round out my statist, political explanations. Structural factors may "set the scene," but they are insufficient proximate explanations of collective action that depended more on dynamic and strategic interactions between economic and state elites.

The Undertheorized State

In Olsonian arguments the state is rarely endogenized, and, if it comes up at all, the state is usually passive and faceless. Frieden, as noted earlier, considered the state to be a passive reactor to demands from organized economic groups. Similarly, Olson's later work (1982) relegated the state to the role of victim to predation by distributional coalitions.[5] Michael Shafer (1994) starts with an extended Olsonian explanation of collective action based on sectoral characteristics and asset specificity but also incorporates a more nuanced view of the state, though still largely as a passive actor. He endogenizes the state by making its development subject as well to the characteristics of the dominant export sector. So, for example, if mining is the main export activity, then not only does the mining industry organize to pressure the state, but the state itself is more receptive to these demands because it depends on the mining sector. John Bowman's (1989) study of collective action in the U.S. coal industry argues that business often relies on outside actors – suppliers, labor unions, and the state – to solve its problems with collective action. However, allowing the state to help them organize is risky for business because states are vulnerable to pressures from antibusiness groups. In the end, though, Bowman analyzes only the demand side – why capitalists would ask the state to organize them – not the supply side – why state actors might take the initiative to organize business.

Some recent studies of civil society acknowledge the heavy presence of the state. In a study of civic engagement in the United States, Skocpol argued that "the story of American voluntarism has been clearly one of symbiosis between state and society – not a story of society apart from, or instead of, the state" (1999a, 70).[6] Similarly, the overview chapter to another volume on civil society argues that "the civil society argument focuses on the ways in which society organizes itself *independently of the state* or *over against the state*. But states arguably shape their societies as profoundly as the reverse. They provide the constitutional, legal, political, and even moral framework within which social organizations arise and operate" (Edwards and Foley 2001, 13). Yet neither "symbiosis" nor "framework" is an adequate starting point for theorizing the more direct

---

[5] Anne Krueger's (1974) theory of rent seeking, which informs much of the work on collective action by business, starts with the state: it is the initial provision of rents by the state that turns capitalists into rent seekers. Much subsequent work on rent seeking ignores this sequence and focuses instead on how predatory groups exact rents from vulnerable states.

[6] Skocpol continues: "huge wars have stimulated the founding of associations and, in their aftermath, renewed associational memberships. Similarly, the growth of federal social spending . . . , has also been good for civic associations, which championed these programs and often grew along with them" (1999a, 70). Later in the same volume Skocpol argues that a variety of factors explain the transformation of civic life in the late twentieth century, "including racial and gender change, shifts in the political opportunity structure, new techniques and models for building organizations, and recent transformations in U.S. class relations" (1999b, 480–1).

and strategic actions by state officials that organized business in Latin America.

Theda Skocpol's introduction to the volume *Bringing the State Back In* summarized major arguments on how the organizational configurations of states, "along with their overall patterns of activity . . . , encourage some kinds of group formation and collective political actions (but not others)" (1985, 21). In general, "state structures, established interest groups, and oppositional groups all may mirror one another's forms of organization and scopes of purpose" (24).[7] Skocpol termed this a "Tocquevillean" approach (based on his analysis of the *ancien régime*) in which "the investigator looks more macroscopically at the ways in which the structures and activities of states unintentionally influence the formation of groups and the political capacities, ideas and demands of various sectors of society" (21). This Tocquevillean view takes a fairly distant, structural, and limited view of state "architecture."[8] This kind of macroscopic perspective may be useful for examining enduring differences among group organization in countries with states as different as those found in Europe and the United States but less so in explaining shorter-term organization in an area like Latin America, where states are characterized by both greater structural similarities and greater volatility over time in the organization of governments and regimes.[9] A more complete and compelling approach for Latin America must incorporate instead a *micro*scopic view that focuses on state actors and their goals and resources and that considers the consequences of intended actions as well as unintended organizational by-products.

The literature on corporatism consistently factors in the state, though usually as a similarly static or structural feature rather than a dynamic participant.[10] Schmitter provided an extensive analysis of states and corporatism, but he was ultimately skeptical about generalizable

[7] William Coleman also argues that the "macropolitical institutions" of the state explain differences in "comprehensive" business associations, and he extends the mirror metaphor: "Different historical experiences of authority and policy styles favoured by a given state appear to foster systems of comprehensive associations fashioned somewhat in that state's image" (1990, 233).

[8] As Skocpol notes of Tocqueville's analysis of the French Revolution, "Effects of the state permeated Tocqueville's argument, even though he said little about the activities and goals of the state officials themselves" (1985, 21).

[9] In her analysis of business politics in the United States, Cathie Jo Martin has a more dynamic analysis of how political actors mobilized business allies to reform tax policy (1991, especially 196–7).

[10] Schmitter's (1974) initial distinction between state and societal corporatism was mostly definitional, though he noted that the travails of late capitalist development prompted

arguments: "the emergence of neocorporatism (and its persistence) cannot be predicted from the micro-motives of interested private individuals or public employees. Nor can it be analysed exclusively in terms of the macrofunctional imperatives of either the capitalist economy or the democratic polity" (1985, 44). However, Schmitter's neocorporatism is the societal variety, where state, business, and labor all have independent power and the institutional arrangements among them are bargained and hence contingent, and cannot be explained by any one set of actors and preferences. His focus is also on tripartite arrangements rather than just collective action by business. The situation in Latin America is distinct: labor unions are weaker, and business is more dependent on, and responsive to, the state. So it makes better sense there to look more closely at the "micro-motives" of state actors.

Overall, what is still lacking in existing statist arguments is a more dynamic and microanalytical appreciation of the impacts of changing contexts, especially economic crises and new development strategies, on the incentives state actors have to shape collective action by business. Schmitter and Streeck offer the most extensive discussion of hypothesized relations between states and collective action in the research framework they propose for the study of business associations in advanced industrial countries. They consider 10 factors that affect how states influence the general organization of business (and an additional 8 factors affecting narrower sectoral associations) (1999, 33–5). Most of these factors are structural or relatively constant features of states such as levels of centralization and of state intervention in the economy. Again the focus is more on how capitalists organize in response to the kinds of states they confront than on how and why state actors might help them organize. However, a subset of their variables deals "with the international economic and political vulnerability of the country, and the hypothesis would be that the greater the perception by those in power of this vulnerability, the greater will be their inclination to intervene to create a 'favorable' set of organizational properties for business associations" (1999, 35). This is the kind of argument I develop, but obviously much needs to be done to specify things like perceptions of vulnerability, opportunities for creating "favorable" business organizations (opportunities constrained by the constellation of preexisting associations), and the unintended organizational consequences of other kinds of state actions.

states to intervene more in the organization of social groups, especially labor. See also Offe (1995, 127).

More recent work in the comparative political economy of developed countries, especially *Varieties of Capitalism*, pulls the state back out of the analytic framework and privileges instead the private sector (Hall and Soskice 2001b, 4–7). My approach shares with this framework a central focus on strategic interactions between firms and their environments, and on the general enterprise of concentrating on the organization of the private sector to discern crucial differences among capitalist systems. Where I part company is on the role of the state, which is surprisingly absent in Hall and Soskice's framework. In addition, Hall and Soskice are less interested in where the institutions of "coordinated" and "liberal" market economies come from, as I am centrally in this book, and more on an equilibrium analysis of institutional complementarities and the consequences of each variety for economic performance, subjects I return to in Part III.

Why State Actors Organize Business

What incentives do self-interested state actors have to organize business?[11] Sometimes the incentives are crudely Machiavellian when state actors seek only to generate support and minimize opposition. In other instances, state actors promote business organization in order to reveal or construct the collective preferences of business, commonly known as "aggregating interests." And sometimes policy makers are motivated to achieve particular policy goals and enlist business collaboration to these ends. The variety of arrangements to further policy goals can range from the simple exchange of information between business associations and government officials to the devolution to associations of full responsibility for policy implementation. Taken together, the goals of state actors are to reduce their vulnerabilities or to enhance government effectiveness, and these ends are distinct from other political goals – more common among politicians in political society – to use policy directly for partisan advantage and electoral benefit.

Empirically, who were the relevant state actors? They usually comprised a small number of people in the president's informal inner circle, cabinet ministers, and officials in the top two or three levels of ministries responsible for economic policies. The level of state actors involved varied with the scope and significance of the policy. For macrostabilization

---

[11] My arguments on how and why state actors help business organize apply to both voluntary associations and corporatist organizations, at least in their formative years. Over time, however, corporatist associations tend to take on lives of their own, and their persistence often has little to do with the political logic that prompted their initial creation.

and changing development strategies, the actors were likely to be at the very top; for sectoral issues, the actors might be senior officials in the ministry responsible for the particular policy area. Significantly, elected politicians in legislatures had little impact on collective action by business. Earlier in the twentieth century, some business associations were drawn into electoral skirmishes (generally to their regret), but the rule later in the century was for associations to steer clear of partisan or electoral entanglements in order to facilitate workable relations with whoever won the elections. If business associations abstained from electoral and party politics, then politicians had little to gain from meddling in their organization. So, beyond initial foundational moments, elected or party politicians rarely attempted to shape business organization. Labor unions in Latin America, in contrast, were often closely allied with parties, and elected politicians (both pro- and anti-labor) were keen to meddle in the organization of labor (see Collier and Collier 1991). Hence, my discussion of microfoundations draws a clear distinction between politicians' self-interest in reelection, which drives the bulk of theorizing about microfoundations of government action, and the interests of appointed officials who do not try to use business associations to promote directly their reelection.

Table 2.1 lists a variety of incentives or goals state actors historically have had to promote business organization and closer business–government relations. These incentives were generally stronger under the conditions of perceived vulnerabilities; however, it is essential to

TABLE 2.1 *Incentives for State Actors to Promote Organization by Business*

Incentive	Mechanism	Vulnerabilities Intensifying Incentives
Generate political support	Privileged access for associations	Changing development strategy; political crises
Aggregate business preferences	Regular consultation	International crises (war, trade); political crises (regime transition); high cost of information (large numbers of firms, few public resources)
Implement policies	Concertation	Policy success depends on rapid coordination; economic crises
Delegate policies	Semiautonomous sectoral governance	Risk of policy politicization; large numbers of firms involved; low administrative capacity

disaggregate the sources of vulnerability in order to understand the variable uses of business associations to mitigate those vulnerabilities. The first set of political incentives in generating support was often evident historically when associations started to emerge. In industry, for example, many associations began forming in the crisis years of the 1930s at a time when state actors saw opportunities for strengthening and institutionalizing support from business associations, especially for new development strategies. In Brazil developmentalism was at the core of the close, mutually supportive relationships that developed in the 1930s and 1940s between newly formed industry associations and the governments of Getúlio Vargas (see Schneider 1999). In Mexico in the same period, presidents used corporatist laws to create Canacintra (Cámara Nacional de la Industria de Transformación), composed largely of smaller national and nationalist firms, that strongly supported the expansion of the developmental state. State actors also encouraged rival business organizations to weaken opposition to new development strategies. In an extreme example, Perón outlawed the adversarial industry association UIA and nurtured a new association, CGE (Confederación General Económica), similar to Canacintra in its overrepresentation of smaller nationalist capitalists, as well as its loyalty to the government. In later periods, more general political crises sometimes prompted governments to seek out business associations. A prime example is Pinochet's turn to business associations in the wake of street protests against his dictatorship in 1983. The sources of vulnerability varied over time and space, but state actors felt that strengthening business associations and consulting with them could mitigate these vulnerabilities.

In other instances, state actors merely wanted to know the existing preferences rather than persuade business to support government policy. To do so, state actors tried to organize business in ways that were most conducive to aggregating and intermediating preferences. Incentives for encouraging business to find a collective voice are higher in periods of rapid change and difficult communication, as during the Mexican revolution or the world wars.[12] The story of the foundation of ANDI (Asociación Nacional de Industriales), the Colombia industry association, is revealing (and is discussed later at greater length). In 1944 President Alfonso López Pumarejo called industrialists together for a meeting and told them he

---

[12] For Europe, Johan Olsen argued generally that "during wars, depressions, or other national crises, as well as during crises in specific sectors of society, integrated organizational participation by peak associations becomes more frequent" (1981, 502).

did not have time to talk to each of them separately; they would therefore have to decide on one spokesman for industry, who would then have open access to the president (Urrutia 1983, 72). Two weeks later Medellín industrialists chose a spokesman, and the formal organization of ANDI followed quickly.[13]

Beyond aggregating and reconciling preferences, policy makers may also seek basic information on economic activity in the private sector such as production, investment, employment, capacity utilization, technology, exports, and prices. Where possible, state actors presumably prefer to rely on their own bureaucracies to collect unbiased information, but in many instances the costs are too high, especially in the short run (see also Schmitter 1985, 46).[14] Therefore policy makers often turn to association leaders for help in collecting information. In the early days of the developmental state in the 1940s and 1950s, good information was especially costly, and valuable, to planners. Subsequent fiscal crises also reduced state capacity and sometimes generated greater dependence of officials on associations. In one extreme example, Marcio Fortes, the secretary of industry of the state of Rio de Janeiro in the late 1990s, relied on the state's industry federation for information, meeting space, research, and even airplane tickets to go abroad to drum up investment, because the state government did not "have the means" (interview, 27 November 1997).

In areas where policies are designed to change the behavior of nonstate actors, policy makers face common implementation problems of how to ensure compliance. Associations can help in a variety of ways. A first, simple issue may be communication, and associations can provide the most effective means of communicating policy changes. Government ministers in Latin America, for example, regularly accept invitations to speak at association meetings and conventions. Policies that attempt to induce new behaviors in private actors may run into resistance, so policy makers may appeal to associations and their leaders to use their persuasive and other

---

[13] Strong encompassing associations can be particularly useful to state actors pursuing policies with differential impacts across sectors, as for example setting tariffs with differential impacts on up- and downstream producers.

[14] Information from associations is not, of course, costless because associations have incentives to bias or manipulate the information. In principle, officials should favor associations with greater institutional capacity, namely, more professional staff, higher density, and better procedures for internal representation (Doner and Schneider 2000). These features of institutional capacity reduce uncertainty for officials on the quality of information associations provide.

powers to elicit cooperation from member firms.[15] Generally, the more urgent the crisis policy makers face, and the more desperate they are to change business behavior (rein in, for example, price increases or capital flight), the more attractive the option of collaboration with associations will be.

Policy delegation takes the process of public–private collaboration further and delegates entirely some aspects of policy making and implementation to business associations. The incentives for such delegation are often similar to those in cases of joint implementation. Policy makers, however, may want to take the extra step if they feel state capacities are not sufficient for effective partnership, or if they feel that state offices are vulnerable to partisan takeover and subsequent politicization of policy. In one extreme example, during the Mexican Revolution the government lost control of currency emission and asked business associations to issue "scrip to provide reliable fractional currency and to retire dubious revolutionary issues" (Shafer 1973, 30). In Colombia the coffee federation, Federacafe, was the most economically significant example of government-delegated sectoral governance in Latin America. Colombian politics stand out in Latin America as extremely partisan, conflictual, and violent. It is remarkable then that coffee policy has, since its delegation to Federacafe in 1928, been so insulated from legislatures, parties, and partisan squabbles. Reflecting on the benefits of this delegation and insulation, both for the coffee sector and for politics generally, Miguel Urrutia, a prominent Colombian economist, wondered how different Argentine history might have been had policies for wheat and beef been so insulated (1983, 134).

In sum, state actors had a variety of incentives to promote collective action by business, and the intensity of those preferences (shaped by perceived vulnerabilities) depended on factors such as the economic and political conjuncture, the resources available to state actors, and the types of existing business organizations they could call on. For newly appointed officials in the Ministry of Finance or the Ministry of Industry and Commerce, the situation, in a stylized account, was commonly the following. The appointees were under pressure to act quickly but soon found out that they lacked information, competent and sufficient staff, and material

---

[15] Cooperation is especially important when policies interfere in traditional management spheres, that is, when states intervene in matters "related to production, investment and employment rather than the more traditional areas of infrastructure provision, income distribution, consumer protection, or social welfare" (Schmitter 1985, 46).

resources; at the same time, they could expect opposition from some sectors of business and other social groups to almost any policy they adopted. Under these conditions of multiple vulnerabilities, turning to business associations for help often made great sense. Of course, some appointees did not turn to associations, as will be seen in Part II, sometimes because they were ideologically indisposed and often, in the later decades of the twentieth century, because state actors deemed existing associations unreliable. However, state officials who avoided contact with associations usually perceived the same vulnerabilities and incentives, and often attempted to bypass associations and devise ad hoc, informal consultations with business seeking the same sorts of assistance: political support, information, or help in implementing policies.

In laying out this framework for the empirical analysis to follow in Part II, it is important to signal some of the empirical limitations that come up later. Precise, concrete documentation of the motives of state actors was not easy to collect, especially from periods earlier in the twentieth century. Even where interview research was feasible, it was not possible to talk directly to all participants. Hence, the evidence presented in the country chapters is sometimes circumstantial. But the circumstantial evidence is consistent: state actors usually helped business to organize at times we would expect conditions to intensify their preferences for stronger business organizations and a closer collaboration with them. Where it was possible to research the motives of state officials directly, their responses generally confirmed the hypotheses presented here.

How State Actors Organize Business

When state actors turned to associations for support, information, or other help, they usually gave business associations access to policy-making circles and other forms of assistance. This assistance often became the core selective incentive that held together "unnatural," encompassing associations in Latin America. To simplify, state actions to dissolve obstacles to collective action, following Olson, were either to remove the free-rider problem by making membership compulsory or to provide significant selective benefits through exclusive access to public resources or policy making (see Schmitter 1995b, 293). Most important in the empirical analysis that follows in Part II were decisions by state actors to grant associations privileged access. It is important to note at the outset that state actors could not organize business whenever and however they pleased (and Chapter 7 offers some contrasts to stronger Asian states that could).

Private business was generally unable on its own to solve collective action problems and form encompassing associations. In this sense, state actions were necessary and usually sufficient to generate an organizational response from business. However, the response was not always what the officials wanted or expected, and in some cases business leaders vetoed state initiatives or successfully pressed for major modifications. In essence, state incentives for collective action had an impact because organizational entrepreneurs in the private sector were eager to use them. Leaders of associations or would-be leaders recognized the value of the public benefits for strengthening the position of association leaders vis-à-vis their members (Schmitter and Streeck 1999).

Table 2.2 captures the diverse range of incentives encountered historically in Latin America for both corporatist and voluntary associations. Nonmaterial benefits like privileged access to government officials or policy forums were common positive incentives for the strong, encompassing associations listed in Table 2.2. For example, in the 1960s, industry associations in Chile and Colombia had seats on scores of public boards,

TABLE 2.2 *State-Provided Incentives for Collective Action*

Country	Association	Selective Incentives
Mexico	CMHN	Privileged access through monthly luncheons
	CCE	Negotiating role in social pacts and Nafta negotiations; privileged access through monthly dinners
Chile	CPC	Privileged access (especially 1984–94)
	Sofofa	Access through representation on public boards; delegated public functions (e.g., vocational education)
Colombia	Federacafe	Revenues from export tax; price stabilization fund; representation on government councils
	ANDI	Access through representation on public boards
	CG	Occasional consultation
Argentina	CGE	Compulsory membership and representation on public boards, though only briefly during Peronist governments
	UIA	Sporadic inclusion on government boards and in social pacts
Brazil	CNI	Compulsory membership; delegated responsibility for government-funded vocational program
	IEDI	None

Note: These and other selective incentives are examined at greater length in the country chapters.

councils, and commissions. CMHN, the exclusive Mexican association, had the most impressive access; a few dozen of its members lunched each month with a minister or another top representative of the government. Access by these multisectoral associations improved during periods of crises when state actors sought business support, but regular access sustained collective action over time. Weaker associations in Argentina sometimes had access, but it was sporadic, ad hoc, and dependent on particular governments. In Brazil, encompassing industry associations had impressive access to policy forums in the 1940s and 1950s but subsequently were largely excluded.[16]

The benefit of privileged access requires some fundamental rethinking of Olson's original theory. Olson claimed that "the provision of public or collective goods is the fundamental function of organizations generally" (1965, 15). Such nonexcludable, collective goods are subject to free riding, which in turn can be overcome only by providing separate selective incentives. But what if the relationship between government and the association generates mostly club benefits available to members only rather than public goods? When, as is common in Latin America, policy decisions are specific – for example, loans, tax exemptions, market restrictions, or quotas for particular products or sectors – associations mediate information on government benefits and make it available collectively to active members only.[17] It is not that access for associations to government policy makers facilitates individualized rent seeking by members, but rather that access for associations to government allows associations, in turn, to disseminate to members, as a selective benefit, information on government policies and distribution of public benefits.

---

[16] Institutionalized access for business associations was also common in Andean countries; (Conaghan 1990, 76; 1992, 225). In Peru business leaders had seats on consultative commissions that dealt with specific issues such as trade and tariffs. In Ecuador representatives of business associations sat on the boards of directors of institutions such as the Monetary Board, the Social Security Institute, and the Industrial Development Center. In Bolivia associations were formally represented in agencies such as the Social Security Institute and state banks. However, these arrangements were sometimes "as frustrating as they [were] useful" because business representatives were often in a minority and because major policy decisions were often decided elsewhere (Conaghan 1992, 225–6). In Uruguay by 1973 there were over 50 different government boards and commissions that included representatives from business associations (Filgueira 1988, 498).

[17] Lichbach notes that making goods more excludable and clubbish or private, as in some selective benefits, is one of the two dozen solutions to the "cooperator's dilemma," but he does not mention the state as a probable source of these solutions. In fact he criticizes the "selective incentives" solution as "logically incomplete" because "it does not specify where the resources required to offer selective incentives come from. This omission is not trivial" (1996, 203). See also Hardin (1982, 19).

Moreover, sitting at the table with government representatives may also yield intangible or indirect, though excludable, benefits. For example, in fluid, personalized economic bureaucracies, just getting to know the bureaucrats who are making policy gives leaders of business associations a sense of where policy is going, reduces uncertainty, and facilitates regular communication outside the ambit of the policy council (Addis 1999, 49). In addition, and sometimes just as important as the positive benefits derived from a policy council, association representatives can block policy initiatives deemed harmful. Although business representatives rarely have a majority on policy councils, they have recourse to common committee tactics of delays, proposing studies, and raising alternatives.[18] In sum, if potential members want input on what information and policy preferences the representative of their association takes to a meeting with government officials, and they value access to the information the association representative brings out of the meeting, then the option of free riding is uninteresting. Rather, potential members will have strong incentives for collective action and for investing significant time and resources in the association.

Of course, the formal existence of a consultative body or public–private committee or board does not necessarily mean that real decisions are taken there. To be meaningful, the consultative body has to meet regularly, foreclose alternative channels of communication, and distribute significant resources. If capitalists continue to have individual access outside institutional channels or a wider portfolio of political options, then privileged access for associations is not as valuable and the incentives for contributing to associations consequently are weaker. In Brazil association representatives sat in some government forums, but they were not viewed as significant venues and policy makers did not close off alternative channels of informal access.[19] Talking about his lack of interest in

---

[18] Miguel Urrutia sums up well the less visible advantages of the access benefit in the case of Colombian agriculture: "this institutional access to various Juntas or Councils does not always give SAC [Sociedad de Agricultores de Colombia] direct influence over the policies discussed in these Forums, but perhaps it offers SAC the possibility to delay decisions, by showing the government possible conflicts, or by using dilatory tactics. This access also keeps channels of communication with the government permanently open, which makes it possible to keep officials abreast of opinions in the association on measures taken, and to pressure, based on technical arguments, for modifications in policies that could benefit the sector. This informal contact is more important for associations than the formal participation in Juntas or Councils" (1983, 40).

[19] Similarly, in France, thousands of public–private committees existed by the 1960s, and nearly all business associations participated in some of them. However, in the 1970s, no

FIESP (Federação das Indústrias do Estado de São Paulo), one prominent industrialist said, "I don't need FIESP; I call whomever I please" in the government (interview with Paulo Villares, 28 January 1993). In contrast, Jaime Serra Puche, the Mexican secretary of commerce and industry in the early 1990s, told his staff to work only through business associations, so firms had strong incentives to invest in them (interview 15 July 1996).

Beyond encouraging simple affiliation, the selective benefit of access also increases incentives for greater member investment of time and resources in the association. In terms of time, struggles over leadership positions are likely to intensify since association leaders are the ones who sit on, or appoint those who sit on, the consultative boards. So, members have strong incentives to promote leaders sympathetic to their concerns. In terms of material resources, association leaders try to extract more funds from members in order to develop in-house technical capacity to allow them to participate effectively in consultative bodies dominated by government technocrats armed with sophisticated data analyses. Chilean associations, for example, invested more in technical staff once they were invited to participate more in policy forums, both in the 1950s and again in the 1980s (Silva 1996, 90, 156, 205). Mexican business leaders, especially members of CMHN, invested millions of dollars in the 1970s and 1980s, once access to the government became more institutionalized, in building the technical staff and capabilities of CCE.[20] Thus this benefit of privileged access can elicit much higher investment in collective action than other kinds of selective benefits and thereby generate stronger, richer associations.[21] Access also shifts relations among associations. If, for example, two associations seek to organize the same members, then granting access to one of them should dramatically shift members' investment. In Argentina, for example, shifting memberships and investments in associations was common after the 1940s as firms joined whatever associations were favored by the government of the moment. In other cases, granting access to the economy-wide association, rather than to sectoral

---

business leaders in one survey (*N* = 33) ranked these committees as the most effective means of action to influence policy. Over 40 percent said that informal contacts with ministers or bureaucrats were the most effective (Wilson 1983, 899–900).

[20] Interview with Francisco Calderon, executive director of CCE from 1976 to 1997, 19 May 1998. CMHN members decided not to hire staff directly for CMHN but rather to build technical capacity in CCE.

[21] This finding contradicts fairly directly the relationship hypothesized by Schmitter and Streeck that privileged access would encourage members to become "passive political customers buying . . . decisions produced by their association on their behalf" (1999, 84).

member associations, strengthened the all-encompassing association and its leadership vis-à-vis member associations (see Schmitter and Streeck 1999, 36–7).

In sum, state actors in Latin America have dissolved obstacles to collective action by providing a variety of selective benefits. The selective benefit of access to policy forums was a common magnet holding together voluntary, encompassing associations. In theoretical terms, this kind of selective incentive requires a further elaboration of Olson's logic. At issue is whether the government provides *collective* or public goods available to members and nonmembers alike, subject therefore to the free riding that is the keystone of Olson's original theory, or whether the government provides *selective* or club, and therefore excludable, benefits. If the latter, research on collective action should move away from a preoccupation with free riding and the characteristics of social groups (numbers, diversity, asset specificity, etc.) and toward the state and the terms of interaction between states and associations.

Labor Unions, Property Rights, and Defensive Encompassing Organization

Several kinds of government policies perceived as threatening to business had the unintended consequence of helping business form or strengthen encompassing associations.[22] Depending on the political context, a range of policies appeared threatening to business at various points in the twentieth century. In the empirical analyses that follow in Part II, the most common threats that triggered an organizational response by business revolved around labor organization earlier in the twentieth century and abrogation of property rights later in the century.[23]

Many governments in Latin America intervened extensively and institutionally in wage negotiations, strikes, and union organization, especially in the wake of the Great Depression and the early years of ISI

---

[22] Many studies emphasize the role of threats in encouraging counterorganization by business, including Acuña (1998, 55–6), Lowi (1964, 707, as cited in Menges 1966, 359), Durand and Silva (1998), and Menges (1966, 359). Frieden also notes that "where class conflict is salient, it overrides sectoral demands" (1991, 34), but he neglects the impact such conflict has on promoting multisectoral organizations.

[23] Some chapters in Part II note that an additional threat that encouraged defensive business mobilization, especially in Colombia, Venezuela, Brazil, and Mexico, was the rapid growth of state intervention into the economy in the 1960s and 1970s. However, the threat of state intervention was historically not as acute as labor organization or direct expropriation and hence had a weaker organizational impact.

(import-substituting industrialization) (see Buchanan 1995; Collier and Collier 1991). Initial state interventions in labor organization were often triggering points for the establishment of employer associations in Mexico, Argentina, and Chile in the 1920s and 1930s. Labor incorporation through legislation favoring workers and unions usually occurred under crisis conditions and populist governments. This form of incorporation initially appeared threatening to general capitalist interests and hence intensified common business opposition to progressive labor legislation. To the extent that common interests gain higher priority, they lower obstacles to collective action in encompassing associations and give business stronger incentives to organize in order to influence state actors.

Parenthetically, deep state intervention into labor markets, wages, unions, and strikes reduced incentives for business to organize lasting employers associations (see Acuña 1998, 51, and Schvarzer and Sidicaro 1988, 233). Business organized not to deal directly with labor but rather to influence state policies concerning labor. Even Coparmex, the only employers' confederation to survive, did not bargain directly with labor, but rather organized to influence government labor legislation and rulings. This is a crucial difference between northern Europe and late industrializers in Latin America and elsewhere. In northern Europe, business invests both in sectoral associations grouped around product markets and in multisectoral employers' associations designed to bargain with labor unions. Elsewhere some compulsory associations like FIESP in Brazil did negotiate with labor unions, but even FIESP was organized on sectoral lines primarily as a trade association. The lack of employer associations in Latin America constitutes an example, following Skocpol (1985), of how the "structure and activities" of the state account for broad differences between Latin America and Europe.

Later in the twentieth century, other state actions threatened property rights and thereby also increased incentives for collective action, especially in the form of encompassing associations. Land redistribution in Mexico and Chile in the 1970s, and attempts to nationalize banking in Mexico and Peru in the 1980s, prompted capitalists to establish new economy-wide peak associations or resuscitate dormant ones. Threats to property rights reduced barriers to collective action by making the common interest in private property more important than contending business or sectoral interests. But in this case, the relevant unit of analysis is not just the individual businessperson but also the leaders of existing associations. In principle, and as discussed further in Chapter 8, when encompassing collective action takes place among associations, not individuals, free riding is less of an obstacle. Associations are few in number and run by professional staffs that reduce the costs of monitoring the contributions of other member associations. The greater obstacle to collective action among sectoral associations is divergent interests of the association members of the peak organization. Once the interests of member associations are "homogenized" by government threats to property, leaders of sectoral associations have relatively less trouble relinquishing some autonomy in order to create all-encompassing peak associations.[24]

Despite important triggering effects from threatening states, lasting institutional strength of associations resulted primarily from positive benefits delegated by state actors. Thus, peak associations were often born in defensive mobilization, but infant mortality was high in the absence of subsequent government support. Many encompassing associations can trace their origins to a particular moment of crisis due to state threats in labor markets or property rights. However, there were also numerous historical instances of ephemeral organization in response to threats, but these associations then evaporated once the threat receded. Argentine capitalists created numerous peak associations, ranging from early employer associations in the 1920s to movements to oppose Isabela Perón's government in the 1970s, that all disappeared along with the initial threat. In Brazil business mobilized against the reformist policies of the Goulart government that favored labor and threatened property rights but demobilized after the coup in 1964. These defensive mobilizations never generated lasting organizations, in large part because governments in Brazil and Argentina never extended to these incipient associations selective benefits like privileged access or public functions.

Arguments that overemphasize the role of strife between business and progressive politics in the formation of encompassing business organization often suffer methodologically from problems of selection bias. That is, while the histories of most existing economy-wide associations include earlier episodes of conflict, the analysis must also include in the sample associations created in moments of conflict that did not outlive the conflict.

---

[24] Finding a common interest is also easier in defensive, rather than offensive, action (Waarden 1991, 5, citing Hardin 1982, 120). There are some exceptions. In Portugal "the radical expropriation of industry and financial institutions [in the 1970s] disoriented the initial response of capitalists and fragmented them by sectors" (Schmitter 1995b, 310). In Peru in the early 1970s SNI (National Society of Industrialists) endorsed confiscatory agrarian reform (in the hope that they might stall reform in other areas) but later joined with agriculture and other sectors in opposing the reformist military government after it outlawed the National Agrarian Society (SNA) and confiscated its assets (Conaghan 1992, 205).

Including these extinct associations in the analysis makes it clear that additional factors – like government-provided selective benefits – helped surviving associations hold together.

To sum up the chapter so far, state actors increased incentives for business to organize either by threatening business interests through reformist policies or, more importantly in the long run, by providing them with public resources or access. State actors often granted benefits to associations in efforts to gain business support, aggregate business preferences, or overcome limitations in state capacity in order to get policies implemented. The remaining sections of this chapter consider a range of additional factors and contending hypotheses. Although none of these contending hypotheses are sufficient to explain the wide variation across the large countries of Latin America, they sometimes bring in factors that complement and round out my core arguments.

Geographic Factors: Country Size and Regional Concentration

In comparisons across a larger number of cases, country size seems to correlate with collective action in ways consistent with microeconomic, Olsonian expectations. In principle, businesses in smaller countries should be less heterogeneous, smaller in number, and better able to communicate and network among themselves. In Europe social groups tended to be better organized in smaller countries (Katzenstein 1985, 93).[25] By one measure of population the correlation also holds fairly well in Latin America, where only one of the three largest countries had a strong economy-wide peak association (and the Consejo Gremial in Colombia was recent and skeletal), while most of the smaller Andean, Central American, and Caribbean countries had them (see Table 2.3). However, Mexico, the second largest country, is a significant outlier with a strong peak association, as are smaller countries like Uruguay and Ecuador that did not have economy-wide associations.

The size hypothesis might hold better in agriculture, where smaller territorial size and greater geographical homogeneity do seem to correlate with collective action. Agriculture is, of course, necessarily geographically dispersed, and the larger and more varied the national territory, the more likely agriculture is to be more diverse among regions. In Brazil and Mexico, two of the largest countries in terms of territorial extension,

---

[25] Wallerstein (1989) argues that union density in advanced industrial countries is largely a function of country size.

TABLE 2.3 *Economy-Wide Peak Associations in Latin America*

Country	Association	Date Established	Population (millions)
Chile	CPC	1933	12
Venezuela	Fedecamaras	1944	16
Bolivia	CEPB	1958	6
Mexico	CCE	1975	68
Peru	CONFIEP	1983	18
Colombia	Consejo Gremial	1991	28
Uruguay	None		3
Argentina	None		29
Brazil	None		127
Ecuador	None		9

Sources: For information on peak associations, see Durand (1994, 109), Conaghan (1990, 77), Filgueira (1988), and the appendixes. Business created a peak association in Ecuador in 1981 but it "never functioned" (Conaghan 1992, 216). Other cases include Panama in 1964 and Paraguay in 1951. All the countries of Central America also have encompassing peak associations. Population is for 1982 from IDB (1992, 285).

agriculture varies greatly from north to south, and only weak corporatist associations exist for agriculture as a whole (Porras Martínez 2000). In contrast, agriculture is more homogeneous in Chile and Argentina, and landowners organized in the nineteenth century associations that were very powerful early in the twentieth century (Wright 1982). Members of the SRA (Sociedad Rural Argentina) dominated Argentine politics until the 1940s (Smith 1969), and even at the end of the twentieth century the SRA had a budget four to five times larger than that of the industry association UIA (see Appendix A). Colombia is an intermediate case, both because Andean geography created greater diversity in agricultural production but, more importantly, because the state created an extremely powerful coffee association. Prior to the creation of Federacafe, large landowners in Colombia had, as in Chile and Argentina, formed an important voluntary association (Bejarano 1985; Urrutia 1983).

In industry, however, country size is not necessarily a good proxy for the heterogeneity and dispersion of business due to the historical tendency in Latin America for industry to concentrate in a small number of cities and regions (see Table 2.4). By international standards Brazil, Mexico, Colombia, and Argentina are all large land masses with great geographic diversity, but the economic elites in their respective industrial heartlands of São Paulo, Valle de México, Bogotá, and Buenos Aires were relatively small and concentrated. This regional concentration should

TABLE 2.4 *Regional Concentration of Economic Activity in Latin America (Percentage of Total Output)*

Country	Center	Second Pole
Industrial production		
Mexico	39	9
Chile	49	19
Argentina	68	9
Brazil	44	~10
Total Production		
Mexico	34	7
Chile	45	11
Colombia	24	15
Brazil	35	12

Sources: For Mexico in 1993, INEGI, "Producto Interno Bruto por Entidad Federativa para el período 1993–1999," Cuadro 81, http://www.inegi.gob.mx/difusion/espanol/fbie.html. For Chile in 1990, Banco Central de Chile, "Anuario de Cuentas Nacionales 1998," http://www.ine.cl/Territoriales/acecoweb.htm. For Argentina in 1974, IEA (1988, 196–7). For Brazil in 1985, Affonso and Silva (1995, 260). For Colombia in 1993, DANE (1998, 45). The "Centers" were Valle de México and the Federal District combined for Mexico, São Paulo, Santiago, Bogotá, and the province and capital of Buenos Aires. The secondary poles were Nuevo León in Mexico, Antioquia in Colombia, Bio Bio in Chile, Santa Fé in Argentina, and Rio de Janeiro in Brazil.

generally facilitate collective action by lowering the costs of communication and social interaction (see Feldman and Nocken 1975, 419 on Germany). However, the relative share of the center of economic production does not in these five cases show any apparent relation to the strength of encompassing organization by business. Argentina's business associations were weak despite very high levels of concentration in the province of Buenos Aires and the capital district, and the concentration of economic activity in São Paulo is on par with the concentration in Mexico and higher than the general economic concentration in Colombia, both countries with stronger encompassing organizations.[26]

---

[26] Levels of regional concentration seem fairly stable over time. About two-thirds of industry in 1939 was located in the Buenos Aires metropolitan area (Rock 1985, 233). In 1970 the Valle de México (composed of the Federal District and the State of México) accounted

Industrial elites in the secondary manufacturing poles were especially important in the history of business politics in Colombia and Mexico. The second-ranked states of Rio de Janeiro, Antioquia (especially Medellín), and Nuevo León (especially Monterrey) produced about 10–20 percent of manufacturing output. These secondary poles might theoretically have posed significant challenges to national-level organizing, but in fact industrial leaders in these second poles, especially Monterrey and Medellín (as discussed further in Part II), did not undermine encompassing collective action; instead they took the lead in organizing and funding national organizations. These are important cases where diversity and heterogeneity (in this example, regional) actually contributed to encompassing collective action rather than detracted from it. The cases of Medellín and Monterrey also illustrate the problems of deducing preferences and strategies from economic position alone. The interests of industrialists in these regions often conflicted with those of industrialists in the major pole, yet industrialists from the secondary pole still opted to invest heavily in encompassing associations.[27]

In sum, microeconomic arguments relating small country size or relative regional concentration to stronger encompassing organization might work better for a larger sample that included smaller countries.[28] For my subsample of larger countries, the relationship is more complex and requires a closer examination of the actual regional and sectoral diversity within each country, as well as an empirical assessment of elite strategies for collective action. Argentina is similar in size to Mexico (territory) and Colombia (population), yet had weaker encompassing associations. The existence of robust encompassing associations in some large countries does not alone disconfirm size arguments, but it does suggest that there are other causes for the variation in collective action within my subsample of larger countries.

for 50 percent of industrial output and the state of Nuevo León for another 10 percent. By 1993 these shares had dropped to 43 percent and 9 percent, respectively (INEGI 1994). In Mexico the distribution was about the same for the 639 largest industrial firms: 49 percent in the Valle de México (Federal District and the State of Mexico) and 12 percent in the state of Nuevo León (Cordero H., Santín, and Tirado 1983, 46).

[27] The evidence is slim, but my hypothesis would be that industrialists in the second pole sought to dilute and balance the influence of the largest industrial region by roping industrialists from the primary region into an encompassing association. Following this hypothesis, the location of the primary pole in the capital also seems to matter. Had Rio de Janeiro been the dominant industrial center instead of São Paulo, the organization of business in Brazil might have looked quite different.

[28] See Collier and Mahoney (1996) on "causal heterogeneity" and selection bias generally.

Corporate Factors: Concentration, MNCs, and Conglomeration (or Why Sectoral Analysis Is So Problematic)

If firms are larger and more concentrated, then fewer firms would control more of the economy and presumably find it easier to overcome free riding and act collectively. For association leaders, high corporate concentration reduces the costs of organizing and increases the incentives for attracting each member on the margin (see Wallerstein 1989). Concentration may correlate inversely with country size, but concentration measures more directly the number of potential members necessary for high-density organization. In addition, the largest firms may, as Olson (1965, 35) hypothesized, have incentives to bear a disproportionately large share of the costs of collective action. Historically, the greater concentration of industry and the larger size of firms in the first round of late industrializers such as Germany are sometimes identified as partly responsible for the early and rapid development of business organizations (for example, Feldman and Nocken 1975, 419).

Although sparse and not directly comparable across countries, some estimates of corporate concentration in Latin America do seem to show a tenuous correlation between high ownership concentration and strong encompassing organization.[29] For manufacturing, aggregate concentration appeared higher in Colombia and Chile, where encompassing industry associations were strong, than in Argentina and Brazil, where encompassing associations were weak (see Table 2.5).[30] For Argentina the figures in

[29] The data in Table 2.5 come from studies that used different methods and may not be strictly comparable. Moreover, these sources and other studies usually include MNCs and state-owned firms in their calculations of concentration, which make the calculations less relevant for assessing the potential impact of ownership concentration on collective action by domestic business. Castañeda estimated the concentration among large firms by calculating the sales of the largest 10 industrial firms as a proportion of the sales of the top 100 firms: 42 percent in the United States, 49 percent in France, 36 percent in Japan, 59 percent in Mexico, 47 percent in Argentina, and 53 percent in Brazil (1982, 86). Again, his data are not very useful since they include Pemex and Petrobrás, the huge state-owned oil monopolies, which make industry in Mexico and Brazil appear very concentrated.

[30] In Brazil aggregate concentration seems fairly low. In 1992 the top 100 private national firms in terms of revenues produced about one-third of GDP (calculated from *Gazeta Mercantil* 1992). In 1974 the largest 100 industrial firms, including state and multinational firms, in Brazil accounted for 27 percent of manufacturing output, compared to about a third for the top 100 firms in the United States (Buarque de Holanda Filho 1983, 92). In Chile in 1957 the 20 largest manufacturing firms accounted for 28 percent of production, 19 percent of employment, and 52 percent of fixed capital (study by Lagos cited in Arriagada 1970, 42). Another study found that in 1966, 284 firms in Chile controlled

TABLE 2.5 *Levels of Aggregate Concentration in Industry (Percentage of Total Manufacturing Output)*

Country	Share of Largest:		
	20 Firms	50 Firms	100 Firms
Chile (1957)	28		
Colombia (1968)	22	37	46
(1984)	24	35	45
Brazil (1974)			27
Argentina (1956)			21
(1966)			29

Sources: For Colombia, World Bank (1991, 48); for Chile, the study by Lagos cited in Arriagada (1970, 42); for Brazil, Buarque de Holanda Filho (1983, 92); for Argentina, the study by Skupch cited in Niosi (1976, 245).

Table 2.5 are the lowest of several estimates of concentration. Other calculations put concentration in Argentina industry at a level comparable to that of Colombia.[31] By a different calculation of ownership concentration in nonfinancial firms, Mexico (.64) and Argentina (.50) rank higher than Chile (.41) and Brazil (.31).[32] These rankings correlate with the relative strength of business associations in Mexico and Brazil, but the rankings are inverted for Argentina and Chile.

A better estimate of concentration would focus on more or less informal economic groups or *grupos* rather than on individual firms because *grupos* control multiple firms. The empirical data are, however, even sketchier and cross-national comparison more problematic. Considering all GDP rather than just industry, in Mexico by 1989 the 37 members of CMHN controlled 70 major *grupos* that accounted for 22 percent of total GDP (Camp 2002, 54).[33] In Colombia only four *grupos* controlled a

all sectors in the economy, and 144 industrial firms had the potential to control all of industry (though the definition of "control" was not spelled out in the study by Garretón and Cisternas cited in Arriagada 1988, 79).

[31] In Argentina in 1954, "69 establishments... were responsible for 20 percent of the value of production of all industry" (Polit 1968, 400). However, according to a report in *La Nación* on 17 December 1955, 53 firms "supply approximately 40 percent of the industrial products consumed" (Polit 1968, 418).

[32] The measure is the average percentage of common shares owned by the three largest shareholders in the 10 largest nonfinancial, privately owned domestic firms (La Porta et al. 1999, cited in Sargent 2001, 22).

[33] Another study estimated that 12 *grupos* controlled firms that produced a third of manufacturing output (*Cuadernos de Nexos*, January 1993, p. VI). In another estimate, by

comparable 20 percent of GDP (Rettberg 2000, Chapter 3, p. 17). In Chile in the 1950s 11 *grupos* had control or influence over 290 corporations that accounted for 70 percent of corporate capital (Lagos 1961, cited in Johnson 1967, 54). In Argentina by the 1990s, 40 conglomerates participated in 700 firms and accounted for 25–30 percent of industrial production (Bisang 1998, 151). In a rare comparative estimate of the percentage of GDP accounted for by the sales of the 10 largest business groups, Colombia ranks first among Latin American countries with 28 percent, followed by Argentina with 11 percent, Mexico with 10 percent, and Brazil with 8 percent (Guillen 2001, 72). In sum, several, but not all, indicators of concentration rank Chile and Colombia at the top and Brazil at the bottom, while rankings for Argentina and Mexico vary substantially from measure to measure.

High economic concentration may have facilitated collective action in Chile, Mexico, and Colombia, but it is not a sufficient competing explanation for overall variations among the five cases. Empirically, the data are too incomplete and inconsistent to support any definitive conclusions. The data are inconsistent because different measures of concentration yield different rankings across countries. The data are incomplete because some studies do not explain their methods of calculation, and if they do, the methods differ across countries, making cross-national comparisons problematic. Analytically, high concentration might in some cases facilitate collective action in particular sectors, but concentration alone does not necessarily help members of encompassing associations overcome divergent sectoral interests. Nor does concentration affect potentially divisive ownership issues, as discussed later. Lastly, at very high levels of concentration, formal collective action becomes dispensable if those who control the largest firms can coordinate better informally and prefer direct individual access to top officials (Rettberg 2000; Schmitter and Streeck 1999, 25). Chapter 5, on Colombia, provides just such an example where the four largest *grupos* undermined collective action by the Consejo Gremial, the formal economy-wide association, in part because of their close informal, individual relations with government. Other things being equal, the portfolios of political investment for the largest firms may favor personal, individualized lobbying over investments in business associations and other forms of open, collective politics.[34]

1998 10 major capitalists controlled 15 percent of GDP and accounted for a quarter of the sales of all firms listed on the Mexican stock exchange (Camp 2002, 54).

[34] Eva Bellin (2002, Chapter 3) makes this argument for Tunisia. The small number of large firms encouraged individual contact with the state instead of collective action.

The banking sector offers another interesting window on possible connections, or lack of connections, between concentration and collective
action. Banking in Latin America is typically highly concentrated, yet not
prone to early or high-profile organizing, especially compared to less concentrated sectors of industry, agriculture, and commerce. For example,
in 1980 the five largest banks accounted for 81 percent of deposits in
Mexico and 61 percent in Brazil (Castañeda 1982, 89), and banking was
highly concentrated in other countries as well.[35] Despite high levels of
concentration, banking associations emerged late in Chile (ABIF, 1945)
and especially in Brazil (Febraban, 1967). In Argentina the first banking
association, ABRA (Asociación de Bancos de la República Argentina),
was founded in 1919, but in characteristic Argentine fashion bankers
created a second rival association, ADEBA (Asociación de Bancos Argentinos), and then a third, ABA (Asociación de Bancos de la Argentina).
Bankers organized early in Mexico (ABM, 1928) and Colombia (Asobancaria, 1936), but in both cases state actors took the initiative and encouraged them to organize. Moreover, outside of Mexico and Colombia,
analyses of business associations and political economy more generally
rarely mention the banking associations in the other three countries. In
sum, high levels of concentration in finance did not result in strong, visible
organizations unless the state provided an additional nudge.

The conditions for collective action vary not only according to the
level of concentration but also, and more importantly for many purposes,
according to who owns the firm. A firm in a given market will have
quite different preferences and propensities to act collectively, depending on whether it is a standalone firm, a firm in a vertically integrated
corporation, a firm in a highly diversified conglomerate, a state-owned
enterprise, or a subsidiary of an MNC (multinational corporation). (see
Schneider 1998a). MNC subsidiaries have exit options not available to
managers of other types of firms, and managers of state-owned enterprises are constrained to follow political directives from superiors in the
government, just to mention two of the many ways that diverse forms

---

[35] See the List of Abbreviations for the acronyms of these banking associations. In Mexico
in 1980, Bancomer and Banamex had 54 percent of all deposits; in Brazil, Bradesco and
Itaú had 36 percent. By 2001 the top 10 banks in Mexico had 90 percent of total assets,
and the 10 largest banks in Brazil had 67 percent (*Gazeta Mercantil*, 11 April 2002, p. 1).
In Argentina in 1925, 36 banks controlled 80 percent of the capital, 96 percent of loans,
and 85 percent of deposits in the entire banking system (calculated from Niosi 1974, 33).
The largest five banks in the United States and France held 53 and 65 percent, respectively
(Castañeda 1982, 89).

of corporate ownership can lead to divergent preferences even among firms in the same sector. In Latin America most of these diverse forms of ownership were common among the largest several hundred firms. In 1983, for example, MNCs and state enterprises in Brazil, Argentina, and Mexico accounted for three-quarters or more of the total sales of the 50 largest corporations.[36] Large domestically owned firms, historically the primary movers in collective action, were a distinct minority. Thus, trying to predict propensities for collective action based on levels of concentration, without accounting for differences in ownership, makes little sense. In the Mexican case, high levels of aggregate concentration might appear to explain high levels of collective action until one discounts the massive presence of Pemex (Petróleos Mexicanos), the state oil monopoly. Pemex does not participate in any voluntary encompassing associations, and aggregate levels of concentration are much lower for Mexico when Pemex is excluded from the calculations.

The large influx of MNC manufacturing firms after the 1950s introduced a deep potential cleavage among economic elites, but in practice MNCs had an ambivalent impact on incentives for collective action.[37] By 1972 MNCs owned half of the assets of the 300 largest manufacturing firms in Brazil and Mexico (Evans and Gereffi 1982, 138). In Mexico foreign control of industrial capacity averaged about a third in the 1970s and 1980s, though MNCs controlled only 7 of the 50 largest manufacturing firms (Camp 1989, 234). Interviewees often agreed that the large presence of MNCs altered the dynamics in their associations, but they disagreed on how they altered those dynamics. In some ways MNCs introduced new divisions that impeded collective action. MNCs were subsidiaries of global corporations, so their preferences reflected those of the corporations' global strategies and could diverge from those of national counterparts.[38] Even among national firms some capitalists were more

---

[36] Of the sales of the largest 50 corporations in Mexico, state enterprises accounted for 66 percent, MNCs for 10 percent, and domestic private firms for 24 percent. In Argentina and Brazil MNCs accounted for closer to a third, but still domestic private firms accounted for 21 percent in Brazil and 25 percent in Argentina of the sales of the largest 50 corporations (Fajnzylber 1990, 18).

[37] Major studies of collective action by business in Latin America such as Frieden (1991) and Durand and Silva (1998) barely mention MNCs as a possible cleavage. See also Coleman (1988, 234) on developed countries and Domínguez (1982) on Latin America.

[38] For Camp, the presence of MNCs makes business elites more heterogeneous (1989, 117). When membership within an association is fairly evenly split, as for example in ABDIB, the Brazilian association of producers of capital goods, reaching consensus within the association is more difficult. See Appendix A and Boschi and Diniz (1978, Chapter II).

closely linked to MNCs than others, which sometimes gave them differ-ent policy preferences.[39] In addition, foreign managers lacked knowledge of the language and local context, and so had less to contribute to de-bates in associations, and were likely to stay out of leadership positions to avoid provoking antagonistic political reactions (to which MNCs were especially vulnerable).[40]

In one extreme example in Chile, subsidiaries of foreign mining com-panies disagreed with the confrontational stance of Sonami (Sociedad Nacional de Minería) and wanted Sonami to allow state-owned enter-prises to join the association (Vera Azargado 1998). Sonami's leaders refused, so disgruntled MNCs formed the separate Consejo Minero and invited the huge state mining firm Codelco (Corporación Nacional del Cobre de Chile) to become a member. This sort of public discord and organizational splintering was rare in Latin America, but the example serves as a good illustration of how preferences can differ by ownership and as a clear warning against using sectoral or other economic indica-tors to predict organizational outcomes without taking ownership into consideration.[41]

In other ways MNCs may encourage collective action. MNCs were large, capital-intensive, and small in number, and, especially if they pro-duced for domestic markets, shared many interests with domestic firms. MNCs might help build institutional capacity in associations because they typically joined associations and paid dues but participated little in meet-ings and politics internal to the association. Moreover, by their presence alone, MNCs reduced the potential size and heterogeneity of domes-tic, national capitalists and thereby reduced barriers to collective action among nationally owned firms on their own; at the same time, MNCs increased their incentives for organizing by posing a common threat.[42]

---

[39] In a comparison of Brazilian and Argentine industrialists in the early 1960s, Cardoso found that those with ties to international capital (about half of the sample in each country) were less likely to accept alliances with agriculture or the popular sectors, though they were evenly split (as were those without international ties) on whether the state should be developmental or laissez faire (1978, 192–204).

[40] Association statutes in some cases, Mexico and Argentina for example, excluded MNCs or foreigners from leadership positions (see Acuña 1998, 63).

[41] In another earlier example, private nationally owned banks in Argentina formed a sep-arate association, ADEBA (Asociación de Bancos Argentinos), that excluded foreign-owned banks (Itzcovitz 1987, 227–9).

[42] In Mexico, Concamin and Canacintra united around restrictive positions on reserving some sectors for national capital, while Coparmex and Concanaco were more open (Luna, Tirado, and Valdés 1987, 22). Surveys of leaders showed less resistance to MNCs; in 1980 three-quarters of 109 leaders of Canacintra and Concamin, the two

These contradictory influences suggest that MNCs are not likely to have a strong net impact, either encouraging or discouraging collective action, though they do further disqualify simple assumptions on the impact of asset specificity or concentration on business organization. Moreover, in the twentieth century, MNC investment followed fairly similar patterns throughout the region, so their presence cannot explain the wide variation in business organization across large countries.

Conglomeration is probably the most important ownership variable for analyzing these variations because multisectoral conglomerates already have more encompassing interests, which should greatly facilitate investment in encompassing associations. Reliable comparative data are again lacking, and only scattered indicators of conglomeration exist. What studies do exist have long suggested that diversified conglomerates were common throughout Latin America and the developing world (Khanna and Palepu 2000; Leff 1978; Sargent 2001). For example, in Mexico by the 1980s, there were 121 major diversified *grupos* (Camp 1989, 174). Mexican banks played a central role in conglomeration, and most major *grupos* had a financial arm.[43] In Colombia the four largest *grupos* (accounting for 20 percent of GDP) controlled 278 firms in 1998 and had minority holdings in other firms. Each *grupo* had member firms in multiple sectors of industry and services (Rettberg 2000, Chapter 3, p. 16). As noted earlier, in the 1950s in Chile the 11 largest *grupos* controlled nearly 300 firms (Lagos 1961, cited in Johnson 1967, 47). This study did not specify the sectoral diversity of these *grupos*, but presumably they were active in multiple sectors. The holdings of the Edwards *grupo*, for example, included a bank, a newspaper, the beer monopoly, coal and gold mining, a real estate firm, and an insurance company, which in turn controlled other industrial firms (Johnson 1967, 53). In Argentina in the 1990s the 40 largest conglomerates participated in about 700 firms, most of which were on the list of the 1,000 largest firms in the country (Bisang 1998, 151, 156).[44] In Brazil, in contrast, private finance and industry were largely unintegrated, and banks did not have extensive industrial holdings (Barker 1990, especially 238–49, 291–317), yet some of the largest companies, such as Votorantim,

---

most protectionist and nationalist associations, were sympathetic to foreign investment (Story 1983, 365).

[43] See Maxfield (1990), and Alcocer and Cisneros (1988). Brandenburg noted in the 1950s a dominance of conglomerates linked to banks (1962, 22).

[44] In a 1971 survey of 112 industrialists, less than half had activities concentrated solely in a single industrial sector, and over a third had activities spread across multiple sectors of industry as well as commerce, finance, and agriculture (Petras and Cook 1972, 389).

were diversified conglomerates (Goldstein and Schneider 2003). Overall, these disparate empirical indicators suggest that multisectoral conglomeration was fairly common in Latin America. However, available data provide no comparative measures that can be related to levels of institutional capacity in encompassing associations.

Although multisectoral conglomeration may reduce some barriers to forming encompassing associations, it can have equivocal impacts on collective action because owners of large conglomerates, due to their great size, may, as noted earlier, prefer to operate alone.[45] Venezuela provides a good example of a country where smaller conglomerates promoted early encompassing organization. Venezuelan firms diversified from the beginning of industrialization yet remained relatively small – "mini-conglomerates" (Naím and Francés 1995, 166–7) – reducing disincentives for encompassing organization, and Fedecamaras (Federación Venezolana de Cámaras y Asociaciones de Comercia y producción) was indeed one of the first peak associations to form. However, as discussed in Chapter 7, state actors also provided strong inducements for these conglomerates to organize.[46]

Beyond its potential impact on collective action in encompassing associations, conglomeration poses serious analytic problems for major theories in international political economy based on asset specificity and sectoral analysis.[47] These analyses are premised on the idea that firms' interests regarding trade and other types of policies derive fundamentally from the kinds of assets they own and how easily these assets can be converted to other uses. Theories based on asset specificity thus work with fairly primitive models of single-sector firms, and these models

---

[45] Conglomeration or business strategies of multisectoral diversification also muted divisions between industry and agriculture, where many observers expected sectoral clashes to be intense. As Chapters 3 to 7 explain, conflicts between agriculture and industry were few, in part because economic elites tended to own operations in both sectors and because industrialization was less directly threatening to agriculture. A survey in the early 1960s of 324 managers in 12 countries in Latin America found that "most enterprises had their roots in agricultural holdings" (Lauterbach 1965, 205).

[46] Ecuador provides an important counterexample. There too large *grupos* emerged, and many businesses diversified into other sectors. By one count, two-thirds of a sample of 43 industrialists had holdings in other industrial firms and 80 percent had business interests in sectors outside industry (Conaghan 1988, Table 2, 46; see also 33–45). However, Ecuadoran business did not create lasting, voluntary encompassing associations despite these high levels of diversification.

[47] See Frieden (1991), Shafer (1994), and Alt et al. (1999). For reviews of asset specificity in the literature on international political economy generally, see Alt et al. (1996). and Frieden and Martin (2002).

fundamentally misrepresent the reality of multisectoral conglomerates that own a wide range of assets with highly variable specificity across sectors.

In sum, there are theoretical grounds and partial empirical evidence in some cases to argue that high levels of concentration and conglomeration provided favorable conditions for collective action. However, in the absence of more systematic evidence and stronger correlations, these factors are best conceived as facilitating variables that lower some obstacles to collective action without determining whether and how intensely it happens. Other ownership types like state enterprises and MNCs have ambivalent impacts on incentives for organizing, and in any case their relative economic weight does not co-vary with levels of encompassing organization.

Macropolitical Factors: Development Strategies, Regime Type, and Party Systems

A range of scholars expect macropolitical factors such as state-led development from the 1950s to the 1980s, market-oriented development since the 1980s, the structure of party systems, military dictatorship, or democratization to affect patterns of business organization. However, in the histories recounted in Part II, much more depended on the actions of particular state actors within a dictatorship, for example, or on events during the process of implementing a new development strategy, than on these macro parameters themselves.

Overall development strategies, first state-led development from the 1940s to the 1980s and then neoliberalism, both seemed to discourage collective action by business, especially encompassing collective action (see Urrutia 1983, 91, for example).[48] The developmental state intervened in the economy in detailed and discretionary ways, as for example in providing subsidized loans for specific projects, which gave capitalists incentives to deal with the state individually and bypass associations (see, for example, Diniz and Boschi 1987; Schneider 1999; Vernon 1963). However, some state actors in developmental states preferred to interact with collective representatives of business and therefore placed association representatives on public boards, as in Chile and Colombia (or in

---

[48] Offe (1995, 127) argues generally that interventionist states tend to promote group formation, while governments inspired by liberal doctrines ignore organized groups or in extreme cases attempt to dismantle them.

Brazil under Vargas), or favored associations in informal consultations, as with the CMHN in Mexico. In these instances, the institutional linkages between the developmental state and organized business reinforced associations.

Similarly, the impact of neoliberal development strategies on collective action depended more on *how* states went about implementing reforms than on the impact of the reforms themselves. In the 1990s neoliberal reforms reduced many areas of state intervention in the economy and subjected most firms to greater competition, which generally reduced incentives and resources for collective action. However, state officials in Mexico, Chile (after the 1970s), and, to a lesser extent, Colombia consulted closely with business associations in designing and implementing specific market reforms. In principle, trade liberalization requires little coordination between business and government, but in practice, as countries dropped tariffs, they also entered into detailed trade agreements. In some cases, state actors consulted closely with business organizations on these agreements, and these consultations then increased incentives for business to invest in their associations. In short, the impact of the many policies associated with first state-led and then neoliberal development strategies depended more on how state officials implemented them than on any inherent features of either development strategy.[49]

Regime type – authoritarianism and democracy – per se also had no single or consistent impact on business associations. Much more depended on the specific acts of dictators or democratic leaders and their top policy makers. Over the course of a single dictatorship, for example, Pinochet first shunned associations in the 1970s but later called them back to play a central role in policy making in the 1980s. Cross-nationally, authoritarian leaders in Brazil and Mexico in the 1960s and 1970s cultivated very different relations with business. In Brazil, industrialists defected from encompassing organizations after the coup in 1964, and policy makers in subsequent authoritarian governments consulted mostly with narrow sectoral associations or individual capitalists. In semiauthoritarian Mexico in the same decades, state actors helped business organize encompassing associations that had privileged access to top officials. Later, democracy and democratization also had no single impact. Democratization shifts attention and resources to elections and parties, but elected leaders may turn to associations for help in managing the transition, as in Chile, or

---

[49] Many associations in developed countries have weathered neoliberal reforms there (Coleman 1997).

they may largely ignore them, as in Brazil. In Argentina, elected leaders like Perón and Alfonsín sought to consult sometimes with business organizations, while Menem mostly ignored them. Historically in Latin America business–government relations varied as much within democratic or authoritarian regimes as between them.

Strong parties and party systems might seem to correlate roughly with strong business associations. At first glance, parties in Chile and Mexico seemed stronger generally than those in Brazil, with parties in Colombia and Argentina somewhere in between. Experts in party politics do consistently rank Brazil toward the bottom on several dimensions of party institutionalization, but party systems in the other four countries show no consistent ranking across these dimensions (Mainwaring 1999, 29–36). Looking only at the right end of the political spectrum, Kevin Middlebrook found stronger conservative parties (defined, following Gibson 1996), as those whose core constituency is business) in Chile, Venezuela, and Colombia than in Argentina, Brazil, and Peru (2000, 4–6). The apparent correlation between stronger conservative parties and stronger encompassing associations is intriguing, but causal connections are lacking. In explaining the emergence of the stronger conservative parties, Middlebrook highlights deeper historical conflicts over the role of the Catholic Church and longer periods of democratic rule in the twentieth century, yet neither of these factors had much direct impact on the evolution of business associations. In some cases, such as Chile in the 1960s, capitalists appear to have invested heavily in both associations and parties with the common motivation of defensive mobilization against the left. In other cases, Colombia during the National Front period for example, associations displaced parties as vehicles of capitalist representation.

Lastly, and most importantly, despite any superficial correlations, there was a notable lack of contact between business associations and parties. As discussed in Chapters 3 to 7, in most instances business associations were legally prohibited from engaging in party politics, and in other instances associations remained neutral in electoral competition in order not to alienate any potential winner. In stark contrast to labor unions and other organized social groups, business associations avoided close connections to individual parties, so there are fewer empirical reasons to suspect that party systems would have an impact on business organization (see Acuña 1998, 58). Overall, it is hard to tease out any systematic causal relationship between parties and business associations, save their occasional competition for political investments by capitalists.

Conclusion

What emerges in this chapter is that more stable structural or institutional features like regime type, geography, or corporate ownership matter less in explaining stronger business organization than more dynamic and strategic exchanges among state officials, leaders of business organizations, and potential business contributors to associations. The analysis of various geographic, economic, and political factors showed the weakness of contending hypotheses and at the same time revealed the wide range of usually conflicting or ambivalent interests capitalists might have in collective action. This broad, ambiguous range highlights the risks of any a priori, deductive assumptions about interests. Moreover, this diversity and ambiguity of structural interests should have made capitalists especially responsive to strong signals from the state, to signals that decisively alter the balance of their ambivalent natural interests in collective action. These signals from the state usually came as short-term, strategic responses by state actors to the changing economic and political challenges they faced. Paradoxically, these fluid, conjunctural interactions often subsequently had cumulative and enduring institutional consequences for the business associations involved. And very different shifts in incentives from state actors, say from reformist threats to privileged access, could work in the same direction to increase investment in institution building in the associations.

In the historical analyses that follow, state actors emerge again and again, in diverse periods and countries, as the primary and proximate causes for collective action by business. The purpose of this chapter was to outline the general comparative argument for understanding these state initiatives to organize business. The point of departure for that argument is that the "solutions" for collective action are political and lie outside the social and economic characteristics of business. To summarize, the core arguments presented here and in the following chapters can be ranked according to the closeness of fit. The primary and strongest argument is that the state provision of benefits to associations best explains the variation in the strength of encompassing organization over time and across countries. Other factors, either structural (e.g., conglomerates or the portfolio of political options) or conjunctural (such as threats from reformist governments), influence organization in some countries in some periods, but these are secondary influences. Put differently, there were no cases of strong, durable encompassing associations that emerged in the twentieth century in the absence of selective incentives from the state.

The second core argument addresses the question of why state actors helped business to organize, and the answer is more probabilistic and depends on more factors than the first argument. Perceived vulnerabilities ranging from low administrative capacity, to political crisis, to international economic shocks increased incentives for top state actors to seek out business associations. Empirically, however, state actors did not always or automatically reach out to business associations to reduce these vulnerabilities. The vulnerabilities and incentives may have existed, but the turn to business associations was more contingent because state actors may have opted for alternative strategies to mitigate their vulnerabilities. The third argument, taken up in Part III, is that stronger encompassing associations can improve economic and democratic governance. This argument is more permissive: encompassing associations can under certain circumstances contribute to democracy and development through various forms of coordination and concertation that are not available to policy makers in countries without strong associations. Strong associations provide additional policy options, but state actors may or may not opt to avail themselves of these opportunities.

This chapter highlighted the role of state actors in organizing business, but this emphasis does not mean to imply that businesspeople were merely inert onlookers. In most cases, some business leaders pressed state actors to help them organize and negotiated with officials the terms of that assistance. However, there was less variation across countries in terms of pressure from business (there were almost always political entrepreneurs ready to lead new or improved business associations) than there was variation in the responses of state actors, so my comparative explanation focuses primarily on the state. Once established, business pressure was also influential in maintaining organizations (and the flow of benefits that sustained them). The fact that state actors sometimes found it difficult to reform business representation was due in part to business pressures to make these institutions "sticky." Lastly, of course, business had a major influence on state actors through its structural leverage. For the core arguments and analytic simplicity, I treat the sources of state vulnerability as largely exogenous, and in cases like World War II and the Depression of the 1930s they were. However, in other cases of political vulnerability or economic crisis, business itself was a source of vulnerability, as for example the threat of capital flight that gave Mexican policy makers in 1987 strong incentives for concerted policy making. Thus, beyond the proximate causal impact of state actions on organization, business pressures and influence are necessary for a fuller account, and Chapters 3 to 7 provide more detail on the business side of the story. Nonetheless, within this broader context, state officials were still the pivotal, proximate causal agents.

This chapter also raised several problems for various conventional, rational choice theories of political behavior, especially those focused on collective action, rent seeking, free riding, and reelection. The problems highlighted here focused on empirical issues and the shortcomings of these theories in explaining the variation in encompassing organization among the five countries. However, if there is a common theoretical shortcoming across these conventional theories, it likely derives from methodological individualism and a resulting neglect of organization. A variety of organizations – corporate, associational, and governmental – are crucial to these theories both as the context in shaping individual incentives and also sometimes as the units of behavior and analysis themselves, as for example in the case of collective action by associations as unit members of economy-wide peak associations. Chapter 8 returns to the broader theoretical task of factoring organization back into individual-based theorizing.

PART II

CASES AND COMPARISONS

3

From State to Societal Corporatism in Mexico

> We must all hang together, or assuredly we shall all hang separately.
>
> Benjamin Franklin, 1776

Introduction

A love–hate relationship is an apt metaphor for relations between business and government in twentieth-century Mexico.[1] This analogy captures the often extreme passions in alternating periods of cooperation and conflict, as well as the complex entanglement of a rocky romance. This chapter tries to make sense of this entanglement by focusing on a few crucial variables – such as privileged access, threats to property rights, and political exclusion – that all encouraged big business in Mexico to invest in collective action. By the end of the twentieth century, big business in Mexico had created a wide range of voluntary associations and endowed them with lasting institutional capacity in the form of resources, professional staff, and capacity to intermediate member interests. These associations stand out as some of the strongest in the region.

The chronological account that follows covers some of the history of corporatist associations like Concanaco (Confederación de Cámaras Nacionales de Comercio), Canacintra (Cámara Nacional de la Industria de Transformación), and Concamin (Confederación de Cámaras

---

[1] Portions of this chapter originally appeared in "Why Is Mexican Business So Organized?" by Ben Ross Schneider, from *Latin American Research Review* 37:1, pp. 77–1180. Copyright © 2002 by the University of Texas Press. All rights reserved.

Industriales), especially the episodes of creation, which reveal the motivations of state actors in seeking policy and political support in times
of economic crisis and political vulnerability. However, the chapter focuses more on the relatively neglected voluntary associations – especially
the economy-wide associations Coparmex (Confederación Patronal de
la República Mexicana), CMHN (Consejo Mexicano de Hombres de
Negocios), and CCE (Consejo Coordinador Empresarial) – that progressively displaced corporatist associations. Although voluntary, these associations all received decisive impetus and support from state actors,
usually in the form of privileged access. Access was sometimes formal,
with special statutes granting associations, both corporatist and voluntary, representation in various councils and policy forums in the government. More important, though, were the informal, though routine, mechanisms of access, mostly through ritualized lunches and dinners, between
representatives of government and business associations. In terms of the
motives of state actors, the chronological narrative reveals a close correlation between the onset of crises increasing the vulnerabilities of state
actors and their overtures to business to help them organize and give them
access in exchange for political support, aggregated information, and help
in implementing policies.

The Construction of State Corporatism

In the 1930s and 1940s, state leaders incorporated business and labor into
formal corporatist organizations. For business, the state resolved problems of free riding by making membership and dues compulsory, which
gave associations a captive membership and guaranteed financing. At the
same time, corporatist legislation distorted and froze internal representation within associations and circumscribed their autonomy. In strong
top-down corporatist fashion, governments in Mexico made membership
in associations mandatory, legislated rules for leadership selection, required state approval for associations to form, and determined internal
representation within associations. Corporatist associations rapidly filled
much of the organizational space for business. Business elites also organized a few independent associations, but from the 1930s to the 1960s
the corporatist associations dominated business representation.

Even before the construction of state corporatism, state actors in
Mexico were active in organizing business. Discussions of corporatism in
Latin America often note its European paternity from the 1930s. However,
Mexican officials had already established a basic, albeit weak, corporatist

framework in the 1908 legislation governing business associations, the Law of Chambers. Among other things, this legislation stipulated that the chambers would be privileged intermediaries with the government, the minister of finance would set membership limits and grant official recognition (or withdraw it) to associations wishing to form, and associations should provide various services (publications, fairs, contacts with foreign associations, etc.) (Shafer 1973, 20).

In 1917, shortly after the promulgation of the new constitution, the government "initiated rather striking efforts to improve the organization of the business community, and to engage its collaboration with government in dealing with the economic disruption resulting from the Revolution and complicated by World War I" (Shafer 1973, 21). The Revolution had devastated the economy and created shortages and severe price fluctuations. Some state actors felt it was worthwhile to invest a lot to organize business so that business could help establish order in the economy and begin rebuilding. In May 1917 Minister of Industry, Commerce, and Labor Alberto J. Pani wrote to the Mexico City Chamber of Commerce and "asked the chamber to organize under government auspices the First National Congress of Merchants, to study: 1) the moralization of commerce; 2) the collective organization of chambers of commerce, for mutual aid, public good, and representation before the federal government; 3) means for development of domestic and foreign commerce, and 4) the high price of necessities" (Shafer 1973, 22). The First National Congress of Merchants convened in July 1917, with President Venustiano Carranza and prominent government ministers in attendance. Later that year, again under government auspices, delegates from local chambers of commerce met for two weeks to create a Confederation of Chambers of Commerce, Concanaco. The statutes of the confederation required it to seek legal recognition from the government and request further recognition as the general representative of business interests.

At the same time that the chambers of commerce were working on their confederation, an association of industrialists in Puebla asked the government to help organize a separate confederation for industry. Minister Pani accepted the invitation, set the agenda, and asked a commission of the Merchants Congress to organize a meeting on industrialists. In November 1917, shortly after the constitution of Concanaco, 112 delegates from sundry industrial associations met to work on the creation of a confederation of industry. In the case of commerce, delegates were from municipal organizations, and there was little debate over whether internal representation in the confederation would be territorial, as it was in most chambers of commerce around the world. The basis for representation in industry was a more contentious issue. From the beginning the congress was divided along sectoral lines, predominantly mining, petroleum, textiles, and other industries. The mining sector in particular wanted to retain separate representation, both within an industrial confederation and in direct representation with government. The mining sector was large and included many foreign firms (which may also have feared conceding too much power to a confederation dominated by Mexican capitalists). The 1917 congress of industrialists, as well as the 1918 meeting of industry delegates, were organized into sectoral commissions and working groups. Sectoral representation came to dominate in the industry confederation Concamin, but the statutes allowed regionally based groups to affiliate as well.

These confederations would dominate the corporatist structure in Mexico throughout the century. The years 1917 and 1918 were a remarkable period of collective action and intense contact between business and government. The congresses and meetings of delegates lasted for weeks; the first industrialist congress lasted from 17 November until the day after Christmas 1917! These congresses set the fundamental bases of representation, regional in commerce and sectoral in industry. The most powerful subgroup of the industrialists, the miners, got their preferred pattern of representation on the industrial confederation, just as the most powerful business group in Brazil, the São Paulo industrialists, would lobby successfully for a territorial organization in the national confederation of industry (as discussed in the next chapter).

However, business and government did not sustain this intense interaction, and in the 1920s both the confederations and chambers foundered. Membership was voluntary, and both organizations remained weak and poor.[2] In the 1930s association leaders successfully lobbied the Cárdenas government for new legislation, exclusively for business associations, which would make membership and dues mandatory. Starting in 1932, the commerce confederation worked with the government on new legislation: "Concanaco collaborated closely with the Secretaría de la Economía Nacional as well as relevant legislative organs in all stages of study and formulation of the new law" (Alcázar 1970, 39). The 1936 Law for Chambers

---

[2] The 1931 Ley Federal de Trabajo provided statutory regulation for unions and employer associations but did not make membership mandatory. However, this law did not replace the 1908 Chambers Law.

of Commerce and Industry even briefly fused industry and commerce in Mexico's first economy-wide peak association.

Direct information on the motives and strategies of government officials in the 1930s is scarce, but the circumstantial evidence fits well the hypotheses outlined in Chapter 2. The decade of the 1930s in Mexico was a pivotal period of economic crisis, political reorganization, and changing development strategies, precisely the conditions that would lead government officials to want to encourage business organization to generate political support, reduce or displace opposition, and aggregate business preferences. The Cárdenas government (1934–40) actively reorganized the representation of labor, peasants, the military, and other groups, so it was not unnatural to include business representation in this general project of political reconstruction. Moreover, business was at least wary of government reforms such as land reform and nationalization, so preemptive corporatist organization could forestall the emergence of business movements more directly opposed to government policy. In this sense, corporatist associations displaced the embryonic and antagonistic employers association Coparmex.

Cárdenas's successor, President Manuel Ávila Camacho, made several crucial changes in a new Chambers Law in 1941. Over the opposition of many association leaders, new legislation split the confederations of industry and commerce, created a special chamber for manufacturing firms, Canacintra, and made clearer the fact that these business associations were "public institutions" (Shafer 1973, 47).[3] The 1941 law enhanced state control, fragmented business, separated government sympathizers from the existing confederations, and gave them a separate voice in the manufacturers' association Canacintra. Among their public functions, the 1941 law made chambers "organs of consultation for the state" and gave the secretary of industry and commerce the job of overseeing chambers (and licensing new chambers). The law stipulated that 80 percent of the board (*consejo directivo*) of the chambers had to consist of Mexican capitalists by birth. Moreover, the secretary had the right to send a representative, with voice but not vote, to the meetings of the chamber's board (Alcázar 1970, 11–14).

The creation of Canacintra demonstrated astute political engineering by state actors who manipulated corporatist regulations to amplify the

---

[3] While Ávila Camacho was generally viewed as more favorable to business than Cárdenas, Concanaco's influence ironically was greater, at least concerning chamber legislation, during the Cárdenas presidency than during his successor's, when Concanaco opposed the separation of the confederations for industry and commerce (see Alcázar 1970, 39–45).

voice of industrialists who supported the government strategy of state-led ISI. State actors authorized the formation of Canacintra only three months after enacting the 1941 Chambers Law to separate the "new industrialists" from Concamin, the more traditional, broader industrial confederation (see Mosk 1950, 52). Canacintra grew quickly from 93 member firms in 1941, to 1684 in 1942, and to 5,080 by 1944 (and to 18,000 by the 1960s). From the beginning, Canacintra "was favored by government, and had direct access to it, without going through Concamin" (Shafer 1973, 54). Canacintra was formally only 1 of 60 industrial chambers in Concamin but came to have about half as many members and twice as much money (see Appendix A). By 1945 Canacintra had "launched . . . the propaganda career that was prominently to mark its role thereafter: ostentatiously nationalistic, progovernment" (Shafer 1973, 56). Canacintra was the first major business organization to fully endorse state intervention, including controls on foreign capital. Canacintra even supported wage increases, social security, and land reform (Alcázar 1970, 54–97; Vernon 1963, 167).[4] Even into the 1960s, other business leaders referred to Canacintra members as "business Marxists" (Shafer 1973, 55). Shafer concludes that "it would be difficult to imagine doctrine more useful to government and national party. . . . It was widely believed that [Canacintra's] leadership was an unofficial adjunct to those institutions" (56). The creation of Canacintra illustrates clearly the political logic of state-induced collective action, of how state actors manipulated the organization of business in order to generate visible support for government policies.[5]

The corporatist associations gained institutional strength by virtue of the material resources they controlled, but were hampered by distorted internal representation and little autonomy from the state. Data from early years on material resources are scarce, but by the mid-1960s the

---

[4] According to Shafer (1973, 56), "the core of the campaign was a cry for more rapid industrialization, and for government intervention in pursuit of economic and social development; with the concomitant demand for closer restriction of foreign economic interests, and strictures on other business organizations for not having dealt properly with these matters."

[5] The other confederations (Concanaco, Concamin, and Coparmex) were more reluctant to embrace developmentalism. On many topical issues they published joint statements of opposition, as in the cases of the nationalization of electricity companies in 1960 and the proposed tax for education in 1963 (Alcázar 1970, 88, 95). However, these confederations were flexible and were considerably more comfortable with developmentalism by the 1960s than they were in the 1940s. Concanaco opposed restrictions on trade until 1954, when "an important declaration," as the confederation called it, came out in favor of import restrictions in the interest of industrialization (Vernon 1963, 169).

major corporatist associations had budgets in the hundreds of thousands of dollars and scores of staff (see Appendix A). In comparative terms, Concanaco had a small budget and staff but a "mass" base of small retailers. Concamin had fewer industrialist members and a similar budget. Canacintra, itself formally only one member of Concamin, was better funded and staffed than either of the peak confederations. Voting regulations, and hence interest aggregation, varied from association to association. In Concanaco each of the 234 territorially organized chambers of commerce in 1964 got one vote despite the fact that the five largest chambers had a third of all of the members and contributed over half of the confederation's total revenue (Alcázar 1970, 21). The Chamber of Commerce in Mexico City (Canaco-DF) accounted for 40 percent of the revenues of Concanaco yet still had only one vote. In Canacintra each of the 60 sectoral sections and 46 regional delegations had a vote. In Concamin each of the various chambers voted in proportion to its financial contribution. Member chambers were mostly national chambers for a particular sector, though a dozen or so of the 60 chambers were regional groups. However, strict proportionality was limited in the case of large contributors. In its early years Canacintra contributed 42 percent of Concamin's income but controlled only 11 percent of the votes (Shafer 1973, 54). Nonetheless, Concamin had better proportional representation (proportional to member output) than most other corporatist associations in both Mexico and Brazil.

By the 1960s Mexican business elites had a set of seemingly strong business associations. They were still constrained, even beyond formal legal restrictions, by the lack of an economy-wide peak association. Merchants, industrialists, and bankers had separate associations, but no formal entity existed to bring them together along with others into a single economy-wide organization. Nonetheless, prior to the creation of such an organization in 1975, association leaders did engage in other forms of ad hoc collective action. The confederations often issued and published joint positions on major political issues.[6]

In sum, the state in Mexico was deeply involved in organizing business throughout the first half of the twentieth century. Major moments

---

[6] For instance, Concanaco, ABM (banking), Coparmex, and Canaco-DF (Cámara Nacional de Comercio, Mexico City) jointly urged Alemán to slow land reform in 1945 (Alcázar 1970, 42). In 1959 Coparmex, Concanaco, and Concamin issued a joint statement lamenting labor conflicts and later sent a joint telegram supporting the president's decision to declare strikes illegal (Alcázar 1970, 73). In 1963, Coparmex, Concamin, Concanaco, and Canaco-DF took out newspaper ads criticizing a proposed tax increase (Alcázar 1970, 95). Canacintra is conspicuous by its absence from these collective actions.

for the installation and consolidation of state corporatism came during turbulent years for Mexican political economy: 1917–18, at the end of the Revolution; 1936, during the Depression and radical restructuring of the PRI (Partido Revolucionario Institucional); and 1941, in the early years of World War II and state-led ISI. At the end of the Revolution and later at the outbreak of World War II, basic economic organization was a major concern to policy makers, and they explicitly enlisted corporatist associations in the task of administering the economy. During the Cárdenas years the goals of organizing business had more to do with the political logic of control or minimizing political opposition.[7] In each period, business leaders were actively demanding state intervention or changes in state intervention, to which government leaders often acceded. However, state actions were decisive, and state officials decided which business groups to court and which to alienate.

Some Early Autonomous Associations

In the late 1920s, even before the consolidation of state corporatism in Mexico, top capitalists formed two important noncorporatist, voluntary associations, Coparmex and ABM (Asociación de Banqueros de México). Formed within a year of each other, these two associations represent different tendencies among Mexican capitalists. With government encouragement, a small group of top bankers formed the ABM, which later became a significant nucleus for organizing business across other sectors. The ABM also became a privileged conduit for discreet communications between government and business elites. Coparmex represents a different trend: ideological, independent, vociferously antigovernment, and Monterrey based. Born in opposition to central government, it languished for many years but survived as the standard bearer of free market capitalism. Coparmex also demonstrated the continuing interest northern capitalists had in investing in collective action and vocal ideological opposition. These two strands would be manifest later in the

---

[7] Shafer concludes that "there is no reason to assign the increased government control of the 1941 Chambers Law either to Cárdenas' known distaste for businessmen or to the oft-mentioned 'turn to the right' of Ávila Camacho. There had been government interest in control before either man was President – such control would occur to any intelligent bureaucrat convinced of the need of government direction of economic development" (1973, 40). Bureaucratic intelligence, though, does not provide much of a working hypothesis for explaining variations over time and countries in state-induced collective action.

CMHN (broader in sectoral terms than the ABM but still elite and discreet) and CCE (broader than Coparmex but also formed to oppose the government).

In 1928 the government pushed bankers to create an independent organization, the ABM. It was initially weak, but by the 1960s "it had become possibly the most prestigious of all the peak associations." In 1966 the ABM had 296 member institutions, and its annual convention became a major political event at which the president and the minister of finance usually spoke (Shafer 1973, 58–9) (see Appendix A). The ABM was also strengthened by government invitations to participate in policy-making forums. The ABM elected one member to the National Banking Commission, the National Securities Commission, and the Mexican Stock Exchange (Brandenburg 1958, 42; Camp 1989, 163).[8] Bankers were often central actors in diversified conglomerates and played crucial intermediary and coordinating roles in both politics and business (Camp 1989). In the 1960s and 1970s bankers were also crucial in promoting formal multisectoral associations like CMHN and CCE.

In 1929, big business from Monterrey founded Coparmex. In Latin America, Coparmex was unique: it survived and grew for over 70 years, it had tens of thousands of individual members who paid dues voluntarily, and it staked out distinctive and coherent ideological positions, mostly socially conservative and economically liberal. Coparmex's founding was a clear response to a perceived threat from the state. In 1928 the government proposed a new labor law that labor leaders welcomed. Economic elites, especially in Monterrey, opposed this new law and created the independent Coparmex, an employers' organization to articulate their opposition. Among other things Coparmex founders wanted a different labor law, less state intervention in the economy, and stronger autonomous business associations without divisions by sector (Shafer 1973, 37–8). Coparmex was thus "patronal," or an employer rather than a trade or producer association. It is the only one of several employers' associations created at around the same time in the larger countries of Latin America that survived (see Chapters 4, 6, and 7). Coparmex accepts voluntary membership from individual business people in industry, agriculture, and commerce. Members affiliate with a regional *Centro Patronal*. In 1931, two years after it was founded, Coparmex already had 18 regional *Centros*. However,

---

[8] By the 1990s, representatives from the Ministry of Finance, the central bank, and the regulatory commision for finance met every other week with the executive committee of ABM (Wood 2000, 62).

after this initial organizational flurry, Coparmex was "very weak" until the 1950s (Camp 1989, 163). Thereafter membership grew steadily from 7,000 in the 1950s to 30,000 in the 1990s (see Appendix A).

However, the survival and growth of Coparmex was not due exclusively to its function as an employer arm of business, but also to the fact that it assumed a gadfly ideological role based on Catholic social doctrine and free market liberalism. Until the end of World War II, Coparmex's central activity was the legal defense of employers in the field of labor law (Alcázar 1970, 45). After 1946, Coparmex added a broader ideological role (see Bravo Mena 1987). In addition, Coparmex was a vehicle for the opposition of northern business to the encroachments of central government developmentalists. Until the formation of the CCE in 1975, Coparmex was the only multisectoral, mass membership, and independent (noncorporatist) association in Mexico. Coparmex was until the 1970s the only independent business association that could voice opinions without the direct threat of administrative retaliation by state actors. The corporatist associations operated under legal restrictions on their political activities and leadership selection, as well as financial dependence on the government.[9] In this sense Mexican business had incentives to contribute to Coparmex because they had few other options in their portfolios of political investments.

Conflict with the state was the most consistent impetus to collective action in Coparmex. Even in periods of relative harmony between business and government, the state's legal and constitutional prerogatives to intervene in labor markets and expropriate property worried Coparmex supporters. Although less than for other associations, the government also provided some direct support for Coparmex by giving it the selective benefit of access, in this case a seat on the boards of several public entities, especially wage and labor relations commissions.[10] The government also made an informal habit of consulting with Coparmex and other

[9] Coparmex's legal independence was, as was often the case in Mexican politics, relative in practice. Coparmex members sometimes adjusted leadership selection in consultation with the government. Rogelio Sada Zambrano was invited by the Coparmex board to be president, but the invitation was withdrawn because the board, on second thought, felt that Sada would signal too much confrontation with government (interview, 6 March 1994).

[10] The boards included Infonavit (National Institute for Workers' Housing), the National Minimum Wage Commission, the Council for Negotiation and Arbitration of the National Commission for the Distribution of Earnings, the National Tripartite Commission, and Fonacot (National Fund for Workers' Consumption) (Bravo Mena 1987, 92; FCPS 1994, 46).

associations before implementing major policy initiatives.[11] The institutional strength of Coparmex (dependent on material resources for staff and propaganda) and leadership came largely from big business in northern Mexico (see Schneider 2002 for details). The founders came from the Monterrey group, especially the Sada family, and half of the leaders through the 1980s came from Monterrey, whereas the great majority of leaders of other associations came from Mexico City (Camp 1989, 158).

Conflicts over labor legislation early in the twentieth century were midwife to the longest-standing, and most ideologically vociferous, employers' association in Latin America. Its survival during subsequent periods of harmony between business and government was due to the exclusion of business from other avenues of political participation (or the lack of other channels for the expression of the political views espoused by Coparmex), government consultation and cooperation with Coparmex, and the sustained investment by big capitalists from Monterrey.

The Developmental State Reinforced Corporatism and Personal Networks

The period from the mid-1940s through the 1960s was one of economic expansion, relative harmony between business and government (save for several years in the late 1950s), and consolidation of the strategy of state-led development (see Schneider 1999).[12] During this period, the corporatist associations were primary vehicles for business organization and representation, in large measure because the state granted them privileged representation at the same time that other avenues of political representation such as parties and appointments were closed off. In addition, the extensive and detailed intervention of the state in economic activity gave business strong incentives to invest as well in informal networks with mid-level officials. Where they were strong, these networks complemented (though sometimes displaced) associations and rose in value in political

---

[11] The importance of this informal access can be gauged from Coparmex's angry reaction to President Echeverría's enactment in 1970 of a new tax policy without prior consultation with Coparmex. Coparmex immediately issued a press bulletin criticizing the government for breaking with the past practice of sending legislation to associations for prior consultation (Bravo Mena 1987, 97).

[12] Developmentalism achieved a fragile predominance, and by the early 1960s there was "no wide ideological barrier" between officials and businessmen (Vernon 1963, 26). For Shafer, after the intense mobilization in the 1930s and 1940s interest in organizational issues subsided; in the following two decades "business profits anesthetized combativeness over organization questions" (1973, 52).

portfolios. In terms of overall patterns of business politics, the political economy of the developmental state strengthened state corporatism and promoted personalized networks.

The expansion of the developmental state in Mexico created new opportunities for representation through corporatist associations. As policy makers established new agencies for promoting development, state actors strengthened corporatist associations by inviting association representatives to sit on new councils overseeing these agencies or coordinating development policy. The incentives government actors had for inviting associations to participate generally conformed to the political logics discussed in Chapter 2. That is, policy makers wanted information and cooperation from business associations in implementing the policies for promoting industrialization and development. By 1945 the merchants' confederation Concanaco, for example, already had a seat on 17 government committees or boards, including those responsible for railroads, social security, tariffs, price controls, minimum wages, weights and standards, and international trade, as well as forestry, illiteracy, and malnutrition (Shafer 1973, 221). In 1965, Canaco-DF, the Chamber of Commerce of Mexico City, was represented on 21 government boards. These forums thus gave associations a selective benefit that was important to their big members and a significant incentive to participate in associations. Moreover, government officials often sounded out business leaders before enacting legislation.[13] More generally, the Chambers Law of 1936 required state officials to consult with business confederations in sectors affected by proposed policies (Alcázar 1970, 10, 17).

However, representation through corporatist associations was not ideal for business because the government continued to exercise control. This control came not only through direct formal mechanisms but also the clever use of indirect leverage. For example, the creation of new sectoral chambers required approval from government officials. Often, manufacturing firms lumped together in Canacintra petitioned the government to leave Canacintra and set up their own chambers. In the early 1960s the chemical industry waged a vigorous campaign to exit Canacintra, but the government denied its petition. The government did allow a weaker voluntary association, ANIQ (Asociación Nacional de la Industria Química), to affiliate with Concamin, though by law without voting rights (see Shafer 1973, 69–71). The automobile industry also struggled unsuccessfully to

---

[13] Brandenburg (1958, 34, 36). Brandenburg further argues that Concanaco "conferences – on corporate taxation, tariffs, subsidies, price control, quality control..., communications, petroleum and foreign investment – led to government reforms" (37).

leave Canacintra. Government decisions had an impact not only on sectors whose petitions were denied but also, more importantly, on other business leaders, who got a clear demonstration of their vulnerability. Canacintra leaders resisted attempts by such large subsectors to exit and knew that if they were not fully cooperative with the government on other matters, officials could let chemical producers and others sectors exit, depriving Canacintra of significant resources and shrinking its "mass" base.[14]

The developmental state also generated incentives for business to cultivate personal networks, or what were known in Brazil as "bureaucratic rings."[15] In Mexico, most of the day-to-day dealings between government and business involved "the humdrum efforts of single enterprises and small groups of companies – operating within an existing framework of laws, regulations, contacts, and friendships – to obtain government credit, tariff protection, sales contracts, tax exemptions, import licenses, and the like" (Vernon 1963, 155). Direct contacts with the many agencies of the economic bureaucracy were crucial: "virtually every business group of note possesses an intimate interrelation with a corresponding organ of the government" (Brandenburg 1958, 49). Story argues that "Monterrey industrialists have been the most active in pursuing individual interests with high-level bureaucrats . . . , but all entrepreneurs engage in rather frequent interaction with the bureaucracy at some level in order to alleviate a problem or gain a favor" (1986, 93).

Yet Mexican industrialists still also relied heavily on industry associations. Most business elites belonged to associations and seemed to go to them often to resolve differences with the state. René Becerra, a top Mexican businessman, explained the practice as follows: "normally, even though we try to directly influence the minister in charge, we first go

---

[14] This dependence is subject to some dispute. Canacintra and Concamin leaders interviewed in 1979–80 claimed "convincingly" "that the government has not controlled their activities, limited their influence, or interfered in their functions" (Story 1983, 371). Such views may be restricted to the harmonious boom years of the late 1970s. By the 1990s, one Canacintra leader claimed that the government used "Nazi" tactics to try to control the organization (interview with Roberto Sánchez de la Vara, 8 June 1996).

[15] Cardoso defined "bureaucratic rings" as ad hoc personal networks created in specific policy areas that included big businessmen and state officials from the various agencies affected by the policy (Cardoso 1975; Schneider 1991). Bureaucratic rings focus on the executive branch to the exclusion of legislatures and the judiciary. Within the bureaucracy they typically revolve around second- and third-level appointees within the economic bureaucracy. Discussions in these networks usually deal with implementation of decisions taken elsewhere rather than focus on proactive policy making. Lastly, these are ad hoc policy networks without formal rules or lasting manifestations. There is a strong family resemblance between bureaucratic rings and iron triangles. Unlike iron triangles in the United States, economic elites cannot count on allies in the state to last more than a Mexican president's six-year term.

through the chamber before approaching the individual personally" (cited in Camp 1989, 142). In the late 1960s Mexican industrialists preferred to work on an individual basis (15 percent), through informal pressure groups (23 percent), or through industrial associations (50 percent) to counteract unfavorable government policies (Derossi 1971, 40 fn). In 1969, 86 percent of one sample of industrialists belonged to one or more such associations, and half of them claimed to prefer to work through them to iron out policy differences with the government (calculated from Derossi 1971, 186).[16] By 1980, "80 percent said they first preferred to depend on their chamber or association whenever they wanted to influence a government decision" (Story 1986, 95). However, in some cases, even those who sought out their associations might only want informal intermediation or an introduction.

Personal networks and bureaucratic rings generally gave state actors the upper hand, both because they had more control over access and because the constant movement of officials through numerous agencies of the developmental state regularly reshuffled personal networks (Cardoso 1975, 209; Schneider 1991). And business had little recourse through courts or elected officials. However, the relationship was not completely one-sided. Economic elites also influenced appointments in the government (Maxfield 1987, 2). Matilde Luna, Ricardo Tirado, and Francisco Valdés claim that participation in appointments was the second common form of influence, after informal consultation on proposed policy, open to economic elites in Mexico, although activities to influence appointments "have always been carried out most secretively and have never been recognized publicly" (1987, 16). Private sector influence in appointments is not just a short-term personnel issue; it also means that ambitious officials will, as they contemplate future promotions, court business support and be more attentive to their views on policy.[17]

Thus the developmental state reduced some incentives for encompassing collective action and channeled business politics through sectoral associations or personal networks. However, by the 1960s these incentives started changing, especially for the biggest firms, whose owners started building independent, voluntary, encompassing associations to complement, coordinate, and sometimes supplant the corporatist associations.

---

[16] "Interestingly, in a political culture which thrives on personal contact, most businessmen believed that the institutional channels were sufficient for access" (Camp 1989, 109).

[17] Escobar claims that "a broad segment of business leadership participated in the selection of de la Madrid as the PRI presidential candidate" (1987, 77). Camp notes such claims about the weight of business in appointments but points out the lack of empirical confirmation (1989, 245).

Exclusion, Threats, and Independent Encompassing Organization

In 1996 Juan Sánchez Navarro, one of the best-known leaders of the Mexican business community, opened a speech at a business luncheon with a lengthy lament about the historical pattern of exclusion of business from Mexican politics (1996, 1). His opening point was that "despite various attempts by businessmen to participate in the official party or to have access to positions in the Public Administration, their participation was viewed as a contradiction with revolutionary postulates and a popular orientation.... Although isolated examples exist of businessmen assuming public offices or of public officials amassing large fortunes and becoming prosperous businessmen, the numbers are quite small." Sánchez Navarro admitted that the government had created conditions for the rapid expansion of the private sector, but "in exchange," businessmen were systematically excluded from serving in the state, especially in "positions of political control." Lastly, he lamented, capitalists were confined to pushing their narrow business interests within official chambers tied to middle level officials.

Available comparative evidence supports Sánchez Navarro's lament. Mexican businessmen were more excluded from politics than they are in most capitalist countries. When revolutionary politicians formed the PRI, they set up worker, peasant, and popular sector branches but denied entry to a business sector of the PRI. Since the 1940s, public, organized participation of Mexican business in both elections and parties has been perhaps the lowest of any country in Latin America that held regular elections. For Mexican capitalists, "the generally satisfactory results that obtain from direct negotiation with public officials make unnecessary expenditures to influence elections" (Brandenburg 1958, 36).[18] A notable exception was business support for the conservative PAN (Partido de Acción Nacional). Economic elites were prime movers in the creation of the PAN in 1939: 11 of the 29 members of the first National Executive Committee were bankers or businessmen (Story 1987, 265). However, in subsequent decades, when relations between business and government improved, the PAN and its prominent ties to business faded. It was not

---

[18] In the 1960s, only 6 percent of industrialists belonged to a political party (Derossi 1971, 187, cited in Camp 1987, 139). In another survey done by the Mexico government in 1982, 17 percent of industrialists and 22 percent of company presidents belonged to a political party (three-quarters of each group to the PRI) compared with an average of 30 percent for all occupational groups (Camp 1987, 139). Analyses of Mexican elites regularly note an almost explicit Brumairian exchange: the political elite guaranteed property and profits in exchange for political abstention (e.g., Casar et al. 1988, 210; Maxfield 1987, 2).

until the 1980s that business again turned to the PAN as a vehicle to express their dissatisfaction with the government and the PRI (Mizrahi 1994).

For most of the post-1930 period, business informally supported the PRI and periodically petitioned the state for formal incorporation. When Cárdenas incorporated other sectors – labor, peasants, the military, and the popular sector – into the PRI in the 1930s, some business leaders petitioned for the inclusion of a business sector. Cárdenas and the PRI rebuffed this overture, which left business with no regular channel of participation in electoral and party politics. In 1957 members of Concanaco requested that the PRI incorporate an industrial-commercial sector, but the government did not respond. In 1984 some industrialist leaders of Canacintra and Concamin declared their support for the creation of a business sector in the PRI (Luna, Tirado, et al. 1987, 33). Economic elites did not spend much on elections or the PRI because the latter had its own resources, which came primarily from the state.[19] The semiofficial associations were prohibited by law from engaging in direct political activity (Camp 1989, 143).[20] The lack of party channels for business is not uncommon in Latin America; what is more unusual about Mexico, in fact almost unique in the second half of the twentieth century, is the near-complete absence of personnel movement between the public and private sectors.[21] In contrast, labor leaders circulated through legislative, party, and minor executive positions far more than business.

[19] Business leaders usually endorsed PRI candidates, but presumably they had little choice but to support the winners. In 1975, the leaders of nearly all the major business associations issued a joint statement supporting the candidate López Portillo. Ironically, the statement also claimed that he would not provoke disinvestment, capital flight, or the nationalization of the banks (cited in Arriola 1976, 481).

[20] There were several breaches of this legal proscription. In the 1950s, Ruiz Cortines asked Canacintra to help design his electoral platform, and Canacintra participated again in López Mateos's campaign in 1958 (Alcázar 1970, 51–2).

[21] The most extensive study of "public–private interlocks" found little personnel exchange (Camp 1989, Chapter 5). The numbers of top officials coming from business declined markedly after 1935, with a temporary resurgence in the 1940s during the pro-business administration of Miguel Alemán. In the contemporary period, 15 percent of leading businessmen ($N = 337$) have "held national political office," and ten percent of cabinet members "have private-sector career experiences at the management level" (Camp 1989, 62). Of all the presidents of major business associations through the late 1980s, only 8 to 15 percent, depending on the association, went on to politics, almost all of them before the 1960s (Camp 1989, 83–4). Patterns of exclusion become clearer if we look at smaller elite groups. In a follow-up study of 100 top capitalists from 1970 to 2000, Camp found no exchange between business and government (personal communication, 17 June 1998). For instance, since its inception in 1962, no member of the 30 or so wealthiest men in Mexico in the CMHN held high appointed office in PRI governments. One partial

Partly in response to these multiple limitations on business representation, big business in Mexico invested heavily in noncorporatist encompassing associations, especially from the 1960s on. The major voluntary associations CMHN and CCE, as well as Coece (Coordinadora Empresarial de Comercio Exterior, discussed further in Chapter 8), represents a different group of Mexican businesses and a different aspect of relations between business and government. None of these organizations had a counterpart in Brazil or most other countries of Latin America. These associations, plus Coparmex and ABM, constituted the core of the greater encompassing organization and institutional strength of business associations in Mexico.

The backdrop for this collective action is the consistent exclusion of businessmen from positions of power in the government. And the timing of greater exclusion after the 1960s corresponds with the rise in investment by big business in encompassing associations. However, exclusion by itself did not trigger the formation of these associations. The state prompted the initial creation of CMHN and CCE, but in each case initial collective action was the unintended consequence of a perceived threat by the state. Capitalists created CMHN in the early 1960s in response to a perceived radical turn by the government. Similarly, the CCE, with essential support from the CMHN, grew out of intense conflicts between business and government in the early 1970s. Once the initial threats subsided, subsequent variations in the institutional strength and evolution of the associations (as well as the creation of Coece) depended on more deliberate efforts by state actors to strengthen business interlocutors. That is, once created, these associations became valuable to state actors who also lacked contact with business and who sought assistance in implementing specific policies or generating support for, and confidence in, the government's general economic strategies. When state actors relied on CCE, CMHN, and Coece for business input, this access to government gave the associations a strong selective benefit that increased incentives by their members for investing time and resources in these organizations.

exception is Claudio X. González, who was an advisor to Salinas on foreign investment. Moreover, "among the wealthiest thirty families in Mexico, only 8 percent were politicians" (Camp 1989, 86). Lastly, Monterrey capitalists are significantly underrepresented among businessmen who go into politics: only 4 of the 55 capitalists in Camp's survey of businessmen turned politicians, despite the fact that Monterrey capitalists constitute almost a third of Camp's total sample of 377 leading entrepreneurs (Camp 1989, 88). It was precisely Monterrey capitalists who later invested disproportionately in sustaining encompassing associations.

CMHN: An Executive Committee of the Bourgeoisie

In 1962 a small group of the owners of Mexico's biggest businesses constituted what would become the innocuous-sounding Consejo Mexicano de
Hombres de Negocios (CMHN). This sort of exclusive, low-profile association of only a few dozen of the biggest firms was rare in Latin America,
and it is difficult to find comparable associations elsewhere.[22] Francisco
Valdés argues that the CMHN "has been the most powerful business organization ever since" 1962 (Valdés Ugalde 1996, 133). Roderic Camp
called the CMHN "the single most important organization of the private sector" (1989, 83). Moreover, the CMHN was the prime mover in
creating and sustaining other business organizations, especially the CCE.
Despite the consensus on the importance of the CMHN, we know little
about it, due in large measure to the successful efforts of its members to
avoid the limelight.[23]

In organizational form, the CMHN has not changed much since the
late 1960s. Its membership expanded gradually from the 1970s to the
1990s from around 30 to over 40 (see Schneider 2002, Appendix, for a
full list of members). The founding members agreed that they wanted the
association to stay small, and established selective mechanisms for incorporating new members. To become a member, a businessman had to be
(1) Mexican; (2) "representative of one or several firms or businesses";
and (3) a "prominent member of the community" in terms of the national
economy (Ortiz Rivera 1997, 301). The admission of a new member was
subject to unanimous approval by existing members. Turnover and expansion were significant in the 1980s and 1990s. By the mid-1990s, only
2 of the 12 founding members in 1962 and only about a third of the
members in 1974 were still active members. Put differently, only about
a quarter of the members in the mid-1990s had been members in the
1970s (FCPS 1994, 51–3). In some instances, sons replaced fathers or
one shareholder of a major group substituted for another, so turnover

---

[22] In Argentina the "group of 12" and the "captains of industry" were small groups of
large firms that government officials consulted in the 1980s, but neither developed into
lasting associations (see Ostiguy 1990 and Birle 1997). CEA may come closest to the
CMHN, but, as discussed in Chapter 7, CEA never dominated the associational landscape in Argentina the way CMHN did in Mexico. IEDI in Brazil looked much like an
industrial CMHN but never flourished (Kingstone 1998). The Turkish Industrialists' and
Businessmens' Association (TUSIAD) was founded by 12 leading industrialists in 1971
and quickly grew to over 200 members by the 1980s (Arat 1991).

[23] Secondary sources on the CMHN were, until recently, very sparse. See Camp (1989),
Valdés (1998), Briz (2000), and especially Ortiz (1997, 1998).

among member firms and families was lower. Initially CMHN membership included both professional managers and owners of large firms, but over time most managers dropped out and new members were owners (Roderic Camp, personal communication, 5 April 1999). CMHN has a president, ad hoc working groups, and a part-time secretary/treasurer, but no other officers or staff, no office space, no publications, and a small budget. According to one founding member, the CMHN "is not secret, but yes discreet" (Juan Sánchez Navarro, 10 June 1996).

The core activity is a monthly luncheon, almost always with a politician or government official, mostly cabinet members responsible for economic policies. The meeting is closed and generally lasts most of the afternoon. CMHN members convene alone at about 1:00 P.M. to discuss internal business for an hour or more until the government invitee arrives for lunch (interview with Rómulo O'Farrill, 27 July 1998). After lunch the government representative makes a brief presentation, and several hours of questions and discussion follow. Since the mid-1970s, the president of Mexico has met with CMHN about once a year.[24]

From its inception, the CMHN illustrated the love–hate relations with government in promoting organization. For some founding members, the CMHN was, like Coparmex, the organized reaction of big business to government actions perceived as threatening to business as a whole.[25] President Adolfo López Mateos, in the first years of his term (1958–64), appeared to be sympathetic to labor, called himself a "leftist," and supported Castro's revolution in Cuba (see Valdés 1998, 142–5). In 1960 business mounted an opposition campaign and Coparmex, Concanaco, and Concamin jointly published a famous newspaper manifesto ("Por cual Camino?") demanding that López Mateos define himself politically. Juan Sánchez Navarro and others wanted united, collective opposition to threatening actions by the government and created the CMHN as an independent vehicle for such opposition. At the same time, or soon afterward, the government promoted CMHN. The president's leftist sympathies had

---

[24] The CMHN had one meeting with Luis Echeverría, six with José López Portillo, and seven with Miguel de la Madrid. The CMHN also had close but more ad hoc contact with President Gustavo Díaz Ordaz in the 1960s (Ortiz Rivera 1997, 305, 318, 362).

[25] See Valdés (1996, 134). Much of the discussion of the history and functioning of the CMHN draws on long and sometimes multiple interviews with early members, especially Juan Sánchez Navarro (10 June 1996), César Balsa (28 July 1998), Rómulo O'Farrill (27 July 1998), and Agustín Legoretta (28 July 1998). Sánchez Navarro was a driving force in business organization throughout the second half of the twentieth century. He was one of the handful of organizers of the CMHN (and later the CCE) and served twice as its president. Ortiz (1997) offers a complete biography.

scared off some U.S. investors, and several big businessmen felt that foreign investors were overreacting and misreading the political situation in
Mexico. So, one of the explicit goals of the dozen founding members was
to improve Mexico's image among foreign investors, and one of the first,
temporary names of the association was the Mexican Council of Public
Relations (see Ortiz 1997, 300). Government officials supported this aim,
and some early members of CMHN claimed that their invitation to join
came directly from President López Mateos (interview with César Balsa,
28 July 1998).[26]

   Although CMHN's form changed little over the following decades, its
function did. In its early years CMHN invested heavily in public relations
for Mexico and Mexican business. The CMHN paid for ads in the United
States, hired public relations consultants there, and promoted Mexico in
discussions with managers in MNCs.[27] In the mid-1970s, the CMHN
changed its statutes to focus more on domestic politics and economics.
This change was again motivated by changes in government, first in conflict and then in cooperation. By the mid-1970s CMHN members felt the
that Mexico's image abroad no longer needed as much help as building
better relations between business and government after the acrimonious
conflicts with the Echeverría administration. It was after Echeverría's presidency that the CMHN established the more routine contact with presidents and ministers that has continued since then. In the mid-1970s the
CMHN gained a higher profile when its members took the lead in creating the economy-wide CCE and incorporated the CMHN as one of the
handful of member associations with a vote in the CCE. By the 1980s,
the president of the CMHN was regularly quoted in the press alongside
other business leaders.

---

[26] Others, especially Juan Sánchez Navarro, thought Ex-President Miguel Alemán also encouraged or at least approved of the organization of CMHN. Given the divergent views
of the several founding members I interviewed, it appears possible that some members
joined because they thought they were creating an independent association to oppose
leftist governments; at the same time, others joined because they thought they had to do
the government's bidding. See also FCPS (1994, 56).

[27] Most of the literature on business organizations and Mexican politics more generally
in the 1960s pays the CMHN little attention. For instance, Arriola, in one of the most
detailed studies of business associations covering the period 1970–82, barely mentions the
CMHN except to note in passing that it was "powerful" (1988, 165). Two comprehensive
surveys of business organizations published in the early 1970s do not even mention
the CMHN (Alcázar 1970; Shafer 1973). This neglect is mistaken because even in the
1960s, the CMHN was developing into a privileged interlocutor with the government.
For example, Sánchez Navarro reveals in his biography that President Díaz Ordaz stayed
in close touch with him, as president of the CMHN, during the days leading up to the
student massacre of 1968 (Ortiz Rivera 1997, 318).

However, the public presence of the CMHN is less significant than what occurs during the monthly lunch meetings, especially in periods of harmony. The format provides the opportunity for extensive discussion. If the invitee is a secretary of government, then he or she will have several hours to exchange views with 25–30 businessmen. Little is known about what exactly transpires over these hours. All interviewees from both the CMHN and government agree that valuable information flows in both directions. CMHN members interviewed for this study were unanimous in emphasizing the value of the high-level access they gained through the CMHN. One member claimed that he owed it to his shareholders and management team to attend the CMHN luncheons, and he made a practice of reporting to his board and managers after each meeting (interview with Gilberto Borja Navarette, 24 July 1998).

The high point of visible political influence of the CMHN probably came in 1987 with the *pasarela*, or parade of PRI candidates for president before the CMHN (see Ortiz 1997, 368–72). President De la Madrid asked the CMHN to interview all six of the PRI candidates for president. In essence, the only real primary election that year for presidential aspirants was in the CMHN, which invited each candidate in turn to a lunch meeting. The CMHN was careful not to take or publicize a formal vote, and members claimed that they expressed their preferences only when asked. In any case, it seems improbable that De la Madrid would arrange the *pasarela*, and suffer the political fallout, without in the end consulting CMHN members on their preferences.

The CMHN also worked actively to enhance coordination and consensus building within the private sector. In addition to the discussions with government officials, CMHN members meet on their own, often before the arrival of the government invitee, or at other times among subgroups and working committees. These internal meetings provide additional time to exchange views across sectors and regions and build consensus (see Schneider 2002, Appendix, for the major regions and sectors represented in the CMHN). In particular, CMHN is the only institutionalized, direct channel between Monterrey's biggest businessmen and their counterparts in Mexico City. Consensus is highly valued, and the CMHN avoids taking votes. The informal procedure is to let all members discuss an issue and voice opinions. Then, if the president detects something close to consensus, he closes the discussion by stating the consensus and the actions following from it (interview with Rómulo O'Farrill, 27 July 1998). This norm of consensus building limits the range of actions the CMHN can take, but it also dampens the centripetal forces that undermine multisectoral associations elsewhere.

Beyond holding internal discussions, the CMHN also has actively promoted other associations. Most importantly, the CMHN played a dominant role in the CCE by providing many of its presidents and most of its funds. In addition, the CMHN provided substantial material support to Coparmex and COECE. The CMHN also orchestrated overall business support for government policies and worked to build investor confidence. At the end of 1995, a year of crisis, capital flight, and recession, the CMHN decided to shore up government credibility and declare publicly its expected investment for 1996. The CMHN leaders met at a press conference at the presidential residence, los Pinos, to announce that their 38 members planned to invest $6.2 billion in productive ventures, or over 10 percent of total private investment. Moreover, the CMHN said it would support government bonds.[28]

Beyond the intrinsic value of these various coordinating activities, it has been the contact with government that has held the CMHN so tightly together. This conclusion is supported by interviews with members as well as by comparative and theoretical analysis. Ministers and presidents in Brazil and Argentina sometimes established regular, informal meetings with a dozen or two top capitalists. However, what is notable about these groups is that they disappear once government invitations stop. From the perspective of microeconomic theories of collective action, the CMHN seems a "privileged" group (in Olson's terms): it is a very small group of extremely rich men, so many of the obstacles to collective action fade away. However, it is also a diverse group with disparate regional and sectoral interests that theoretically should be difficult to hold together, especially over long periods, in the absence of selective incentives (Olson 1965, 1986). The regular presence of top government officials provides the strong "selective incentives" for collective action. The strongest positive incentive is to be at the lunch table for lengthy conversations with government ministers. A secondary, more negative incentive is that capitalists likely want to be at the table to make sure that the government hears their preferences on policy issues and to counter contrary views from other members.

In sum, the CMHN resembles a substitute "executive committee" for managing the common affairs of the bourgeoisie as a whole and communicating to government the concerns of Mexico's largest business groups.

---

[28] This announcement became an annual ritual with regular investment promises by the CMHN: $7 billion in 1997, $8.4 billion in 1998, $7 billion in 1999, and $8.5 billion in 2000 (Schneider 2002, 93).

Exclusion, cooperation, and conflict have all pushed big capitalists to maintain their investment in CMHN, though the impact of each factor has varied over time. The general exclusion of business from politics consistently increased the value of contact through the CMHN. Periods of conflict with government in the late 1950s, early 1970s, and early 1980s all contributed to member investment in collective action and to the reorientation of CMHN to the important role it has come to play in domestic politics. Since the mid-1980s very close cooperation and communication between government and the CMHN has maintained the high value of membership and active participation in CMHN.

The Consolidation of an Encompassing Peak Association

In 1975 big business in Mexico overcame deep sectoral, regional, and corporatist divisions to create an encompassing peak association, the Consejo Coordinador Empresarial (CCE). Such encompassing peak associations are rare in large, late-developing countries. CCE may not have been as institutionally strong as some peak associations in developed countries, but its very existence in Latin America was remarkable. By the 1990s, the eight associations that made up the CCE included, on paper, almost every type of firm in every sector in Mexico, from the largest conglomerates to hundreds of thousands of small retailers. By 1992 the member associations had over 900,000 member businesses and covered most of the economy. The largest numbers of members came from the traditional corporatist confederations Concanaco (commerce, 500,000 members) and Concamin (industry, 125,000 members), as well as the CNA (Consejo Nacional Agropecuario) (agriculture, 250,000) (Luna and Tirado 1992, 34). The addition of finance, represented through the ABM (banking, 18 members), AMCB (Asociación Mexicana de Casas de Bolsa) (stock brokerage, 26 members), and AMIS (Asociación Mexicana de Instituciones de Seguros) (insurance, 59 members), completed the sectoral membership of the CCE (Tirado 1998, 188). With these six, CCE would seem a fairly typical peak association with one vote per sector, though the votes were skewed in favor of large financial firms.[29] The CCE also included on an equal footing Coparmex and CMHN, which further

---

[29] In addition, Canacintra and Canaco-DF (commerce in Mexico City) had a voice but not a vote (until 2001). The formal representation of finance in CCE underwent several permutations after the government nationalized the banks in 1982. AMCB replaced the ABM during the 1980s. When the government resold the banks in the early 1990s the new owners reconstituted the ABM. See http://www.cce.org for more information.

distorted sectoral representation. Coparmex was a multisectoral employers' organization, and its members also belonged by law to a corporatist sectoral association. Through the CMHN (whose membership overlaped with the small ABM), the CCE formally overrepresented a small number of Mexico's largest firms. Several dozen members of CMHN and ABM had the same vote as the hundreds of thousands of members in Concanaco.

Where did the impetus for CCE come from? The simple and most common answer is: President Echeverría (1970–6), who did many things that displeased business (see especially Arriola 1988). The government's general leftist rhetoric was disconcerting. The Echeverría government supported labor more than past governments and encouraged the formation of the Congreso de Trabajo (CT), a peak labor organization, which some capitalists wanted to counter with a peak association of business.[30] State intervention into the economy, especially in the guise of state-owned enterprises, expanded dramatically under Echeverría and crowded out and competed with private firms on many fronts. Moreover, Echeverría broke an unwritten rule that top officials consult with the private sector before adopting any policy of significant interest to capitalists (Luna 1992, 38). Lastly, Echeverría ended his term with a series of land expropriations that further threatened property rights. In short, Echeverría made it easy for capitalists from all sectors to find common ground in opposition to him and in agreement that the private sector needed a united voice to counter the multiple threats coming from the state. In theoretical terms, Echeverría subordinated divergent interests (that in other times and places impeded encompassing collective action) to common opposition to the state. As in the case of the economy-wide confederation in Chile in the 1960s, Mexican associations feared that if they did not hang together they would hang separately. That is, if the heads of Concamin or Concanaco challenged the president, they would be vulnerable to reprisals against only their associations or sectors. If the challenge came from the CCE, member associations and sectors were less vulnerable (interview with Juan Sánchez Navarro, 10 June 1996).

Surprisingly, Echeverría did not discourage the CCE, and once it was in embryonic form he gave it subtle encouragement. When Echeverría heard that business leaders were planning the creation of the CCE, he

---

[30] Interview with Francisco Calderón, 12 June 1996. This was one of the few times that interviewees mentioned labor organization as an impetus for collective action by business. However, here and elsewhere, business saw the hand of the state behind labor.

told Juan Sánchez Navarro that business should organize as it saw fit and that he would be interested in knowing about the proposed statutes for the new association. So, Echeverría invited the organizing committee for the CCE and the heads of the member associations to breakfast at Los Pinos, the presidential residence. To the surprise of the invitees, most members of the cabinet also came to the breakfast. This was a clear signal that the government was taking the CCE seriously and a boost therefore to incentives for collective action (see Schneider 2002 for more details on the founding of the CCE).

Some of the biggest firms or *grupos* largely financed the CCE, as in the case of Coparmex, by making large "voluntary" contributions, beyond the equal dues charged the eight associations.[31] In the early years the member associations paid very little. Most of the costs were covered, in roughly equal thirds, by (1) the Monterrey group, (2) the bankers, and (3) other firms, such as Bimbo, and the member associations. The owners of many of these contributing firms were also members of the CMHN, so the CMHN in effect carried the CCE for its first years. By the 1980s the CCE had diversified the revenue sources for what would be a fairly constant budget of about $2 million per year. One quarter came from member associations and another quarter from the sale of services, lectures, and publications. A full half of the CCE's budget, or roughly $1 million per year, came in voluntary contributions. By the 1990s nearly 350 firms were making voluntary contributions, but the bulk of the funding came from a few dozen large firms: mostly members of the CMHN, bankers, and Monterrey firms.[32]

Why did these large firms assume so much of the cost of the CCE and tolerate so much free riding by the rest of business? Each of three overlapping sets of huge businesses wanted to support the CCE in order to reduce their vulnerability or increase their influence. The CMHN wanted to remain a discrete association without a public profile, and the CCE offered it a privileged position from which to go public, though not in the name of the CMHN alone. Similarly, the bankers have traditionally had image problems in government circles and public opinion, so that

---

[31] Unless otherwise attributed, these and subsequent financial data come from an interview with a top staffer at CCE who requested anonymity, as well as Juan Sánchez Navarro. Documentary evidence is incomplete but generally corroborates the oral testimony. For fuller data and sources see Schneider (2002).

[32] The top five contributing firms include Bimbo, Alfonso Romo (Monterrey), Vitro (Monterrey), Visa (Monterrey), and Grupo Herdez. Contributions from many firms were highly variable and could disappear from one year to the next, depending on firm profits.

demands coming solely from the bankers' association lacked legitimacy and efficacy (see Camp 1989). Lastly, voluntary contributions gave big business further influence, as discussed later, in CCE policy and leadership selection.

From the CCE's first documents, it is clear that the founders wanted a peak association with institutional capacity, including research, dissemination, and proselytizing (Sánchez Navarro 1996, 9). The target audience was not only business, but also public opinion and political leaders. The staff of the CCE began at around 40–50, in part because it absorbed the already existing CEESP (Centro de Estudios Económicos del Sector Privado), which accounted for half of the starting staff. The staff reached a maximum of 82 in 1982 and stayed at around 80 until 1993, when it dropped to 61, in part because the CCE had, through the reforms of the government of Carlos Salinas (1988–94), achieved so much of what it had been pressing the government to do.

The centripetal impetus Echeverría generated through conflict was dissipated by initially harmonious relations with his successor. President López Portillo (1976–82) was initially more sympathetic to business, thereby diminishing the common interest in the CCE. At the same time, the oil boom of the late 1970s gave capitalists incentives to neglect organizing and tend to business. However, big firms did not completely abandon the CCE, as often happened over the decades in Argentina and Brazil. When members debated possible dissolution in CCE meetings in the late 1970s, the collective decision was to maintain the CCE. When López Portillo nationalized the banks in 1982, business roused the CCE from its relative hibernation to channel business opposition (Tirado 1998, 193–5).[33]

The love–hate cycles intensified and accelerated in the 1980s and strengthened the CCE institutionally. While the intense conflicts of 1976 and 1982 strengthened the CCE, subsequent close cooperation with the de la Madrid government (1982–8) increased incentives for big business to invest in the CCE. After taking office at the end of 1982, De la Madrid made the CCE one of his key targets for efforts to win back "*confianza*" and private sector support. Meetings between top government officials and the CCE became as frequent as those between the CMHN and government. For example, from May 1986 to May 1987 the CCE had 18 "extraordinary" assemblies (in addition to is ordinary meetings), mostly with secretaries and subsecretaries of economic ministries. Over the same

---

[33] The nationalization of the banks, of course, eliminated the single largest sectoral source of CCE revenues and thereby caused CCE a severe financial crisis.

period, CCE delegations met with President De la Madrid 9 times and with economic ministers over 40 times (CCE 1987, Coord-9–10).[34]

The high point of organized collaboration between business and government came at the end of De la Madrid's term. In late 1987, as macroeconomic variables worsened dramatically, government officials sounded out business on the possibility of an anti-inflation pact (discussed further in Chapter 8). Informal discussions led quickly to the first of many regular agreements on taxes, exchange rates, prices, and wages signed by representatives of business, government, and labor. The CCE was the central coordinator on the business side, and its leaders and backers contributed a lot of time and money to organize and enhance business representation in the pacts. The CCE could not compel members to abide by the agreements, and CCE leaders had to spend a great deal of time persuading them to do so (interview with Agustín Legorreta, 28 July 1998). The CCE also benefited from the broad public approval the pacts won as inflation rapidly subsided in 1988 and 1989. Contact between the government and the CCE was intense in the first years of the pacts, and entailed marathon weekend negotiations and lengthy, regular monitoring meetings each week. Even after inflation fell the pacts, under changing names, continued into the mid-1990s (see Ortega 2002).

At the same time that the associations enhanced the pacts, the pacts strengthened the associations, even corporatist organizations. In terms of participation, the pacts automatically boosted incentives for firms to participate in their respective associations. The number of meetings naturally increased, at least in the early years of the pact, when negotiations were most intense. As noted earlier, CCE staff and budgets expanded. The president of Concamin, Vicente Bortoni, used the organization's presence in the pacts to cajole members into paying their dues and stem the association's steady economic decline. Bortoni told the members that Concamin needed funds to improve the staff and Concamin's bargaining position within the pacts. By one estimate, Concamin's staff was around 100 in the 1970s, dropped to 50 during the 1980s, rose to 80 with the pacts, and dropped again to about 40 in the 1990s (interview with Jaime González Graf, 10 June 1996). In sum, the selective benefit provided by the state of sitting at the negotiating table significantly enhanced collective action by business and the institutional strength of its associations.

---

[34] In the early 1990s the presidents of CCE member associations met on Wednesday evenings for lengthy dinners, attended about once a month by a top government official (interview with Roberto Sánchez de la Vara, 8 June 1996).

In the late 1980s and 1990s, in part because of the pacts, the CCE went through some internal conflicts that showed how well the CCE represented big business (see Tirado 1998). Through the late 1980s three presidents of the CCE were members of the CMHN, and two of the three were owners of large, financially centered conglomerates.[35] At the end of the term of the last of these three, Rolando Vega, other CCE members voiced their opposition to the dominance of big business and demanded greater internal democracy and stronger representation of small and medium-sized firms. The impasse was first postponed by keeping Vega on for another year and later was "resolved" through the automatic rotation of the presidency among the heads of the member associations. The CCE dropped the rotation scheme several presidents later, and big business restored its strong hold on the CCE over the course of the 1990s. The president in 1998–9 was Eduardo Bours, officially from the mass agricultural association CNA. But Bours's firm was the huge conglomerate Bachoco, and his father was a member of the CMHN. Big business also retained overrepresentation on the CCE board, and big business continued to foot at least half the bill of the CCE.

In 2000 big business and CMHN returned to more overt control over the CCE. In 1999, Claudio X. González of the CMHN lost the CCE's first contested election for president to Jorge Marín Santillán, a smaller industrialist and ex-president of Concamin. Marín Santillán won this battle but went on to lose the war. Voluntary contributions from big business dropped dramatically in 1999 (interview with Alejando Martínez Gallardo, 11 May 2001). In early 2000, Marín Santillán resigned (or rather announced his decision not to seek a second term, as had been the long-standing custom in CCE) due to opposition from the CMHN (*Reforma*, 17 February 2000, p. A3). Claudio X. González won the presidency in June 2000, but at a cost. Concanaco, the commerce confederation with a preponderance of small and medium-sized firms, withdrew from the CCE, charging it with not representing small firms (*El Universal*, 1 June 2000, electronic version). Concamin also withdrew in solidarity, demanding new statutes, but rejoined later that year.

In sum, the CMHN was always a major force behind the CCE. Exclusion and threatening acts by government during the Echeverría administration gave each member association strong incentives to cede some

---

[35] Claudio X. González was president of Kimberly-Clark in Mexico. Augustín Legorreta was the scion of a traditional banking family and president of the Inverlat group. Rolando Vega Iñiguez was also from a traditional banking family.

authority to a central peak association. The elitist associations like the CMHN and the bankers lacked legitimacy as high-profile political activists and needed mass business allies. The mass corporatist associations were vulnerable individually to government retaliation and needed the cover of a joint spokesperson for business. Renewed conflict in the early 1980s radicalized the CCE. It was De la Madrid's consistent pressure and courtship of business that helped bring moderation to CCE and closer collaboration between the CCE and the government that ended with the successful stabilization pacts of the late 1980s. The unusual absence of both conflict and collaboration in the 1990s translated into somewhat lower investment in the CCE and a reduction of its staff and activities. Nonetheless, the CCE retained a strong public presence and an extensive research capacity that maintained its high profile. In Mexico the years just before and just after a presidential succession are politically intense and especially formative for new political actors like the CCE, formed at the end of the Echeverría's term, cauterized by the bank nationalization at the end of the López Portillo's term, and called into active service in the fight against inflation in the last months of De la Madrid's term. The Salinas government inverted this pattern in relying heavily on organized business, especially the CCE and CMHN, in the first years of his term in the pacts and later in negotiations over Nafta, and then abandoned meaningful contact with business associations at the end of his term. In essence, Mexico's encompassing associations were born in fear, but they thrived only when presidents and ministers made them privileged interlocutors.

When the Mexican government announced plans in March 1990 to pursue Nafta, the CCE – with government approval – quickly created Coece. Coece adopted a decentralized and fluid structure and maintained very close contact with government negotiators. Although difficult to quantify, Coece represented a very large additional investment in collective action, both sectoral and encompassing. This investment came directly from firms (that paid the expenses of representatives who accompanied the negotiatiors) but also from the CCE and CMHN. Collective action and contact with government were intense in the two years after the government's announcement, yet business did not invest in lasting institutional capacity in Coece. However, even less intense participation by existing associations encouraged more investment in their professional staff and their ability to process information (Puga 1994, 190–2).

The desire on the part of Secretary Jaime Serra and other officials in Secofi (Secretaría de Comercio y Fomento Industrial) to work with business illustrates several of the political logics introduced in Chapter 2 (and considered further in Chapter 8). Secofi officials sought overall political support for Nafta in order to overcome anticipated opposition, and businesses active in Coece became strong and vocal supporters. Government negotiators also wanted aggregated preferences. Negotiating variable levels of protection can pit up- and downstream producers against each other, with government negotiators squeezed in between. Coece encouraged up- and downstream producers in various productive chains, though not always successfully, to reconcile their preferences before meeting with government negotiators. Lastly, officials, some of whom had no previous experience in trade or trade treaties, needed basic background information on sectoral performance and trade patterns and logistics (interviews with Jaime Serra, 15 July 1996 and 16 July 1998; Aslan Cohen, 7 June 1996; and Santiago Macias, 16 November 1993).

The Twilight of State Corporatism

The year 1997 marked a watershed for corporatism in Mexico. The Supreme Court forced the issue of modernizing the existing 1941 Chambers Law by ruling that compulsory membership was unconstitutional because it abridged citizens' right to freedom of association. In response, the Chambers Law of 1997 made membership officially voluntary (Ley Cámaras 1997). On the face of it, the end of compulsory membership appeared to sound the death knell of state corporatism; however, the law was remarkable in its efforts to retain state control while acquiescing to voluntary membership. Through dramatic neoliberal economic reform and expanding democratization, top government reformers relinquished state control of much of the economy and PRI control of much of the political system, but they resisted letting go of state control of business associations.

Among other things, the 1997 Chambers Law prohibited the chambers from engaging in political or religious activities, made the chambers partly responsible for collecting information for the government, detailed various sanctions the government can impose on associations, convoked the general assembly of the association, and set the maximum dues associations may charge (Articles 2–6). Associations still required state licensing. The state even reserved the *appellation contrôlée* "chamber" or "confederation" and prohibited other nonlicensed groups from using these labels. The law also gave the chambers and confederations responsibilities "to represent and defend the general interests of commerce or industry" and "to be an organ of consultation and collaboration with the State for the design and execution of policies, programs, and instruments that facilitate the expansion of economic activity" (Articles 10.I and 10.II).

The preamble to the law noted briefly the explicit interests of the state in organizing business. Specifically, the organization of the confederations "allows the government to know, in a timely manner, the positions and proposals that concern industry and commerce throughout the country" (Mexico 1997, 3). The preamble also notes that in the past the corporatist associations "had rendered great service to the country," and notes two recent examples in particular, the pacts and the negotiation of trade agreements (p. 2). In proposing the creation of the Sistema de Información Empresarial Mexicano, the document notes that this *sistema* will "constitute an instrument of planning for the State" (p. 5). Although not part of the Chambers Law, ex-corporatist associations retained representation in the state. In 2001 the industry confederation Concamin, for example, had seats on the boards of a dozen or so public entities, including Nafinsa (Nacional Financiera) and Seguro Social.[36]

Continued access notwithstanding, the end of compulsory affiliation caused membership and revenues to fall precipitously. In the manufacturing chamber, Canacintra total membership fell in the five years after 1997 by nearly two-thirds, from 87,000 to 35,000 members (*Reforma*, 19 February 2002, electronic version). By another measure, the proportion of all manufacturing firms organized by Canacintra dropped from its highest level of over 50 percent in the 1980s to under 5 percent in 1998 (Shadlen in press, Figures 5.2 and 5.3).[37] In Concamin in 1997 the member *cámaras* contributed $2.5 million (over 80 percent of the total budget of around $3 million; interview with Martínez Gallardo, May 2001). After 1997 these contributions plummeted to $400,000 and recovered to around $800,000 by 2000. To make up the shortfall, Concamin approached large national and multinational firms for voluntary contributions. As in the case of CMHN, these voluntary donations gave large contributors considerable, immediate leverage over the association. Other associations tried to raise new revenues by offering services. If successful, these commercial activities may come to overshadow representational functions and grant association leaders organizational autonomy from their members, or "clients" (Schmitter and Streeck 1999, 81–8). In

---

[36] Interview with Martínez Gallardo (11 May 2001). Martínez confirmed that the meetings of many of these boards were important enough that he, as president of Concamin, attempted to attend them all.

[37] Membership in fact dropped in 1998 to only 15,000 and then gradually recovered after 2000 (Kenneth Shadlen, personal communication, 25 February 2002).

short, either strategy – services or voluntary contributions – to attempt to make up for lost revenues due to the change in the Chambers Law had profound impacts on the structure of representation (beyond the loss of thousands of members). These recent changes in Mexico are vivid examples of how shifts in state regulation can have immediate and dramatic consequences for resources, institutional capacity, and internal representation in associations.

Despite the dramatic impact on some of its member associations, CCE was otherwise not much affected by the 1997 Chambers Law.[38] Revenues continued at about $2.7 million in 2002. However, the CCE began its own internal restructuring in 2002 and reduced its staff from 50 to 30. This restructuring was designed in part to reduce the dependence of CCE on voluntary contributions from large firms, which accounted for only 10 percent of CCE's budget after the downsizing compared to over half in the 1980s and 1990s. In principle, the reduction in CCE financial dependence on voluntary contributions reduces the leverage of CMHN members within the CCE.

Certainly the context of business politics changed dramatically with the national elections of 1997 and 2000. The elections opened up new avenues for business politics and widened the portfolio of political investments. When the PRI lost control of Congress in the 1997 elections, the legislature became an important actor in politics generally and in economic policy in particular, so associations reorganized to learn how to communicate with Congress. Vicente Fox's election signaled the importance of two further avenues for political participation by big business. The first was campaign financing and electoral endorsements, as important business groups lined up publicly behind the candidacies of Fox or Francisco Labastida in the 2000 elections. The second was the opening of top appointed positions in the Fox government to businessmen. The prevalence of capitalists in the cabinet was still not as great in Mexico as it has been at times in Brazil, Argentina, and Colombia, but it marked a watershed in Mexican politics. At a minimum, these new alternatives attracted time and resources that might previously have gone into associations. In the first years of the government of Vicente Fox (2000–6), associations maintained good access to the president and top economic policy makers, and this access helped sustain incentives for business investment in associations, though these incentives were diluted by an

---

[38] Much of the information in this paragraph comes from an interview with the general director of CCE, Luiz Miguel Pando, 26 February 2003.

expanding portfolio of options for political participation. Also, a common business complaint was that access to the Fox government was less valuable than access to previous governments because the Fox government was unable to accomplish much (interviews with Pando, 26 February 2003, and Martínez Gallardo, 24 February 2003).

Summary and Conclusions

How did state actors help Mexican business organize some of the strongest encompassing associations in the Americas? Over the course of the twentieth century, government officials used direct regulation, reformist threats, and privileged access, all of which strengthened incentives for business to invest time and money in encompassing associations. Over time, corporatist controls lost importance and love–hate relations with voluntary associations became the main factor influencing changes in business organization. The lack of alternative political investments through the 1990s magnified the importance of associations. That is, business leaders were more likely to accept invitations from government to communicate through associations when they lacked alternative channels through either personal networks, appointments, party politics, or legislative lobbying. In other countries, as seen in the following chapters, state officials might well have wanted to organize business, but their invitations and inducements often had less effect precisely because big business knew that other doors for communication and influence were open.

Why did state actors in Mexico seek out business and promote its organization? Political and economic vulnerabilities were recurring challenges for state actors throughout Mexico's tumultuous twentieth century. Although the crises were quite different, the vulnerabilities of state actors in 1917 (after the ravages of the Revolution) and in 1987 (a time of extreme macroeconomic volatility) were dire and made organizing business to manage the economic transition an attractive option for economic policy makers. More specific and less dramatic vulnerabilities prompted state actors at other junctures to seek out general political support (in the early 1960s and mid-1980s, for example), support for changing development strategies in the 1930s, 1940s, and 1980s, and help with policy implementation, most recently in anti-inflation pacts and Nafta negotiations.

State officials prompted voluntary encompassing collective action both among individuals (in CMHN) and among associations (in CCE). However, the evolution of the CCE reveals a different logic of collective action. The main obstacles to collective action among associations were less free riding than divergent interests. Associations of associations, CCE in this case, had fewer problems with free riding because the number of potential members was quite small, only a handful or two, and richer members, in this case the CMHN, were willing to take on a disproportionate share of material and leadership expenses. If free riding is less of an obstacle, then finding common ground becomes the greater remaining difficulty impeding the formation of peak associations of associations (Chapter 8 discusses the issue of collective action among organizations, rather than among individuals, at greater length). Creating common interests, then, is where threatening state actions come in. If governments attempt to isolate some sectoral associations for retaliation, then these associations have even greater incentives to engage in collective action and to pay the costs of organizing economy-wide peak associations. In other countries, threats from government also prompted business to organize more encompassing associations. However, the lack of subsequent state support for these incipient organizations deprived business of reasons to continue to invest in them. In Brazil, as discussed further in the next chapter, business organized in opposition to Goulart in the 1960s and again in the late 1980s to influence the constituent assembly that was charged with writing Brazil's new constitution. However, government actors did not make these organizations lasting interlocutors, so these associations faded.

This chapter stressed the impressive organizational accomplishments of Mexican business. However, I should emphasize, in closing, that my argument is comparative: Mexican business was strongly organized relative to business in other countries in Latin America. This relative argument should not be construed to mean that Mexican business always acted collectively; in many instances, Mexican business was deeply divided and could not act collectively.[39] The comparative differences will become clearer in the next chapters which document how business elsewhere failed to organize encompassing associations comparable to Coparmex, CMHN, and CCE.

---

[39] In his overview of Mexican business associations, Camp concluded that "Group behavior has not reached its maximum fruition, not only because the state does not permit it to do so, but because businesspeople themselves do not utilize the primary strength of any organization – its collective power" (1989, 172). Story also found that many industrialists lamented the fact that the "industrial sector does not *act* as a unified political force" (1983, 369). Neither study, though, puts these conclusions in comparative perspective.

4

From Corporatism to Reorganized Disarticulation in Brazil

> The presumption that one will not be heard discourages by itself interest in participating, given the skepticism in the efficacy of this participation. The certainty of the futility of action precludes the participation of many industrialists who, otherwise, would be active.
>
> Brazilian industrialist, 1976[1]

Introduction

An examination of business associations in Brazil raises several major questions. Why were some of the wealthiest and best-staffed associations in Latin America so poorly equipped to represent business? Comparatively, why were encompassing associations so much weaker in Brazil than in other countries of the region? And why did some of the most powerful industrial associations in the region in the 1940s and 1950s degenerate over time into much weaker and politically marginal organizations? On the first question, appearances in Brazil were deceptive. On paper, Brazilian associations organized nearly all of business, had massive resources that they spent on sophisticated research and coordinating departments, and appeared regularly in the press to air business's views on the issues of the day. Yet, most prominent businesspeople and top government officials readily admit that these impressive-looking associations

---

[1] Cited in Diniz and Boschi (1978, 182).

Portions of this chapter originally appeared in "Organized Business Politics in Democratic Brazil," *Journal of Interamerican Studies and World Affairs* 39:4 (Winter 1997–8), 95–127.

were in fact weak and unrepresentative, and economic and political elites regularly circumvented them in order to communicate. In his earlier incarnation as one of Brazil's leading sociologists and students of business politics, Fernando Henrique Cardoso concluded that the Brazilian "bourgeoisie never had effective political organization and pressure instruments" (Cardoso 1973, 148).[2]

The misleading appearances of organizational strength make it advisable at the outset to look beyond the imposing façade to the less visible structural debilities. By the mid-1990s the industry confederation CNI (Confederação Nacional de Indústria), for example, had around 500 employees, a budget of $42 million (*Globo*, 25 October 1995, Sect. 1, p. 19), and a range of political and semipolitical programs. Another 1,000 or so CNI employees administered an additional $600 million in compulsory contributions to funds for education, training, and social programs for workers. Despite these resources and compulsory membership for all industries, the CNI had feeble political projection and little capacity to aggregate, and therefore represent, industrial interests.[3] On the aggregation side, the fundamental flaw was that the CNI was composed of 27 state-level federations, each with one vote, so that the federations of tiny rural states had the same vote as the industrial association of São Paulo, FIESP (Federação das Indústrias do Estado de São Paulo). One result of this corporatist misrepresentation was that most of the presidents of CNI since the 1950s were from the northeast, which made little sense in a country where São Paulo accounted for more than half of total industrial output and the center-south for more than two-thirds.[4]

Due in part to CNI's defects, FIESP emerged as the de facto national mouthpiece for industry (Diniz and Boschi 1988, 308; Toledo 1992, 78).

---

[2] Moreover, the "nearly unanimous view of those interviewed is that industrialists view business associations as something foreign to them" (Cardoso 1972, 174).

[3] CNI leaders implicitly acknowledged their difficulties in aggregating interests when in 1988 they began a series of national surveys of 500–700 managers of large and medium-sized firms to find out how industrialists viewed the major issues of reform such as trade liberalization, industrial policy, and privatization (CNI 1990, 1991, 1992).

[4] In terms of political impact, the voice of CNI in Brasília has historically been muted, in part because its staff of hundreds worked in Rio de Janeiro. Until the 1990s CNI lacked even a minimal lobbying operation in Brasília. In some periods, CNI certainly had political access, if for no other reason than that its presidents were also politicians. Albano Franco and Fernando Bezerra, presidents of the CNI in the early and late 1990s, respectively, were both at the same time senators from small northeastern states. This dual role was at best a mixed blessing for industrialists since they represented not only industry but also their parties, regions, and political factions, and the latter political factors were more important to their future political careers.

Public opinion gives one indication of FIESP's predominance: in 1991 only 27 percent of respondents knew of CNI compared with 65 percent who recognized FIESP.[5] FIESP/CIESP (Centro de Indústrias do Estado de São Paulo) had an imposing organizational presence including 121 member associations, about 500 employees, a budget of $41 million, and a 15-story landmark on the Avenida Paulista.[6] Yet, behind the imposing façade was an organization that suffered from its own corporatist distortions. Marginal sectors, and the small and medium-sized firms in them, remained overrepresented. By the 1990s traditional sectors (food, clothing, construction, and furniture) accounted for 16 percent of value added in São Paulo industry but had 44 percent of the votes in FIESP. Modern sectors (chemicals, pharmaceuticals, metal working, and electrical equipment) had only one-third of the votes yet produced nearly two-thirds of value added (calculations by Rubens Figueiredo cited in Kingstone 1999, 130). Not surprisingly, the president of FIESP was often a marginal figure in Paulista industry not drawn from the ranks of São Paulo's best-known and respected industrialists (Schneider 1997–8, 103). One past president acknowledged later that the president of FIESP was essentially a "*despachante de luxo*," an elite broker hired to sort out problems for individual member firms.[7]

Business elites themselves clearly felt that their associations lacked political influence. In a 1990 survey they ranked these associations 12th out of 14 different groups, and well below individual companies, in terms of influence in the government of José Sarney. Not surprisingly, business associations were more powerful in the eyes of other elites in government

[5] CNI and FIESP jointly commissioned a survey of 13,000 respondents in July 1991. CNI was, however, recognized by more respondents than the other corporatist confederations in agriculture, CNA (Confederação Nacional de Agricultura), 21 percent, or commerce, CNC (Confederação Nacional do Comércio), 15 percent. Reported in *Journal da Tarde*, 3 September 1993, p. 10.

[6] *Exame*, 22 July 1992, p. 29, and Toledo (1992, 80). References to FIESP usually subsume the nominally independent CIESP. CIESP is an independent civil association founded three years before FIESP in 1928. By the 1990s its 8,764 members were individual firms rather than sectoral associations. The president of FIESP was always also the president of CIESP.

[7] Luís Eulálio de Bueno Vidigal, cited in *Playboy* 12 December 1991, p. 119. He continued, "the main task of a FIESP president is to solve problems firms have with official agencies," for example, "speed up the disbursement of a loan from the Banco do Brasil, get an import authorization more rapidly, convince some authority that it is important to grant a fiscal incentive." Bueno de Vidigal was in fact one of the few FIESP presidents to come from a prominent, large firm, but to achieve the presidency he ran a two-year campaign against the entrenched leadership of the time to win the first contested election in FIESP in 1980 (Skidmore 1988, 202).

and civil society. However, these other elites still ranked business associations only seventh out of 14 and, most significantly, below unorganized business. Nonelites had similar views. Nearly 5,500 voters surveyed in mid-October 1992 in five state capitals ranked business associations lowest of 24 different groups and institutions in terms of prestige and second lowest in terms of power. On both dimensions associations ranked lower than private national firms, banks, and MNCs. All respondents in these surveys agreed: the whole was less influential than the sum of the parts.[8]

The second, comparative puzzle in Brazil is how one of the largest and most dynamic industrial sectors in the Latin America – and the largest coffee sector in the world, as noted at the beginning of this book – could have such weak organized political projection. Not only were industry associations internally flawed, but business also lacked economy-wide associations. Nothing like the strong multisectoral Mexican associations – CMHN, CCE, or Coparmex – existed in Brazil. Part of the explanation for this puzzle lies in the comparatively hospitable political environment in which Brazilian business flourished in the second half of the twentieth century. Despite some difficult moments, Brazilian business did not face the sustained challenges of labor and leftist politics (as in Chile) or arbitrary state actions (as in Mexico). Moreover, in sharp contrast to Mexico, representatives of business, especially industry in São Paulo, regularly figured prominently in top positions in all sorts of governments. Most importantly, even when business formed temporary economy-wide coordinating bodies, state actors never granted them privileged access or other benefits. So, Brazilian business had fewer incentives to invest time or resources in encompassing organizations.

Another large part of the explanation lies in the early history and distorting legacies of the initial corporatist organization of business. In the 1930s and 1940s corporatist laws regulating compulsory membership and representation helped industrialists create powerful associations in a short time. In this early period, intense conflict with government and labor unions, as well as subsequent government support for the new business associations, generated strong and influential business associations, especially in industry. The third historical puzzle is how these vibrant industry

---

[8] For sources and background on both surveys, see Schneider (1997–8, 103–4). In another poll of business in 1992 "72 percent still believed that FIESP played an important role in the national political and economic scene" (Kingstone 1999, 127). It is harder to interpret this view without explicit comparisons to the influence of other groups and actors.

associations degenerated by the 1970s into much weaker and less representative organizations. As these associations ossified, they not only ceased to represent big business but also filled the organizational space and thereby impeded efforts by big business to find alternative channels for collective action and representation. Many overall political analyses of Brazil highlight low levels of formal institutionalization and very fluid, informal, and constantly changing political arrangements. So, it is noteworthy to come across an example of long-lasting, albeit unintended, consequences of early institutional choices. In the case of the corporatist framework for business organization, decisions in the 1930s and 1940s on regional (instead of sectoral) organization, dual representation (both state-licensed federations and independent associations), and generous state-mandated funding all shaped business organization and ultimate disarticulation for the rest of the twentieth century. Moreover, after the 1940s, the strong industry associations lost their privileged access to core policy councils. Later, many narrow sectoral associations were so favored, which consequently encouraged participation in those associations rather than in encompassing ones. Mutual uninterest created a reinforcing cycle in the last decades of the twentieth century where government officials found business associations weak and unrepresentative and excluded them from policy-making forums. Business, in turn, had fewer incentives, such as institutionalized access to the government, to invest in these associations.

Of course, any analysis of the organizational weakness of business should not lose sight of the fact that Brazilian business – both as individuals and as loose movements – was a major political force throughout the twentieth century and has participated dramatically in major regime changes, both authoritarian and democratic. However, by the close of the twentieth century, all this political activity had left little institutional residual: no parties of business, no economy-wide associations, and greater fragmentation than ever in business representation. This chapter first analyzes the rise and decline of corporatist associations in industry from the 1930s to the 1970s and then turns to a closer examination of later frustrated attempts to create alternative, voluntary, encompassing organizations.

Strong Industry Associations Emerged under Vargas

Some business associations emerged earlier, but in the 1930s and 1940s Getúlio Vargas transformed the organizational landscape for the rest of the century.[9] From Vargas's first decree in 1931 regulating business and labor associations through the Constitution of 1934, the Carta of 1937, major decrees in 1939 and 1940, to the final 1943 Consolidação das Leis do Trabalho (CLT), São Paulo industrialists and officials of various Vargas governments struggled over the terms of organization of both labor and business. State actors took the initiative to organize business, especially industry, but São Paulo industrialists prevailed in a number of battles over legislation that set the terms of organization, including, among other things, a federal structure for the organization of industry (and hence FIESP's original structure), management autonomy on the shop floor, and exclusive business control over state-created training and social funds. In the short term, these victories granted enormous influence to São Paulo associations, but the historical irony is that these same victories contributed by century's end to undermining institutional capacity in the industrial federations, especially in comparison to voluntary industry associations in Chile and Colombia.

The hate–love relationship between business and government that generated such strong associations in Chile and Mexico was compressed into a shorter time span across the changing relations between business and various Vargas governments from 1930 to 1945. Relations were conflictual in the first Vargas years but improved markedly by the mid-1930s. The result by the end of the period was amazingly strong industry associations, beyond the dreams of the São Paulo industrialists who first created CIESP in 1928. CIESP became FIESP to conform to the 1931 decree creating official *sindicatos* (sectoral associations) and encompassing federations of these sectoral sindicatos (Weinstein 1990, 384).[10] In 1938 FIESP had over 1,000 direct members and several thousand more firms affiliated through its member *sindicatos*.[11] By 1941 membership and revenues had doubled. According to FIESP estimates, its member firms

---

[9] Excellent studies on the history of business associations in Brazil include Boschi (1979), Costa (1992), Diniz and Boschi (1978), Diniz (1978), Cardoso (1964), Schmitter (1971), and Weinstein (1996). In finance, see Minella (1988) and Barker (1990). Schmitter characterizes Brazil as a case of state corporatism. The label applies better to labor. Business, as the next sections show, heavily influenced the shape of corporatist regulations on business so that is it better termed "societal" (Schmitter 1974, 103–5), "liberal," or "private" corporatism (Leopoldi 1984).

[10] In Latin America, *sindicato* usually refers to labor unions. In Brazil, the same corporatist legislation created *sindicatos* for both business and labor. In this chapter, *sindicato* refers to these state-chartered organizations; "business association" connotes all forms of business organization generally and voluntary organizations formed outside of the corporatist legislation.

[11] FIESP began with direct voluntary members. When corporatist *sindicatos* joined, FIESP created a dual structure of individual and *sindicato* membership. In the 1940s FIESP

in 1940 accounted for two-thirds of Paulista industry (in terms of capital and number of workers) (see Appendix A). National-level organizing also proceeded quickly. In 1933 state federations from São Paulo, Rio de Janeiro, and Rio Grande do Sul created the Confederação Industrial do Brasil, renamed the Confederação Nacional da Indústria (CNI) in 1938.

Conflict between CIESP and the first Vargas government was initially intense. CIESP opposed new labor legislation from the 1920s (including restrictions on child labor), and Vargas's decrees on paid vacations "directly contributed to the CIESP leadership's decision to join the abortive Paulista rebellion against Vargas in 1932" (Weinstein 1990, 383). Later in the 1930s business was less suspicious of Vargas's initiatives to organize labor (and conservative industrialists endorsed Vargas's repression of leftist movements), but business nonetheless organized to block less favorable elements in corporatist legislation that regulated both labor and business. On the regulation of business organization, a major conflict erupted over regional (or federal) versus sectoral organization. Government officials like Francisco José de Oliveira Vianna favored national associations for each sector of industry, as in Mexico, but Paulista industrialists mobilized successfully, especially in 1939 and 1940, to block the government proposal and restore a regional basis to industry representation (Costa 1991, 137–42).

In terms of positive incentives for business organization, state actors directly fostered business organization through several mechanisms: institutionalized access to policy making, compulsory membership and financing, and representational monopolies. Some early forms of privileged access for representatives of business associations in fact predated Vargas,[12] but access expanded rapidly under Vargas, beginning with the 1931 decree that gave the new Ministry of Labor, Commerce, and Industry the authority to recognize *sindicatos* of labor and business. The decree stipulated that these *sindicatos* (and higher-level federations and confederations) were to have representation in government councils.[13] Within three months, CIESP metamorphosed into FIESP and began "an intensive

---

leaders resurrected CIESP for individual, voluntary members and kept FIESP for compulsory *sindicatos*.

[12] In 1923 the government created the Higher Council of Commerce and Industry and granted representation in it to business associations from Rio de Janeiro and São Paulo (Leopoldi 1984, 47). Paulista industrialists were also pleased with representation in the Conselho Nacional do Trabalho and the Conselho Superior do Comércio e Indústria (Costa 1991, 135).

[13] In the early 1930s, Mário de Andrade Ramos, director of FIRJ and one of the vice presidents of CIB, presided over the government's Conselho Nacional do Trabalho (Gomes 1979, 296).

campaign to recruit members" using the attraction of this consultative function (Leopoldi 1984, 50).[14]

The privileged access for associations even included, at least for a few years, legislative representation. In line with some of the corporatist and antiliberal thinking popular in the 1930s, the first Vargas government granted special legislative representation to business associations. The Constituent Assembly convened in 1934 to draft a new constitution reserved 40 of 254 seats for representatives of functional groups. To select these delegates, the Ministry of Labor, Industry, and Commerce brought together 74 credentialed representatives of new business *sindicatos* to elect the 17 employer representatives to the Assembly (Gomes 1979, 279–81). Most of the 17 selected "employers" deputies were from industry, and most came from São Paulo and Rio de Janeiro. Not surprisingly, the draft 1934 constitution that these employers deputies helped write set aside a fifth of the seats in Congress for representatives of functional groups. Under the 1934 Constitution, business associations could send 21 deputies, 7 each from agriculture, industry, and commerce (Gomes 1979, 302 fn).[15] These representational opportunities provided strong incentives for business to invest in the associations that would select delegates to the legislature. Although many preexisting associations opposed the corporatist legislation of 1931, most business leaders rushed to take advantage of the opportunities for special legislative representation. The number of business *sindicatos* officially recognized by the government rose from 4 in 1932, to 79 in 1933, and to 273 in 1934 (Gomes 1979, 285).

After Vargas disbanded Congress in 1937, business associations were still well represented in major policy councils, especially those dealing with crucial issues of tariff protection and credit for industry.[16] Although never implemented, the Carta de 1937, the supposed constitution of the Estado Novo, created a Conselho de Economia Nacional (CEN), with representatives from industry associations, that would have had the authority to

---

[14] Six months later, in December 1931, the Centro Industrial do Brasil (CIB) followed suit and became the Federação das Indústrias do Rio de Janeiro (FIRJ) (Leopoldi 1984, 51).

[15] Ecuador was one of the only other cases, and a more recent one, of functional representation in the legislature. Prior to 1978 the Constitution granted representation to the Chambers of Commerce, Agriculture, and Industry (Conaghan 1992, 240). On functional representation in Colombia, see the next chapter.

[16] Among others, business associations were represented on the Conselho Federal de Comércio Exterior (CFCE or CFCEX, established in 1934), the Conselho Técnico de Economia e Finanças (CTEF, established in 1937) in the Ministry of Finance, and other general planning councils such as the Conselho Nacional de Política Industrial e Comercial (CNPIC) and the Comissão de Planejamento Econômico (CPE) (Diniz 1978, Chapters 4–6; Leopoldi 1984, 384; Wirth 1970, Chapters 1, 2).

vet all laws and decrees relating to the economy (Costa 1991, 124–5), and the enormous potential power of this Conselho was yet another incentive for business to organize. In terms of real impact on industrial policy, the international trade council, CFCE (Conselho Federal de Comércio Exterior), was probably the most important *conselho* throughout its 15-year existence (1934–49). In the 1940s the CFCE met weekly and made policies important for a wide range of sectors (Diniz 1978, chapter 5; Monteiro and Cunha 1974, 6–7). Despite several changes in internal composition, it was always presided over by the president and always included representatives from industry associations (Monteiro and Cunha 1974, 4).

Over time the statutory provisions for financing compulsory associations bankrolled some of the wealthiest business organizations in Latin America.[17] Beyond the compulsory membership dues, the *imposto sindical* (union tax), Vargas also created, with the support of FIESP leaders, an additional 1 percent tax on payrolls to fund worker training through Senai (Serviço Nacional de Aprendizagem Industrial).[18] In 1946 Roberto Simonsen proposed a new social program to be structured like the training program, and the Eurico Dutra government decreed a further payroll tax of 2 percent to fund the new Sesi (Serviço Social da Indústria) (Weinstein 1990, 397–9). These funds were administered exclusively by the corporatist business associations, and the state-level federations and the CNI were granted a percentage of these funds as a sort of management fee. Partly in response to these financial incentives, the number of

---

[17] Formally, the consolidated labor code (CLT) of 1943 regulated workers' and employers' organizations in detailed ways. The CLT gave the state the power to recognize *sindicatos*, approve their leaders, audit their accounts, and prohibit their participation in party or electoral politics (Schmitter 1971, 116). In return, *sindicatos* gained a monopoly on official representation, guaranteed financing through the union tax (*imposto sindical*), and gained a privileged voice at least initially in discussions with government policy makers. In 1964 the military government considered abolishing the *imposto sindical*. CNI opposed abolition, and FIESP claimed that many of its member *sindicatos* could not survive without it (Schmitter 1971, 120).

[18] In the late 1930s, officials in the Vargas government began discussions with São Paulo industrialists on vocational training. Initial proposals, inspired in part by the German apprenticeship programs, included tripartite funding by labor, business, and government and significant government control (Weinstein 1990, 391–4). However, in 1940 Roberto Simonsen proposed instead that employers alone finance the program; in exchange, program administration would be the sole responsibility of business associations. Vargas accepted this proposal and appointed a commission of three industrialists (Simonsen, Lodi, and Valentim Bouças) to draft the legislation. Later, in 1946, President Eurico Dutra adopted the same formula to fund and administer the social program SESI. As Weinstein concludes: "SESI and SENAI were organized to combine the best elements of both worlds: the state's capacity for coercion and the private sector's preference for autonomy" (Weinstein 1995, 329).

industrial federations tripled from 1946 to 1952. One federation leader admitted that the motive for such collective action was access to funds for social programs (Schmitter 1971, 186). By 1954 industrialists in all but four states had formed federations, and "the CNI had become the most prominent representative association in the country" (Schmitter 1971, 182).

The Vargas government and its new project for state-led industrialization received a lot of support from these newly organized industry associations.[19] Despite intense conflict with Vargas in the early 1930s, "by the late 1930s the leading industrial spokesmen had shifted to a position of almost unqualified support for the Vargas administration" (Weinstein 1990, 385). These were good economic times: industrial and agricultural production rose by half over the 1930s (Levine 1970, 179). Industry was also very well represented in the major new economic agencies Vargas created. Representatives of industry did not always win disputes over economic policy, but they were at the table for the debate (see Diniz 1978, 124–8).

Businessmen were often also appointed or elected to prominent positions in the Vargas and later Dutra governments. Roberto Simonsen was a constant interlocutor between Paulista industry and the first Vargas government (1930–45) both as a "class" representative to the legislatures of the 1930s and as a representative on government councils. President Dutra (1946–51) later appointed Simonsen to head the Department of Industry and Commerce in 1946 before he was elected senator in 1947.[20] Other examples include Jorge Street, president of CIB (Confederação Industrial do Brasil) (1912–26) and cofounder of CIESP, who went to work in the newly created Ministry of Labor, Industry, and Commerce in 1931 (Leopoldi 1984, 38); José Maria Whitaker, finance minister in Vargas's provisional government; Dutra's minister of labor, Morvan Dias de Figueiredo (former president of FIESP) (Weinstein 1990, 401); and Dutra's

---

[19] As president of FIESP and CNI, Simonsen created research departments and regular publications to disseminate developmental discourse (including works by Prebisch) (Bielschowsky 1988, 93–6). These departments continued their work of research and dissemination beyond Simonsen's death in 1948 well into the 1950s. Some key developmentalists who went on to prominent positions in government started their careers in CNI and FIESP.

[20] In contrast to the general lack of meddling by electorally motivated politicians in business associations (see Chapter 2), Simonsen appears on occasion to have used his organizing efforts on behalf of FIESP to further his own electoral career. When Simonsen ran for senator in 1947, he "used SESI employees to help recruit working-class support for his campaign" (Weinstein 1990, 402).

minister of finance, Gastão Vidigal (1946, ex-president of the Associação Comercial de São Paulo).[21] Also included by 1935 in Vargas's inner circle were several members of the Guinle family, João Daudt de Oliveira of the Rio de Janeiro Commercial Association, and Euvaldo Lodi of the Brazilian Federation of Industry (Levine 1970, 30). The fact that so many of these appointees came from business organizations tended to strengthen the associations as a major conduit for business–government relations, as in Colombia, rather than displace them (as would happen later in Brazil).

The second Vargas government (1951–4) represented the high water mark for the corporatist associations of industry. Revenues increased over the 1940s and 1950s, especially those collected through Senai and Sesi, which allowed corporatist associations like FIESP and CNI to hire professional staff and fund publications and dissemination (and even establish a surveillance service on communist activities) (Leopoldi 1984, 412). By 1954, Sesi alone had revenues of $58 million ($9 million in 1954 dollars; Leopoldi 1984, 414), 25 percent of which went to CNI, 32 percent to FIESP, and 16 percent to FIRJ (Federação das Indústrias do Rio de Janeiro). FIESP and CNI became major protagonists in propagating developmentalist ideas that became very popular in the 1950s (Leopoldi 1984; Trevisan 1986). Formal and informal access to Vargas and other government agencies was excellent. Many political appointees were businessmen, often with past leadership positions in FIESP or CNI (Leopoldi 1984, 242), including Finance Minister Horácio Lafer (1951–3), and associations had formal representation in such key agencies as CDI (Conselho de Desenvolvimento Industrial). Economic policy making was informally centralized in Vargas's Assessoria Econômica headed by Rómulo de Almeida. Not only was Almeida formerly an economist with the CNI, but the CNI continued to pay his salary while he was working in the Assessoria (Leopoldi 1984, 245). Lastly, CNI president Euvaldo Lodi was very close to Vargas and met weekly with him and the minister of finance (Leopoldi 1984, 211).

Corporatist legislation greatly helped industrialists create strong industry associations, but it did not provide for an economy-wide peak organization. Business in other sectors of the economy were also setting

---

[21] In 1929, the government appointed a textile industrialist from Rio de Janeiro, Manoel Guilherme da Silveira, to head the Banco do Brasil (Leopoldi 1984, 361). During the Estado Novo, the government created CEXIM (Carteira de Exportação e Importação) do Banco do Brasil. The second director was a businessman, Gastão Vidigal (Diniz 1978, 78).

up new associations; organizing in commerce and agriculture, while not as prominent as in industry, was intense in both Vargas governments. In addition, business leaders from all sectors came together regularly in major conferences in 1943, 1944, 1945, and 1949 (Leopoldi 1984, 426). Despite these propitious developments, government officials did not support the formation of an all-encompassing, economy-wide confederation, and leaders of sectoral associations never managed to create one on their own.

While the early 1950s appeared to be the high point of FIESP/CNI influence, factors were already at work – and would become more evident during the presidency of Juscelino Kubitschek (1955–60) – undermining their collective influence. As the institutions of government intervention into the economy multiplied into state enterprises, specialized agencies, commissions, and executive groups, business representation became more fragmented, especially with the creation of noncorporatist, sometimes parallel associations like ABDIB (capital goods), Anfavea (automobiles), ABIMAQ (machinery), ABINEE (electrical equipment), and ABIQUIM (chemicals)(see the List of Abbreviations for the acronyms). In earlier periods, representatives of FIESP and CNI sat on councils with broad mandates for setting economic policies. However, in the 1950s, many important economic policies devolved to specialized bodies with representation only by sectoral bodies such as Sindipeças (auto parts: Sindicato Nacional da Indústria de Componentes para Veículos Automotores) and ABDIB (Leopoldi 1984, 262). Industry-wide associations lost relevance, and overall coordinating bodies like the Conselho de Desenvolvimento (Development Council, 1956–64) and the Comissão Nacional de Planejamento (National Planning Commission, 1961–4) lacked representatives from industry associations (Monteiro and Cunha 1974, 22). Regional federations "were left to devote themselves to the interests of small and medium industry, the traditional sector, and the macro-problems of economic policy" (Leopoldi 1984, 428).

Although association resources continued to expand in the 1950s, distortions in corporatist representation became more apparent. One good indicator of these distortions was the changing patterns in leadership selection. In the 1950s, leadership in the industrial associations passed to a new generation of more marginal industrialists. When Lodi was forced out of the presidency of the CNI in 1954, CNI member federations elected an industrialist from the rural northeastern state of Bahia. The federal structure that FIESP had fought to maintain would, of course, inevitably overrepresent nonindustrial states at a time when almost three-quarters of industrial production was concentrated in a few southern states.[22] What began as an attempt by Paulista industrialists to preserve their state-level representation later became the basis for national organization and ultimately undermined the authority of the CNI and ironically reduced the influence of São Paulo industry in it. At the level of state federations, the representative structure was frozen in the interests of small sectoral *sindicatos*, while new, large industrial sectors grew up with little or no voice in the federations. In FIESP in the 1950s, for example, two contending factions settled on Antônio Devisate as president (1952–62); however, he "was an honorary figure rather than an effective leader of a regional class fraction" (Leopoldi 1984, 265).

In sum, from the 1930s to the 1950s, successive Vargas governments gave business strong incentives to organize. These incentives included compulsory dues and membership, delegated public functions like the provision of worker training and other social services, and extensive representation by associations in core policy arenas. These regulations transferred to associations massive material resources that gave them great organizational capacity on the level of staff and budgets; however, corporatist statutes on regional and sectoral voting froze internal representation in industrial federations. Beginning in the 1950s, these regulations started to diminish institutional capacity on the level of internal intermediation of interests, especially in the national industry confederation CNI. Moreover, privileged access to core policy forums began a secular decline after the mid-1950s that further reduced incentives for aggregating and reconciling member preferences with corporatist associations. In terms of the incentives facing state actors, the 1930s (and the 1940s to a lesser extent) were years of enormous political and economic vulnerabilities. By the end of the 1930s, Vargas had handled the political vulnerabilities masterfully by building a strong coalition among labor, business, and the military. Granting business organizational advantages and privileged access was a key component of this coalition building.

Collective Action against Goulart: Effective but Ephemeral

The transfer of the presidency to Jânio Quadros in 1961 seemed to pose few threats to business. Quadros appointed several businessmen to

---

[22] The electoral dominance of northeastern states made it more likely that a northeasterner would be elected to head the CNI. However, rivalry between the two major industrial states, Rio de Janeiro and São Paulo, likely encouraged representatives from these states to favor anyone not from the rival state.

head key economic ministries and many others to lower-level positions (Dreifuss 1981, 127). However, before the year was out, Quadros had resigned, and his vice president, João Goulart, elected independently and from a different party, replaced him. Throughout the political turmoil of the following two years, Goulart took several actions that industrialists perceived as threatening, and business, in turn, demonstrated an impressive ability to mobilize collectively against him (Dreifuss 1981; Payne 1994). As in Mexico, threatened business leaders in Brazil created new associations and bypassed the existing corporatist organizations.

The main organization for business mobilization against Goulart was a new think tank, IPES (Instituto de Pesquisas e Estudos Sociais), and the associated IBAD (Instituto Brasileiro de Ação Democrática), which provided forums for interelite strategizing and for disseminating anticommunist, procapitalist discourse. From 1962 to 1966 IPES in Rio de Janeiro went through rapid mobilization and demobilization (Blume 1967–8, 211–19). In late 1961, several months after Quadros resigned, prominent economic, military, and intellectual elites founded IPES. By 1963, IPES had 500 members (including Conclap [Conferência das Classes Produtoras], the forerunner of FIRJ, and other business associations) and a budget of over $2.2 million.[23] In 1963 IPES sponsored research, distributed 182,144 books, devised policy proposals, and hosted debates. In response to Goulart's reform agenda, IPES offered 23 detailed alternative reforms (Stepan 1971, 186 fn 38). Although FIESP and CNI were not, as organizations, actively involved in IPES, 27 of 36 FIESP directors and 21 of 24 CNI directors belonged to IPES (Dreifuss 1981, 173).

Although not formally spearheading the opposition to Goulart, corporatist associations like CNI and FIESP suffered politicized internal conflicts in the early 1960s similar to the politicization of Argentine associations after the 1940s, with damaging consequences to their longer-term development. For example, in 1961 José Villela de Andrade Junior asked Quadros to intervene in the CNI, as authorized in the corporatist legislation, to clean up alleged irregularities in the use of funds (Leopoldi 1984, 317). Quadros obliged and installed Andrade as president of the CNI. When Quadros resigned, so did Andrade, and the new Goulart government appointed an interim president until regular elections could be held in 1962, when an industrialist from the small rural state of Paraiba was elected. FIESP tried to maintain a working relationship with Goulart (though many of its members did not), and did not formally break with

---

[23] 220 million 1963 cruzeiros.

the government until four months before the 1964 coup, when FIESP too started working for Goulart's removal (Leopoldi 1984, 319).

Once the military deposed Goulart in early 1964, economic elites, individually and collectively, endorsed the coup and promptly demobilized. The new military government invited many IPES members, though significantly technical and professional members rather than business members, to join the new government and adopted many of IPES's previous proposals (Stepan 1971, 186 fn 38). One of the organizers of IPES was disgusted with members who withdrew support for IPES after the coup (Payne 1990). By 1965 IPES's budget had dropped to $230,000 (81 million 1965 cruzeiros) (over a quarter of which came from the Antunes group alone), or by almost 90 percent in two years, a dozen or so key IPES organizers were in the government, and only 13 members showed up for the general assembly (Blume 1967–8, 218–19). By 1966 IPES had ceased distributing books and sponsoring research. However, membership had only dropped to 300 (half corporate and half individual), suggesting that business elites wanted to maintain membership to keep IPES alive at least on paper but did not want to contribute time or money.

Much has been written about the role of business in the 1964 coup, and conclusions vary. Some think the coup was essentially orchestrated by business, others conclude that business was a strong member of the coalition supporting the coup, and still others largely ignore business.[24] My goal is not to resolve these disputes, but rather to assess how business reacted to the changed political context created by Goulart. Goulart reduced barriers to encompassing collective action by threatening many business interests, including property rights (especially on the issue of land reform), and thereby allowed diverse business interests to unite around the common goal of opposing and ultimately overthrowing Goulart. In a short-term sense, anti-Goulart businessmen got what they wanted. However, and more importantly for my general argument, they did not achieve lasting organization and representation, as business had in other countries when they opposed reformist governments. Brazilian business expected the military to depose Goulart and then call new elections, as the military had done in the past (Payne 1994, 53–4). Not only did the military stay,

---

[24] Payne (1994) provides a broad review of the various arguments. Dreifuss (1981) argues most strongly that the coup was mostly a business creation. Skidmore (1967) and others note the mobilization of business without assigning it preponderant weight. Santos (1986), Cohen (1987), and Stepan (1978) argue that the coup was predominantly the result of political factors such as gridlock with Congress and strategic miscalculations by Goulart.

but organized business, especially encompassing business associations, quickly discovered that they were excluded from policy making under authoritarian rule.

Distortions and Fragmentation in Business Representation under Military Rule

By the 1970s, most observers were characterizing Brazilian business associations as weak in internal organization and not very forceful in representing business interests in national politics. Schmitter concluded that "the associations themselves have no institutionalized means for assessing and interpreting the opinions of entire sectors. The result, as one respondent put it, is that the leadership abdicates its responsibility and permits the association to be used to express the views of an adversely affected minority of its members" (1971, 292). One central bank official summed up his interaction with business leaders: "they don't anticipate; they only react" (cited in Schmitter 1971, 291). Public officials in the 1960s complained that associations were unrepresentative, poorly prepared, and usually made demands that were "'too specific,' 'concerned only with small measures,' 'mere movements without substance,' 'too many palliatives,' and 'too many special favors.' Associations at all levels were repeatedly criticized for their immediatism, i.e., their unwillingness or inability to take a longer or broader perspective" (Schmitter 1971, 291).

What were the sources of this increasing weakness? For one, corporatist distortions in internal representation continued and worsened. In addition, individualized contacts between business elites and government officials, as well as a lack of government support for associations, further discouraged business investment of time and resources in formal organization. As discussed in the previous chapter, Fernando Henrique Cardoso (1975) coined the term "bureaucratic rings" to describe the interaction between the state and business in Brazil during military rule.[25] Where bureaucratic rings (personalized networks) predominated, firms had fewer incentives to invest in associations.[26] Although informal, personalized

---

[25] As the developmental state evolved, economic elites in Brazil concentrated their attention on the executive branch and within it the economic bureaucracy (Leff 1968, 111). For business associations in the 1960s, "the federal bureaucracy stands out unequivocally as the primary focus of Brazilian interest politics" (Schmitter 1971, 285).

[26] In a clear earlier example of this trade-off, in the early 1950s some auto parts producers who "had good government contacts and could easily cut through extensive bureaucratic red tape" *objected* to creating Sindipeças, a formal corporatist organization (Addis 1999, 48).

access was generally good, especially during the heyday of the economic miracle, when Finance Minister Antônio Delfim Netto (1968–73) dominated economic policy making, institutionalized channels for participation by associations in policy making, like those involving encompassing associations in Mexico and Chile, became increasingly rare in Brazil.

Military governments continued the practice of relying on scores of special councils to coordinate economic policy making, but did not incorporate encompassing associations into these councils, most of which were created after 1964 (Barros 1978, 255). One of the most important economic councils in the 1960s and 1970s was the Conselho Monetário Nacional (CMN), which became under Delfim Netto the central forum for economic planning. Major ministries and state banks had representatives in the CMN but, in contrast to the *conselhos* in the Vargas governments, only two seats were reserved for nongovernment appointees, and these went to personal nominees of the president rather than to representatives selected by business associations.[27] President Ernesto Geisel (1974–9) strongly recentralized economic coordination through the Conselho de Desenvolvimento Econômico (CDE), which included representatives from economic ministries and agencies as well as three members from outside the government, but these seats again went to presidential appointees rather than delegates from business associations.

Price control was another preoccupation of military governments, and another area where interactions between business and government were mostly informal and individual (Diniz and Boschi 1987). The first price-control agency, CONEP (Comissão Nacional de Estímulo à Estabilização dos Preços), included representatives from corporatist associations of labor and business. From 1965 to 1968, despite several changes in statutes and membership, the presidents of CNI and CNC (commerce) were on CONEP's decision-making council. In 1968 CIP (Conselho Interministerial de Preços) replaced CONEP, and private sector representation was downgraded from "deliberative" to "consultative" (Diniz and Boschi 1987, 62). In 1975 the government eliminated the remaining consultative role for business associations. Contact between CIP and individual businesses, though, remained regular and intense.

---

[27] Vianna (1987) provides the complete story. The two members from outside the government did not act as representatives or bring demands from the private sector to the CMN. In fact, they were often the last to know what was on the agenda. The original organization chart of the CMN provided for subcommissions on specific issues like rural or industrial credit, and these subcommissions did include representation by business associations. However, in practice, these subcommissions never really functioned and rarely met (Vianna 1987, 157ff.).

The lack of institutionalized access worried some associations. For example, capital goods producers, one of the sectors most favored by industrial policies of the 1970s, lamented the lack of access to timely information and input into policy making. In 1976 ABDIB formally proposed to the government the creation of an interministerial commission with representatives from business associations (Boschi and Diniz 1978, 197).[28] Despite its strong support for the capital goods sector, the Geisel government did not adopt ABDIB's recommendations. The interviewee, cited at the beginning of this chapter, who argued that capitalists will not participate if they do not think they will be listened to, also applied his argument specifically to FIESP:

> It happens that FIESP is, according to the law that created it, a consultative organ of the government. However, it does not have the capacity to fulfill this function because it is not listened to, since it lacks representation in the organs that advise the government. . . . There exists the possibility of coordination, of an understanding among the representative organs of industry, in order to undertake common action. But, there are no incentives for this. (Diniz and Boschi 1978, 182)

Formal exclusion discouraged investment in encompassing associations, and, as discussed later, helped push business into the opposition camp.

Considering the abundant resources at their disposal, corporatist associations might have offered members more attractive selective benefits to encourage participation. However, most of these resources came from Senai and Sesi, and the structure of these programs favored instead the expansion of the association bureaucracy and autonomy for association leaders, later criticized as "Fiespocratas," and at the same time encouraged exit by large firms. As mentioned earlier, the "management fee" granted by the government to the associations for running Senai/Sesi gave association leaders enormous revenues, tens of millions of dollars by the 1980s.[29] Therefore, leaders did not have to worry about responding to large contributors and, most importantly, association leaders had strong incentives not to cross government officials who controlled the collection and disbursement of their funding. In principle, the Senai training

---

[28] An additional motivation for the ABDIB proposal was to force various ministries and agencies to coordinate their policies (Boschi and Diniz 1978, 195). Fragmentation within the economic bureaucracy meant that policies and projects involving large investments in things like capital goods were often buffeted about and revised many times over through bureaucratic infighting (Schneider 1991b).

[29] By the 1990s, CNI was receiving a fee equal to 4 percent of total SESI revenues and 2 percent of total SENAI revenues. Together these fees accounted for three-quarters of CNI resources, which in 2001 were US$27 million (R$ 64 million; personal communication from Luiz Eduardo Pedroza, administrative director, CNI, 19 June 2002).

program should have encouraged greater efforts by big business to influence FIESP policies and leadership. The Senai law created a large fund for worker training, and large firms in principle would have wanted to participate to determine which workers got trained and in what areas. The design flaw (in terms of motivating participation in associations) was that large firms could create their own in-house training programs that, with Senai certification, would exempt them from participating in Senai programs (Weinstein 1990, 395). So, big firms opted out of Senai and had few incentives for participating in other Senai programs or in the corporatist associations that managed them.

Under military rule, the associational universe for Brazilian business also became increasingly fragmented and decentralized. By the 1970s, significant collective actions by Brazilian business largely bypassed the existing corporatist *sindicatos* with the expansion of *"associações"* (Boschi 1979). These associations were formally independent of the corporatist structure, although informally they often shared space, staff, and leaders with the officially sanctioned *sindicatos*. Leaders created these associations because they could do things the *sindicatos* could not, such as engage in more public relations and political activities; seek sector-specific access to government officials, bypassing the cumbersome corporatist organizations; represent businesses internationally; manage their resources flexibly; raise funds; and provide an alternate channel of representation in the event that the government ever threatened the official *sindicato*.[30] In other cases, the new associations did not overlap with the preexisting *sindicato*. Economic diversification produced new groups not foreseen in the archaic structure of corporatist industry groups. While these associations helped represent new sectors such as computers, software, petrochemicals, and, by the 1990s, Internet providers, the overall effect was to further fragment business representation. To the extent that economic policy makers listened to business associations, they were more likely to involve these associations rather than encompassing corporatist associations, shifting incentives for investment to narrower sectoral associations.[31] In sum, there were multiple channels of communication between business and military governments, but government officials mostly avoided corporatist associations, especially the encompassing federations

---

[30] Schmitter (1971, 197–8), Kingstone (1999, 115–18); see also Boschi (1979, 189) and interview with Paulo Butori, 20 November 1997.

[31] For example, in one major policy area, officials in government worked closely with ABDIB, ABINEE, and ABIMAQ in designing huge hydroelectric projects in the 1970s. Conspicuously absent from the policy story are references to FIESP or CNI (Klein 1987).

and confederations, and thereby reduced incentives for industrialists to invest time and resources in them.[32]

Active but Not Organized: Business Opposition to Military Rule in the 1970s

After the turbulent 1960s, business became increasingly dissatisfied with military rule. One visible rift surfaced in the early 1970s over the issue of state intervention in the economy. Disenchanted capitalists launched a *desestatização* ("de-statization" literally) campaign against state intervention in the economy that reverberated in the private sector and in the military. It was the first significant break between capitalists and the military in what many observers had considered a cozy, supportive relationship. It was also noteworthy that the campaign was organized outside of corporatist federations (Cruz 1984). It was more of a movement-type, spontaneous collective action with an "amorphous" organizational structure (Payne 1994, 62).

In the late 1970s the target of business criticism shifted from specific economic policies to military rule itself. In June 1978 a group of eight business leaders issued a manifesto, popularly known as the "Documento dos Oito" (Document of the Eight), that endorsed an end to military rule, and marked a further rupture between business and the military regime. At first glance, it appears to be a major instance of encompassing collective action, but in fact it was more a media creation. The *Gazeta Mercantil* (the *Wall Street Journal* of Brazil) conducted a mail survey of its readers to elect the business leaders of the year. Then "a journalist drafted the Documento dos Oito and secured industrialists' signatures, and the media then sponsored round-table discussions and extensively covered the attitudes, statements, and actions of these prodemocracy business leaders . . . , the media transformed this group of important but isolated individuals into a prodemocracy 'movement'" (Payne 1994, 79). Even this small group of like-minded industrialists required external prompting in order to act collectively.

---

[32] Complete data are lacking, but the number of businesspeople appointed to top positions in the economic bureaucracy fell during military rule. For example, during the preceding democratic regime from 1945 to 1964, five ministers of finance had a business background (Sebastião Paes de Almeida, 1959–61; Clemente Mariani Bittencourt, 1961; and Walter Moreira Salles, 1961–2, banker, n.b., in the Goulart government), in addition to Vidigal and Lafer, mentioned earlier (Brazil 1983). After 1964 economic policy makers were more likely to have academic and technical backgrounds. Significant exceptions were Severo Gomes (1974–7) and Angelo Calmon de Sá (1977–9), appointed by Geisel to be ministers of industry and commerce.

FIESP, CNI, and other corporatist associations were significantly absent from the Documento dos Oito. Among the eight signers of the Documento were several industrialists who were directors of FIESP, and several had been leaders in noncorporatist associations like ABDIB and ABINEE (Motta 1979). However, the current presidents of FIESP and CNI figured neither among the top 10 business leaders elected in the *Gazeta Mercantil* poll, a significant reflection in itself of the marginal position of these associations, nor at the vanguard of industrialists pressuring the military to leave.[33]

Transitologists seem to agree that the Documento dos Oito was crucial in sustaining the gradual movement to civilian rule, yet observers differ on what exactly provoked this prominent faction of industry to join the opposition camp (Bresser Pereira 1978; Payne 1994; Remmer 1993). Some analysts argue that the motivations were primarily economic; as the economy slowed, business pushed for change and new political management (Frieden 1991; Haggard and Kaufman 1995). There are several problems with this argument. Growth may have been slowing in the late 1970s, and dipped to 3 percent in 1977, but growth for industry still averaged around 7 percent for most of the 1970s (Payne 1994, 62). Growth rates were even higher for capital goods, due in part to government promotion, yet capital goods producers were prominent in the Grupo dos Oito (Motta 1979, 125–6). In 1977, even before the Documento dos Oito was published, Einar Kok and Cláudio Bardella, both capital goods producers, publicly called for a transition to democracy (Payne 1994, 58). Moreover, as discussed in Chapters 3 and 6, authoritarian governments in Chile and Mexico, when faced with periods of even worse economic performance, found ways to reassure businessmen and keep them from joining the opposition. A more plausible interpretation is that what most angered business was not economic management or performance but rather exclusion from policy circles (Remmer 1993). The most extensive survey of industrialists' opinion concludes that "industrialists universally felt that they had lost political influence during the second decade of the military regime" (Payne 1994, 78).[34]

---

[33] Business was not, of course, unanimous in its opposition to the military. Later in 1978, 102 capitalists signed a counter letter of support for the regime (Payne 1994, 60).

[34] Individual access, however, was not a problem. As one of Payne's business interviewees noted: "I do not know of any members of the business community who, if they wished, have not had the opportunity to converse with a government authority. But at the moment a decision is made, they have not had even a small amount of influence" (Payne 1994, 78).

In sum, collective action by business during military rule came primarily in unorganized waves of opposition, first to the economic policies of military governments and then to the dictatorship itself. Both movements, and the strong impression they made on policy makers and public opinion, along with continued lack of access by associations, marginalized encompassing corporatist associations and reduced incentives for voluntary investment of time or money in them. In the 1960s and 1970s, businesses in Brazil rebalanced their portfolios of political investments to favor individual politicking and narrow sectoral associations. In contrast, their counterparts in Mexico, Colombia, and Chile in these same decades were weighting their portfolios in favor of encompassing associations, largely because governments in these countries granted encompassing associations new or continued access to policy making, access that military governments in Brazil denied.

New Voluntary Encompassing Associations[†]

The amount of money and time industrialists invested in the 1980s and 1990s to bypass or reform existing corporatist organizations was a good indication of the dissatisfaction with them. The late 1980s, in the new civilian regime, seemed a golden age for political activity by the captains of industry. As opponents of military rule, capitalists had gained a new legitimacy to engage in politics, and they took advantage of opportunities to accept government appointments, join parties, run for office, and talk about politics in the press. Their participation in Congress was extensive and constituted a form of elite circulation rarely seen elsewhere in Latin America, except perhaps Chile. Somewhere between one-fifth and one-half of the deputies elected in 1986, 1990, and 1994 had business backgrounds (see Schneider 1997–8 for details and references).[35]

Outside the electoral arena, industrialists in São Paulo embarked in the late 1980s on two more lasting organizational initiatives, the Pensamento Nacional das Bases Empresariais (PNBE) and the Instituto de Estudos para o Desenvolvimento Industrial (IEDI).[36] Both new initiatives were

---

[†] This section draws on a lengthier treatment in Schneider (1997–8).

[35] DIAP (Departamento Intersindical de Assessoria Parlamentar) estimated that the number of businesspeople in the Chamber of Deputies fell by half, from 201 in the early 1990s to 104 in 2003 (*Folha de São Paulo*, 9 February 2003, as reported by Radiobrás e-mail summary).

[36] There is no easy translation for PNBE. Literally, it would be National Thinking of the Business Bases. Payne captures the guiding idea of PNBE with her translation: National Grassroots Business Association (Payne 1994, 113). The analysis of PNBE draws on

designed to rectify the perceived representational deficiencies of FIESP. Businesspeople from smaller firms criticized FIESP for representing only big business, while big business complained that smaller firms had too much influence in FIESP.[37] Paradoxically, both criticisms were at least partly true; the corporatist structure gave equal votes to *sindicatos* for marginal sectors like leather and furniture, with a lot of small firms, yet most leaders in the FIESP directorate came from larger firms. Although also inspired by substantive goals, business organized new associations in part to redress these flaws: IEDI to represent better the largest industrial firms and PNBE the smaller firms.

In 1987 Emerson Kapaz and other disaffected businessmen founded PNBE. Its members were young, came from small and medium-sized firms from both the service sector and industry, and spouted progressive ideas. Kapaz had been active in FIESP (starting in 1986 as the president of the association for toy manufacturers) but quickly became impatient with its outmoded structure. In contrast to FIESP, PNBE was voluntary, encompassing, organized on the principle of one capitalist/one vote, and willing to engage more directly and actively in politics. PNBE attracted a lot of attention in the first year of the government of Fernando Collor (1990–2). Its leaders went to Collor in mid-1990 and suggested that he attempt to negotiate a social pact with business and labor. Government representatives subsequently met several times with those of business and labor but the negotiations collapsed, due mostly to government uninterest (see Schneider 1991a). Later, when the Collor government became mired in corruption scandals, the PNBE was also visibly engaged. In 1992 PNBE was one of the groups in civil society, and one of the only business groups, to take to the streets demanding Collor's impeachment.

By 1995 PNBE had 480 members, mostly from small and medium-sized firms. Its membership base grew more diverse as more entrepreneurs from the service sector joined (close to half of all members by 1995). While 80 percent of the members were from the state of São Paulo, PNBE also established branches in other major cities. In contrast to the flush corporatist associations, PNBE scraped by on about $350,000 a year, with a small staff of a half dozen financed by voluntary member contributions ranging

---

interviews with PNBE leaders Emerson Kapaz (27 January 1993), Eduardo Capobianco (27 January 1993), and Pedro Camargo Neto (24 May 1995). See also Kingstone (1999, 132–7).

[37] In a 1992 survey, 60 percent of businesspeople interviewed said that FIESP "represented only big business interests" (Kingstone 1999, 127). Complaints of big business came largely through my personal interviews.

from $60 to $230 per month. The major themes in PNBE's politics in the mid-1990s continued to be labor relations, corruption, ethics in politics, poverty, and citizenship. PNBE leaders generally tried to stimulate public debates on these issues rather than attempt to push a specific legislative agenda in Brasília. PNBE was one of the first business associations to seek out labor unions in an effort to find a common agenda for constitutional reform. What is remarkable about the PNBE story is that a handful of political entrepreneurs could get together a few hundred members (mostly from small firms), raise a few hundred thousand dollars, and articulate a national presence in the media and a major challenge to corporatism as represented in FIESP. However, after Collor, PNBE did not have much influence in Brasília and no institutionalized representation.

The second initiative, IEDI, created in 1989, also emerged from frustrations with FIESP and with the Sarney government.[38] Many of IEDI's founders were also members of FIESP, but unlike the young grass-roots organizers of PNBE, they were the captains of about 30 of Brazil's largest industrial groups. IEDI's members were also less concerned about issues of democratic politics, social welfare, and relations between capital and labor. They wanted industrial policies and found the Sarney and Collor governments especially deficient in providing them. FIESP did not help advance the agenda of industrial policy and at times made matters worse.[39] In contrast, the idea behind IEDI was to conduct studies, disseminate research, and formulate proposals for a new industrial policy. IEDI hooked up with economists at the University of Campinas and started publishing studies and proposals (e.g., see IEDI 1992). Their target audience was restricted to the elites of the economic bureaucracy and of industry, and they did not initially seek great visibility or a mass base.

However, IEDI got more media exposure when Emerson Kapaz launched his opposition candidacy in the 1992 elections for president of FIESP. IEDI members Paulo Francini, Paulo Villares, Claudio Bardella,

---

[38] Background on IEDI came also from interviews with Mauro Arruda (15 December 1993 and 23 May 1995), Paulo Cunha (18 November 1997), Sergio Mindlin (29 January 1993), and Paulo Villares (28 January 1993). See Kingstone (1998; 1999, 138–42).

[39] During Mário Amato's term (1986–92), FIESP's long-term proposals were essentially neoliberal and against state intervention in industry. Industrial policy is barely mentioned in the book FIESP published with great fanfare in Collor's first year (*Livre para Crescer* [FIESP 1990, especially 291–323]). In the view of *Isto É*, "FIESP came into the 1990s without having formulated important proposals for industrial policy or even having sought a solution to the economic crisis" (5 August 1992, p. 63). A *Veja* report on FIESP carried the subtitle, "Without Ideas of Its Own, FIESP Follows Brasília" (6 January 1993, p. 69).

and Eugênio Staub were either on Kapaz's ticket or prominent supporters of it. PNBE and IEDI had begun with different motives but united in
their opposition to FIESP's traditional leadership, whom Kapaz belittled
as "Fiespocratas" (Kingstone 1999, 144). The election of August 1992
was the second contested election in FIESP/CIESP's 64-year history and
the first since 1979. A contested election was already a clear sign of dis-
content with the existing leadership. Carlos Eduardo Moreira Ferreira
ultimately won both elections, though by a much slimmer margin in the
voluntary association CIESP: 80 percent of the 121 associations in FIESP
but only 52 percent of the over 8,000 individual members of CIESP (*Isto
É*, 5 August 1992, p. 62).

After this brief moment of media attention, IEDI stabilized in the mid-
1990s at a fairly low level of activity. A few members left and a few joined,
so the total stayed around 30. The budget remained constant at about
$350,000 (about the same as PNBE's). IEDI also promoted debates with
public officials and continued to advocate industrial policy, though usually
in targeted and discreet ways, as in presenting president-elect Fernando
Henrigue Cardoso in 1994 with a blueprint for industrial policy. Overall,
though, IEDI was marginal to national debates because industrial policy
was not a core concern in Brasília in the 1990s. By 1997 members were
admitting that IEDI had become largely "irrelevant" (Kingstone 1999,
142).

The specific goals of the organizational entrepreneurs who formed
PNBE and IEDI differed, but they were all dissatisfied with FIESP and
CNI. IEDI was predominantly an attempt to get big industrialists more
involved collectively in setting the policy agenda. PNBE had many goals
but fundamentally challenged existing patterns of interest aggregation,
while also trying to get business more involved in public debates on broad
social and political issues. Organizations such as IEDI and PNBE demonstrated the perceived inadequacies of FIESP at the same time that they
further fragmented the organization of business.[40]

Policy makers in government still felt the need to consult with business, yet sometimes found the existing associations lacking. For example,
Collor's second minister of the economy, who was chosen precisely to
mend fences with business, created his own informal groups for consulting

---

[40] Big farmers and agribusinesses also organized a number of new encompassing, multisectoral associations in the 1980s and 1990s, which resulted in a similar fragmentation and
duplication of the representation of big agricultural interests (Porras Martínez 2000).
Kingstone concluded that by the mid-1990s "the business community was more fragmented . . . than it had been for years" (1999, 225).

business.[41] Rather than work through CNI, FIESP, or Firjan, Marcílio Marques Moreira created small groups of capitalists in São Paulo and Rio de Janeiro that he relied on for feedback on particular policy ideas and overall evaluation of the government. The Marques Moreira still talked with the heads of associations like FIESP, but more as a political courtesy than as a source of real aggregated business preferences.[42]

The leaders of corporatist associations also attempted to reorganize business input into politics – especially the drafting and later reform of the 1988 Constitution – by creating several new economy-wide coordinating bodies. The União Brasileira de Empresários (UBE) was a collective, encompassing effort by major sectoral associations created to lobby the constituent assembly (1987–8). The UBE initially appeared to be an appropriate vehicle for taking advantage of a golden opportunity for collective input into the most general policy debates over the Constitution. However, it lacked staff and institutional means for interest aggregation. The UBE "suffered from constant internal divergences" and "its coordinating capacity was always limited" (Weyland 1996, 64). In order to balance the representation of the participating associations, UBE adopted the practice of rotating presidents every six months or so, which ensured a further lack of experience and institutionalization on the part of UBE leaders. In the end, the rotating presidents often used UBE to pursue their own agendas rather than seeking a common one (interview with a senior CNI staffer in Brasília, 27 May 1995).

Some argue that business was effective in reorganizing to influence Congress and the Constituent Assembly (Dreifuss 1989). The UBE, in conjunction with the National Front for Free Initiative, raised an impressive $51 million ($35 million in 1988 dollars) for lobbying the Constituent Assembly (Kingstone 1999, 52). The UBE managed to achieve "modest" changes on many proposals they opposed and several victories on labor rights (Kingstone 1999, 56). However, most observers, including many of

---

[41] Collor sent one of his ministers, Jarbas Passarinho, to São Paulo to invite a prominent business leader, and member of both FIESP and IEDI, Sergio Mindlin, to be minister of the economics. Mindlin declined but recommended Marcílio Marques Moreira. Interviews with Mindlin (29 January 1993) and Marques Moreira (26 November 1997).

[42] In an earlier attempt to calm business fears, as economic policy unraveled in late 1991, President Collor met for three hours with nine representatives of business. The representatives included presidents of CNI, FIESP, FIERGS (Federação das Indústrias do Estado do Rio Grande do Sul), and IEDI, but significantly included five other businessmen who were listed in press reports, and presumably invited, because they came from important firms (*Diário do Comércio e da Indústria*, 6 September 1991, p. 7, and *Folha de São Paulo*, 6 September 1991, pp. 1–7).

the business participants themselves, viewed the glass as more than half empty (Lamounier 1992). According to one report, UBE prepared a list of 24 essential, "non-negotiable" demands (on labor law, interest rates, regulations on MNCs, etc.) on which to concentrate business lobbying, yet only one of them was approved (*Jornal do Brasil*, 4 September 1988, as cited in Figueiredo 1993, 58; Kingstone 1999, 56).

The Constitution of 1988 included a provision that the Constitution be opened to amendment by simple majority vote five years after its adoption. In fact, the Constitution was slated for major overhauls every year from 1993 to 1997. Over the 1990s, business leaders experimented with a number of different political strategies to press for reform, though none left a lasting organizational legacy.[43] In 1992 CNI leaders began mobilizing for the revision slated for the following year. For CNI leaders, part of the aggregation problem in UBE in 1988 derived from the fact that each association hammered out a specific and detailed wish list before discussing its position with other associations. In 1992–3, the CNI held a lot of meetings just to discuss principles, without drawing up a detailed platform. Once CNI and other associations had reached agreement on principles, they found it easier to reach agreement on specific amendments. This procedure had come about by coincidence and was quite successful initially, in the narrow reform of port legislation (Doctor 2000). The issue of ports had come up in a separate congressional debate. It was a relatively narrow issue, and all the business associations agreed, in principle, on lobbying for the breakup of state ownership and labor monopolies in Brazilian ports. Jorge Gerdau Johannpeter, the head of a large steel conglomerate, assumed informal leadership of business lobbying on ports because he was well known and knew a lot about ports. Members of CNI subsequently asked Gerdau to assume the same informal leadership for the constitutional revision.

In 1993 business associations formed a loose coordinating body, Ação Empresarial (Business Action), for lobbying on the Constitution. Ação Empresarial was well coordinated, yet almost completely informal and only dimly visible, especially after 1995. It had no office, no staff, no

---

[43] My focus is on collective lobbying by encompassing associations. For more extensive discussion of all forms of business lobbying in Congress, see Diniz and Boschi (1997). They find increasing interest and activity by sectoral associations in lobbying Congress. They show that legislation concerning ports and pharmaceuticals, in particular, coincided with positions advocated by sectoral associations, but they hesitate to draw a strong causal connection. The fact that these two narrow sectoral "victories" stand out in an overall survey confirms indirectly the weakness of business input into broader issues of constitutional reform.

position papers, and no blueprint for lobbying.[44] The work of Açao Empresarial was divided up among working groups headed by staffers from each of the major participating associations. In this way, Açao Empresarial had no staff of its own (though it did have a small budget of several hundred thousand dollars, mostly for office expenses). Açao Empresarial was active in interest aggregation and in lobbying, but rarely in the name of Açao Empresarial. In curious fashion, the coordinating body would reach a consensus position that was documented in a specific platform, though not distributed in the name of Açao Empresarial. Actual lobbying based on this consensus was left up to members but only in the name of each member association. The leaders of Açao Empresarial decided that the whole was less influential than the sum of the parts.[45] Even that was not very influential; Kingstone concluded, "Ação Empresarial registered scarcely any successes" (1999, 192).

Given the perceived failures of more visible lobbying through the UBE and the preferences for the low profile of Ação Empresarial, there was little indication by the late 1990s of interest on the part of big business in trying to create a stronger, institutionalized, economy-wide peak association. In addition, state actors in the 1990s showed little interest in promoting encompassing organization. Many state actors agreed with the agenda of Ação Empresarial for reforming the Constitution, and sometimes encouraged business to lobby Congress in favor of particular pieces of legislation, but they did not provide Ação Empresarial with privileged or institutionalized access.

Circumventing Corporatism through Mass Mobilization and Internal Reform

While Ação Empresarial continued its loose coordination and low-intensity lobbying, reformers in CNI adopted a very different strategy in the late 1990s. In May 1996 nearly 3,000 industrialists flew to Brasília to pressure the government, especially Congress, to accelerate the pace

---

[44] My analysis of Açao Empresarial owes a great deal to lengthy interviews with a long-time member of the Legislative Action Council of the CNI on 27 May 1995 and 9 September 1996.

[45] The bankers' association had a similar practice, since the "bank lobby cannot be seen" walking around the halls of Congress. Febraban coordinated campaign contributions, later aggregated interests, but sent individual bankers, rather than officers of Febraban, to Brasília to talk with legislators (interview with an executive of the Banco Real and director of Febraban, 22 May 1995).

of constitutional reform. This meeting represents perhaps the largest collective investment in lobbying of the decade, considering the opportunity cost of taking the day off from business. The impetus for this mass mobilization can be traced to several sources. First, CNI President Fernando Bezerra embraced a different political strategy when he took office in 1995 (see *Gazeta Mercantil*, 19 October 1995, p. A-6 and 4 November 1996, p. A-6).[46] In his first speeches, he declared that CNI was primarily an institution for lobbying and representing industry. In an interview, Bezerra called the May 1996 demonstration in Brasília "a lobby with a capital L. We are not doing anything in secret" (*Gazeta do Povo*, 18 May 1996, p. 12). In addition, he was concerned with the sectoral fragmentation of industry and wanted to use the May demonstration to promote a unified position by industry. Bezerra offered an interesting interpretation in a column he wrote just before the Brasília demonstration:

The fragmentation of business that exists today is reflected in the way the government discusses issues with the business classes. Although we have the best understanding with and great access to President Cardoso, we have not managed to institutionalize negotiation with other levels of government. We are constantly taken by surprise by initiatives that go completely against our interests and on which we were never even consulted. (*Estado de São Paulo*, 20 May 1996, p. 2-2)

Lastly, President Cardoso provided a last-minute nudge by encouraging industrialists to come to Brasília to pressure Congress. He had suggested a Brasília meeting in March, and once CNI had issued invitations for the May meeting, Cardoso personally telephoned key figures like the keynote speaker Antônio Ermírio de Moraes to convince them to come (*Estado de São Paulo*, 22 May 1996).

In terms of mobilization and collective action, the meeting was a great success. The press issued amazed reports on the planeloads of industrialists who made their way to Brasília. Moreover, the meeting presented a relatively unified voice (and Bezerra [CNI] and Moreira Ferreira [FIESP] had managed to put aside their differences on specific issues like interest rates). However, the meeting was a stark failure in terms of bringing pressure to bear on Congress. In a remarkable feat of bravado, Congress voted down, the same day thousands of industrialists were walking the

---

[46] After an uncharacteristic interregnum by an ex-president of FIESP, Mário Amato, the presidency of the CNI reverted to an industrialist from the northeast. And, like the last president from the northeast, Albano Franco, Bezerra was also a senator in the national Congress. However, Bezerra was a marginal figure in industry; he was the Coca-Cola bottler in the small state of Rio Grande do Norte (*O Globo*, 24 May 1996, p. 4, and *Estado de São Paulo*, 19 June 1996, p. B6).

halls of Congress, a proposal for reforming social security, which had the explicit support of the industrialists. Bezerra called it "lamentable" and an "affront" to industry (*Folha de São Paulo*, 23 May 1996, p. 14).

On another front, Bezerra worked to reform the internal structure of CNI in order to improve its capacity for interest intermediation. Over the course of 1996 Bezerra informally incorporated sectoral associations into CNI's working committees on such issues as labor relations and international trade. The innovation in this strategy was that the associations were voluntary organizations outside the corporatist structure and historically had little to do with CNI. The idea was to have a dual structure within CNI with the state federations voting on some issues, including leaders, while association leaders and other industry "representatives" appointed by CNI leaders did the real work of aggregating interests across sectors on various policy issues (interviews with José Augusto Coelho, 10 December 1993 and 2 September 1996). Bezerra also expanded CNI's use of opinion surveys to canvass the preferences of industrialists (Schneider 1997a–8).

A major obstacle to reform that association staffers often point to is the CLT, the consolidated labor laws that govern not only the usual regulation of labor markets (working hours and conditions, maternity leave, child labor laws, etc.), but also the structure of wage negotiations, the *imposto sindical*, the regional organization of both labor and business, and the Sistema S (the compulsory contributions to the business-controlled training and social funds, Senai and Sesi). Proposals to reform the CLT come up often and regularly generate conflict, so much conflict that governments back away (Cook 2002). Both the labor confederation CUT (Central Única dos Trabalhadores) and the major industry associations claimed that they wanted to end the *imposto sindical* and compulsory membership, as well as government authority over permissible forms of business and labor organization. However, other associations and unions, especially smaller ones, opposed these reforms. Moreover, though an association like FIESP might relinquish the *imposto sindical*, other business associations would oppose any reduction in contributions to Sistema S (Cook 2002, 20).

By the end of the 1990s, Bezerra had accepted an appointment to Cardoso's cabinet, CNI was in the hands of an interim president, and most of Bezerra's reform strategies had been tabled. Nonetheless Bezerra's reform initiatives demonstrate that industrialists working within the corporatist structures were investing a lot of time and energy to redress corporatist distortions in representation, just as other industrialists were investing in new voluntary associations. However, by the end of the decade, both sets of reformers had made little progress in revamping overall business representation and organization.

Beyond exceptional moments like the Brasília demonstration, big industrialists generally invested little time in the regular activities of corporatist associations. The main reasons for this lack of interest were the corporatist distortions in representation – regional in CNI and sectoral in major state-level federations like FIESP – and the fact that industrialists had other avenues for attempting to influence policy. The corporatist associations did have enormous resources they could have used to provide selective benefits, and, curiously, associations retained some representation on policy councils, a major factor encouraging participation in associations in other countries. Several reasons contributed to their lack of effect on collective action in Brazil. For one, as discussed earlier, representatives from corporatist associations were progressively removed from the core policy councils in the 1960s and 1970s. Other councils were less important for policy making, and associations themselves attached little value to them and delegated representation to a wide variety of members.[47] Nonetheless, the resources and access of corporatist association occasionally attracted the attention of big industrialists, as evidenced by the several costly attempts (most prominently in FIESP in the late 1970s and early 1990s) to contest internal elections and wrest control from the internal oligarchy.

A final comparative and theoretical question for the crisis and transition period of the 1980s and 1990s is why state actors did not feel moved to incorporate associations into policy making. According to the arguments laid out in Chapter 2, the vulnerabilities experienced by state actors should have prompted them to seek support from business associations. There are several key reasons state actors did not. In comparative terms, there is evidence that political leaders were more complacent about the economic crisis and political transition in the 1980s (see Schneider 1997). On the economic front, for example, and in contrast to Mexico in 1987, state actors in Brazil were less vulnerable to massive capital flight. On

---

[47] In 1972 the predecessor of Firjan, for example, had representatives in 76 different councils, commissions, and institutions (FIEG 1972, ix–xi). Many of these were narrow sectoral bodies, and representation in them was apparently delegated to the relevant member association of the federation. Staffer interviews in the 1990s indicated that some of these councils existed into the 1990s but were not important to the association (interview with Luciana de Sá, 28 May 2002). Other interviews as well as policy studies generally did not even mention these councils. A proliferation of councils in the 1990s became much more important for representation of other groups in civil society (Friedman and Hochstetler 2002, 26–30).

the political front, in contrast to the center-left coalition that succeeded the military dictatorship in Chile, the Sarney government came from the center–right and included a lot of business appointees. Some state actors, especially in the 1990s, did perceive serious vulnerabilities and did seek out business interlocutors, but they mostly avoided CNI and FIESP. President Collor initially eschewed contact with organized business (as had been his campaign strategy; Kingstone 1999). Later, when Collor's vulnerabilities increased, he consulted sporadically with business, but usually individuals or the embryonic PNBE. Similarly, some of Collor's top policy makers also consulted with business, though mostly again with informal groups or narrower sectoral associations (as in the "sectoral chambers" considered in Chapter 8). Ultimately, neither this consultation nor the Collor government overall lasted long enough to institutionalize new patterns of consultation with business.

Conclusions and Comparisons

Business leaders were active in the 1980s and 1990s inventing new kinds of associations to represent their interests. None of the new associations scored high on an index of institutional strength: PNBE, IEDI, and Ação Empresarial lacked sufficient capacity to intermediate interests, material resources, and staff to become strong institutions. Despite the effervescence of new, voluntary organizing, the new associations did little to dislodge the corporatist associations from their dominance in the organizational domain of business. Corporatist associations were weakened by criticism from multiple sources and felt threatened by rival new associations, but they were still there: prominent in the press and flush with involuntary contributions. Several governments debated an end to the *imposto sindical*, and many associations supported its disappearance. However, the proposals never got very far. In the end, Brazilian business ended up with even greater associational fragmentation or reorganized disarticulation.

What stands out in comparative perspective is the absence in Brazil of deeper, ongoing meddling by state actors in the associational landscape of business. Most of that landscape still lay in the long shadows of Vargas and Simonsen. Their corporatist legislation represented decisive state intervention, but it is not something that state actors subsequently reformed or manipulated on a regular basis. State actors had little role in PNBE or IEDI. Had state actors drawn IEDI or PNBE into policy deliberations, incentives for investment in these associations would have been much higher and more lasting. Similarly, had UBE or Ação Empresarial found a niche in Brasília, either could have developed a more institutionalized presence.

Comparative analysis generates another major question for Brazil: why did business never establish a lasting, economy-wide peak association? One simple answer is that the corporatist legislation prohibited it. However, Mexican business and Brazilian labor overcame similar formal obstacles. Moreover, from the 1940s on, business in Brazil did regularly try to promote coordination across major sectors: Conclap, Forúm Informal (in São Paulo), UBE, and most recently, Ação Empresarial. In comparative perspective, two factors were missing in Brazil that might have transformed these passing attempts at coordination into a lasting peak association: threats from labor and the left (which were pivotal in Chile and Mexico) (Kingstone 1999, 245; Payne 1994), and especially privileged access to state officials (as was crucial in Chile, Mexico, and Colombia).

In the absence of state support, the mobilization of Brazilian business in politics, outside of the corporatist structure, exhibits a wavelike quality, similar in some respects to the "movement" quality of Argentine business associations. After each successive wave of mobilization – against Goulart in the 1960s, against state intervention and military rule in the 1970s, and lastly in favor of constitutional reform in the 1990s – business disbanded with little interest in institutionalizing the new bases of collective action. This repeated demobilization is very different from the story told in the previous chapter. In Mexico, business mobilized against labor law in the 1930s, against López Mateos in the 1960s, against Echeverría in the 1970s, and against the bank nationalization in 1982. However, as each mobilization receded, it left an institutional moraine, an association that survived, often adapted its functions over time, and grew in strength, in large part because subsequent governments granted these new associations access or other benefits.

The lack of organization of Brazil business is noteworthy compared to business in other countries of Latin America; it is also remarkable compared to the evolving political organization of Brazilian labor. Corporatist legal constraints were much greater for labor than for business, yet from the 1970s on, leaders of the "new unionism" overcame these constraints, founded lasting encompassing labor confederations (not provided for in the corporatist legislation), and created the PT (Partido dos Trabalhadores), the most strongly institutionalized party in the Brazilian political system. A full comparison of the incentives for, and obstacles to, collective action by various social groups is beyond the scope of this chapter. However, the CUT and PT are compelling indications that Brazilian business is not just conforming to some overall Brazilian pattern of social and political disorganization.

After six months, it is too early to assess how business–government relations will evolve through the new PT government (2003–), but, by way of speculative epilogue, some possible sources of change are worth noting. For many years, and continuing into the electoral campaign of 2002, Lula (Luiz Inácio "Lula" da Silva) and the PT were perceived as threatening to business (see Kingstone 1999), and conceivably might have had a centripetal impact in promoting defensive business organization. However, Lula moderated the PT's electoral appeals in 2002, and by mid-2003 business support for Lula was running high. In a survey of São Paulo business commissioned by FIESP in April 2003, 82 percent of businesspeople interviewed thought that the government was average or better, while just 17 percent rated it as bad or worse (*Jornal do Brasil*, 18 April 2003, p. 2, in Radiobrás e-mail summary). Beyond this overall approval, other specific issues may generate more conflict. For one, Lula and other members of the PT have long argued for the need to reform the CLT generally and the corporatist regulation of business and labor specifically. If they succeed, the impact could be similar to the profound transformation of corporatist associations in Mexico after the end of compulsory affiliation in 1997.[48]

On other policy fronts, the Lula government actively sought out dialogue with business and worked to incorporate representatives of business, as well as other social groups, into new consultative policy bodies. Lula also appointed businessmen to head the ministries responsible for industry and agriculture as well as the Central Bank. This close communication and consultation, at least in the first months of the PT government, exceeded communication in the previous governments since 1985 (and most before that). This new access too, if sustained over the longer term, could have a profound effect on incentives for collective action. However, existing business associations had no monopoly on mediating relations between business and government, and thus the incentives to invest in them were still weak. For example, on his first day in office, Lula created the Conselho de Desenvolvimento Econômico e Social (CDES) to coordinate dialogue between the government and civil society (see www.presidencia.gov.br/cdes). CDES was charged with generating

---

[48] According to the president of Sindipeças, one of the larger member sindicatos of FIESP, all but about 10 of FIESP's 112 *sindicatos* depend primarily on compulsory dues and would suffer greatly if membership were made voluntary (interview with Paulo Butori, 20 November 1997).

proposals on taxes, social security, and labor law, the core reform agenda for the PT government. The government rapidly invited 82 members of society to join 11 representatives from government and formally installed CDES in February 2003. Half of the 82 representatives from society were from business, and of these 41 business representatives, 23 were from industry. The other business representatives came from finance, agriculture, and services, including some from MNC subsidiaries.[49]

Business representation in CDES is certainly encompassing, but most revealing from the perspective of institutionalized collective action was that only 15 of the 41 businesspeople, just over one-third, represented existing associations. These 15 associational representatives included the presidents of the four federations of industry from Rio de Janeiro, São Paulo, Minas Gerais, and Paraná, states that accounted for a majority of industrial production, as well as noncorporatist associations for finance, automobiles, capital goods, and other major sectors. Conspicuously absent was the CNI. The membership list revealed Lula's view of business representation: it favored individuals and informal business leaders over presidents of associations, and among associations it favored voluntary over corporatist associations, and, of course, excluded formally the largest encompassing association of all, the CNI. Labor representatives to the CDES, in contrast, were all drawn from union confederations, and all major confederations were included. The potential impact of CDES on business politics will depend on how the Conselho participates in policy over the medium term. The immediate message, though, was not that business should invest in reinvigorating associations. On the contrary, CDES sent a clear signal that the government wanted input from prominent individual businessmen as much as or more than it wanted to listen to the collective, albeit distorted, voices of associations.

---

[49] Information on members is from www.presidencia.gov.br/cdes/pg/cons 1.htm on 12 June 2003 and from *Folha de São Paulo*, 6 February 2003, pp. 1, 4, as reported in Radiobrás, "Sinopse."

5

Business in Colombia

Well Organized and Well Connected

> At bottom, group interests are the animating forces in the political process. The exercise of the power of governance consists in the promotion of group objectives regarded as legitimate, in the reconciliation and mediation of conflicting group ambitions, and in the restraint of group tendencies judged to be socially destructive.
>
> V. O. Key (1952, 23)

Introduction

Colombia is often neglected in general theories and comparative studies of Latin America in part because its political economy in the twentieth century was so anomalous. Colombia enjoyed greater political and economic stability than most of the rest of the region while also suffering lasting civil violence and the corrosive effects of a booming underground drug economy. Colombia is also an intriguing outlier on several empirical dimensions of business politics. For most of the twentieth century, relations between government and business were very close and congenial, consistently more so than in any of the other large countries of Latin America. For sectoral governance, the strongest and most entrepreneurial association in all Latin America was the coffee growers' association, Federacafe (Federación Nacional de Cafeteros de Colombia). Government officials later extended the Federacafe governance model to rice and other agricultural sectors, and the flower association, Asocoflores, recently contributed to making Colombia the world's second largest exporter of cut flowers.

In Colombian politics, contestation by organized business against particular governments and in favor of democracy was remarkable by the standards common in Latin America. The most famous incident was business mobilization in 1957 to bring down the dictatorship, but thereafter business associations remained prominent and sometimes obstreperous actors in national politics. Lastly, the overlap between business leaders, especially leaders and staffers from prominent business associations, and top government offices was striking. Even several recent presidents of Colombia began their careers in business associations. The boundary between business and the state was more porous in Colombia, and more consistently so, than in any of the other countries considered here.[1]

Theoretically, however, the Colombian case is not so anomalous and provides strong evidence to support the argument that states organize business, even in voluntary associations. In Colombia state actors from the 1920s through the 1990s provided business associations with significant benefits – privileged access and sometimes material resources – that gave capitalists strong incentives to invest in these associations. In particular, their representation on government boards and councils was widespread. By the 1970s, business associations had 30 percent of the seats on boards and commissions dealing with general economic policy and 24 percent of the seats on boards charged with sectoral policy (Revéiz Roldán 1981, 60). Informal and ad hoc access by associations to government officials was also quite open.

The story of the economy-wide Consejo Gremial is revealing, especially in comparison with the economy-wide associations that emerged earlier in Mexico and Chile. Colombian sectoral associations engaged in occasional joint activities but lacked any lasting organization prior to the founding of the Consejo in the 1990s. Comparisons with Chile and Mexico suggest that two main factors contributed to the absence of an economy-wide association. First, Colombian business rarely confronted major political and ideological threats or lengthy periods of antagonistic relations with the government (see Losada Lora 2000). For example, among the five countries analyzed in this book, Colombia had the weakest labor movement. By one estimate, only about 10 percent

---

[1] Overall, Colombian business politics have been characterized historically by strong societal corporatism. John Bailey (1977) rejects the label "state corporatism" in favor of "elite pluralism." Bailey rightly notes that even state-chartered business associations have wide autonomy from government. However, he downplays the pervasive state funding and statutory representation, which are more consistent with the characterization of societal corporatism than pluralism. Hartlyn also uses the term "societal corporatism" to characterize the coffee sector (1988, 135).

of workers belonged to labor unions (Collier and Collier 2002, 680; Osterling 1989, 202). And policy makers in Colombia undertook fewer threatening reformist policies, so the unintended centripetal consequences of progressive policies like land reform or laws favorable to unions did not promote defensive organization. The second main factor was that the membership of associations in industry and coffee, Federacafe and ANDI (Asociación Nacional de Industriales), the strongest associations in Colombia, was fairly encompassing and included major firms in other sectors. So the incentives were weaker for business to create another separate economy-wide association. Nonetheless, state action altered these incentives. When in the early 1990s officials asked business to organize an economy-wide association to consult on trade negotiations, existing associations quickly created the Consejo Gremial.

In terms of the motivations of state actors, various political logics were visible in the efforts of officials to organize business. At important turning points in the twentieth century, state actors wanted coffee growers to organize in the 1920s in order to develop the sector, then industrialists to get together in the 1940s to manage wartime shortages, and later flower growers, for example, to coordinate export strategies in the 1980s and 1990s. In these and other instances the goals were largely pragmatic and short-term – how best to manage various challenges in economic and sectoral policies. Efforts to organize capitalists to generate overall political support were less in evidence in Colombia, in part because shifts in development strategies were more gradual and piecemeal compared to much of the rest of Latin America. Lastly, policy makers sometimes delegated benefits and policy responsibility to associations because they felt that partisan politics were too polarized and would undermine policy making, were responsibilities not shifted beyond the reach of party politics and clientelism.

The following sections analyze the three major associations. Other chapters are organized chronologically in order to illuminate major variations over time – both in government policy (and usually regime type) and in business organization. Several short-term ruptures notwithstanding, relations in Colombia between business and government were characterized by greater continuity than in most other countries of the region, so this chapter is divided into sections on each of the main associations: Federacafe, ANDI, and the Consejo Gremial. Nonetheless, this chapter retains some chronological structure by examining the associations in the order in which they were created.

Federacafe: State Actors Dissolved Obstacles to Collective Action in the 1920s

In the universe of business associations in the large countries of Latin America, Federacafe was the strongest and richest, with the most diversified organization of staff and activities. Federacafe was not only the sole conduit for the representation of the interests of coffee growers; it was simultaneously a mammoth multinational commercial enterprise as well as a central provider of public goods and services to entire regions of Colombia, not just to coffee growers. Observers sometimes call Federacafe "a state within a state" (Rodríguez Vargas 1997b). Through the marketing of Juan Valdez as the symbol of Colombian coffee, Federacafe became the only major business association in Latin America with a regular presence in American media.[2] The statutes of 1971 charged Federacafe with 24 duties and functions including agricultural extension and training services, international advertising, provision of infrastructure such as warehouses and transportation, setting quality standards, promoting research, disseminating information to members on markets, buying up excess coffee in periods of low prices, compiling complete statistics on the coffee sector, and intervening in salary and labor disputes (ANIF 1975, 94–5).

By 1997, Federacafe had 248,000 members comprising 80 percent of the coffee growers and 95 percent of the production in Colombia.[3] Already in 1980 Federacafe marketed 95 percent of exports, up from 30 percent in the 1960s (Thorp and Durand 1997, 220). In 1980 the Departmental Committees of the federation had 2,200 employees, and the central office employed another 800 (Urrutia 1983, 116–17). In the early 1990s Federacafe had 5,000 employees, far more than any other association in Latin America (interview with Jorge Cárdenas, 29 August 2001; Rodríguez Vargas 1997b, 75). Federacafe had one or more technical staff in each of the federation's 604 municipal offices (Rodríguez Vargas 1997b, 74). In a retrospective study in 1980, Federacafe estimated that in its first 50 years it had constructed 2,300 aqueducts, extended rural electrification to 110,000 homes, built 14,000 schoolrooms, maintained 460 school lunchrooms, and constructed or improved 15,000 kilometers of roads. In 1980 alone the federation provided agricultural extension

---

[2] According to one survey in the 1990s, 87 percent of U.S. respondents recognized Juan Valdez more than any other trademark, save one, included in the survey (Junguito and Pizano 1997, 65).

[3] www.cafedecolombia.com/70anhos/datos/ori.html, 31 December 1997.

services to 130,000 growers and granted 18,000 loans (Urrutia 1983, 126, 128).

Federacafe did not evolve into a major player in Colombia's political economy; it was born strong and thereafter thrived. The Colombian state created Federacafe, but not as a compulsory corporatist association.[4] In 1927 the provincial government of Antioquia convened the Second National Coffee Congress, which voted to create Federacafe. Before adjourning, this Coffee Congress appointed a National Committee to continue working to try to organize a permanent association. However, the half dozen members of this committee faced a daunting task: to organize tens of thousands of small producers, dispersed throughout many regions of Colombia, without the benefit of material resources or modern communications. In fact the Coffee Congress itself was so penurious that it asked another association, SAC (Sociedad de Agricultores de Colombia), to organize publication of the report from the Congress and requested paper from the government (Cortázar Toledo 1968, 49).

It was Alfredo Cortázar Toledo, a second-level official in the Ministry of Industries, who solved their collective action problem. Appointed chief of information and propaganda, Cortázar decided to make organizing the federation his top priority. The president of Colombia and the minister of industries agreed with this plan, and Cortázar proceeded to call the first meeting of the National Committee. Cortázar proposed a tax on exports to finance the association, but the coffee growers demurred. The Second Coffee Congress had even passed a resolution expressly opposing any taxes on coffee. After several meetings, Cortázar finally convinced the National Committee to accept an export tax, in part by arguing that no association would be possible without the tax and also by giving his assurance that the tax would not get folded into general government revenues.

Cortázar then drafted Law 76 creating Federacafe, and once the law was approved, the National Committee voted unanimously to elect Cortázar as the first manager of the new association. For the first six months before the tax collections started, Federacafe had a precarious existence. At one of the early meetings of the National Committee, Cortázar asked everyone, including himself and another ministry employee, to

---

[4] Much of this history is drawn from Cortázar (1968), Koffman (1969, á81–3), and Junguito and Pizano (1997, 1–8). Business associations required state licensing in Colombia, but the government generally granted recognition to any association that requested it. The government used coercive corporatist controls more often with labor and religious associations (Bailey 1977, 266, 272–3).

contribute $50 toward the first budget of $350 ($5 and $35 in 1928 dollars). Later, Cortázar loaned the legally constituted but revenueless federation $50,000 of his personal funds and subsequently gave his personal guarantee for a bank loan of another $50,000 ($5,000 in 1929 dollars). Cortázar did not receive any salary during his first year as director, and another federation employee was still getting paid by the ministry (Cortázar Toledo 1968, 51, 54). Even discounting for possible exaggeration in Cortázar's personal account, this is a remarkable story of organizational entrepreneurship by a government official. Robert Bates's (1997, 61) argument that Federacafe was "created by local and regional politicians" is misleading because it fails to distinguish between elected politicians and state officials like Cortázar. Local politicians did help organize the second National Congress in 1927, but this Congress, like the two before it, generated no lasting association. It was Cortázar and his export tax that laid the foundation for one of the most remarkable associations on the continent.[5]

The incentives for state actors to organize coffee growers were strong and several. For one, coffee prices were falling in the late 1920s at the same time that the Colombian economy was becoming increasingly dependent on coffee exports.[6] State actors confronted major problems or vulnerabilities (weak administrative and political capacity) in designing effective state promotion of coffee. Coffee production in Colombia was dispersed among many producers (in contrast to the more concentrated plantation production in other countries), and the state's administrative capacity was low, especially before the 1960s. The costs of exclusive state action in collecting information, setting standards, and promoting coordination were consequently high. Moreover, speed and flexibility in adjusting coffee policy were essential in order to respond to rapid changes in international markets. So, political executives worried that leaving tax policy to the legislature, as normally required by law, would result in inevitable and damaging delays. More generally, since the performance of the coffee sector had such a large impact on overall economic performance, political

---

[5] The source of the novel solution of an earmarked tax is apparently the subject of continuing controversy with Cortázar, the minister of Industries Montalvo, and another ministry official all having some claim to paternity (Junguito and Pizano 1997, 6, fn 26). All three claimants were, however, top officials in the key economic ministry, which conforms to my general argument about the usual source of efforts to organize business.

[6] Thorp (2002) emphasizes the crisis conditions of the late 1920s in the creation of Federacafe, which presumably increased the willingness of growers to accept the tax solution proposed by state actors.

executives feared subjecting coffee policy to the then intense partisan conflict between the major parties (Urrutia 1983).[7]

The interests of coffee growers in creating an organization like Federacafe were also intense. Colombian coffee was high quality and high priced but faced formidable obstacles in getting to the market, especially for small producers, including difficult and costly transportation, warehousing, and monitoring for quality (Thorp and Durand 1997, 219). In all these aspects, collective action was clearly optimal, yet free riding would have been irresistible without the state. Tellingly, previous national meetings of coffee growers in 1904 and 1920 failed to overcome free riding and generate a national coffee association (Urrutia 1983, 119).

Federacafe celebrated its first contract with the government in 1928 (renewed every decade since). This contract removed the free-rider problem by granting Federacafe control over a tax on coffee exports. Overnight Federacafe had a large budget, and it has never lost control over this tax. In its first year Federacafe had a budget of $1.4 million, a staff of at least 10, and 2,000 members.[8] In 1940 the government created FONAC (Fondo Nacional del Café), a fund to stabilize the prices paid to Colombia producers. The idea for this fund, unique among coffee-producing countries, was for Federacafe to pay producers less than the international price during boom years and put the difference into the fund (Rodríguez Vargas 1997b, 85–6). Then in years of low international prices, Federacafe would tap into the fund to pay producers more than the going international prices. The fund expanded greatly after the 1950s, and Federacafe used it as a financial fulcrum for spinning off a host of subsidiaries in finance, shipping, warehousing, and other related activities (Junguito and Pizano 1997; Rodríguez Vargas 1997b).

Material resources alone do not generate institutional strength. It was the effective use of these resources to build transportation and warehousing infrastructure, as well as the effective policing of coffee exports, that gave the federation legitimacy and coercive powers over its members. Part of Federacafe's effectiveness, in turn, can be attributed to its insulated

---

[7] As the Colombian economy grew and diversified, it became less dependent on coffee. By the early 1990s, coffee accounted for 5 percent of GDP, one-quarter of agricultural production and of foreign exchange earning, but 40 percent of agricultural employment (Rodríguez Vargas 1997a, 202).

[8] $139,000 in 1928 dollars (Cortázar Toledo 1968, 54, 56). Palacios emphasizes that Federacafe was "weak and uncertain" in its first three years (1980, 219). Federacafe was certainly weak compared to the imposing institution it would become decades later, but it was still well endowed compared to fledgling associations born elsewhere without an earmarked tax.

and professional staff, which was "one of the largest, best remuner-
ated, and most competent in Colombia" (Rodríguez Vargas 1997b, 74).
Federacafe is famous "for having had only three general managers in the
course of its nearly seventy years of life – all of them people of enormous
stature and quality" (Thorp and Durand 1997, 221). This effectiveness
was also in the interests of Federacafe members, whose profits depended
heavily on Federacafe's infrastructure, financing, technical assistance, and
marketing.

This insulation and stability of Federacafe's president and technical
staff did not, however, degenerate into what some characterize as the bureaucratic capture of corporatist associations in Brazil (by Fiespocratas),
largely because there were stronger incentives and more opportunities
for Federacafe members to participate actively in association affairs.[9] For
example, the investment of Federacafe's resources in infrastructure and
assistance to growers was decided largely by municipal and departmental committees (Thorp 2002, 13), which increased incentives for growers,
even small holders, to join and participate at the local level. Another
strong incentive to participate, more for the coffee elite, was the position
of Federacafe within the state. Federacafe, like other Colombian associations, had seats on many public councils, but in addition had a seat on the
board of the central bank (through the 1990s) and was the only association on the council of economic ministers (Consejo de Política Económica
y Social (CONPES) created in 1967 (Thorp 2002, 12)). Most observers
agree that the coffee elite dominated the governance of Federacafe to
the exclusion of the mass of poor, small producers. However, among the
elite, interest intermediation was effective and representation was largely
proportional (by geographic area and production; see Rodríguez 1997a,
1997b).

The sources of Federacafe's impressive institutional strength and capacity for collective action are relatively straightforward. What is harder
to explain is why government actors created Federacafe rather than a government coffee agency, as the Brazilian government did at around the same
time. Of course, there was strong opposition from parts of the coffee elite

[9] Some observers criticize the growth, cost, and self-interested behavior of the Federacafe
bureaucracy. A bill proposed in 1992 in the Colombian Senate would have limited
Federacafe's administrative costs to 10 percent of its budget. The bill lost by a vote of 49
to 3. Rodríguez concludes that "no measure unfavorable to the interests of [Federacafe's]
bureaucracy has ever passed in the National Congress" (1997b, 76). However, Federacafe
members still had relatively greater control over the bureaucracy compared, for example,
to FIESP members.

who wanted to limit government intervention (see Pécaut 1979). And, from the beginning, state actors were in fact worried about losing control of coffee policy and worked to maintain detailed oversight and institutionalize mechanisms of control over the federation. The first contract contained many provisions for submitting reports to the government on Federacafe activities. Moreover, budgets and key personnel decisions had to be approved by the National Coffee Producers' Committee, which usually had near-parity representation by government.[10]

In practice, though, the coffee elite dominated Federacafe and the association operated with a good deal of autonomy from government. Although evidence on the exact motivations of state actors at the moment of creation are scarce, depoliticization and delegation seem to have been important goals in the creation of self-governance in the coffee sector. For example, the Constitution granted the legislature the exclusive right to set taxes. Obviously, setting tax rates is a long and conflictual process for legislators, and any legislature would have had a difficult time keeping abreast of rapidly changing conditions in international markets. The political solution was hence to delegate the collection and administration of taxes on coffee (Urrutia 1983, 134). Moreover, in 1935, to depoliticize further the association, the federation statutes were amended to prohibit the election of government officials as delegates to Federacafe conventions (Urrutia 1983, 121).

Federacafe leaders worked to maintain relative autonomy from the government. Federacafe appeared dependent when it stayed on the sidelines when other associations engaged in confrontational contestation, particularly joint business demands for presidents to resign in both the 1950s and 1990s. Nonetheless, most observers consider Federacafe to be a sophisticated, largely independent, and effective lobby for coffee interests as well as more general business causes. Despite formal administrative controls by the government over Federacafe and representation of the government on Federacafe councils, government officials were at a disadvantage in dealings with the federation (Rodríguez Vargas 1997b, 68).[11] First, the government had no independent or complete source of

---

[10] In the 1950s the committee had five representatives of government and six from Federacafe. In 1979 the committee was expanded to include eight representatives each from government and from Federacafe (Urrutia 1983, 122).

[11] Palacios concludes that "the formal and informal power of the body is based on these four elements: (a) its ability to act as a quasi-state entity in areas such as legal initiatives" and enforcement of laws (most of which FNCC originally drafted), b) economic resources, c) "oligopolic agent in the internal coffee market" and d) "control of information" (1980, 248–9).

information on the coffee sector, so deliberations between government and the federation relied on Federacafe's information. Second, Federacafe managers and delegates to the National Coffee Producers' Committee enjoyed much longer tenure than government representatives. The average tenure for Federacafe representatives was 15 years, while government representatives rarely lasted as long as 4 years. At the top level between 1958 and 1979 there were 15 different ministers of finance, while Federacafe had the same general manager (Urrutia 1983, 122–3).[12]

The careful regulation of representation of the coffee elite within the federation also made its voice authoritative. Unlike corporatist associations that overrepresent small business on the basis of one vote per business, regardless of the size of the business, Federacafe statutes granted representation on the basis of proportion of production. Big producers were naturally well represented, and their voices were aggregated on a regional basis, again in proportion to their production (Rodríguez Vargas 1997a, 205). Despite the bias favoring the coffee elite, voluntary participation by the mass membership was often high. Over 160,000 members voted in the 2002 elections for municipal and departmental representatives (Federacafe 2002, 33–4). At each level there were at least twice as many candidates as there were seats, and combined turnover was 51 percent. Overall, 59 percent of eligible members voted, which represented a higher voter turnout than that for national political elections. So, when Federacafe representatives defended the sector's interest, they could claim a legitimate mass mandate.

The intense and often violent partisan conflict that characterized Colombian politics for much of the twentieth century may also have worked to enhance Federacafe's autonomy. On the one hand, opposition politicians would have been especially upset if the president and ruling party used their formal powers to appoint sympathizers to Federacafe's management. On the other, even ruling politicians might have realized that subjecting Federacafe to partisan considerations was too dangerous, given the government's and the country's great dependence on competent management of the coffee sector (Thorp and Durand 1997). Such concerns likely contributed to the high technical qualifications of Federacafe's

---

[12] This asymmetrical pattern of turnover seems to characterize other public–private boards. Generally, the average tenure of ministers from 1930 to 1970 ranged from a low of 10 months in Education to a high of 18 months in Public Works. On the directorate for the national apprenticeship program, private sector representatives averaged five years compared with one year for the representatives from the public sector (1957–72) (Bailey 1977, 292–3).

staff and the longevity of its top managers. Long tenure and technical competence, in turn, contributed to both the authority of Federacafe positions and the willingness of managers to defend Federacafe as an institution. Overall, Hartlyn concluded that "the relationship between the state and the coffee sector approximates that of 'societal corporatism'" (1988, 135).

Federacafe also served at times as a functional equivalent for a multisectoral peak association. Like Brazil, Colombia had no peak association that united Federacafe with associations in other sectors. However, leading members of the decentralized, department-level committees were either professionals or prominent businessmen (with minor interests in coffee) or were big producers with diversified holdings in other sectors of the economy (Adelman 1981, 460, 467 based on Koffman 1969). Federacafe "was principally controlled by people whose interests lay in diverse fields, always including the commercialization of coffee but rarely its production except in small scale. From the early days, the federation was in effect a multisectoral association."[13] In sum, encompassing interests filtered unintentionally through Federacafe because of the strong representation of coffee elites who had multisectoral holdings. Colombia found "ways to build in the interests of both industry and agriculture in response to the encompassing nature of the interests behind" Federacafe (Thorp and Durand 1997, 222).

Returning to the framework in Chapter 2, state actors granted Federacafe public authority over collective governance functions like taxation and price stabilization. Federacafe passed on these selective benefits and services, which made membership highly valuable to most producers. In addition, state actors granted Federacafe privileged access, which was another attractive benefit for the coffee elite. State actors, in the 1930s and 1940s especially, faced a number of vulnerabilities that Federacafe served to mitigate. For one, the administrative tasks of grading and marketing coffee initially exceeded the capacities of the Colombian executive bureaucracy. Moreover, officials charged with making macroeconomic policy and overall development strategy were vulnerable to incompetent or politicized governance of the sector that generated for decades over

---

[13] Thorp and Durand explain further that "what contributed to this was the fact that coffee production in itself requires little subsequent investment once the plantation is established. There was thus a need for deployment of surplus funds in other ways. From early on, important coffee people were also looking for outlets in commerce, real estate, industry, shipping, and finance" (1997, 220). Kline writes that "in Colombia . . . , there is a tendency toward overlapping ownership of industry, commerce, and agriculture" (1974, 287).

half of the country's export earnings. Lastly, depoliticizing governance of the crucial coffee sector reduced some overall political vulnerability for national leaders familiar with the often hyperpartisan party strife.

ANDI Developed Institutional Capacity and Encompassing Representation

Although the industrialists' association, ANDI, lacked the massive resources of Federacafe, it was still institutionally strong in terms of staff and interest intermediation. ANDI was a close interlocutor with government and was generally considered the most influential association in Colombia after Federacafe (Kline 1996, 30; Osterling 1989, 206; Urrutia 1983, 72).[14] As in the case of Federacafe, ANDI's creation came in response to state initiatives, but ANDI was never as dependent on the government for resources and maintained greater independence. ANDI grew strong in the 1940s largely because of its privileged access to government, and then further mobilized in the 1950s to oppose many policies of the dictatorship of Gustavo Rojas Pinilla. Later it maintained its privileged connections, both formally through representation in policy councils and informally.

Three things stand out in the early history of ANDI that illustrate clearly several of the core arguments in this book.[15] First, state actors had strong political motivations to organize industry, especially to aggregate preferences and manage the economic disruptions caused by World War II. Second, state actors could not impose unilaterally the organization they wanted, but rather negotiated an organizational compromise with business. And third, privileged access by ANDI strengthened incentives for collective action and investment in the institutional capacity of the association.

The difficulties of managing a wartime economy in the 1940s led state actors to promote the formation of ANDI. In 1940 the government drafted a decree creating the Asociación Nacional de Manufactureros. The decree

---

[14] For a minority, contrary view, see Mares (1993, 460).
[15] Industrialists attempted to organize earlier (Poveda Ramos 1984, 1–11). In 1929 Medellín industrialists created the Industria Nacional Colombiana, which functioned from 1930 to 1937. This association was based in Medellín but also opened offices in a few other cities. In 1930 industrialists in Bogotá created a rival association, Federación Nacional de Industriales, that had offices in a few other cities (though not in Medellín). This association also fizzled by the end of the 1930s. Poveda is the only source on these associations, but he does not provide information on why they emerged or why they folded. The fact that Bogotá and Medellín industrialists maintained separate "national" associations for most of the 1930s suggests that regional rivalries were not trivial.

would also have established a policy forum, the Comité Nacional, with five members appointed by government and five by the new association. This statist format was similar to those adopted in the 1930s and 1940s in Brazil and Mexico, but Colombian industrialists opposed the decree and the Supreme Court blocked its implementation (Poveda Ramos 1984, 13). ANDI was born later as a purely private body, though President Alfonso López Pumarejo pressed for its formation and used the promise of institutionalized access to help industrialists organize.[16] Miguel Urrutia's account is worth quoting at length:

During some time, President Alfonso López Pumarejo lived in Medellín, where he had many friends. In his second presidency, during a period when due to the shortages created by the war the state had to administer import ceilings and price controls, his industrialist friends from the region called him constantly for help resolving their problems. During one visit to Medellín, the President called the industrialists together ... and explained to them that he could no longer hang on the phone talking to all his friends who called to tell him of their problems, and he asked them to organize, to name one spokesman for all of industry, and that for this person, yes, he would have time to attend to his concerns. (Urrutia 1983, 72)

The selective incentive for potential members to join was that the president made clear that the association would be the privileged interlocutor for industry.

State actors subsequently relied regularly on ANDI for ad hoc consultations and later institutionalized this access by putting ANDI representatives on the boards of scores of public entities and commissions. For example, in the late 1940s, industrialists and economic policy makers engaged in protracted discussions over the future of the oil industry.[17] A subsidiary of Standard Oil held a concession to the Mares oil fields that expired in 1951, and in 1949 the company decided not to seek a renewal. Government officials then recommended that a Colombian firm, a joint venture between the public and private sectors, take over the concession. In early 1950 the minister of mines and petroleum, José Elias del Hierro, and other government officials traveled to Medellín to meet with 50 members of ANDI to discuss raising investment from the private side. Over the following months President Mariano Ospina Pérez formed a government commission of three ministers (mines and petroleum, government, and finance) to continue negotiations with a commission from

---

[16] Revéiz (1981, 52). For a full history of the period see Sáenz Rovner (1992).
[17] The full story comes from Sáenz Rovner (2002, Chapters 2, 3).

ANDI, headed by ANDI's first president, Cipriano Restrepo Jaramillo. Negotiations continued through 1950 and into the new government of President Laureano Gómez, but the new government was not as keen on including the private sector and ultimately, in early 1951, created a state firm, Ecopetrol, to take over the concession. In the end, ANDI negotiators failed to secure a place for private capital in the oil industry. However, during these years of intense negotiations, government officials relied on ANDI to represent the private sector, and this privileged access via ANDI gave industrialists strong incentives to continue to invest in their new association. In 1953, in another instance of privileged representation, the government convened the Asamblea Nacional Constituyente (ANAC) to draft a new constitution. Just as in the constituent assembly in Brazil in 1934, ANAC reserved seats in its senate for representatives from functional groups, including ANDI (Sáenz Rovner 2002, Chapter 7). Later in 1953 ANAC endorsed the coup by Gustavo Rojas Pinilla.

ANDI had an erratic relationship with the mercurial dictatorship of Rojas Pinilla (1953–7) that resembled the love–hate relationship Mexican business had with several PRI governments. For ANDI this volatile relationship gave industrialists strong incentives to invest in the association, both for defense against adverse policies and for effective participation in the forums where the dictatorship still granted ANDI privileged access. ANDI initially went along with ANAC's endorsement of the coup, but relations between ANDI and the government began to deteriorate almost immediately afterward when the government proposed new, progressive taxes. This conflict provoked countermobilization by ANDI and other associations. In October 1953 ANDI convoked a national three-day conference of its directors that issued a very critical assessment of the proposed tax reform (Sáenz Rovner 2002, Chapter 8). Although some government policies in the 1950s provoked business opposition, others were more favorable to industry, and government officials regularly sought out ANDI leaders for consultation. For example, in June 1954 the government created a commission to study the economic conjuncture and invited the director of the Banco de la República, the director of Federacafe, the president of ANDI, José Gutiérrez Gómez, and five ex-ministers to staff the commission. In addition, ANDI retained its representation in ANAC, which continued to meet during the Rojas Pinilla dictatorship (Sáenz Rovner 1992, Chapter 9).

ANDI's membership (a mixture of individuals, firms, and associations) responded to incentives for collective action and invested in creating an association with impressive institutional capacity.[18] ANDI's membership grew from 540 members in 1963 to 861 members in 1981 before falling to 732 by 2001 (see Appendix A for sources and more information). By 1981 ANDI had a budget of about $4 million (120 million 1981 pesos; Urrutia 1983, 82), and by 2001 ANDI's budget of $5 million supported a staff of 161 (interview with Juan Carlos Beltrán, 27 August 2001). The proportion of industry represented by ANDI is difficult to estimate and subject to some dispute. ANDI sources estimated that the association represented between 65 and 85 percent of industrial production (Rettberg 2000, Chapter 3, fn 23).[19] ANDI membership and budgets are small compared to those of the corporatist associations of industry in Brazil but larger than those of most other voluntary industry associations in Latin America.

Over time ANDI became more encompassing by including nonindustrial firms in commerce, transportation, agroindustry, insurance, finance, and other services (Juárez 1995, 90).[20] For Kline, ANDI "approximates an overall peak organization of all producer associations" (1996, 30). In part because of Federacafe's close and discreet relation to the state, ANDI emerged as the major association representing the private sector, especially in moments of public confrontation with the government. By the year 2000 ANDI's website was proclaiming that "we are the private sector of Colombia."[21] Some saw ANDI's power and prestige peaking in the 1940s and 1950s; however, ANDI's continuing institutionalized presence within the state gave it lasting institutional capacity and influence (Rettberg 2000, chapter 2).

By the mid-1980s ANDI representatives had seats on over 60 public boards and councils (Osterling 1989, 206). By another count of representation in the 14 consultative boards coordinated by the Ministry of Development, ANDI had the widest representation, with seats on all 14 boards, followed by an exporters association with seats on 6, and other associations with fewer seats (studies cited in Giacalone 1999, 72).[22] ANDI's

---

[18] Data on the early years are scarce, but one indication of ANDI's institutional strength was the publicity campaign it launched in 1954 in print and affiliated radio stations (Sáenz Rovner 1992, Chapter 9).

[19] In 1951 SMEs created Acopi (Asociación Colombiana Popular de Industriales) to represent the interests of smaller firms not adequately represented in ANDI.

[20] See www.andi.com.co/dependencias/sriagra1.dirciiu.htm, 1 September 1999.

[21] www.andi.com.co/presentacion/informacion_central.htm

[22] One hypothesis, plausible also for Sofofa in Chile, is that ANDI became more encompassing, in part by virtue of its access to broader macro policy entities or forums. Nonindustrial firms had incentives to seek membership in ANDI in order to gain indirect access to these macro policy discussions.

retrospective publication on the occasion of its 50th anniversary high-lighted some of the councils and boards on which it was represented, including those responsible for wages, regulation of labor markets, vocational training, social security, and the central bank (though apparently only through the 1960s) (ANDI 1994a, 24–5). This publication made special reference to ANDI's participation in the national vocational training program SENA (Servicio Nacional de Aprendizaje). In the 1950s ANDI lobbied the government to create a training program and helped draft the legislation establishing the program in 1957. The legislation naturally included provisions for active ANDI participation in operating SENA. In the 1990s ANDI was again active in drafting legislation to reform SENA (ANDI 1994a, 70–1).

Over time ANDI's institutionalized representation in government forums expanded. By 1980 ANDI had an additional 46 sectoral committees that met with government planners to work out sectoral programs. In these discussions the "detailed technical knowledge of the representatives from the private sector influences a lot the final form the plan takes" (Urrutia 1983, 78). ANDI later played an important role in mobilizing business input into international trade negotiations (Giacalone 1999).[23] In the 1990s the president of ANDI usually appointed a staff member instead of a member firm to represent ANDI in specific policy councils. These staff members then devoted much of their time to interest aggregation and technical research (interview with Ricardo Correa Robledo, 29 August 2001). In sum, this guaranteed policy input strengthened incentives for investing in the professional and organizational capacity of ANDI.

In addition, continuing concerns about an overly interventionist state led ANDI members to strengthen interest intermediation and develop the capacity for resolving conflicts among sectors within the association. In one example, ANDI brought together printing firms that were complaining about paper prices with the offending monopoly paper producer and successfully intermediated a pricing agreement. In another instance, ANDI brokered negotiations between sugar producers and soft drink bottlers. In these and other cases of in-house intermediation, ANDI leaders feared that unresolved conflicts, and aggrieved parties, would invite government intrusion (Urrutia 1983, 75).

---

[23] Additionally, the nine regional branch offices of ANDI had representation in the regional operations of a variety of government programs including social security, vocational training, local public enterprises, free trade zones, and other social services (ANDI 1994b, 26).

In Colombia ANDI was the largest and most encompassing association of industry and the private sector as a whole. The government also nurtured associations in other sectors of industry, agriculture, and services, sometimes delegating self-governance functions similar to Federacafe's. For example, rice producers founded the Federación Nacional de Arroceros (Fedearroz) in 1947, but it was not until the government copied the Federacafe model in the rice sector that Fedearroz became a significant factor in rice production.[24] In 1963, the government imposed a tax on rice and turned the proceeds over to Fedearroz to be used, according to a contract between the government and Fedearroz, to develop rice production. The 1960s were the heyday of the green revolution in rice, and Fedearroz took as its main function the introduction of new seeds and cultivation techniques into Colombian production. By the late 1960s it had developed extensive research and extension programs and was selling millions of dollars worth of seeds, herbicides, pesticides, fertilizers, and machinery. In terms of area sown with "modern" seed varieties, Colombia went from last place, out of 10 major rice producers, in 1968 to first place in 1974 (Urrutia 1983, 60).

Delegating various kinds of authority for sectoral governance to other sectors, such as sugar, banking, and cotton, became a common option for state actors facing changing sectoral challenges. Asocaña (Asociación de Cultivadores de Caña de Azúcar) allocated export quotas among sugar producers and provided a number of other technical services (Urrutia 1983, 89). In 1960 the government granted the Federation of Cotton Growers, Federalgodón, authority to market and export cotton (Hartlyn 1988, 137). The bankers' association, Asobancaria (Asociación Bancaria de Colombia), provided an impressive array of services and extensive sectoral governance for banks. Created in 1936, again with government encouragement and support, by 1981 Asobancaria had a budget of over $2.7 million (78 million 1981 pesos) (of which more than half came from the sale of services to members) and 165 employees (Urrutia 1983, 108–9). Among other things, Asobancaria provided technical training, security advice (and had its own team of investigators), credit ratings on clients throughout the banking system, a personnel office and screening service, administration of government-financed credit for agriculture, and sectorwide standards on check bouncing and procedures for closing delinquent accounts.

---

[24] The government also extended the model and control over "parafiscal" resources to cacao, grains, milk, unrefined sugar, and meat (Rodríguez Vargas 1997b, 79).

From the 1940s to the 1970s, close government collaboration with business and the government practice of inviting association representatives to join policy councils helped generate a broad set of business associations, with ANDI and Federacafe at the core. Many of these associations had significant organizational capacity, measured both by their large technical staffs and by the ability of their members to reconcile differences and thereby participate more effectively in policy making.

Economy-Wide Coordination and the Creation of the Consejo Gremial

At first glance, it is somewhat puzzling that these well-endowed and well-organized sectoral associations did not form an economy-wide peak association. What was missing in Colombia, from a comparative perspective, were the sorts of threats from labor or labor-backed and reformist governments that in Mexico and Chile triggered the creation of peak associations. Urrutia noted that industrialists "felt that the government was dangerous," and for this reason sought consensus within ANDI (1983, 75). However, threats from the Colombian government were milder than those from reformist governments in Chile and Mexico or even from the governments of Perón and Goulart (threats, as defined in Chapter 2, that involved expropriation of private property or government support for labor organization and militancy). In addition, several peculiarities of Colombian associations further reduced incentives for organizing a peak association. As noted earlier, several major sectoral associations, especially ANDI and Federacafe, had a more encompassing membership than their names implied. Other associations deferred informally to ANDI as the spokesman for the private sector, reducing the need to create a separate peak organization of sectoral associations. In addition, Federacafe's unique status so closely associated with government (both revenue dependence and government representation on its board) kept it from joining other, less constrained associations in joint opposition to government policies (a common path to the formation of peak associations in other countries).

Despite the lack of a formal peak association, major sectoral associations demonstrated the capacity for joint action with other associations through ad hoc arrangements. In the 1950s, some policy initiatives of the Rojas Pinilla dictatorship, especially tax and social spending proposals, encouraged efforts for united opposition from industry (ANDI), commerce (Fenalco, the Federación Nacional de Comerciantes), and agriculture (Federacafe and SAC). In 1954, for instance, the presidents of ANDI and Fenalco drafted a letter opposing a government proposal for obligatory bond purchases by all businesses, and other associations such as Asobancaria (bankers) and SAC (agriculture) signed on (Sáenz Rovner 2002, Chapter 9). Federacafe, though, did not sign. However, other major policies on tariffs and exchange rates pitted agriculture (with preferences for low tariffs and undervalued exchange) against industry (with preferences for high tariffs and overvalued exchange).[25] This kind of intersectoral divergence reduced interest in bringing all associations together in one peak organization.

In subsequent decades, sectoral associations demonstrated a further capacity for ad hoc coordination. In early 1965, in the midst of threats of general strikes and military coups, ANDI took the initiative to organize the Comité Privado de Cooperación, which included Fenalco, ANDI, Asobancaria, SAC, and the small business association (Acopi) (Hartlyn 1985, 117). In February 1981, five major associations from industry, commerce, construction, and finance (but not Federacafe or other agricultural associations) created the Frente Gremial in order to pressure the government for policies favorable to business.[26] This Frente, though, fell apart over intersectoral differences in policy preferences (Osterling 1989, 207–8; Rettberg 2000, Chapter 3, fn 22). Up to the 1980s, these ephemeral, efforts at coordination looked much like the UBE and Ação Empresarial in Brazil and similar ad hoc coordinating bodies in Argentina.

In 1991 a stronger and more enduring coordinating entity, the Consejo Gremial (CG), emerged. The initiative for the CG came from an invitation from then Secretary of Development Ernesto Samper to consult with government on trade and other macroeconomic policies (interview with Samper, 24 August 2001). Promoting encompassing organization was a natural step for Samper. He had participated from the business side, as president of ANIF, in the Frente Gremial in the 1970s, and from the government side helped promote encompassing organization among labor unions as well. He thought the institutionalized encompassing

---

[25] In the late 1940s ANDI supported tariff protection. Fenalco opposed it vociferously (as did SAC and Federacafe more moderately and quietly) (Pécaut 1979, 334).

[26] The five associations were ANDI, Fedemetal (Federación Colombiana de Industrias Metalúrgicas), Camacol (Cámara Colombiana de la Construcción), Fenalco, and ANIF. Later, in December 1982, ANDI met frequently with SAC, Fenalco, and Acopi to devise a common strategy for negotiating wage increases (Kalmanovitz 1990, 199, 205–6).

association Fedecamaras, in neighboring Venezuela, was an appropriate model for Colombian business. In terms of motives, Samper was primarily interested in organizing the CG in order to get business to aggregate and reconcile interests across sectors, as in the 1940s when the government promoted ANDI, more so, at least initially, than in generating overall political support or specific kinds of policy-relevant information. The members of CG were 15 major associations from agriculture, finance, industry, transportation, commerce, and construction (Rettberg 2000). Federacafe again was not a member. However, CG remained an ad hoc coordinating body rather than developing into a more strongly institutionalized peak association like the CPC in Chile or the CCE in Mexico. The CG had one staff person, no offices, and a presidency that rotated every six months among the heads of the member associations.

Despite its debilities in terms of staff and material resources, CG's institutional capacity for mediating interests, reconciling differences, and voicing collective concerns, sometimes radical, was impressive. This capacity is best revealed in CG's opposition, ironically, to its creator, Ernesto Samper. Frankenstein-like, CG turned on its creator shortly after he was elected president and by 1996 demanded his resignation (see Rettberg 2000 for the full story). The Samper administration (1994–8) ran into deep political and economic trouble in the middle of his term. The economy slid into recession, the United States "decertified" Colombia's efforts in fighting drug trafficking, and Samper struggled through a political crisis after his campaign manager admitted taking funds from drug traffickers. In this context, the CG decided unanimously in January 1996 to call publicly for Samper's resignation.

Although reminiscent of the successful campaign to oust the dictator Rojas Pinilla in 1957, CG was not able to force Samper out of office. Conditions were, of course, quite different 40 years later: Samper was a constitutionally elected president, he was already halfway through a fixed term, and business and the economy were far more diversified. Samper played on this diversity by sowing divisions within CG and courting successfully support from some of Colombia's huge conglomerates. While perhaps a failure compared to 1957, the call by an economy-wide CG for Samper's resignation was still a remarkable feat of interest aggregation and collective action, certainly compared to other similar incidents in Latin America. When other governments in the region became mired in corruption scandals, as in Brazil under Collor or Argentina in the later Menem years, business was not nearly as active or united in contesting the president. Colombian business, in contrast, was much more independent and politically mobilized.[27]

Political Portfolios: Parties, Circulation, and Associations

Relations in Colombia between economic policy makers and business associations were especially close and knit together by extensive formal representation, epidemic elite circulation, and dense informal networks. So, it is not surprising that parties, elections, and legislative lobbying were underweighted components in the portfolio of political investments by Colombian business. Parties and legislatures were historically less important channels of interaction between business and the state. The two major parties, Liberals and Conservatives, were open to capitalists and to business lobbying, though both parties were catchall, multiclass parties and neither could claim to represent business better than the other (Dix 1987, Chapter 5). Many studies note the eclipse of the power of the legislature, especially during the National Front period (1958–74). By the 1970s, economic policy makers usually announced new policy initiatives in assemblies of major business associations rather than in Congress (Cepeda cited in Revéiz Roldán 1981, 40). A survey of legislators in the early 1970s revealed that (1) business associations ranked last among associations of all types in terms of frequency of contact with legislators; (2) 40 percent of legislators reported no contact with business associations; (3) those legislators who did have contact were evenly distributed across parties; and (4) legislators ranked ANDI and Federacafe as the most influential of all types of interest groups (Kline 1974, 281, 290, 294). Overall, since the 1960s, during the National Front period, business associations "increased in numbers and influence in the wake of a corresponding relative decline in the influence of the parties" (Dix 1987, 127). However, the end of the National Front and the revival of electoral and party politics have increased incentives for business investment in parties and campaigns (see Rettberg 2000).

Elite circulation was very high in Colombia. There was a rapidly revolving door between business and government, with a steady stream of people moving in both directions. Moreover, it appears that there was movement not only of top capitalists into government, but also of leaders

---

[27] Business opposition to corruption in the Samper government was not motivated exclusively by civic outrage. The economy was performing poorly, and Samper's political crises hurt the economy. In addition, decertification imposed high costs on Colombian exporters. See Rettberg (2000).

and professional staffers at business associations into top appointed and elected positions in government. One study concluded that 56 percent of ministers and higher government officials, 42 percent of congressmen, and 43 percent of high-level bureaucrats "had held a position in an association."[28] Later studies confirm this channel of recruitment; "practically all government ministers in positions important for national economic development have been presidents of business associations and top executives in the private sector" (Juárez 1996, 23; see also Juárez 1995). Associations also brokered some of the movement in the other direction, from the government to the private sector, by hiring ex-ministers and even ex-presidents to run their affairs.[29] Although such movement between the private and public sectors was common in other countries of the Americas, what stands out in Colombia was that this exchange was mediated centrally by associations. Miguel Urrutia concluded that "many association presidents are on their way to a political career and others find themselves oscillating between public administration and the private sector" (1983, 105).[30]

Even at the very top, many Colombian presidents were businessmen or combined political and business careers. Alfonso López Pumarejo was the son of a prominent businessman and coffee exporter in the early twentieth century and worked in the family business for several decades before entering politics and serving two terms as president (1934–8, 1942–5) (Dávila 1986). Roberto Urdaneta Arbeláez was one of the first directors of Asobancaria before becoming president (Urrutia 1983, 109). Mariano Ospina Pérez was a delegate to the second National Coffee Congress in 1927, the second general manager of Federacafe (1930–4), and later was elected president (1946–50).[31] Presidents Carlos Lleras Restrepo (1966–70) and Misael Pastrana Borrero (1970–4) had been president

[28] These percentages seem very high, but are cited by Colombian specialists such as Bailey (1977, 302, fn 56) and Dix (1987, 124).

[29] See Pécaut (1979, 337–8) on movement from government into associations in the 1940s and 1950s.

[30] Movement between associations and government was common at other levels as well. For example, after two decades in ANDI, Fernando Ruibe Restrepo was nominated to Colombia's Supreme Court (Osterling 1989, 205). Of seven executive presidents of the bankers' association Asobancaria from 1960 to 1981, six held top positions in the economic bureaucracy before or after working at the association (Urrutia 1983, 109).

[31] In addition to Presidents López Pumarejo and Ospina Pérez, five other presidents had personal and family investments in coffee. From the creation of Federacafe through 1997, close to half (7 of 16) of the presidents of Colombia had close ties to coffee (Rodríguez Vargas 1997a, 221).

of Celanese Colombiana, one of the country's largest textile enterprises (Dix 1987, 70). The first president of ANIF (Asociación Nacional de Instituciones Financieras) was Belisario Betancur, previously a Conservative minister and legislator and later president (1982–6). The second president of ANIF was Ernesto Samper, who built a very successful political career through exposure as association president on his way to the presidency of Colombia (1994–8). The business experience of at least four of these presidents from the 1930s to the 1990s (Urdaneta, Ospina Pérez, Betancur, and Samper) included prominent positions in business associations, a pattern of circulation seen nowhere else in the region save Argentina prior to 1940.

Thus, on inauguration day, most incoming governments took office with dense built-in networks to the private sector. These readymade networks no doubt contributed to the generally congenial relations between business and government (as well as to the exclusion of nonelite groups). For the portfolio analogy, this near fusion of business and state elites raises the question of why business bothered to invest in associations if they already had open individual channels of communication with government. In Brazil and Argentina the strong presence of capitalists in top executive positions seemed to reduce incentives for investing in associations by offering big business alternative channels of representation. This effect is muted in Colombia for two reasons. First, associations remained an important avenue for formal access to policy boards and commissions, and business influence in these commissions still flowed through associations. State actors, despite their strong informal networks, still turned to associations for input on aggregate preferences. Second, incentives for investing in associations were higher because recruitment of business leaders into government often happened through associations. In other countries, personal networks bypassed associations and made them dispensable, but in Colombia associations often mediated and channeled network relations.

Conclusions

Direct state action accompanied the formation and maintenance of all major Colombian associations. Unlike the corporatist interventions in Mexico and Brazil, state actors in Colombia promoted business associations by providing selective benefits, either material (as in the case of Federacafe and Fedearroz) or access to and participation in the many public/private boards and commissions. Later, when state intervention in the economy decreased and the importance of these policy boards waned, business associations were invited to participate in new policy initiatives like the trade negotiations for the Group of 3 (Giacalone 1999). Colombian associations depend heavily on the state for these selective benefits. However, in contrast to state corporatism, these associations were still much freer to decide issues of internal representation and structure.

In terms of political logics, the need of state actors for political support during periods of economic crisis and changing development strategies was somewhat weaker in Colombia because economic downturns were comparatively less severe (especially in the 1980s) and shifts in the development strategy were more piecemeal and gradual than elsewhere in Latin America. Political logics were evident in the promotion of sectoral policies and associations in coffee, rice, and other sectors where association representatives were invited to sit on policy councils. In these cases, the motives of government policy makers focused more on the weakness of the executive bureaucracy to formulate and implement policy and on the perceived need to enlist organized business for information, aggregate policy input, and in several cases delegation of policy responsibility. The desire for interest aggregation was clear in the state promotion of ANDI when, during the economic difficulties caused by World War II, President López Pumarejo asked industrialists to channel their communication through one spokesman. Similarly, half a century later, Samper's initiative to form the CG in 1991 was an effort to get business to aggregate and reconcile preferences.

The unintended consequences of threatening state actions in promoting defensive collective action by Colombian business were generally weaker. State-sponsored labor incorporation was mild and conservative by regional standards, and did not generate pressures for countermobilization by business. The developmental state that emerged in Colombia (1940s–1970s) had less pervasive control over the economy than its counterparts in Brazil and Mexico and fewer disarticulating effects on business. As in Chile, the proliferation of decentralized agencies was accompanied by corporatist efforts to provide direct representation by encompassing associations, thereby strengthening them rather than promoting exclusively personalized, bureaucratic rings, as in Brazil. Lastly, there were few government actions as threatening to property rights generally as the kinds of progressive politics that provoked encompassing collective action by business elsewhere. These kinds of threats, and their impact on business organization, will be more evident in the next chapter on business politics in Chile.

6

Consultation and Contention in the Making of Cooperative Capitalism in Chile

> Today we are strong because we are organized, tomorrow we will be invincible because we will have improved our organization.
>
> President of the National Agricultural Society, 1934[1]

Introduction

The Industry Building or Edificio de la Industria is a gleaming high rise in a prime area of Santiago's new business district. Sofofa (Sociedad de Fomento Fabril), the long-standing industry association, constructed the Edificio de la Industria in the 1990s in order to move out of its old quarters in the declining city center. Sofofa occupies the first three stories of the building, and made a lot of money selling space on the floors above. Similar stories of wealth, modernization, and institutional strength could be told about other peak sectoral associations in mining, construction, and agriculture, as well as for the economy-wide peak association, the CPC (Confederación de la Producción y del Comercio). In organizational terms, business in Chile ranks on the high end of the continuum of strong encompassing associations along with Mexico and Colombia.

The similarities and contrasts among these three countries are revealing. As in Colombia, Chilean business organized voluntary associations with significant institutional capacity that derived strength from their institutionalized access to policy making. Business elites also frequently circulated through top policy positions in government, though this circulation was more variable and ended with the return to civilian rule in

---

[1] From a speech at the inaugural convention of the CPC, cited in Drake (1978, 102).

1990. Beyond these broad similarities, the contrasts with Colombia are significant. Most importantly, in Chile the CPC, the oldest economy-wide peak association in the region, had grown strong by the 1990s at a time when Colombian business was only just forming a weak coordinating body, the Consejo Gremial. The evolution of Chile's all-encompassing association shows greater similarity with the Mexican experience. As in Mexico, the policies of left-leaning governments on labor legislation and property rights generated intense conflicts with business that led big Chilean firms to invest in encompassing associations. However, these investments were less consistent in Chile than in Mexico, in part because periods of reformism were often followed by profound political changes, such as the bloody military coup of 1973, that effectively removed the kinds of threats that were perceived by Mexican business as more constant. Also, the collaboration between business and government that evolved in periods of greater harmony in Chile often involved sectoral rather than economy-wide associations. In Mexico, access for associations was better for economy-wide associations, whereas in Chile the government institutionalized access for sectoral associations like Sofofa. As a result, in Mexico the stronger associations were economy-wide associations like the CMHN and CCE, whereas Chilean sector-wide associations like Sofofa and SNA (Sociedad Nacional de Agricultura) were organizationally stronger and better funded than the peak association they belonged to.

The following sections proceed chronologically through major periods of transformation in business–government relations, business organization, and business politics in Chile generally. As elsewhere in Latin America, the 1930s and 1940s were a period of economic and political turmoil, labor organization, and industrial growth. In Chile these factors combined to fortify business organization and intensify the incentives of state actors to incorporate business representation into new agencies designed to promote development. Institutionalized consultation sustained incentives for business to invest in sectoral associations in the 1950s, but the economy-wide association, CPC, languished. Reformism and radicalism in the 1960s and 1970s again prompted business to invest more in encompassing associations. Shortly after the coup in 1973, the government of Augusto Pinochet excluded associations and removed most incentives for collective action until the government ran into political trouble in the early 1980s, when a new cohort of government ministers began consulting again closely with encompassing business associations. This privileged consultation continued into the 1990s, when the new civilian government negotiated with encompassing associations to help smooth the transition to democracy and higher social spending.

From Depression to Consultative ISI

The history of business organization even in the nineteenth century shows that Chilean capitalists organized earlier than their counterparts elsewhere and that state actors were active from the beginning in promoting their collective action. As early as 1838 it was a government decree that created the agricultural association SNA. Merchants formed a national association in 1858. In 1883 the minister of finance asked the SNA to organize industrialists into Sofofa, and later to help mining firms create the Sociedad Nacional de Minería (Sonami).[2] By the 1920s Chilean capitalists had organized "powerful sectoral peak associations" (Silva 1996, 31). These associations went through consistent organizational development; "from the nineteenth to the twentieth century, the employer associations became 1) social clubs for the upper class, 2) pressure groups for their constituents, 3) internal regulators of their economic areas, and 4) technical advisers and decision-makers for the government" (Drake 1978, 89).

In 1933 the four major sectoral associations (mining, agriculture, industry, and commerce) formed a comprehensive peak organization, the CPC. The initial impetus for this economy-wide collective action came largely from perceived threats from government, leftist parties, and labor unions. The 1930s in Chile were politically turbulent and witnessed the rise of organized, radical labor, the growth of leftist parties, and several socialist or populist governments.[3] Membership in industrial labor unions more than tripled from 1932 to 1940 (Cavarozzi 1975, 153). In 1934 the two major labor unions formed a national confederation, and the government enacted the Labor Code (which business later endorsed). In 1935 labor leaders called a unity conference that eventually led to the Popular Front, which took power in 1938.

In sum, business elites first designed the CPC to respond "to the specter of 'socialism' and worker mobilization" (Drake 1978, 102). The CPC's statutes make clear its political function: "To assure that national

---

[2] As the name suggests, Sofofa was created in part to promote industry before there was much industry to organize (Drake 1978, 89). See Appendix A for more background information on individual associations.

[3] Of the eight major countries in Latin America, Argentina and Chile had the conditions most favorable to the early development of labor movements and the "most extensive early labor movements" (Collier and Collier 1991, 95–6).

legislation proceeds in accordance with the just interests of commerce and production" (Menges 1966, 345). Once formed, the CPC received further encouragement from the government. In 1934 President Arturo Alessandri (1932–8) "attended the Confederation's inaugural convention and assured it the desired voice in policy-making" (Drake 1978, 102).[4] In later years, as the perception of threats to common capitalist interests faded and representation by sectoral associations expanded, capitalists reduced their investment in the economy-wide CPC and the association languished.[5] The official acts of the "semidormant" CPC in the 1940s and 1950s revealed only "sparse activity – mostly symbolic – in comparison with that of its member organizations" (Cusack 1972, 70; Menges 1966, 360).

In the wake of the Great Depression parts of a developmental state emerged, and Chile developed a kind of "cooperative capitalism" (Muñoz 1986, 103). The establishment of Corfo (Corporación de Fomento de la Producción) in 1939 was one of the first efforts in Latin America to create autonomous agencies charged primarily with promoting industry (Mamalakis 1969). Thereafter the public sector continued to expand at a rapid pace, and by 1967 it accounted for 71 percent of gross internal investment (Soares 1975, 65). The initial impetus for developmentalism in Chile came from Popular Front governments in the late 1930s and 1940s and carried the birthmark of its leftist origins. The law creating Corfo was hotly disputed and barely passed the Senate (Pinto 1985, 24). However, the Popular Front government (1938–41) and successor center–left governments turned out to be less threatening than business initially feared and even worked to institutionalize the privileged access of business associations in various public entities, especially Corfo.[6] Because business

---

[4] In addition, the "leading *gremial* movement in the 1930s, the SNA achieved – in its own words – very 'tight collaboration' with the government and with the other sectoral organizations" (Drake 1978, 102–3). See also Wright (1982).

[5] Industry and agriculture, of course, differed on some policy preferences (Cusack 1972). For example, SNA joined the mining and commerce associations in favoring freer trade against the protection preferred by industry. But, even in the nineteenth century, "from the beginning, rural and urban economic leaders engaged in cooperation more than in conflict" (Drake 1978, 89). One factor that mitigated sectoral conflict in Chile was that big landowners diversified into industry (Zeitlin and Ratcliff 1988, 207).

[6] Cavarozzi offers the most thorough analysis of business influence in the Radical governments in the 1930s and 1940s and generally concludes that business interests were well represented, despite the radical rhetoric of members of the government (1975, 199). Chile lacked subsequent conservative developmentalists like Alemán in Mexico or Kubitschek in Brazil. In contrast, in Chile, the right-wing president in the late 1950s, Alessandri, tried to roll back the increasing state intervention of the previous two decades (Moulian and Torres 1986, 80; Pinto 1985, 31–6).

worried about how state actors in earlier leftist governments might use their new powers of intervention in the economy, business associations lobbied effectively to gain representation on new decentralized agencies and allied with others in government who wanted agencies to be run technocratically (Cavarozzi 1975). Overall, this major selective incentive for collective action (formal representation on government boards) was the result of political exchange; business withdrew its opposition to state intervention in the economy in return for institutional guarantees of oversight (if not direct influence) and depoliticization of agencies directing the intervention. Summarized in the terms used in Chapter 2, the state actors who were adopting the new development strategy felt vulnerable to political opposition, especially from business, and therefore granted business associations representation to mute their opposition. This representation, in turn, increased incentives for business to invest in the institutional capacity of the associations.

Compared to Brazil and Mexico (and even Colombia in the case of Federacafe), Chilean business was generally freer in the mid-twentieth century to decide independently how to structure business representation. State corporatism for business was weak and ineffective in Chile, and major business associations were voluntary and autonomous throughout the twentieth century. Legislation for unions (*sindicatos*) was more state corporatist in providing for state licensing, automatic financing, and representational monopolies. However, this legislation was applied only to labor, and businesses, although they could use the corporatist legislation to form business *sindicatos*, usually opted for voluntary organization under different legislation. Some formal legal restrictions on business associations remained, even if they opted to organize outside the Labor Code. For example, in 1951 a presidential decree created a new sectoral peak association, the Chilean Chamber of Construction (Drake 1978, 106). Later, when the CPC decided to incorporate the construction chamber in 1966, the decision provoked heated debate in Congress. Ultimately the Supreme Court ruled that the CPC could incorporate new members (Cusack 1972, 73–4). Business associations were also legally proscribed from party politics, a provision that President Salvador Allende later attempted to use in the 1970s to dissolve Sofofa (Drake 1978, 111).

By the 1960s the major sectoral associations enjoyed significant institutional strength. They had professional staffs, frequent publications, and high public profiles. Internal representation was effective in that major associations balanced regional and sectoral representation and granted proportional representation to economically powerful sectors. Moreover, leaders tended to be drawn from the pool of the most successful businessmen (Menges 1966, 346–7). The CPC and its five member associations together employed 250 people and had combined annual budgets of around $5.3 million. Of the member associations, SNA in agriculture was the largest, with a budget of $2.1 million and a staff of 171. A partial list of another 53 associations had combined expenditures of $8 million and 385 employees.[7] These were voluntary associations, so many smaller firms did not belong. By CPC estimates in the late 1960s, 15 percent of all business associations were affiliated with CPC and its five member associations, but these affiliated associations included around 30 percent of entrepreneurs and, most importantly accounted for about 80 percent of total production (Arriagada 1970, 41).[8] Despite the smaller numbers of firms, this constellation of encompassing associations represents a great deal of voluntary investment in collective action for a small, poor society.

In industry, Sofofa built up significant organizational capacity on the dimensions of technical staff and interest intermediation among large firms. Sofofa membership represented only a small proportion of the total number of industrial firms, but it organized most large firms. In 1941 Sofofa represented 792 plants or about 18 percent of industrial plants (Cavarozzi 1975, 108–9). By the 1960s Sofofa's 2,200 members represented only 6.5 percent of all industrialists in the country but accounted for 60 percent of private capital in industry and comprised 80 percent of private industrial capacity.[9] Sofofa's budget reached $1.1 million ($200,000 in 1966 dollars) and its staff numbered about 40 (Cusack 1972, 46). By comparison, in Mexico, where industrial output was several times larger and where dues were compulsory, Concamin had revenues of only $700,000 and Canacintra had $1.5 million (Shafer 1973, 94–5). On the intermediation side, an important indicator of the effectiveness of internal representation is the fact that Sofofa had up to the 1970s brokered several important reconciliations among contending sectoral interests. For example, it was customary for Sofofa to review plans for new investments by members

---

[7] All staff and budget figures are calculated from Cusack (1972, 66) and converted from 1966 dollars to 2000 dollars. See Appendix A for further details.

[8] Of the 85 percent of associations that did not belong to the CPC, the vast majority were local associations for agriculture and commerce.

[9] In a sample of 138 medium-sized and large firms in the 1960s, three-quarters belonged to Sofofa (though only 15 percent participated actively) (Johnson 1968–9, 80). Of those surveyed, half had a negative opinion of Sofofa, and of those, many criticized the association for representing only a minority (which, unsurprisingly, is what large contributors would favor).

to determine if the Chilean market could absorb the new production. In one instance of conflict among two members, Sofofa brokered an agreement whereby the new investment would produce for export (Menges 1966, 348).[10]

What accounts for this comparatively high degree of voluntary collective action by large industrialists, despite the apparent free riding of a majority of industrialists? The small size of the economic elite and the high geographic concentration of industry meant that industrialists probably knew each other socially, so presumably social interaction facilitated monitoring and peer pressure not to free ride.[11] These factors are permissive in reducing barriers to collective action – without, however, providing any positive incentive. The technical business services provided by Sofofa do not appear to have been important, especially to large firms.[12] The more important selective benefit was access through Sofofa. Large industrialists needed to belong in order to have a chance for input into the dozens of policy councils on which Sofofa had a seat. By 1967 Sofofa, "the most widely represented association, had voting representatives on twenty-six state and semiautonomous policy boards, and vocal representatives on eighteen others" (Cusack 1972, 109; see Menges 1966, 350).

The most important of these boards was Corfo, where Sofofa was well represented. Corfo accounted for 8 percent of the national budget in 1941–2 (Cavarozzi 1975, 115). Sofofa,

as well as the other sectoral peak associations, had representation on Corfo's board of directors. More importantly for industrialists, however, they took part in Corfo's planning commissions to a much greater extent than the representatives of other economic sectors. Not once did [Sofofa] raise a serious complaint against Corfo policy. In short, industrialists had ample input in policy formulation and in the design of policy implementation. (Silva 1996, 35)

---

[10] Of course, this cartel-like behavior to regulate markets may have raised barriers to entry, with negative consequences for competition and consumer welfare. The point here is to highlight the institutional strength required to regulate market entry.

[11] In one estimate of the corporate elite or oligarchy, only 169 businesspeople had a combined total of 1,081 positions on boards of directors, giving them control or influence over 60 percent of the publicly listed firms in Chile (Johnson 1967, 62). See Chapter 2 for other indicators of very high economic concentration in Chile.

[12] Cusack (1972, 47) claims that in the 1960s Sofofa had "the most professional and differentiated organization and member services of any private-sector organization," but he does not elaborate on what the services were. In a 1960s survey of 138 medium-sized and large firms, many complained about Sofofa's disorganization and poor services (Johnson 1968–9, 80). Menges (1966, 347) argues that member services were significant, especially from the SNA.

Sofofa representatives also had half of the seats on the board of the state-owned steel company (Cusack 1972, 66). To enhance their ability to participate in these boards, Sofofa leaders established a technical research department in 1956 and invested in it heavily, at least through the 1970s (Cavarozzi 1975, 125).

This pattern of representation on policy boards was a common incentive for collective action in other major associations. From the 1940s to the late 1960s, business associations were widely and deeply represented in the policy process within the state. Sectoral associations in the first half of the century "each lobbied for and obtained the creation of line ministries related to their economic sectors. The directors of these business and landowning associations then gained ample representation in, and access to, the new ministries charged with regulating economic activity in their respective sectors. These linkages became stronger over time" (Silva 1996, 31). By the 1960s in most councils, the pattern was to assign roughly a third of the seats each to government, to the private sector (with few exceptions the CPC business associations), and to "neutral" experts (Cusack 1972, 109). Moreover, in the legislature, associations lobbied, gave testimony, provided data, and "in many instances actually draft[ed] legislation on policy matters pertaining to their economic sector," as well as participating in various ad hoc policy commissions set up by the government (Menges 1966, 352).[13] As one major study from the 1960s summarized: "managing a business association means in Chile having a not insignificant quota of the power of the State, and exactly in those institutions of greatest interest to the business leader" (Arriagada 1970, 21).

Representation on policy boards usually meant more oversight than direct participation in day-to-day policy making. The internal bureaucracies of agencies like Corfo were relatively professional and Weberian, and their decisions were rarely overturned. In addition, since many decisions affected single firms, representatives of business associations on Corfo's board did not want to be perceived as defenders of one firm's interest (Cavarozzi 1975). Moreover, initial business lobbying for representation

---

[13] Given such active interaction with the executive and legislature, it is surprising that there were "*no formal* contacts at all between the business associations and political parties" (Menges 1966, 354). Even in the highly polarized election of 1970, the associations refused to endorse any candidates, and later said they were willing to work with the winner, Allende (Campero 1984, 35, 42). Decades earlier, Sofofa had given "full and public support to Arturo Matte Larraín – undoubtedly 'one of them' – in the 1952 elections as the Liberal and Conservative candidate" (Cavarozzi 1975, 186).

on agency boards was also motivated by a desire to keep politicians out rather than just to let business run the agencies, and business representatives did work to insulate and depoliticize agencies. An indirect indication of the real significance of this formal representation is the extent of the conflict over how many representatives associations were allowed on these boards. Associations complained loudly about underrepresentation and when reformist governments tried to reduce or circumvent formal association representation (Menges 1966, 350).

The pattern of business representation on state boards helps explain the greater investment by business in sectoral rather than encompassing associations and, by extension, helps explain the relative institutional weakness of the CPC compared to its economy-wide counterparts in Mexico. At least through the 1980s, the CPC did not have any representatives on public boards; most representatives of the private sector came from the CPC's member associations (Dugan and Rehren 1990, 121–7). Capitalists in Chile consequently invested more in the long-term institutional capacity (human and material resources) of their sectoral associations than in the CPC.[14]

The appointment of prominent capitalists to high positions in government was common from the 1930s to the 1960s, though the number of appointments could vary greatly from one government to the next.[15] In 1938, the Popular Front government appointed Roberto Wachholtz, from a private oil monopoly, to head the Ministry of Finance in an explicit effort to calm business fears (Cavarozzi 1975, 117). At least four of the seven finance ministers over the period 1938–45 were from business (calculated from Cavarozzi 1975, 158). A minister of the economy in the late 1940s, Fernando Müller Bordeu, was an industrialist, a member of Sofofa, and a landowner (Cavarozzi 1975, 169). Over the middle decades of the twentieth century, Chilean capitalists also became very active in electoral party politics, as Brazilian businessmen would after 1985. In the mid-1960s, 28 percent of 229 higher executives of the 37 largest nonfinancial corporations held national political office, which indicates "an extraordinary level of political consciousness and activism" (Zeitlin and Ratcliff 1988,

---

[14] Cavarozzi claims that the CPC "never became a very effective tool for the representation of entrepreneurial interests" (1975, 110). This characterization was more true of the period of Cavarozzi's study, 1938–64, than later. The CPC became much more important in the late 1960s and again in the 1980s and 1990s.

[15] Before 1973, "almost all middle and upper administrative posts" were filled by appointment (Cleaves 1974, 1).

196). Moreover, a quarter of those who had never held office were related to immediate family members who had (199).[16]

The career of Jorge Alessandri and the composition of his government epitomize the fusion of politics and business. Alessandri's father, Arturo, was president in the 1920s and again in the 1930s. Jorge Alessandri became president of the CPC in 1943 (a position he held on and off for 16 years), then finance minister in 1948–50, senator in 1957, and then president in 1958–64.[17] In his years out of government Alessandri was also a director of Sofofa, president of one of the largest industrial firms, and a director of other industrial and financial corporations (Stallings 1978, 60). His election in 1958 was called the "revolution of the managers," and Alessandri appointed many representatives of the emerging manageriat to government positions (Pinto 1985, 30). Of the 37 ministers Alessandri appointed in his six years in office, 12 were "owners of large farms, and 21 were owners, managers, or directors of industrial, financial, or commercial corporations" (Stallings 1978, 60). Some of these ministers were double-counted as both landowners and industrialists, but in any case, a good majority of his appointees were prominent capitalists.[18] The Alessandri government marked the high point of business appointees in government. Subsequent governments, reformist and military, would not include so many businesspeople.

How did this porous boundary between business and government affect the portfolio of political investments? In early periods, "representation" through appointment seemed to dampen incentives for formal collective action. For example, "in 1928 and 1930 two 'businessmen' conventions were called as a public protest against the lack of influence in Chile's . . . military government. Both conventions quickly dissolved when their leaders were given ministerial posts by the government" (Cusack

---

[16] However, this political activism was more characteristic of big business. Another survey in the 1960s focused on 69 capitalists from medium-sized firms (50–200 workers) and 69 large firms (over 200 workers). Of these, only a handful belonged to a political party and only 20 percent reported participating in the presidential election of 1964 (Johnson 1968–9, 78).

[17] Sofofa was very pleased with Alessandri's nomination as finance minister, called him "one of us," and stated that "Alessandri's ideas are our own ideas" (cited in Cavarozzi 1975, 175). After Alessandri was reshuffled out of the cabinet in 1950, two other businessmen were appointed ministers (Cavarozzi 1975, 184).

[18] Of course, capitalists are often disappointed by businessmen politicians once they take office. In a survey during the Frei government, nearly a third of the business respondents felt that industrialists' interests would be better served by the reformist president, Eduardo Frei, than by Alessandri ($N = 138$; Johnson 1968–9, 83).

1972, 14). However, by the 1960s other factors worked to maintain incentives for investing in associations, parties, and elections, even though representation by appointment in the Alessandri government was so high. For one, associations had privileged formal access to public boards and intermediated informal contacts with capitalists in government (Stallings 1978, 80–1). More importantly, the electoral expansion of the political center and left encouraged business simultaneously to invest defensively in associations, parties, and elections, since they could not count on the electoral success of candidates like Alessandri in the future.

Government Reformism Strengthened Encompassing Associations, 1964–1973

After the mid-1960s, reformist threats to property rights and the closing of some prior channels of communication led business leaders to resurrect the CPC, which had lain dormant since the late 1930s. In 1966 its annual budget was only $165,000 ($31,000 in 1966 dollars), just a fraction (a little over 3 percent) of the total spent by its five member associations, and it had a small staff of eight people (Cusack 1972, 66). After 1966, CPC associations elected new leaders and embarked on a major program of mass mobilization and contestation, which some argue was so effective that it contributed to the rightward shift of the government in the last year's of Eduardo Frei Montalva's presidency (see Cusack 1972 for the full story; see also Garcia 1973, 73). Landowners and their association, the SNA, felt acutely both the loss of influence of business associations through existing channels and the threat to property rights presented by government proposals for land reform. Although SNA representatives had seats in various policy councils, they were ignored by government representatives, who held a majority (Dugan and Rehren 1990, 126). SNA leaders felt excluded and singled out, and turned to the CPC. They argued to other CPC members that agrarian reform presented a general threat and that business should mobilize collectively in the defense of private enterprise. In the end, the other associations agreed to join with SNA in reviving CPC and opposing reforms of the Frei government, even if they did not feel equally excluded.[19] Sofofa and other

---

[19] Initially, a faction of industry argued that Sofofa should endorse agrarian reform as a means to expand the domestic market, but they were dissuaded from pressing this position (Menges 1966, 360). On other issues, CPC was unable to broker a compromise

sectoral associations maintained their institutional representation on government commissions and boards. Sofofa in fact increased its representation from 34 public entities in 1965 to 39 in 1968 (Dugan and Rehren 1990, 127). Although unintended state actions prompted this encompassing collective action in CPC, once business mobilized, the government, especially President Frei, provided further support for the CPC by commending the democratic participation by business and by attending CPC conventions.

The Allende government intensified business exclusion and threatened property rights across all sectors. It reduced the representation of Sofofa on the boards of public enterprises from 27 to 8 firms and twice threatened to cancel its legal recognition (Dugan and Rehren 1990, 130). The CPC abstained from endorsing any candidates in the 1970 elections and vowed to work with the winner, Allende (Campero 1984, 35). However, before long, CPC and especially Sofofa were active coup conspirators (Silva 1998, 222). Orlando Sáenz, president of Sofofa during the Allende government, said that "Allende managed things so badly, so badly that he did not succeed in dividing the private sector" (Campero 1984, 58). By 1972 encompassing associations were joining together to oppose Allende. For example, Sofofa, SNA, other members of CPC, and other associations joined the trucker strike of October 1972 (Drake 1978, 114). This opposition mobilization tended to strengthen the associations and compensate, in terms of organizational incentives, for the loss of privileged access.

After the military coup in 1973, temporarily restored access by associations to government policy makers revived incentives for collective action. In the months leading up to the coup, a select group of representatives from business, working in Sofofa offices, devised an economic program for the military government. This program was later endorsed by a CPC convention three months after the coup. The pre- and post-coup involvement of business associations in designing economic policy briefly reinvigorated major business associations, especially Sofofa and CPC, and was initially very different from the pattern in Brazil (Silva 1996, 90). In Brazil in the early 1960s, capitalists mobilized to depose Goulart, though not through a peak association, and the Brazilian generals did not consult with

among the sectoral associations. In one instance in the 1960s, Corfo was going to finance the establishment of a tractor factory. Sofofa and the Chamber of Commerce endorsed the project. But SNA opposed it, and "after several years of bitter SNA–SFF [Sofofa] repartee, Corfo finally dropped the idea" (Menges 1966, 362).

business associations in designing economic policy. As a result, encompassing collective action waned quickly in Brazil shortly after the coup. Chilean associations went through a similar cycle, but in slow motion.

From Demobilization to Remobilization under Military Dictatorship, 1973–1989

By 1975 Pinochet had consolidated personal power and appointed a team of neoliberal economists, the "Chicago boys," to restructure the economy. At the same time, some leaders from sectoral associations and association staffers were also appointed to top positions in line ministries. Leaders from SNA or from Sonami were appointed, for example, to top positions in the ministries of agriculture and mining, respectively (Dugan and Rehren 1990, 132). However, the radical neoliberal technocrats quickly expanded their control over economic policy. In the process, they excluded business associations from access to policy making; instead they developed close informal ties to a few of the largest conglomerates (Schamis 2002, Chapter 3; Silva 1996, 107, 130).

The second half of the 1970s was a debilitating period for business associations. Government officials reversed nearly all of the policies that had previously encouraged collective action in associations. Top economic policy makers were generally wary of contact with organized interest groups and worried that consultation would contaminate their reforms (Silva 1998, 227). The Pinochet government rapidly dismantled the representative structure constructed over the previous decades. The boards of core government agencies such as Corfo and the Banco Central were purged of the many representatives from business associations. The boards of the remaining state enterprises (most were privatized) were also reduced, and military officers replaced representatives of business associations (Dugan and Rehren 1990, 132–3). Other indirect incentives for encompassing collective action also faded because the dictatorship thoroughly repressed labor and leftist parties and staunchly defended property rights. Moreover, the economic restructuring divided member associations within CPC, some of which favored radical trade liberalization and others, especially Sofofa, did not. Lastly, the government imposed controls on leadership selection in business associations through 1981, which in practice froze in place the leaders of 1973, so members had few incentives to participate in the association with a view toward influencing internal succession (Silva 1998, 227). Sofofa's budget reflected these changing incentives: it rose over the 1960s to $2.2 million by 1971 but then fell to $1 million in the late 1970s. By the 1990s the budget was back to around $2 million (see Appendix A).

Relations between business associations and the Pinochet government changed dramatically in the early 1980s and recast associations as the primary intermediaries in a much closer and more encompassing relationship between business and government. The economic crisis that swept Latin America in 1982–3 was particularly virulent in Chile. After the initial shock, business leaders came to the conclusion that the sectoral associations would have to work through the CPC to develop a joint position on what package of policies the government should adopt to confront the crisis. This decision was at least partly due to the signals from government that they would not consider special requests for emergency relief from isolated sectors and that business therefore had to come to a consensus on a joint program (Silva 1998, 229).

Consensus was not easy to reach, and sectoral leaders labored hard through the CPC in a series of meetings (including a retreat to the country estate of the CPC president) in early 1983 to work out a common program, which they launched publicly in July 1983 (Silva 1998, 230).[20] This instance of consensus building was an important indicator of CPC's strength in periods of crisis. Although the CPC lacked organizational resources like a large professional staff, it still showed remarkable institutional strength in key moments along the other core dimension of institutional strength, interest intermediation. Among numerous divisions across the sectoral associations, Sofofa pushed for differentiated tariffs against the preferences of the other associations for uniform tariffs. In the end, the CPC president gave Sofofa an ultimatum: either accept uniform tariffs or be excluded from drafting the overall CPC plan for economic recovery (Silva 1998, 230). Sofofa acceded. In the end, the efforts at interest reconciliation within CPC paid off. After 1983, government officials rapidly adopted many of the CPC's proposals, as well as sectoral programs proposed by CPC member associations (Silva 1998, 232; see also Campero 1995, 140).

After 1983 Pinochet offered many top government positions to business. Elite circulation expanded, but as in Colombia, business associations were important conduits for this circulation (Silva 1996, 163). Starting in

---

[20] Consensus building involved intense discussions not only among CPC members but also within member associations, some of which had suffered internal rifts in the 1970s. Sofofa, for example, was unable to maintain unity throughout the radical neoliberal restructuring of the 1970s (Silva 1996).

early 1984, "most economic ministers were leaders of organized business," and many of them helped to draft the CPC's economic program (Silva 1998, 232). Modesto Collados headed the construction association before his appointment as minister of the economy (1984–5). His successor as minister from 1985 to 1987, Juan Délano, was previously the president of the Chamber of Commerce. Ministers of agriculture and mining during this period were also drawn from the leadership of agricultural and mining associations, respectively (Campero 1995, 140).

This representation through appointments did not displace representation through associations but rather, as in Colombia, paralleled and reinforced the role of associations. State actors worked closely with business associations and reincorporated representatives from associations into various councils and commissions. In 1984, for example, Pinochet created the 100-member Consejo Económico y Social (CES) and appointed members from associations to it. The CES both responded to government requests for opinions on policy proposals and made proposals of its own (Dugan and Rehren 1990, 133). In addition, CPC leaders had regular access to top economic policy makers to discuss macroeconomic policies such as those concerning interest and exchange rates. Other associations had privileged access to numerous commissions and subcommissions that dealt with policies like those on housing, agricultural prices, and drawback schemes. Collaboration with government did not revolve just around negotiating broad policy goals but also included detailed negotiation between mid-level officials in the ministries and the technical staffs of associations over drafting specific legislation (Silva 1998, 233).

These various forms of regular consultation by government officials with business associations renewed incentives for investing in business associations in several specific ways. First, the associations needed much better technical staff. Silva concludes that

one of the positive consequences of this system of interaction for organized business has been its professionalization. In the 1970s, only the SFF [Sofofa] had a technical department capable of analyzing and developing policy proposals. Ten to fifteen years later, each of the other five sectoral associations and the CPC established sophisticated technical departments of their own. Meanwhile the SFF's department of studies expanded even further." (Silva 1996, 205)

The informal access by association leaders, as well as their occasional appointment to ministries, increased the value of participating in leadership selection. Lastly, the premium associations and the government placed on reaching consensus positions in the CPC and other associations increased the value of participating at meetings. Although it is hard to quantify, big business invested a great deal more time and resources in their associations.[21]

Why did the Pinochet government change its relationship with business so dramatically and greatly increase the incentives for business to invest in their associations? On the economic front, the crisis years of 1982–3 increased vulnerabilities for economic policy makers and increased their incentives to work with business associations to manage the policy response to the crisis. The political logic of seeking general political support from business associations was also clear, especially in the timing of overtures to organized business during 1983 in the midst of the most active and vocal political opposition to the military regime. The government met the street demonstrations that began in May 1983, and the intensified opposition by labor and the left, with renewed repression. What was more worrisome was the prospect that moderate and business supporters might break with the military government and join the opposition. Smaller firms organized several meetings in 1982 that generated declarations critical of government policy (Campero 1995, 135–6). The CPC and the big businesses it represented avoided open confrontation. Nonetheless, the military regime was more politically vulnerable than it had been in the 1970s, and its overtures to business associations helped it weather the protests of 1983 and bolstered the authoritarian regime for the rest of the decade. The CPC remained a staunch supporter and later in the decade led business support for the "yes" vote to extend Pinochet's rule in the 1988 plebiscite (Campero 1995, 146).

Democratization and Business Politics in the 1990s

The Concertación coalition of parties headed by the Christian Democrats also maintained close contact with business associations before and after the transfer of power from Pinochet in 1990. This contact helped smooth the transition to democracy. Unlike most other countries in Latin America, Chile's transition to democracy occurred during an economic boom, and many in business feared that the new center–left government would snuff it out. Concertación members used consultation with

---

[21] Campero (1995) provides a chronology of the many meetings, discussions, negotiations, and conferences business organized in the 1980s to generate consensus and overcome old divisions.

associations to attempt to assuage investors and assure them that they were not going to roll back the neoliberal development strategy. Once in office, officials in the government of Patricio Aylwin (1990–4) continued negotiating with business associations, especially over sensitive policy areas like taxes and labor law (see Chapter 8). The CPC was the major protagonist from the business side. The issues of political transition, taxation, redistribution, and development strategy all affected business as a whole and, where sectoral preferences diverged, required intermediation by a multisectoral association like the CPC.

In 1994 and 1996 the administration of Eduardo Frei Ruiz-Tagle (1994–2000) convoked National Production Forums to bring together representatives of government, business, and in the second forum labor (though in a subordinate role). In the context of these forums, the Ministry of the Economy and the CPC set up long-term "working commissions" in which "the leaders of the CPC and the sectoral associations meet with government officials to define an agenda for action, after which the research departments of the sectoral peak associations and the relevant government agency hammer out the details of the policy based on technical criteria" (Silva 1998, 240). This sort of interaction maintained the incentives for simultaneous investment by business in consensus building in the CPC, in active participation in associations, and in technical personnel in the sectoral associations.

However, over the course of the 1990s, some of the core issues in business–government consultation became more detailed and often sector specific. So, for example, integration into regional trading blocs became a major issue in the mid-1990s. Regional integration held variable prospects, especially for industry (Sofofa) and agriculture (SNA). In the end, the divergences were too great for the CPC, and SNA and Sofofa dealt separately and directly with the government (see Chapter 8). When trade topped the list of members' concerns, CPC was increasingly dispensable. At the same time that Sofofa was disagreeing with SNA and CPC, it also began attracting nonindustrial members, and to the extent that Sofofa became encompassing, it had even less need for interest aggregation in CPC. Differences between Sofofa and CPC widened over the 1990s. In the mid-1990s, Walter Riesco (ex-president of Sonami), with support from landowners (SNA), defeated Pedro Lizana (ex-president of Sofofa) in the first contested elections for the presidency of CPC. By late 1998 relations had deteriorated to the point where Sofofa President Felipe Lamarca stopped attending CPC meetings. After a year of abstention, Sofofa withdrew its economic contribution in early 2000.

The crisis was apparently resolved in May 2000 through some tinkering with the CPC statutes (mostly designed to exclude past presidents) and streamline decision making within the CPC (see *El Diario*, 10 May 2000, p. 27).

Sofofa, in contrast, adapted well to policy shifts in the 1990s, grew more encompassing, and maintained its institutional strength. The shift in the policy agenda, and government invitations for associations to participate in trade negotiations, generated important changes within Sofofa (interview with Hugo Baierlein, 9 May 2000). In 1995 Sofofa hired an ex-government official with long experience in international trade, who, in turn, transformed Sofofa's international trade department from a skeleton crew of two people into Sofofa's largest department, with over a dozen professional staff. Sofofa members and staff worked closely with government officials in all aspects of trade negotiations. Moreover, by entering into various trade treaties, Chilean negotiators committed Chilean exporters to abide by the rules of origin stipulated in these agreements. Certifying manufacturing exports then became a major administrative task that the government decided to delegate to Sofofa. Sofofa charged for this service, open to all manufacturers, whether or not affiliated with Sofofa, and these charges not only covered costs but also contributed another 10 percent to Sofofa's overall operating budget (interview with Pedro Lizana, 10 May 2000).

In the 1990s, as in previous decades of political change, Chilean capitalists adapted their organizations rapidly to the changing relation between business and government. In particular, government consultation was initially intense with CPC but then shifted more toward sectoral peak associations like Sofofa. CPC consequently weakened as incentives to compromise among sectors faded. Sofofa, in contrast, maintained its institutional capacity and shifted it to focus heavily on international trade. As in the late 1980s, business–government relations were largely harmonious and largely channeled through associations.[22] It was no longer defensive mobilization that provided centripetal incentives but rather positive incentives of access and delegation that supported encompassing collective action. Moreover, the Concertación government reversed the practices of the 1980s and did not appoint businesspeople to top government posts. In terms of the portfolio analogy, democratization opened up opportunities

---

[22] Pedro Gúzman, president of CPC in 1990–6, claimed that during his term and afterward, "the government prefers to consult with a single interlocutor" for the private sector (interview 9 May 2000).

for business to participate in parties and elections, but the new center–left government closed off representation through appointments and at the same time maintained close contact with associations.

Conclusions

Throughout the twentieth century, the high density of civil and political society in Chile stood out in Latin America. Parties were among the strongest in the region, and labor unions, business associations, church, and other civil organizations were all vibrant. For a nation of "joiners" it comes as less of a surprise that business too should be well organized. However, there was much more to the evolved strength of organized business in Chile than a cultural proclivity to belong. The state, in intended and unintended ways, gave business consistent and powerful incentives to invest in associations.

Political logics for the state promotion of collective action regularly stood out in Chile. Struggling governments repeatedly called on business associations. Popular Front and Radical presidents in the 1930s and 1940s, Pinochet in the 1980s, and Aylwin in the 1990s all worried about business defection and courted business support through consultation with business associations and, with the notable exception of Concertación governments, appointment of businessmen to top government positions. During the Radical governments, political leaders attempted to assuage business fears about the expanding developmental state by granting them representation on public boards of new developmental agencies. Pinochet and Aylwin turned to business to gain support or at least reduce or fragment political opposition. In each period the formal incorporation of representatives of associations in policy making increased the incentives for member firms to invest in their associations. State actors provided access to mitigate short-term political and policy vulnerabilities, and as a by-product contributed to building longer-term institutional capacity in business associations.

The experience of Chilean associations earlier in the twentieth century also highlights the salience of defensive organization. Labor was better organized and more radical than in the other four countries. Movement towards labor unity helped sectoral business associations to overcome their differences and create the CPC in 1933. Labor and leftist resurgence in the 1960s prompted capitalists to resurrect the CPC and invest in a general campaign in defense of free enterprise. However, business associations did not negotiate directly with labor unions. Hence, the targets of business mobilization against labor and the left were the state, public opinion, and electoral politics.

In terms of the overall portfolio of investment options, Chilean business (like Colombian business) was less singleminded in investing in associations than was big business in Mexico. In Mexico, the lack of options for business representation through parties, legislative lobbies, or ministerial appointments channeled political investment into associations. In Chile, in contrast, pro-business parties were stronger, as was the legislature in democratic periods, and appointed positions in government were sometimes open to business, yet business still invested a great deal in associations. Chilean businesspeople invested more in parties and elections than did their counterparts in Mexico during PRI hegemony prior to the 1990s; however, they rarely won elections. In the context of intensely polarized electoral politics, business also needed nonpartisan entities like a business associations to negotiate with the parties that regularly defeated pro-business parties. Most importantly, though, besides access through parties and appointments, state actors usually provided privileged access only through associations for some policy areas, so that investment in associations still yielded important returns.

The balancing of political portfolios in Chile can also be viewed in the shifting roles and relative power of the CPC vis-à-vis its member associations. The CPC played a central role in aggregating business interests and negotiating with the state in the late 1930s and early 1940s, the late 1960s and early 1970s, and the late 1980s and early 1990s. In the intervening periods the CPC was sometimes characterized as dormant. A graph of investment over time in CPC, and in its institutional capacity, would show fluctuations over the course of the twentieth century. Similar graphs for sectoral associations would show less variation in capacity because sectoral associations had, at least through Pinochet, institutionalized access. The lines on the graph representing investment in sectoral associations would be straighter, rising through the 1950s and into the 1960s, then falling sharply (along with the CPC) in the late 1970s and rising steadily from the 1980s into the 1990s. The key dimension of organizational strength in the CPC was not its staff, which was always small, but rather its ability to reconcile differences and promote consensus. The CPC could do this in periods of crisis, both political and economic in the Great Depression, in the reformism of the late 1960s and early 1970s, in the debt crisis of the early 1980s, and finally in the transition of the early 1990s. In these periods business invested enough resources (mostly time) to build that consensus.[23] In other periods, state actors encouraged greater participation by sectoral associations, most recently in trade negotiations, and big business reduced its investment in consensus building through the CPC.

---

[23] Measured just in terms of opportunity cost, consensus building can be an extremely costly process involving hundreds of person-hours of those attending meetings of the CPC and thousands of person-hours for meetings among members of the sectoral associations, as well as travel time, preparation time, premeeting sidebar discussions, etc. Hiring an economist, by comparison, is relatively inexpensive.

7

Business Politics in Argentina

Fragmented and Politicized

> If the liberty of association is a fruitful source of advantages and prosperity to some nations, it may be perverted or carried to excess by others, and the element of life may be changed into an element of destruction.
>
> Alexis de Tocqueville, 1835[1]

Introduction

Rivalry, politicization, and weak institutional capacity characterize most of the history of business associations, especially encompassing associations, in Argentina. For the second half of the twentieth century the associational domain for business was unstable, partisan, fragmented, and competitive for firms within the same sectors. By the end of the century, the outcomes in terms of organization and business–government relations could hardly have been more different from those in Chile. In contrast to Chile's strong encompassing associations and multiple institutional channels for associations to participate in policy making, Argentina lacked a single stable economy-wide association (despite repeated attempts to create one), and other associations had few consistent channels, either formal or informal, for input into policy making.

Chile, Colombia, and Mexico all tend to the more organized, societal corporatist end of the continuum in Latin America. Brazil and Argentina cluster on the disorganized end of the continuum. Business is disorganized in different ways in Brazil and Argentina, though in both cases mostly as the legacy of meddling by state actors in business organization.

[1] Cited in Dahl (1982, 1).

In Brazil the distortions of state-regulated corporatism discouraged investment in voluntary encompassing associations. In Argentina state actors, especially in the governments of Juan Perón, rendered business politics more politicized and fluid. As for Brazil, the analytic challenge in the Argentine case is not only to explain why strong associations did not exist by the late twentieth century but also why previously robust, institutionalized associations, backed by steady investment in collective action by elite members, degenerated over the second half of the century. The explanation lies mostly in the actions of political leaders who attempted to use associations to mobilize support or undercut opposition. Over time these attempts exacerbated and reinforced existing economic cleavages, making encompassing collective action increasingly difficult. Among the various political logics analyzed in previous chapters, the logic of organizing supporters and disorganizing opponents was clearly dominant for state actors in Argentina. Other more practical motivations for officials to collaborate with associations – such as seeking to aggregate business preferences or to enlist business assistance in policy implementation – occasionally arose, but were usually drowned out by partisan conflict or abandoned due to the institutional weakness of associations.

In comparison to the other countries, the Argentine case highlights the relative causal weakness of defensive mobilization in generating lasting associations, especially in the absence of positive selective benefits such as privileged access. The history of business associations in Argentina is littered with acronyms of associations (see Appendix A for a partial list) created to combat perceived threats, yet quickly discarded once the threats had passed, usually after the military had forcibly removed the offending government. Beginning in the 1920s with efforts to counter labor organization and continuing through many opposition movements, especially against Peronist governments (and against the rival associations these governments supported), big business created numerous encompassing associations. However, the jumble of acronyms generated by these mobilizations signified little more than transitory coordinating efforts without any deeper organizational grounding in formal by-laws, staff, or offices. By the 1980s coordinating groups had dropped the custom of creating new acronyms and referred to themselves simply by the number of associations involved: "*grupo de los 8*" or "*grupo de los 12.*" None of these coordinating bodies were granted, after the initial threats had past, any special or lasting benefits by the government. They had little therefore to do and subsequently disbanded.

The exception in Argentina, which highlights the general rule, is the CGE (Confederación General Económica), the Peronist-backed economy-wide association. The CGE received significant benefits from Peronist governments in the early 1950s and again in the early 1970s. These benefits, especially high-level access, helped the CGE associations attract members and resources but only so long as Peronists were in power. Once Peronist governments were forcibly removed, new military rulers rescinded CGE privileges, members defected, and its institutional capacity plummeted.

Agriculture and Industry Developed Strong Associations before Perón

Starting in the nineteenth century and building through the end of World War II, big business organized strong, voluntary associations for agriculture and industry. Economic elites in Argentina organized early and independently: the Sociedad Rural Argentina (SRA) in 1866 and the Unión Industrial Argentina (UIA) in 1887. Both associations were encompassing in their respective sectors and beyond. Moreover, both associations enjoyed close relations with most governments through 1946. In this period SRA had more members in government than perhaps any association in the region ever since.

The Sociedad Rural organized the landowning elite. Between 1910 and 1946, membership varied between 2,000 and 5,000, usually averaging around 2,500. The SRA had a secret admissions procedure that favored the ranching elite (around three-quarters of SRA members listed residences in Buenos Aires). SRA members represented only 10 percent of all ranchers; "as much as any other single institution, the Rural Society stood for the landowning aristocracy" (Smith 1969, 50). SRA was an association of the largest agricultural interests and allowed other associations to emerge to represent smaller farms and tenant farmers. And the SRA elite dominated politics. From 1910 to 1943, five of nine presidents of Argentina, over 40 percent of all ministers ($N = 93$), 12 of 14 ministers of agriculture, and roughly 15 percent of all members of Congress belonged to the SRA (Smith 1969, 48–50).

In industry, fractious infighting, which was to plague relations among industrialists in the late twentieth century, erupted in the late nineteenth century even before the formation of the UIA and before there was much industry to organize. In 1874 industrialists formed the Club Industrial Argentino. Only four years later, a dissident group left the Club to found a rival Centro Industrial Argentino. A variety of issues divided capitalists in the Club and Centro including ideology, national political factions, firm

size (Club members included more small-scale artisans), and sector (the
Centro included members from agriculture and commerce). Although the
participants and context were completely different a century later, state
actors and politics had reinforced similar divisions among industrialists.
It was only in 1887, 13 years later, that the 500 members of the Club and
400 members of the Centro agreed to merge into the UIA.[2]

After this rocky start, the UIA grew to become a major industrial association for the representation of big business. By 1946 UIA had around
3,000 individual members and 91 affiliated associations (Lindenboim
1976, 169). By mid-century UIA seemed to presage the similar evolution of voluntary industry associations in Chile (Sofofa) and Colombia
(ANDI). For example, by 1944 UIA was represented in 24 government
commissions or organs, including the board of the recently created Banco
Industrial, where UIA had three representatives (Schvarzer 1991, 84).
UIA's membership also included firms in finance, commerce, and agriculture, and many industrial firms also had interests in other sectors, so,
as in ANDI and later in Sofofa, UIA was more encompassing than just
industry from an early date (Brennan 1998, 83).[3]

Although the SRA and UIA, along with several other sectoral associations, dominated the associational landscape in the first half of the twentieth century, business also invested in several economy-wide associations,
including the Asociación de Trabajo, CACIP (Confederación Argentina
del Comercio, de la Industria, y de la Producción), and the Federación
Argentina de Entidades Defensores del Comercio y la Industria. SRA
and UIA dominated their respective domains for elites in their sectors;
however, representation at the economy-wide level remained fragmented
among these rival and overlapping associations. In response to growing labor organization and radicalization after 1916, business created
several encompassing employer associations (Acuña 1998, 61–2). The
Asociación de Trabajo, created in 1918, was designed to confront new
labor organizations and included provisions for an employers' defense
fund. Other business leaders formed a second encompassing association,
CACIP, also to oppose labor and to present the employer perspective in
political debates over state regulation of labor. Later in the 1930s, business
created the Federación Argentina de Entidades Defensores del Comercio

---

[2] On the early history, see Schvarzer (1991), Cúneo (1967), and the UIA's websites,
http://www.uia.ar/ pages lauminar.htm, elclubi.htm and elcentr.htm (as of 29 April 1998).
See Appendix A for more background on members and changes in organization over time.
[3] By one calculation, nearly one-quarter of the capital of UIA members in the 1940s was in
firms outside of industry (Lindenboim 1976, 180).

y la Industria (Lindenboim 1976). Each of these associations staked out distinctive political positions and targeted different, though overlapping, membership bases (see Lindenboim 1976 for the full story). For example, the Asociación del Trabajo focused on labor issues and tended to assume more right-wing positions (associated with the Liga Patriótica Argentina). CACIP was more moderate and brought together a larger number of firms, many foreign owned, in agriculture and commerce. The Federación drew more members from national industry and from provinces outside Buenos Aires. However, none of these encompassing associations developed much institutional capacity, and none endured beyond the 1940s.

Overall, the trajectory of Argentine sectoral associations as of 1945 did not look very different from developments across the mountains in Chile. Business had strong encompassing associations in major sectors like agriculture, industry, and commerce. In Argentina the associations were voluntary, and some, like UIA, had institutionalized access to the state. Economy-wide associations in both countries were also embryonic before the 1940s, but significantly, they were multiple and fragmented in Argentina. However, a decade of Peronist government would decisively alter the trajectory of all Argentine associations, transform business organization, and deepen economic and organizational cleavages that would continue to thwart efforts at encompassing collective action for decades afterward.

Perón Politicized Business Representation, 1946–1983

From a comparative perspective, it is somewhat puzzling that Perón did not develop a more collaborative relationship with business, as Vargas had in Brazil and as post-Cárdenas PRI governments were doing in Mexico in the 1940s. Economically, industry fared very well under Perón from 1946 to 1955. Government support helped industry expand, and profits were higher than ever before (Brennan 1998, 82; Polit 1968, 404). Carlos Alfredo Tornquist, a big industrialist and UIA leader, emphasized "the fact that we industrialists have never made as much money as in the past few years" (*Acción Industrial*, 15 June 1948, cited in Cúneo 1967, 181). Decades later, industrialists still remembered Perón's first government as a golden age for industry. When asked in 1971 in a survey of 112 industrial elites what was the best period for industry, 30 percent – a higher percentage than for any other period – named the years 1945–55 (Petras and Cook 1972, 394). Although a full examination of this counterfactual – why a more cooperative relationship between Perón and organization business never emerged – is beyond the scope of this section, comparisons to other cases suggest several plausible hypotheses including Perón's relative political uninterest, the more accommodating environment of the postwar international economy, and the high degree of prior organization by industry in UIA, as well as UIA's electoral forays against Perón.

The UIA was the only encompassing association for industry until the Perón government "intervened" it in 1946 and then outlawed it in 1953. The intervention in 1946 had several motives: the UIA had supported Perón's opponent in the elections; the UIA had opposed many of Perón's social and labor policies (Cappelletti 1985, 13); and Perón wanted to create an officially sanctioned business counterpart to the labor confederation. Over the course of Perón's rise to power in the 1940s, UIA split among those who favored working with him and those who preferred active opposition. UIA member Raúl Lamuraglia led the movement to muster UIA support for the candidate running against Perón in the 1946 elections. Lamuraglia channeled several million dollars into his campaign (see Schvarzer 1991, 92–4, for the full story).[4] Shortly after Perón won the election in 1946, UIA held its own internal elections. Members of the faction that favored open opposition to Perón had a hard time keeping a candidate in the running. Every time they found a member willing to head the slate, Peronist officials talked him out of running. The anti-Peronist faction managed to keep one candidate, Pascual Gambino, out of the country during the UIA campaign and get him elected. The government "intervened" UIA several months later and apparently retaliated against Gambino, who rapidly lost most of his personal fortune (Schvarzer 1991, 95).

After intervening in the UIA for several years in an attempt to transform it into an official Peronist business association, Perón "liquidated" the UIA in 1953 and confiscated its assets. In its stead Perón promoted the rival CGE (preceded briefly by ephemeral acronyms like AAPIC, CEA, and CAPIC; see Appendix A). The fact that Perón waited until 1953 to liquidate the UIA suggests that he was looking for ways to establish some kind of working relationship with the UIA, and that he found other associational initiatives wanting (Brennan 1998, 84, 89). Other reports indicate

---

[4] Business contributions to campaigns were common practice, though rarely public. In this election campaign, an attentive, and possibly Peronist, employee of the Central Bank's clearing house came across one check for over $500,000 (300,000 pesos in 1946) that he took to the press, fueling public antagonism between Perón and UIA opponents (Schvarzer 1991, 93).

that organizing business support was not a top priority in the early years of Perón's government. Compared to state actors in other countries in the difficult years of the Depression and World War, Perón faced less daunting political and economic vulnerabilities. He had just won a resounding electoral mandate, and the international economy was very accommodating. According to former Minister of Economy Alfredo Gómez Morales,

> while Perón had frequently suggested that it might be useful to develop and institutionalize private-sector collaboration with the government, he was too much in a hurry to complete his economic reforms to expend the effort needed to build such collaboration. Instead, he preferred either to speak directly with individual cattlemen and industrialists when help was needed or, more often, just to ignore them.... (Interview cited in Manzetti 1993a, 289).[5]

State actors like Vargas in the 1930s or leaders of the Popular Front in Chile faced more difficult environments when they sought out business support and therefore had stronger incentives to help business organize.

In the early 1950s, economic and political conditions in Argentina took a turn for the worse and increased the vulnerabilities of the Peronist government. As hypothesized in Chapter 2, these vulnerabilities, in turn, raised the incentives for state actors to consult with business, and Perón returned in earnest to the issue of organizing business and formalizing its representation in his government (Mainwaring 1986, 24). Perón decided to foster new organizations to supplant the UIA and turned to an incipient CGE that had formed in 1952 in the provinces. In the worsening context of the early 1950s, Perón's vulnerabilities increased on multiple fronts. Perón's goal in seeking business support was partly to manage "the severe economic problems of his second administration," but "above all, ..., Perón used the CGE to strengthen business in order to lessen his dependence on the unions and reverse declining labor productivity and increasing labor demands" (Brennan 1998, 96). In contrast to the UIA and to Perón's previous halfhearted attempts to organize business support, both of which focused on large firms in and around Buenos Aires, the CGE represented provincial, small, and newer business and supported a more nationalist, protectionist development strategy of import substitution (Imaz 1964, 140–1).

---

[5] Perón had earlier expressed a preference for dealing individually with industrialists rather than with UIA: "I call the owners of the factories and I do not call the Unión Industrial ... I do not accept the Unión Industrial, the frontmen (testaferros) paid by employers organizations. Therefore I call the owner of the factory and not the director of Unión Industrial. I do not accept intermediaries" (Perón quoted in *La Prensa*, 27 December 1944, as cited in Cúneo 1967, 175–6).

Perón employed state corporatist mechanisms to help the CGE organize. The CGE was an encompassing peak association composed of three
confederations of industry, commerce, and agriculture; informally the industry confederation CGI (Confederación General de la Industria) dominated the CGE (O'Donnell 1988, 35)). The 1953 decree on Asociaciones
Professionales de Empleadores made dues but not membership obligatory
(Cappelletti 1985, 39). Government decrees also established an internal
structure for the CGE, similar to the structure that Vargas promoted in
Brazil, that overrepresented small firms and less industrialized provinces
(Brennan 1998, 95–6). Perón established official business representation
through the CGE and gave its president, José Gelbard, representation on
the Comisión Económica Consultiva, as well as a seat at cabinet meetings
(Schvarzer 1991, 102; Teichman 1981, 150).[6] CGE representatives also
sat on the numerous subcommittees of the Comisión Consultiva, and
overall "the CGE exercised a considerable degree of influence on government economic policy in the final years of Perón's government" (Brennan
1998, 96). Not surprisingly, capitalists flocked to join the CGE, and the
CGE, in turn, provided political support to Perón. However, the CGE's
loyalty to Perón would soon become a liability when Perón was out of
power.

After Perón's ouster in 1955, subsequent political conflicts deepened the
cleavages and animosity between Peronist (CGE) and non-Peronist associations (UIA, SRA, CAC [Cámara Argentina de Comercio], and others).
The military government that deposed Perón in 1955 almost immediately
outlawed the CGE and later barred past CGE leaders from assuming
leadership positions in other business associations (Cúneo 1967, 230).
Industrialists migrated back to the resurrected UIA (Brennan 1998, 100).
In 1958 the new government of Arturo Frondizi reinstated the CGE. In
response, anti-Peronist associations – UIA, SRA, CAC, the Stock Market
Association, the Grain Exchange, and the Banking Association – counter
mobilized to establish ACIEL (Acción Coordinadora de las Instituciones
Empresariales Libres).

Thus, from the late 1950s through the early 1970s, Peronist and anti-
Peronist businesspeople maintained parallel, redundant, and competing
business associations. The CGE had sectoral member federations in industry, agriculture, and commerce that duplicated and competed with those

---

[6] Maria Seaone (1998) gives a complete account of Gelbard's remarkable career both in
creating the CGE and his later return to the center of power in the second Perón government.

of ACIEL. Generally, the UIA represented big industry and accounted for a majority of total production but had territorial gaps; the CGE covered more territory, had more members (smaller firms), and hence counted a greater proportion of all firms in its membership. Both associations claimed, with differing justifications, to be more representative of industry. To hedge, industrialists often affiliated with UIA sectorally and CGE regionally (Cappelletti 1985, 82). But conflict between the CGE and ACIEL continued and often turned nasty. For example, in the early 1960s ACIEL campaigned to have CGE assets returned to the firms that had been forced through compulsory dues to pay into the CGE (Cúneo 1967, 272 fn).

A survey of leaders of rival industrial associations in the 1960s captured the spirit, or dispiritedness, of the times. Among other things, the survey found that two-thirds of the leaders felt that their efforts to influence politics had failed (Freels 1970, 443). UIA leaders viewed the rival CGI as a Peronist "creation" led by "political hacks who sought to . . . satisfy ego needs frustrated by their failure" in business. CGI leaders, in turn, viewed the UIA as "foreign dominated," undemocratic, and unresponsive to the needs of small business (Freels 1970, 445). Despite these animosities, nearly 80 percent of respondents from both camps favored unity between CGI and UIA (Freels 1970, 446). Such widespread sympathy for unity suggests that organizational divisions among industry associations were as much the result of politics as of natural cleavages within industry.

Despite the strong endorsement by UIA and ACIEL (though not the CGE) of the coup that brought the government of Juan Carlos Onganía to power in 1966, "these organizations had no institutionalized access to the new regime's decisions" (Manzetti 1993a, 300). These associations mobilized business opposition to the previous civilian government but, as in Brazil, languished after the military coup because the government did not invite them to participate in policy making. After 1971, first in the authoritarian regime during the term of President Alejandro Lanusse and later during the Peronist governments (1973–6), state actors invited business, especially the CGE, to join various forums for concertation. This was the high point for the CGE and its leader, Gelbard. Gelbard was pivotal in Perón's return from exile and then a powerful economic minister in Perón's government. Many other CGE members were appointed to positions in various other ministries (Brennan 1998, 106), and the Peronist government attempted more intense concertation with business, represented by a revived CGE (see Ayres 1976; Cappelletti 1985). The government convened several social pacts designed to contain inflation, and the CGE represented business in these negotiations and monitoring commissions. Although the UIA did not suffer intervention, as in the previous Peronist government, state officials nonetheless explicitly excluded the UIA. In part to gain access, a conciliatory UIA leadership agreed to merge with the industrial confederation of the CGE to form CINA (Confederación Industrial Argentina). Although never fully consummated, the plan to merge showed how government access and the potential menace from the state encouraged business to reorganize.

The high point for economy-wide collective action by big business came with the political mobilization to bring down the tottering government of president Isabel Perón (Cappelletti 1985, 95).[7] Anti-Peronist associations, mostly previous ACIEL members including SRA and UIA, formed APEGE (Asamblea Permanente de Entidades Gremiales Empresarias) in 1975. APEGE was another coordinating body without much organizational substance. However, it was powerful in coordinating joint action against the government. It was particularly effective in organizing an economic lockout (as Colombian associations had in 1957 to bring down an authoritarian government) in February 1976, a month before the military coup. APEGE also made open "incendiary" demands for military intervention (see Schvarzer and Sidicaro 1988, 234).

As in the coup of 1966, the generals who took power in 1976 accepted business support for the return of military rule but did not offer associations any institutional channels of participation in policy making. In fact, the generals rapidly intervened the UIA, then outlawed the CGE and its member confederations, and in 1977 expropriated CGE assets (Acuña 1995, 8). APEGE quickly disbanded. In 1981 the military government loosened controls and allowed UIA to elect its own leaders, though the CGE remained closed until an act of Congress allowed it to reopen in 1984 (Acuña 1995, 5). Given the continued proscription on the CGE, its members decided to enter UIA (consummating finally the merger attempted several times before) and constitute themselves as an internal faction, MIN (Movimiento Industrial Nacional). This fusion gave UIA a near "monopoly of representation" and much greater coverage of smaller firms and industries outside of Buenos Aires (Manzetti 1993a, 307).

For most of the second half of the twentieth century, sectoral and partisan conflict, as well as instability, meant that business associations in Argentina never developed much institutional strength. Kathryn Sikkink,

---

[7] Formally, her name was María Estela Martínez de Perón. She was Perón's third wife, who became president on Perón's death in mid-1974.

for example, concluded that ACIEL "had no organizational structure and mainly existed as a vehicle for the expression of the shared liberal world view of the member groups and as an opposition front to CGE" (Sikkink 1991, 106). The CGE briefly participated in corporatist fashion on government councils during two Perón governments (1952–5 and 1973), which strengthened incentives for collective action, but this participation did not last long enough to generate much institutional strength, let alone a monopoly on business representation.[8] Subsequent military governments shut the CGE down completely from 1955 to 1958 and again from 1976 to 1983. Overall, Sikkink concludes that "Argentine business associations were structured and behaved more like political movements and less like organizations. They lacked strong institutional and organizational structures" (Sikkink 1991, 108). Acuña (1998) also labels Argentine associations "movements" without stability or internal capacity to reconcile conflicting interests.[9]

Other Encompassing Associations and Patterns of Elite Circulation

The SRA was a significant exception to this rule. While associations like the CGE, UIA, and ACIEL might not know from year to year whether they would have legal status, members, or access to policy makers, the SRA maintained a strong institutional capacity straight through the turbulent postwar decades. Membership rose steadily from 2,300 in 1940 to a high of nearly 12,000 in 1975 and then tapered off to 10,000 in 1984 (Palomino 1987, 149–50). The budget varied from around $2 million to $3 million for much of the period 1955–83 (converted from Palomino 1987, 32, 34).[10] Moreover, the SRA managed internal conflicts without long-term schisms or mass defections and administered valuable self-governance services.[11]

How was the SRA able to survive and thrive in turbulent Argentine politics? First, state actors did not close it or actively promote substitute

---

[8] Ducatenzeiler calls the 1973 *pacto social* the most important experience of concertation in Argentina (1990, 241). For a full historical review of various failed efforts at concertation, see Cappelletti (1985).

[9] Ayres concludes with "another significant generalization about Argentine politics, viz., the relative weakness of business interest associations as compared to organized agriculture and organized labor" (1976, 498).

[10] This institutional strength continued into the 1990s. Membership stood at 8,881 in 1999, and the budget was about $12 million in both 1998 and 1999 (SRA 1999, 78, 274).

[11] The SRA was relatively encompassing in agriculture, but it did not try to monopolize representation and allowed several other agricultural associations to emerge – for example, for breeders (CARBAP, Confederación de Asociaciones Rurales de Buenos Aires y La Pampa) and smallholders (FAA, Federación Agraria Argentina).

associations, as they did in the case of the UIA. The Peronist government in the 1950s did confiscate major SRA assets such as the genealogical registry and the Palermo exhibition building, but the military government returned them shortly thereafter in 1955 (Palomino 1987, 25, 28–9). Second, the SRA maintained economic governance functions crucial to the sector, in particular genealogical records on pure-bred cattle and the annual SRA exhibition in Buenos Aires. These activities generated the bulk of SRA income and occupied most of its staff. For example, in 1955, only 11 percent of SRA income came from membership dues compared with 83 percent from exhibitions, the genealogical registry, and other services. The breakdown was similar in 1972 with 15 percent from dues and 67 percent from exhibitions and services (Palomino 1987, 34). Third, agrarian reform and political attacks against *latifundios* were more prominent in the early 1970s, and perhaps partly in response, SRA membership and revenue peaked in the mid-1970s before declining again in the 1980s. Contrary to strong associations elsewhere and to some of the arguments developed in Part I, the SRA seemed to lack institutionalized channels of access to the state, and apparently self-generated governance functions provided most of the SRA's institutional capacity.[12] Yet, informal access in most governments throughout the twentieth century was apparently impressive since most ministers of agriculture and many other officials in top positions in the economic bureaucracy were members of the SRA.

One lasting alternative effort to organize big business into an economy-wide association was the Consejo Empresario Argentino (CEA).[13] Founded in 1967, apparently with the encouragement of Minister Adalbert Krieger Vasena, the CEA had about 30 members, expanding later to 40

---

[12] By the late 1990s, the president of SRA was meeting, along with the presidents of three other associations from agriculture, with the minister of agriculture on the first and third Wednesdays of each month (SRA 1999, 102). However, it is not clear how long this pattern of consultation existed or how important it was to the SRA.

[13] This *consejo* is not to be confused with the earlier CEA, the Confederación Económica Argentina (sometimes also referred to as the *Congreso* Empresario Argentino) that existed briefly in the late 1940s. That acronyms get recycled in Argentina is itself a telling indication of the high mortality and turnover among associations. Most scholarship on Argentine business pays scant attention to this later CEA, so we know little about its organization and its relationship to government. Manzetti's (1993) exhaustive study of interest groups in twentieth-century Argentina does not mention the CEA, nor does O'Donnell (1988) in his book on Argentine political economy from 1966 to 1973. By one account, "the biggest industries, mainly multinationals, withdrew from the UIA, forming the Consejo Empresario Argentino (CEA) in 1967 in alliance with the ACIEL" (Brennan 1998, 109). See also Castell (1987).

(CEA n.d.). The superficial resemblance to the elite Mexican CMHN is striking. The CEA was a very elite club of owners and chief executive officers of top corporations from all major sectors of the Argentine economy. Membership was by invitation only and, like the CMHN, the CEA's primary activities were meeting with government officials and funding studies. CEA members usually met once a month from 6 to 9 in the evening. Representatives of some government were frequent guests (occasionally at their own request), but their attendance depended on the receptivity of particular governments to contact with CEA. So, access was poor with Peronist governments in the 1970s and the Alfonsín administration but improved with Menem (interview with José Alfredo Martínez de Hoz, 5 May 2000). By the 1990s the CEA was meeting regularly with officials from the Menem government and spending hundreds of thousands of dollars to finance studies on a wide range of policy issues (CEA 1994 and subsequent *memorias*). In some activities the CEA tended more toward civic responsibility, such as helping in the renovation of the Biblioteca Nacional, rather than strict business representation. The CEA in the 1990s had a small office and a staff of two.[14]

However, in contrast to the CMHN in Mexico, CEA membership was subject to higher turnover and included managers, rather than owners, of both Argentine and foreign firms. Annual reports in the 1990s each year thanked several departing members for past services and welcomed several incoming members. Moreover, unlike the CMHN, the CEA did not develop into an "executive committee for the bourgeoisie," and was not active in coordinating and financing other business associations.[15] In Mexico the CMHN financed most of its studies and reports by funding the institutionalized research wing of the peak association CCE. The CEA, in contrast, spent its research money through consulting firms. Overall, CEA never developed much institutional capacity either in terms of staff and resources or in terms of intermediating divergent preferences across cleavages within the business community. The reasons for this lack of capacity,

---

[14] Total CEA expenditures were $456,000 in 1994, $796,000 in 1995, $813,000 in 1996, $559,000 in 1997, and $518,000 in 1998 (CEA 1994–8). These figures are in pesos, which at the time were pegged at parity to the U.S. dollar.

[15] Partisan polarization may also have marginalized the CEA. For example, Martínez de Hoz had a long association with the CEA, and he was president of the CEA before being appointed minister of the economy in the military government in 1976. Because of the brutality of the military regime and the radicalness of the monetarist policies he adopted, Martínez de Hoz became a lightning rod for the far right, which in turn tainted the CEA, in which he was again active after leaving the military government.

especially compared to the CMHN, are several, including high membership turnover, disarticulation with other associations, and especially the
lack of consistent access to government.

Presidents across all types of governments in postwar Argentina appointed capitalists to top government positions, though business appointments after 1945 never approached the degree of penetration or capture
enjoyed by the SRA in the first half of the twentieth century.[16] Some illustrative examples include the following. In the mid-1940s, the military
government created the Banco de Crédito Industrial and named UIA Vice
President Ernesto Herbin its first director (Brennan 1998, 83). Miguel
Miranda, a prominent UIA member and the losing candidate in UIA
elections in 1946, was Perón's main economic adviser in the late 1940s
(Manzetti 1993, 289). After reorganizing business into the CGE in 1953,
Perón appointed its president, José Gelbard, and other CGE leaders to
important positions in the waning years of his first government (Manzetti
1993, 290), and Gelbard and other CGE members returned to prominent appointed positions in the Peronist government of the 1970s. In the
early 1960s Alfredo Concepción, ex-member of the executive council of
UIA, was appointed secretario de industria y minería in the government
of Arturo Illia (Cúneo 1967, 275 footnote). In a survey of 112 industrialists in 1971, 20 percent had held a public office and 8 percent had been
ministers, cabinet advisors, or ministerial subsecretaries (Petras and Cook
1972, 389).

Although less visible than earlier in the century, the SRA was still well
represented in appointments in a range of later governments. From 1955
to 1983, 74 members of the SRA were appointed to 94 government positions, with wide variation among governments from zero appointments
in Peronist governments (1973–6) to a high of 30 appointments in the
military government preceding them (1966–73) (Palomino 1987, 165).[17]
In the Proceso governments (1976–83), José Martínez de Hoz, the main
architect of economic policy, was prior to his appointment the president

---

[16] In contrast to their Chilean and Brazilian counterparts and SRA members earlier in the
twentieth century, most Argentine businesspeople steered clear of electoral politics. By
one calculation, of 249 prestigious entrepreneurs (in *Quien es Quien* of 1959), only 3 had
held or run for national office (Imaz 1964, 148).

[17] Palomino includes second-level positions in national government, as well as top positions in the governments of major provinces. The breakdown for all governments is
as follows: 12 appointments of SRA members in the military regime (1955–8), 19 in the
Frondizi government (1958–62), 17 in the Guido government (1962–3), only 3 in the Illia
government (1963–6), 30 in the military governments (1966–73), none in the Peronist
governments (1973–6), and 13 in the military regime (1976–83) (Palomino 1987, 165).

of a big steel firm (Acindar), a long-standing member of the SRA, and head of the CEA.[18]

Scholars have long debated the salience of sectoral and distributional conflict in Argentine politics. One side sees relations as deeply conflictual, due in part to the fact that exports of beef and wheat could be consumed domestically as wage goods, which naturally exacerbated distributional contention between urban consumers and rural exporters. In this view, cleavages between industry and agriculture, and later among factions of industry, were greater in Argentina than elsewhere in Latin America and, for some, contributed to Argentina's long record of political instability.[19] O'Donnell, for example, argues that much of Argentina politics from 1956 to 1976 can be interpreted by assessing the instability of alliances between big agriculture and big industry on the one hand versus smaller, national business and urban popular sectors on the other. However, even these groups and conflicts among them were not merely natural and spontaneous expressions of economic cleavages: "the actors were not classes, fractions and organisations which retained their 'structural' characteristics unchanged, beyond these struggles. Rather, they were the political, organisational and ideological expression of classes and fractions created and transformed during and through this pattern of alliances and oppositions" (O'Donnell 1978, 23). In this sense, Perón was critical in "creating and transforming" the factions of industry represented in the UIA and CGE as well as other, less durable organizational breaches.

From a different view, these surface divisions masked a deeper harmony within the business community premised in part on patterns of diversified ownership that spanned several sectors, especially agriculture and industry. Prior to the 1940s, Argentine industry and agriculture had a "symbiotic relationship" in that much of industry processed agricultural goods; "as late as 1935, foodstuffs still accounted for 47 percent of all industrial production" (Smith 1974, 5). Gustavo Polit argued that "industrialists and landowners, are intertwined: the vague boundaries that separate them are attenuated through the investment of agrarian rent in industry and the investment of industrial profit in agriculture, converting

---

[18] Martínez de Hoz had also been minister of economy briefly in 1963. Even Perón invited him to be minister of public works in the 1970s, though he declined the invitation (interview, 5 May 2000). Guillermo Livio Kühl, president of Saab Scania and Celulosa Jujuy, was appointed minister of industry and mining for four months in 1981 (Ostiguy 1990, 26).

[19] Among those who emphasize sectoral and distributional conflict are Manzetti (1993), O'Donnell (1978), Waisman (1987), and Acuña (1998). Mallon and Sourrouille titled their book *Economic Policy Making in a Conflict Society* (1975).

the landholders into industrialists and the industrialists into landholders"
(1968, 399–400).[20] From the side of agriculture, the core leaders of the
SRA over the period 1955–83 maintained diversified business interests in
finance, commerce, and industry. One study identified a *"grupo de control"* in the SRA composed of 24 people who were members of Comisión
Directiva for nine or more years over the period 1955–83. Of these 24, 17
appear 109 times on the board of directors of 102 *sociedades anónimas.*
Of these 102 firms, 23 are in agroindustry, 17 in finance, 29 in commerce,
10 in real estate, and 23 in industry (Palomino 1987, 43–5).

Leaders of major sectoral associations, especially the SRA and UIA,
generally got along well (Cúneo 1967, 192). Interestingly, in one poll of
leaders of industrial associations in the 1960s, 55 percent said that conflict between industry and agriculture was minor or nonexistent (Freels
1970, 448). And Argentine capitalists did in fact manage to overcome
sectoral divisions, if only temporarily, to create several economy-wide associations, from the Asociación de Trabajo, CACIP and the Federación in
the interwar period, to the government-mandated CGE under Perón, to
ACIEL and APEGE in opposition to the CGE and Perón. Moreover, even
associations like the UIA, constituted as a sectoral association, included
many nonindustrial members. Hypothetically, multisectoral diversification in business ownership and prior intersectoral coordinating should
have facilitated economy-wide organization, had, for instance, state actors provided strong and consistent incentives to organize.

Clearly, the partisan conflicts between Peronists and anti-Peronists
politicized various distributional cleavages among agricultural exporters,
urban workers, and various factions of industrialists. Even after discount-
ing patterns of diversification, the remaining economic and social differences among various latent factions of business – agrarian elite, big
business, MNCs, and small business – were susceptible to rapid and lasting politicization and polarization. However, political actors were still
necessary catalysts to activate these cleavages, and Perón's actions – such
as closing the UIA and opening the CGE – may have provided the maximum activation. Detailed data comparing the underlying economic and
social cleavages between big and small industry in Argentina with similar

---

[20] Although much later, and only in one case, it seemed incongruous when I went to interview Jorge Blanco Villegas, president of UIA from 1993 to 1997, to find the office
of this ex-industrialist adorned with pictures of prize-winning livestock. Blanco Villegas
began his business career in agriculture and had returned to it, as well as other diversified
investments, after leaving UIA (interview, 3 May 2000).

cleavages in other large countries of the region are lacking. At various points in the later twentieth century, conflicts between big and small firms emerged in business politics in all countries, but more comparative economic evidence is required to link these conflicts primarily to differences in their underlying economic interests.

The comparative organizational evidence is, however, clearer. Where political leaders helped smaller industry organize separately, lasting political divisions complicated subsequent business politics and attempts to organize economy-wide associations. Where political leaders did not help small business organize on its own, conflicts were muted and had less influence on business organization or business politics overall. In both Mexico and Argentina, for example, political leaders created separate associations composed largely of smaller, provincial, protectionist industrialists, Canacintra and CGI, respectively, that subsequently fought with associations composed more homogeneously of larger, internationalized firms located in major industrial cities. In contrast, in Colombia and Chile, political leaders did not create rival associations, and did not therefore politicize and divide industry. Over time associations of small industry did emerge in these countries, but they lacked powerful patrons, and focused more on pragmatic concerns of small firms rather than engaging in high politics of national development strategies.

In sum, in Argentina the tumultuous postwar years buffeted business associations about and left them on the eve of the transition to democracy in 1983 with little institutional capacity (especially in industry and economy-wide organizations) either in resources and staff or in the ability to intermediate members' interests. Fragmentation, political rivalry, and competition sapped the strength of associations that survived and contributed to the demise of others, especially the several attempts to establish economy-wide organizations. By 1983 Argentine business, like business in Brazil, had no economy-wide peak association that brought together other major sectoral associations. The only surviving economy-wide association, the very elite CEA, was organizationally weak and isolated from other associations. The sources of most cleavages and organizational weaknesses in Argentine business associations can be traced back to state actions. As in other cases, state actors in Argentina responded to political and economic vulnerabilities by supporting various associations. However, in sharp contrast to other countries, state actors in Argentina also closed opposing associations, confiscated their assets, and persecuted their leaders. Motivations among political leaders were heavily political, though in particular crises, notably those of the 1950s and early 1970s,

Peronist officials invited representatives of business associations to consult on economic policy. Overall, though, none of the periods of repression or support and consultation lasted long enough to end fragmentation and politicized rivalry.

Redemocratization and Continued Weakness in Business Organization, 1983–2000

The victory of the Radical Party (UCR, Unión Cívica Radical) in the 1983 elections changed dramatically the context for business politics (Acuña 1995). For business associations it was, for the first time in many years, not a question of which associations would experience intervention and which would be favored. Rather, UIA, CGE/CGI, and other associations were free to develop as voluntary associations and recast themselves as nonpartisan representatives of all of business. However, their historical weaknesses and loyalties were not immediately forgotten, and both business and government often bypassed associations seeking alternative means of interest aggregation and negotiation. Overall, the Alfonsín government, especially in the late 1980s, drew associations into closer contact with the government and thus helped them restore some institutional capacity. However, the Menem government largely ignored business associations, and its economic policies undercut the membership basis of associations like UIA, so that by the end of the 1990s many associations were in even greater disarray.

Officials in the Alfonsín government attempted initially to bypass formal associations. In 1984, Dante Caputo, minister of foreign relations, called a meeting at his home with a dozen or so capitalists from the largest conglomerates in Argentina. These meetings continued, at government invitation, with minor changes in the list of invitees. The press dubbed this group the "captains of industry," though it was also known as the Grupo Maria (Castell 1987; Ostiguy 1990). These meetings represented the view among some government officials that existing business associations, including the elite CEA, did not adequately represent big business, and that it was better for government to hand pick the businesses they wanted represented. The immediate motives for Foreign Minister Caputo and Secretary of Industry Carlos Lacerca were to enlist business collaboration in efforts to overcome the economic crisis of the early 1980s (Ostiguy 1990, 324). In addition, Alfonsín wanted to improve ties to business (historically weak with the Radical Party) and supplant traditional links between big business and the military (Ostiguy 1990, 325).[21] Coincidentally, this logic resembled that animating the Pinochet dictatorship at about the same time – court business to keep it from joining the opposition – except that the Chilean government promoted contact with associations, while the Alfonsín government met with the informal grouping of the "captains." These informal meetings signaled that consultation with business would not run exclusively through associations, thereby discouraging investment in associations. By some accounts, business resisted government efforts to formalize their consultations with the captains (Castell 1987, 21; Ostiguy 1990, 325), despite the misgivings prominent capitalists had about existing business associations.[22]

By 1985 state actors, especially the new economic team under Juan Sourrouille, had made several attempts to establish closer formal ties to business associations. In the context of severe inflation, the international debt crisis, and initial attempts at structural reforms like further trade liberalization, state actors in the economic ministries sought out business to support these policies and help implement them. However, most of these overtures were short-lived (as were the policies associated with them), involved concertation with labor, and often ended up exacerbating sectoral divisions among associations rather than promoting more encompassing collective action. A month after enacting the heterodox Austral Plan in June 1985, officials in the economic ministries established the Economic-Social Conference to promote tripartite dialogue (Acuña 1995, 15–20). By 1986 industry associations were still supporting the Austral Plan, but agricultural associations had begun mobilizing against it.

The last years of the Alfonsín government, 1987 and 1988, brought new stabilization plans, new efforts at concertation, and ongoing divisions among business. The Spring Plan of 1988 "included an alliance with the UIA and CAC" (industry and commerce) but generated almost immediate opposition from agricultural associations (Acuña 1995, 24–5). In these and other forums, business also attempted to establish loose coordination through things like the Group of 11 in the early 1980s that included representatives from major business associations as well as labor unions,

---

[21] A top official in the Alfonsín government explained that the government was open to business participation in part because of a tradition of distance and mutual mistrust between business and the Radical Party (interview, May 2000).

[22] One small survey in the 1980s of about 15 top managers of Argentina's largest *grupos* found a universally negative view of associations, which among other things were viewed as "unrepresentative," "segmented," and abused to further the interests of a few (Sguiglia 1988, 60).

or the Group of 8 in the late 1980s and 1990s that brought together the major business associations. However, efforts at all-encompassing collective action did not go beyond these temporary attempts at coordination, and even weak peak associations like ACIEL or APEGE were not revived.

The appointment of businessmen to top positions in government continued after 1983 across all types of governments. The Radical government in the 1980s made key appointments of big businessmen to head state enterprises (Schvarzer and Sidicaro 1988, 235, 239). In 1986 Alfonsín appointed Ernesto Figueras to the Ministry of Agriculture as a close representative of the SRA (Acuña 1995, 16). Later, as the economy began to unravel in 1988–9, Alfonsín appointed an UIA leader, Murat Eurnekian, as secretary of industry. Compared to the 1990s, when business appointees to government came mostly from the biggest firms, Alfonsín was more likely to appoint people who had closer contact with associations, as in the Colombian tradition.

The Alfonsín government was better in many respects for business associations, especially in industry, than governments before or since. The incorporation of much of the CGI into UIA, and the more conciliatory management of cleavages within UIA, rather than through competing associations, strengthened UIA and industrial representation. Regular invitations from government to participate in negotiations over social pacts, stabilization programs, and economic integration with Brazil gave business further reasons to revive and remodel UIA. Despite these improvements, UIA still remained weak and divided compared to industry associations in other countries. Internally, political intrigue and factional fighting continued, while outdated statutes impeded better representation (interview with Blanco Villegas, 3 May 2000). Sympathetic treatment by one government, especially one beset by so many crises, was not enough to revamp representation for organized industry.

In contrast to the Alfonsín government, the Menem government (1989–99) largely excluded associations. State actors in the Menem government were more reluctant to consult regularly with organized business, though Menem and many of his top policy makers communicated with individual businessmen, especially those from the largest firms.[23] In contrast to the

---

[23] In October 1999 the CEA organized a lunch to honor outgoing President Menem. Various speakers from the CEA highlighted how many of the structural reforms of the Menem government had addressed recommendations made in earlier CEA studies. The CEA reported on some of the comments at the meeting: "Dr. José A. Martínez de Hoz made special reference to the fact that it was with this government that the Consejo Empresario Argentino has maintained the most fluid dialogue" (CEA 1999, 13).

collaborative arrangements between business and government that had developed in Chile and Mexico to manage and promote market-oriented reform, economic officials in the Menem government preferred to act alone, and quickly. Even in the case of Mercosur, as discussed in the next chapter, government officials negotiated without much input from business associations.

Ad hoc access for associations was, though, fairly open. Jorge Blanco Villegas, president of UIA for most of the 1990s, conversed regularly with Domingo Cavallo and other ministers, but the UIA had no institutionalized representation during the Menem government (interview, 3 May 2000). Institutional capacity of the UIA was drained by this lack of institutional channels of representation, as well as by the de-industrializing reforms of the period (especially trade liberalization and the overvaluation of the currency) that hit many member firms hard. One indication of fading institutional capacity was that UIA downsized by almost half, from 65 employees to 35 (interview with Eduardo Cassullo, 4 May 2000). In addition, according to Blanco Villegas, UIA's greatest strength was its visibility in the press, not its capacity for interest intermediation: "the circumstances preferred by each one of the sectors are many times opposed. What is best for the automobile industry or freezer manufacturers is not what is best for those who produce steel. In this the Unión Industrial does not have real power. Where it has power is in the enormous attention given it by the media" (interview, 3 May 2000).

Appointments of businessmen to top government positions continued after 1989. Menem's surprise appointment of a top manager of the huge Bunge y Born conglomerate as his minister of economics was one of the clearest instances of using an appointment to signal the government's commitment to maintaining good relations with business (see Schneider 1998b). Cavallo, a later economics minister, was not a businessman; however, he had developed close links with business through many years of directing a research institute funded by business, the Fundación Mediterránea (see Huneeus 1998, 189). Appointments after Menem seemed to draw again more on businessmen from associations. The government of Fernando de la Rúa (1999–2001) included some "business" appointees. Although de la Rúa's economy minister, José Luis Machinea, had been president of the Central Bank in the Alfonsín government in the 1980s, he spent much of the 1990s as a consultant and staffer to the UIA. When Eduardo Duhalde took power in the crisis of late 2001, he appointed José Ignacio de Mendiguren, then secretary of the UIA, to be his minister of production (at least for the first several months of 2002).

In sum, the return to democracy in 1983 removed the specter that had haunted business associations for nearly four decades, the specter of being intervened in or legally extinguished by the next government. Industrialists took advantage of this openness to work to overcome their differences (or at least internalize them within UIA) and achieve single representation. However, state actors did not provide any consistent incentives to invest in these associations, either negatively by threatening broad business interests or positively by institutionalizing consultation with business associations. Murat Eurnekian, active in various leadership positions in UIA from 1962 to 1996, summed up the resource problems thus: "one of the biggest problems facing the Unión Industrial is resources to subsist. Of course, to the extent that the Unión Industrial is not representative and does not act as an intermediating body in interactions with the government and with various agencies of the state, its power decreases, as does its revenues" (interview, 4 May 2000).

Conclusions on the Argentine Case

Although Argentina's famous fractiousness is evident in the tortured history of its business associations, state actors, especially since the 1940s, were central protagonists in exacerbating differences and impeding, or not helping, efforts by business to achieve stronger, encompassing, collective action. State actors in Mexico, Colombia, and Chile helped business organize mostly by granting existing associations privileged access. Such formal access in Argentina was either denied or sporadic (or superseded by informal individual access). Furthermore, leftist threats from labor and government in Mexico and Chile helped unify business, while pro-labor Peronist governments divided economic elites. Perón was not as leftist as, for example, Chilean socialists, and Perón courted some segments of business, so he did not have the same centripetal impact on business preferences for encompassing organization. Counterfactually, had Perón redistributed rural property through land reform and threatened other property rights, he might have helped business unite, as reformers in Chile and Mexico did in the 1960s and 1970s.[24] But even this hypothetical scenario would likely have been insufficient to sustain strong encompassing associations without further selective benefits.

---

[24] Perón agreed with SRA that land reform and redistribution were not suitable policies for Argentina (Cúneo 1967, 219). SRA was publicly supportive of the first Perón government, more so than the divided (and later intervened) UIA (Cúneo 1967, 160).

In the portfolio analogy, business has incentives to shift investments among associations, parties, and personal politics according to the expected return from each. In Argentina, through the transition to democracy in 1983, associations were embattled and parties were weak (especially parties linked closely to business), so business tended to shift investment toward personal politicking, business "movements," and conspiracies with the military (see Acuña 1995; Gibson 1996; Schvarzer and Sidicaro 1988). In a survey of 100 leaders of industrial associations in the late 1960s, 57 advocated an active political role for associations. Of these 57 leaders, 77 percent thought that "industrial associations should participate directly in government commissions and bureaus," 12 percent felt that "industrial associations should place members in key ministries," and 11 percent favored working to get an industrialist elected president (Freels 1970, 444). Although partial, these data confirm several arguments presented in this book. First, industrialists valued privileged access and seats on commissions. Moreover, the fact that three-quarters of industrialists (who favored political activism) felt that associations ought to be so represented is an indirect indicator that associations were not sufficiently represented at the time. Lastly, this group of industrial leaders had a collective notion of a portfolio of political strategies that ran the spectrum from abstention, to lobbying for appointments, to electoral politics. Industrialists differed on the primary political investment they preferred, and they made calculations on the relative merits of, or returns on, alternative political investments.

Outside the special case of SRA, Argentine associations generated little institutional capacity in the late twentieth century. A crucial prerequisite of nonrivalry was not met, especially by industrialists, in the postwar period. By the 1980s, UIA, though representing most of industry, was itself formally split internally into two contending factions. There is little associations can hope to accomplish if they are warring with other associations or factions. Because of these competing associations and factions, the cost of defecting has rarely been great for firms. In addition, the state offered few benefits, either access or subsidies, that associations could use to increase incentives to belong, participate, and compromise. Thus, associations in Argentina continued to be movements of small numbers of like-minded capitalists.

Given the strength of organized labor, one question is, why did business not invest more in encompassing associations in order to counter or negotiate with labor unions? The economy-wide associations Coparmex in Mexico and CPC in Chile (both in the 1930s and 1940s and later in the

1960s and 1970s) were created and strengthened in periods of labor in-corporation and organization by left-leaning governments. In Argentina, economic and especially political cleavages predominated over employers' common concern with what became a very strong Peronist union move-ment (Acuña 1998). Moreover, labor after World War II in Argentina was not radical and autonomous. Rather, its strength varied with Perón and Peronists, and for employers the core challenge came not directly from labor, but rather from labor backed by Peronists in government. So cap-italists organized and politicked over state power rather than organizing to negotiate directly with labor (Schvarzer and Sidicaro 1988, 234).

The lack of institutional capacity in Argentina's associations cannot be explained without reference to the state. State actors intervened con-sistently and dramatically, usually closing an association and opening a closed rival. The motivations of state actors conformed usually to the most instrumental of political logics: strengthen supporters and weaken oppo-nents. Some moments of deteriorating economic conditions increased the vulnerabilities of state officials and prompted them to seek out business and in some cases strengthen their organizations. Despite clear vulnera-bilities and potential interest in collaborating with business, state actors often faced associations they ultimately preferred to avoid. Thus, as the economy ran into trouble in the early 1950s, Perón sought business sup-port but opted to close UIA and create a new CGE. In the early 1970s, governments consulted again with CGE and almost drew UIA into the CGE. The Alfonsín government took office as the debt crisis of the 1980s deepened. Government officials in the 1980s first created various informal forums for consulting with business and later turned to more traditional associations, especially the UIA. Overall, these kinds of economic vul-nerabilities – and consequently increased incentives for officials to draw associations into joint economic governance – were weaker than political and partisan logics. Moreover, threats to property rights were compar-atively less common in Argentina, especially compared to the impact of partisan conflict, as consequently were defensive incentives for economy-wide collective action.

By the 1990s business associations in Argentina were among the weak-est and most fragmented in the region. No economy-wide associations existed, and other encompassing associations in agriculture and indus-try faced competing associations and lacked institutional resources. Yet this outcome was not inevitable. There were several turning points in the history of business–government relations when state actors sought out business consultation and gave associations privileged access in ways that in other countries gradually strengthened the associations. However, in Argentina these consultations usually had a partisan and exclusionary edge. More importantly, political instability meant that no single attempt at institutionalizing business representation had enough time to become consolidated.

Broader Comparisons

To conclude the empirical discussion of Part II, the final sections of this chapter summarize the main findings and extend the empirical comparisons beyond the five core cases. The central question posed at the outset of this book was, why were voluntary encompassing business associations stronger in Mexico, Chile, and Colombia than in Brazil and Argentina? The primary and proximate answer was that behind strong encompassing associations were state actors who granted these associations selective benefits, often in the form of institutionalized access to policy deliberations. Historically, these government officials were more likely to grant these benefits according to political logics, and seek out organized business collaborators to reduce their vulnerabilities during periods of economic and political crisis. In response to the crises of the 1930s and 1940s (and 1950s in Argentina), state actors in all five countries promoted new forms of collective action by business. However, by the 1980s, the responses of state actors to fairly similar crises varied more, because by the 1980s and 1990s the organizational domain for business differed greatly across the five countries. Stronger economy-wide associations had evolved with government support in Chile, Mexico, and Colombia. In these countries, state actors in the 1980s and 1990s turned to these encompassing associations to reduce new vulnerabilities and in the process further strengthened these associations. In contrast, state actors in Brazil and Argentina had no economy-wide associations to turn to, and major associations in sectors like industry were weakened by previous decades of state intervention, partisan in Argentina and corporatist in Brazil.

Might the arguments developed in this book be useful for understanding business politics and organization in other countries and regions? In fact, state intervention in organizing business seems to be the rule in larger developing countries.[25] In Venezuela, to take a first example from another

---

[25] Although beyond the scope of this section, the experiences of associations in more developed countries often reveal the important role of the state, even in the United States. Moreover, even earlier industrializers' state initiatives in organizing business often coincided

country in Latin America, business created in 1944 one of the earliest economy-wide peak associations in the region, Fedecamaras (Federación Venezolana de Cámaras y Asociaciones de Comercio y Producción). By the 1960s, Fedecamaras had grown institutionally strong and was a major participant in economic policy making (Bond 1975 provides the most complete early history). As noted in Chapter 2, the extensive corporate conglomeration and diversification of big business in Venezuela likely facilitated encompassing collective action. However, much of Fedecamaras's evolution came in response to state actions. In 1946, for example, the government created CVF (Corporación Venezolana de Fomento) with the mission of lending 10 percent of the government's budget to private industry. Fedecamaras played a major role in designing CVF, and, similar to the arrangements for Corfo in Chile some years earlier, CVF statutes reserved two of five seats on its board for representatives from Fedecamaras (the president was to pick two members from a list provided by Fedecamaras) (Bond 1975, 66). Privileged access initially strengthened the fledgling federation, but shortly thereafter the access was withdrawn and the organization suffered. The authoritarian governments from 1948 to 1958 generally excluded Fedecamaras from policy making and removed its representatives from CVF. For Fedecamaras, the 1950s was a period of organizational decline: "annual conventions were poorly attended, member groups complained, and financing activities of the federation became a problem" (Bond 1975, 70).

After the return to democracy in 1958, access for Fedecamaras and other business associations expanded dramatically. By one calculation, business came to have 67 seats on the boards of 68 decentralized agencies and 663 seats (15 percent of all seats) on 314 consultative commissions (Crisp 1996, 37, 39, 41; Corrales and Cisneros 1999, 2107). Fedecamaras gained institutional representation in core planning entities like Consejo de Economía Nacional and Sistema de Planificación Venezolana (López Maya, Gómez Calcaño, and Maingón 1989, 88–9). Members of Fedecamaras also invested in the federation to counter perceived threats from government. Similar to Mexico, another large petroleum producer, business worried that political leaders would use oil resources to expand state

with moments of international and economic crisis. For example, predecessors of voluntary encompassing associations like the CBI (Confederation of British Industry), CNPF (Conseil national du patronat français, France), and BDI (Bundesverband der Deutschen Industrie, Germany) "were all created between 1916 and 1920 at the urgings of governments seeking assistance in dealing with the end of the first world war" (Coleman 1990, 251).

activity in the economy and crowd out private business (Bond 1975, 59). Also, similar to the Mexican peak association CCE, a small group of the wealthiest capitalists in Venezuela provided most of the funding for Fedecamaras (Bond 1975, 121). In the early 1970s Fedecamaras had 168 member associations, representing 75 percent of the Venezuelan economy, as well as a staff of 25 and a budget of about $1.4 million ($400,000 in 1974 dollars) (Bond 1975, 63, 93, 151). After the 1970s, Fedecamaras declined somewhat and may have been partially displaced by narrower sectoral associations that gained enhanced access, especially during the price control negotiations in the 1980s (Naím and Francés 1995, 178–82). Overall, the organizational strength of encompassing organization in Venezuela covaried over time with the level and extension of institution-alized access to economic policy makers.

In developing countries of Asia, state actors were often very intrusive and controlling in their efforts to organize business. In South Korea and Taiwan, for example, state actors actively organized business associations, both sectoral and encompassing, and granted them access often through formal consultative bodies (Campos and Root 1996, 79–106; Fields 1997).[26] In South Korea the state created and controlled most business associations in a system scholars generally categorized as state corporatism (Kim 1993, 34–5). Most business associations were statutory bodies under the jurisdiction of specific ministries that had the right to intervene in the associations' management and leadership selection. In addition, elite bureaucrats often retired to top positions in associations (Kim 1999, 286, 298). However, business also organized a few voluntary associations outside the corporatist framework. The history of the en-compassing Federation of Korean Industry (FKI) bears some resemblance to the conflict-then-cooperation relationships that Mexican and Chilean associations had with their states. In 1961, 78 top Korean industrialists formed the predecessor of the FKI to defend themselves against a pro-posed Illicit Wealth Decree. After this early antagonism, the FKI grew strong and enjoyed good access to officials in the military regime (Fields 1997, 136–7; Kim 1993, 35).

---

[26] Reliance on public–private consultative bodies was also extensive in Japan. The numbers of consultative councils peaked at 277 in 1966 and declined to 214 in 1986. In these councils "business has enjoyed wider representation . . . than any other interest group," and representation usually came through associations. Business and agriculture were represented on 80 percent of these councils, and 84 percent of the councils with business representation included people from associations (Schwartz 1992, 219, 221, 224–5).

In Taiwan the state was also heavy-handed.[27] After 1949 the Nationalist government transplanted legislation from the 1920s that mandated compulsory membership and structured representation in associations. Moreover, in the 1950s the government added control over personnel and party monitoring to the structure of state corporatism. The government also delegated numerous functions of policy making and implementing (Kuo 1995, 68–74). Where these sectoral governance functions were crucial to members, some associations, as in textiles, grew quite strong (Kuo 1995, Chapter 4). However, in other associations, especially encompassing ones, state control undermined associations: "the government deliberately fragmented authority among three different peak groups to dilute their influence. Staff and activities were meager. Leadership was concentrated in the hands of a few figures with close ties to the government and party" (Noble 1998, 45).

Data on the motivations of state actors in these countries are slim, but a plausible starting hypothesis is that incentives for state actors in Asia to help business organize were not very different in kind from incentives in Latin America, though in some periods they were probably much more intense in Asia.[28] During the Cold War, for example, leaders and economic policy makers in frontline states like Korea and Taiwan

---

[27] Other cases where state actors have been more authoritarian in imposing state corporatism on business include Egypt (Bianchi 1989, 162–72), Jordan, and Kuwait (Moore 2002). China represents a recent extreme case where state agencies directly created and controlled business associations (Foster 2001, 2002). In Tunisia, state elites were less heavyhanded in organizing business but still maintained tighter control than was common in Latin America (see Bellin 2002, especially Chapter 3). UTICA (Union Tunisienne de l'Industrie, du Commerce et de l'Artisanat) gained official status and state funding (to support a large staff of 150), but along with this support came deep meddling by state actors in selecting leaders of the association. UTICA and other, more independent associations were also undermined by personalized relations between big capitalists and state officials. In some cases, capitalists were formally appointed to government boards, not as representatives of associations but rather as prominent businesspersons (as in Brazil). In other cases, individual access was informal, but regular and equally discouraging to formal organization.

[28] In his general discussion of corporatism, Kuo offers a series of rationales for state interest in working with business associations that sounds similar to the political logics discussed in Chapter 2: "first, the state reduces the costs of collecting information. Business associations can provide timely and well-formulated policy proposals. The state gains legitimacy when it implements proposals initiated and supported by the business community. The state can reduce its political burden and risks by allowing the business community to hammer out their own differences and conflicts of interest. And, finally, by delegating parts of policy implementation to business associations, the effectiveness of public policies can be improved and the administrative costs of the state reduced" (Kuo 1995, 38).

had strong incentives to seek out business support for their development strategies and assistance in policy implementation. State actors in this context would have had strong, sustained incentives to reduce their multiple international, political, and economic vulnerabilities through policies like organizing business.

In Thailand the evolution of encompassing associations shows some close similarities to the history of business associations in Latin America.[29] Overall, business–government relations in Thailand bear a surprising resemblance to those in Colombia (Doner and Ramsay 1997; Thorp and Durand 1997). Among other things, in both countries the state was comparatively less intrusive in promoting industrialization and social welfare, political and economic elites were more closely fused (e.g., businessmen were commonly appointed to cabinet positions), labor and the left were relatively weak, and business associations by the late twentieth century were well represented on public boards. In the early twentieth century business associations in Thailand were few and weak. The Thai Chamber of Commerce (TCC), the earliest encompassing association for Thai business, was created in 1933 but remained embryonic until 1966, when the government made its president the ex-officio president of the Board of Trade. A government decree in 1954 had established the Board of Trade to regulate exports of agricultural commodities. As in the case of the Colombian coffee federation Federacafe, the Board of Trade was delegated public functions and authority but remained under the control of private agricultural exporters. Other sectors later organized voluntary associations, for example the Association of Thai Industries (ATI), in 1967, but had few members and little institutional capacity until the 1980s.[30]

In 1981 Prime Minister Prem Tinsulananda created the Joint Public and Private Sector Consultative Committee (JPPCC), which rapidly transformed the organization of Thai business. The JPPCC included representatives from the major business association (TCC, ATI, and TBA [Thai Bankers Association]) and ministers from economic areas. In its first five years JPPCC met 46 times and passed resolutions on 34 issues, mostly on issues put forward by business (Laothamatas 1992, 70). This privileged consultation through the JPPCC had an immediate and dramatic impact on business investment in collective action. In the early 1980s

---

[29] Unless otherwise noted, all the information on Thailand comes from Laothamatas (1992).
[30] Bankers formed the Thai Bankers Association (TBA) in 1958. It did not develop much institutional strength despite the high concentration – 16 banks controlled 94 percent of all bank assets (Laothamatas 1992, 50).

membership grew 37 percent in the Chamber of Commerce and over 80 percent in the industry association. Staff in the TCC grew sevenfold.[31] JPPCC meetings tapered off in the late 1980s, in part for lack of urgent new business. However, by 1990 the major encompassing associations had institutionalized access throughout the government: the Chamber of Commerce had representatives in 56 government committees, the Board of Trade in 81, the industrialists (ATI) in 256, and the bankers association in 81 (Laothamatas 1992, 47–50).

Why did state actors in Thailand grant business privileged access through the JPPCC? According to Anek Laothamatas, the primary motives for state actors – the political logics – were to manage the economic crisis and shore up wobbling political support.[32] More than other countries in Asia, and similar to much of Latin America, Thailand suffered a deeper economic crisis in the early 1980s. Probably most important in the immediate calculations of government leaders was the attempted coup, two months before the creation of JPPCC, by junior officers who had previously backed the Prem government. Faced with uncertain military support, Prem courted business by creating the JPPCC and appointing more businessmen to his cabinet (to nearly half of the positions by one calculation; Laothamatas 1992, 34) to reduce vulnerabilities on several fronts.

In a range of other developing countries political leaders, especially long-standing dictators, showed little interest in strengthening associations and preferred instead to deal with big business through personal and clientelist networks, or what became known as "crony capitalism." This was more the pattern in the Philippines, Indonesia, some countries of Central America, and parts of Africa.[33] These patterns of individualized

---

[31] Membership rose rapidly in TCC (from 778 in 1980 to 1,066 in 1985) and even faster in ATI (from 758 in 1981 to 1,377 in 1985). The staff of TCC also grew by leaps and bounds, from 10 in 1977 to 70 in 1987. By 1991 the ATI (then renamed FTI, Federation of Thai Industries) had the largest staff of all associations, 84 people (Laothamatas 1992, 48–9, 71).

[32] Laothamatas identifies four sets of explanatory factors: "the rise of the Sino–Thai business class, the economic crisis of the early 1980s, the government's need for political support, and external influences" (1992, 76). However, the first and last sets of factors were more background or facilitating factors than direct motivations for state actors. The expansion and diversification of Sino–Thai business made possible and more desirable some sort of organized consultation, at some point, while international factors included modest financial support from the U.S. government and the widely admired model of business organization in Japan.

[33] See, for example, Kuo (1995) and Kang (2002) on the Philippines, Macintyre (1994) on Indonesia and Southeast Asia, McCleary (1999) and Spalding (1998) on Central America, and Boone (1992) and Evans (1995) on Africa.

interaction, similar in some ways to those of Chile in the first half of the Pinochet dictatorship or to those of Argentina under Menem, reduced incentives for business to invest in associations. Over time this individualized clientelism, or crony capitalism, inhibited associations from developing institutional capacity, and therefore further encouraged both state and business elites to bypass associations.

These brief comparisons help situate the five Latin American cases in this book between extremes of state corporatism and individualized clientelism. The extremes were more common where political leaders enjoyed greater personal power and had greater autonomy to set the terms of interaction with business. The private sector, or select groups within it, may, of course, ultimately have prospered under either type of relation, as it did in Indonesia and Taiwan, but business leaders still had little choice in how they interacted with the state. My argument spotlights the role of state actors because strong associations did not emerge in Latin America without state support; however, interregional contrasts show that these state actors in Latin America were also relatively constrained compared with their counterparts in other regions. State actors in Latin America rarely had such free rein, and their interactions were guided more by strategic *exchanges* with business than by unilateral imposition. Strong presidents like Perón, Vargas, or a succession of semiauthoritarian PRI leaders had decisive impacts on business organizations, but even these presidents were unable to coerce business to organize exactly the way they wanted. The organizational outcomes, especially in cases of voluntary associations, were comparatively more negotiated and interactive in Latin America. Another significant interregional contrast is the relative absence in other developing countries of defensive organization by business to counter pressures from labor, leftist parties, or state threats to property rights. Land reform, for example, was more extensive in Korea and Taiwan than in Mexico and Chile, yet was less threatening to urban business and to property rights generally because it was undertaken by more conservative governments.

The contrasts with clientelist and state–corporatist relations help situate and delimit the range of my argument. Other cases of strategic exchange, especially Thailand, as well as the common occurrence of important consultative forums, suggest that the core arguments – especially the positive impact that privileged access had on collective action – have relevance beyond Latin America.[34] And recent developments may make my

---

[34] Privileged access is also common in advanced industrial countries: "the structure of the modern state is shot through with consultative and decisional bodies composed of functional representatives. Virtually all empirical research to date reveals that [business

arguments more relevant outside Latin America. With the end of the Cold
War and the further development of business communities, governments
are less likely to be able to continue to impose one-sided corporatist or
clientelist relations. Moreover, with democratization, disadvantaged social groups may increasingly mobilize to demand redistribution, and such
popular mobilization may, in turn, give business more incentives to organize defensively.

Institutional Formation and Change

In nearly all the case studies, it was state actors who triggered initial
institutional formation, deliberately or unintentionally, and who shaped
subsequent institutional reproduction or change by granting or withhold-
ing selective incentives (see Thelen 2002; Thelen and Steinmo 1992). The
origins of these institutions, business associations, derived largely from
the interests of government officials in managing conjunctural political
and policy problems, sometimes in negotiation with business leaders or
organizational entrepreneurs in the business community. However, these
short-term interests had longer-term institutional and distributional consequences. In general the design of institutions, if it involves a third party,
as in this case, leads to the suspicion that the third party (in this case,
primarily state officials) will mold the institutional design to suit their
interests (Bates 1988, 395–7).

Yet what stands out in most stories of association formation is that
those creating these institutions seemed to have had little notion of exactly how their decisions would shape future institutional evolution. On
the side of the state, the officials who set up privileged access usually did
so to get immediate information and political support, without necessarily
thinking through how this access might over time change business representation and institutional capacity in associations. Where state actors
seemed to be more deliberate was in Mexico – where state actors were
consistently concerned about how all social groups organized – and in
Argentina – where state actors from Perón on had clear ideas about which
supportive associations they wanted to strengthen (and have win in the
long-term rivalry) and those they wanted to undermine. On the business
side, organizational entrepreneurs like Roberto Simonsen in Brazil could

interest associations] are prominently, even quite disproportionately, present in such forums and it seems that this represents a particularly privileged arena of influence for
business interests" (Schmitter and Streeck 1999, 36).

not have been thinking about disenfranchising big business over the long run when they successfully pressured the Vargas government to structure representation regionally and to grant full control over training programs to corporatist federations. Yet the short-term actions of Simonsen and like-minded business leaders had profound institutional consequences in distorting business representation.

In other words, to return to Bates's suspicion about third-party motives, even if the suppliers of institutions try to design them to further their interests these institutions may turn out later to serve other interests, for at least two reasons. First, even for political actors who can foresee the long-term institutional consequences, their own time horizons are short. For political executives who can be fired at any moment, their concerns about long-term organizational consequences are likely secondary, as are considerations of whose interests stronger associations will favor later on. Second, the mechanisms of institutional evolution are often opaque. Economic policy makers, operating in crisis circumstances, may have little time to assess how the granting of privileged access to an association might enhance members' interest in sustained investment in organizational capacity or strengthen association leaders vis-à-vis passive members in ways that give leaders strong incentives to defend their privileged access. Whether such calculations should be appropriate criteria for policy analysis is an issue I return to in the final chapter. Suffice it to say for now that there is little evidence that such considerations were carefully factored into the cases of policy making considered in this book.

Institutional change in associations was also largely the result of changing interests among state actors, except that each institutional innovation narrowed the range of options for later modifications. Institutional maintenance was primarily a function of the continuing provision by the state of selective benefits, in many cases even in the absence of the interests that motivated the initial concession of benefits. Again, for major changes in business associations, state actors often showed little appreciation for the longer-term consequences of changes they introduced. So, for example, Colombian officials could introduce in 1940 an emergency fund to stabilize coffee prices during World War II without imagining how this might transform Federacafe during subsequent coffee bonanzas into something resembling more a vast holding company than a representative association. And in Brazil, officials in the Kubitschek government could take industrial federations off key policy councils without thinking through how their lack of access would change internal dynamics in these associations. Again, in these comparisons, Mexican officials seemed to appreciate how, for example, their support of new voluntary associations in the 1970s and 1980s would help them displace older corporatist associations.[35]

If selective incentives provided by the state hold these institutions together, then relatively small changes in state policy can be crucial sources for institutional change. For example, the rescinding of compulsory dues in Mexico in 1997 dramatically reduced membership and revenues and prompted associations to search for new benefits to offer members. At the same time, state actors may provide new selective incentives to alternative associations in order to meet new policy challenges. Regional integration and the negotiation of trade agreements has, especially in the Mexican and Chilean cases, led political executives to provide associations with the selective incentive of accompanying the negotiations. There were some early indications that negotiations over the Free Trade Area of the Americas (FTAA) might breath new life into Brazilian associations like the industry confederation CNI, because government negotiators wanted business included (in contrast to their exclusion from Mercosul negotiations discussed in the next chapter) (interview with Ricardo Markwald, 28 May 2002).

Business associations, and likely other institutions dependent on voluntary contributions, may constitute a subset of institutions with distinctive dynamics of institutional change. General theories of institutions regularly emphasize their inertia and stickiness, absent exceptional periods of institutional transformation or "punctuation" (Krasner 1984). Yet as institutions, business associations seem relatively less sticky in that they respond quickly to the changes in benefits provided by the state. Business associations seem especially unsticky on the down side, as evidenced by the common cases where capitalists abandoned associations from one day to the next when either a government threat or a benefit disappeared. The overall point for understanding longer-term institutional change in associations is to identify changing challenges and incentives facing political executives that, in turn, prompt them to change the types of selective incentives they offer to business associations.

---

[35] Perón is somewhat more puzzling in this regard because he had a clearer strategy for organizing labor, but he was unable to put a lasting mark on business associations, though perhaps because he had less time and "institutional space" than his Mexican counterparts to reorganize Argentine society.

PART III

IMPLICATIONS AND CONCLUSIONS

8

Economic Governance and Varieties of Capitalism

> People of the same trade seldom meet together, even for merriment and diversion, but the conversation ends in a conspiracy against the public, or in some contrivance to raise prices.
>
> Adam Smith[1]

The Discrete Charms of the Organized Bourgeoisie[2]

Previous chapters worked to untangle the often turbulent histories of major business associations in the larger countries of Latin America and pinpoint moments of foundation and transformation. These moments were almost always associated with state actions, either deliberate or unintended, that significantly altered the incentives for big business to engage in collective action. The end result was that for most of the second half of the twentieth century, Chile, Mexico, and Colombia had the strongest business associations and the closest approximation overall to liberal or societal corporatism. The two concluding chapters of Part III shift the focus from the causes of greater organizational capacity in business associations to some of the consequences. This chapter considers the question of whether stronger organizations mattered to economic policy making and performance; the next chapter assesses how they affected democracy.

[1] Cited in Cohen and Rogers (1995b, 15).
[2] I borrow this subtitle from Levy (1999, 169) and emphasize "discrete," or separate, rather than "discreet" to signal the distinct ways that associations resolve some coordination problems in the economy. The concluding chapters further argue that the some charms of the organized bourgeoisie lie precisely in the ways that organization makes business–government relations less discreet and instead more open and transparent.

The general argument to be developed across these concluding chapters is that stronger associations in Mexico, Chile, and Colombia made more visible and consistent contributions to economic governance and democratic governability than their institutionally weaker counterparts in Brazil and Argentina.

As signaled in Chapter 1, there is considerable disagreement over the question of whether an organized bourgeoisie can be expected to have any charms. Although Olson admitted the possibility that encompassing associations might make positive economic contributions, his theory predicted that encompassing associations would be rare and short-lived. Olson takes up where Adam Smith left off in the quote at the beginning of this chapter and argues that more numerous narrow associations were likely to form "distributional coalitions" and behave like "bandits" and "wrestlers in a china shop." This chapter first analyzes some of the empirical exceptions to these prevalent Olsonian views. The concluding section then delves further into theoretical problems in the microeconomic literatures on distributional coalitions and rent seeking.

The literatures on corporatism, governance, and some variants of historical institutionalism generally differ from Olson in their answers to the question "what do associations do?"[3] Since Schmitter's rediscovery of corporatism in the 1970s, most studies of European political economy have emphasized the central roles of business associations in tripartite bargaining with labor and government to stabilize the macroeconomy and in the governance of particular sectors of the economy. The key benefits or public goods that corporatism was to deliver were macroeconomic stability and more flexible and lower-cost ways to manage adjustment to exogenous shocks. This management required centralized and concentrated associations for business and labor (Katzenstein 1985). Summing up the results of two decades of research on advanced industrial countries, Schmitter concluded that tripartite bargains "under corporatist auspices seemed not only to have a significant impact on rates of inflation, levels of unemployment, and fiscal equilibria, but to contribute to the 'governability' of the polity" (1992, 434). After a lull in the 1980s, incomes policies and tripartite bargaining reemerged in the 1990s in many countries of Europe (Baccaro in press; Schmitter and Grote 1997). Other scholars emphasized the role of business associations, at sectoral and micro levels, in performing essential governance functions. Hollingsworth and Boyer argue that

---

[3] Even the World Bank admitted the possibility of positive economic contributions from business associations (2002, 62–3). See also Picciotto (1995, especially 10–12).

"neocorporatist state–society interfaces enable economic actors to cooperate in developing long-term obligations for themselves and others. . . . And it is the state, interacting with the organized interests, that permits neocorporatist institutional regimes to outperform liberal ones in a variety of areas" (1997, 14). Most recently, Hall and Soskice (2001a) argued that "coordinated market economies," coordinated in part by strong employers associations, have distinctive strengths – such as highly skilled labor, incremental technological innovation, and greater equality – compared to "liberal market economies."

Such blanket statements are harder to make for Latin America, where it is important from the outset not to overstate the contributions of strong business associations to economic performance. It might be tempting to try to link societal corporatism and strong encompassing associations to overall economic outcomes. For instance, Colombia and Chile in the 1980s, and Mexico and Chile in the 1990s, were at times growth leaders in the region, and Colombia had greater macroeconomic stability over the postwar period than the other large countries (Stallings and Peres 2000; Thorp 1991).[4] However, aggregate outcomes like sustained growth and enduring macroeconomic stability depend on many factors, so it is unwarranted to try to link them causally to a single institutional dimension of variation such as the level of organization by business. Hence, subsequent sections of this chapter disaggregate economic performance into separate, discrete dimensions on which stronger associations had more visible and direct impacts: concerted inflation reduction, collaborative implementation of major economic reforms, consultative negotiation of trade agreements, and sectoral governance.[5] Nonetheless, the ranking of countries with well-organized business at the top of various lists of overall economic performance does invite skepticism toward the argument that strong business organization necessarily stands in the way of economic progress.

This chapter takes a closer look at some of the various functions strong associations pursued. While many associations sought rents and special benefits for their members, the activities of the encompassing associations

---

[4] In the 1980s, the five cases ranked as follows in terms of average percentage growth in real GDP for 1980–90: Chile 3.5, Colombia 3.4, Mexico and Brazil 1.5, and Argentina – 1.4. The rankings for 1995–2000 were: Mexico 5.5, Chile 4.6, Argentina 2.7, Brazil 2.3, and Colombia 1.0. Argentina's GDP grew rapidly in the early 1990s, but the economic collapse of 2000–2 erased many of the gains of the 1990s (UNCTAD 2002, 322–8).

[5] For a broader comparative and theoretical analysis of the contributions of associations to development, see Doner and Schneider (2000).

encountered in Chapters 3 to 7 cannot be classified exclusively, or even primarily, as rent seeking. In fact, weaker associations in Brazil and Argentina were more likely to engage in a narrower range of purely self-serving behaviors in part because their lack of institutional capacity limited their options for more public-spirited activities. However, most of this chapter focuses on a selective assessment of some of the contributions strong associations made in their "more coordinated" economies without attempting a full comparison with the behavior of weaker associations in the "less coordinated" market economies of Brazil and Argentina.

In broad terms, much of the history of policy reform in twentieth-century Latin America can be summarized by the pendular movement from attempts after the Great Depression to use state intervention to remedy market failures to later efforts at the end of the century to push market reforms to correct state failures. A general goal for this chapter is to look beyond state and market solutions and consider whether some coordination problems, derived from either state or market failures, are best addressed by associational solutions.[6] After decades of market reforms in Latin America, other scholars are also looking to business and business–government relations for novel solutions to continuing obstacles to equitable growth. For example, in concluding their extensive review of the disappointing results of market reforms in Latin America, Barbara Stallings and Wilson Peres argue that the now stronger private sector, combined with poorer governments and new challenges of globalization, make it "therefore essential for the government and private actors to work together more closely" (2000, 220). Where strong associations exist, they can become the pivotal private actors in this new collaboration.

Concerted Macroeconomic Coordination

Latin America has a long history of inflation and emergency stabilization policies, a history littered with failed policies and austerity programs with deep and prolonged social costs. These failures and costs regularly led policy makers to explore heterodox options, sometimes including incomes policies. Incomes policies, or the simultaneous setting of wage and price increases, in turn, usually required tripartite negotiation among representatives of government, business, and labor. Ideally, the participating organizations of business and labor would be encompassing enough to

[6] For a summary of coordination problems and the limits of markets and hierarchies, see Hall and Soskice (2001, 6–12).

cover most major sectors of the economy, as they were in Mexico's successful concertation in the 1980s. Where economy-wide encompassing associations did not exist, as in Brazil and Argentina, and where fragmented sectoral associations did not have common experiences reaching compromises, negotiating incomes policies was fraught with difficulties. The failure of past attempts at social pacts in Brazil and Argentina had multiple causes, but the relative disorganization of business was clearly among them.

The best positive case for illustrating the benefits of business organization and concerted stabilization comes from the Mexican Pacts. These pacts received much of the credit for reducing inflation at the end of the 1980s: "as a result of the *Pacto*, monthly inflation rates dropped from an average of about 15 percent in January 1988 to only one percent for the second half of the year" (Cardoso 1991, 175).[7] The pacts contributed to the success of the stabilization plan in multiple ways. Concertation, especially through the weekly meetings of the Price and Monitoring Commission, provided *information* to policy makers so that they could anticipate problems (Lustig 1992, 54). Government officials watched carefully for shortages, which were rare, certainly compared to the Brazilian experience with the short-lived Cruzado plan several years earlier. By providing complete information on the contribution of each party to the accords, or overall *transparency*, concertation reduced incentives for free riding (see Córdoba 1991, 35). Concertation enlisted firms and business associations in the tasks of *monitoring* and *enforcement* (see Streeck and Schmitter 1985). The government signed numerous "concertation accords" with particular firms, groups of firms, or associations and created the tripartite Price and Monitoring Commission, which met weekly to assess compliance. Of the associations involved, those representing retail trade, cement, chemicals, and autos were pivotal. In retail trade, members of ANTAD (Asociación Nacional de Tiendas de Autoservicio y Departamentales) controlled 35–60 percent of the retail market, and they bought only at prices authorized by the government (Kaufman, et al. 1994, 388–9).

Concertation greatly enhanced the *credibility* of the stabilization program; it "coordinated expectations" (Cline 1991, 14). The pacts became a crucial conduit for communication, especially on government

---

[7] This section draws on my earlier treatment in Schneider (1997). For the full story of the pacts see Zuckerman (1990) and Kaufman et al. (1994). Biddle et al. (2000) provide the full story on the first year of the pact and include an appendix on why it worked so well. For other favorable reviews, see Cline (1990), Lustig (1992), and Córdoba (1991).

intentions. In particular, the government used the pacts to demonstrate commitment to fiscal discipline (despite election year pressures) and over-all policy continuity. The commitment to fiscal austerity was one of the core components of *reciprocity* for business: "both publicly and in in-terviews, representatives of the leading business organizations identified quantified commitments to reduce expenditures as a key condition for their participation in the pact" (Kaufman et al. 1994, 382). Concertation also permitted more *flexibility*, especially in adjusting individual prices without causing irreparable damage to credibility (Cline 1991; Córdoba 1991, 35; Kaufman et al. 1994). Price freezes always get some prices wrong, and concertation provided a means for ongoing adjustment. The government in fact did not make open-ended promises on exchange rates and public prices precisely to maintain credibility after the inevitable ad-justments. In principle the terms of the pacts were subject to revision at each meeting: "this was a precaution to preserve government credibility in the event conditions were not sustainable" (Lustig 1992, 54). Lastly, the incomes policy in the pacts reduced the social costs associated with the more orthodox elements of the stabilization program and thereby made the program more politically *sustainable* (Córdoba 1991, 34). Some busi-nessmen found the concertation relationship so cozy that they lambasted the leaders of major participating associations for being ministers of the private sector (*Secretarios de Estado de la Iniciativa Privada, Proceso* 597, 11 April 1988, p. 10). While levied as a criticism, this transformation is exactly what concertation is designed to effect – to broaden the hori-zons of business leaders and enlist them in the task of providing collective public goods.

State actors instigated the pacts, set the agenda for negotiations, and contributed greatly to monitoring and implementing the accords, but in-stitutional strength on the part of the participating business associations was also a necessary complementary ingredient for success. Diverse asso-ciations and sectors had to be able to reach basic compromises and con-sensus on the pacts. Government officials signed agreements with some sectors individually, but these usually conformed to overall parameters ne-gotiated with the economy-wide CCE, and agreeing on these parameters involved intense intersectoral discussions among CCE members (inter-view with Agustín Legorreta, 28 July 1998). Technical staff in the associ-ations also contributed to the joint monitoring. Lastly, the high density of membership in business associations was essential to coordinating price reductions, monitoring, and reducing free riding. Less organized sectors revealed the importance of dense representation by negative example. Small-scale service firms, like private schools, restaurants, and beauty parlors, created problems for the pacts because they lacked associations that organized a significant proportion of the firms. Density was also crucial for the enforcement and cooperation of ANTAD, the supermarket association. Depending on the product, the members of ANTAD controlled large shares of total sales and could exercise monopsonistic power to encourage suppliers to exercise price restraint (interview with Jaime Serra, 16 July 1998).[8]

In Brazil and Argentine governments sometimes experimented with social pacts, especially in the 1980s, to coordinate macroeconomic policy but without any notable successes. These failures were in some ways overdetermined by multiple divisions within labor unions, within government, and within business associations. In Brazil in 1986, in the context of the Cruzado Plan to reduce inflation, the Sarney government invited representatives of business and labor to discuss a possible social pact. These discussions did not get very far, in part because their was little to negotiate, since the government had already set incomes (prices and wages). Moreover, this attempt "floundered on governmental indecision, inept use of incentives to elicit labor support, and union hostility" (Roxborough 1992, 652). In 1990 President Collor called together representatives of business and labor to discuss measures to sustain his rapidly unraveling stabilization program (Kingstone 1999, 136, 168; Schneider 1991a). These meetings fell apart for several reasons, among them a lack of prior coordination among fragmented representatives of both business and labor and a "lack of enthusiasm on the part of the government" (Roxborough 1992, 655). In one instance of successful concertation in the auto sector (discussed later), stabilization concerns did give government officials stronger incentives to reach an agreement, though it was only in one sector where the representation of business and labor was far less fragmented.[9]

In Argentina, political and economic elites have attempted concertation more often than elites elsewhere but to little effect. In the early 1970s and again in the 1980s, governments of all sorts – military, Peronist, and Radical – initiated concertation with business and labor, but none of the agreements lasted or had appreciable effects on macro instability. In the

---

[8] The pacts continued even after inflation dropped, though under different names and with new functions. The pacts became increasingly marginal to economic policy toward the end of Salinas's term. However, the pact was implicated in the capital flight and the peso collapse at the end of 1994 (Ortega 2002, 2003).

[9] Isolated regional experiences with concertation have generated some more positive results. In the state of Minas Gerais, for example, the industrial and commercial associations sat on the state's Industrial Council, which "improved decisionmaking capacity" (Montero 2001, 60).

early 1970s General Lanusse invited business to join the Gran Acuerdo Nacional. The following Peronist government, under the coordination of Gelbard (ex-president of CGE and minister) convoked another agreement. The Alfonsín government initially avoided negotiating with business associations but in the late 1980s turned to them several times in efforts to use concertation to control inflation. As in Brazil, the ineffectiveness of pact making in Argentina had multiple causes (Ayers 1976; Cappelletti 1985). Yet the lack of success stories confirms the expectation that concertation is less likely to work where encompassing organizations are weak.[10]

Coordinated Policy Reform

Major structural adjustments were not uncommon in twentieth-century Latin America, coming often on the heels of acute external shocks or dramatic domestic political transitions. As discussed in Chapters 3 to 7, in the wake of the Great Depression of the 1930s, government officials (in Chile, Mexico, and Brazil especially) sought out business associations and enlisted their support for changing the development strategy toward state-led ISI. Again after the debt crisis of the 1980s, economic policy makers sometimes turned to business associations, especially where business was well organized, to help in the transition to more open market economies. These reform policies affected large groups of businesses, and government officials therefore tended to seek out representatives of encompassing associations, both economy-wide and in major sectors like industry and agriculture. Where no such associations existed, policy makers tended to act in isolation or consult informally with major capitalists.

Chilean officials and associations illustrate best the form and benefits of close collaboration during both the neoliberal reforms of the 1980s and the redistributive reforms of 1990s. The decade from the outbreak of mass protests against Pinochet in 1983 through the first years of the democratic Concertación government put the economy-wide CPC at the center of business–government relations. After 1984 the military government's new economic ministers, especially Hernán Büchi, actively cultivated consultation and collaboration with business associations, especially the CPC (Silva 1996, 1998). Later the CPC became a privileged locus for deliberating a common position of the private sector for the plebiscite in 1988 and

---

[10] Tripartite bargaining was rare in Colombia, as was very high inflation. The Samper government experimented with a *pacto social* in the mid-1990s, but it had little impact on inflation (CNP 1997, 203).

presidential elections in 1989, as well as for negotiating major changes in tax and labor laws in the early 1990s (see Rehren 1995). Manuel Feliú, president of the CPC in the late 1980s, called this the "golden age" of the CPC (interview, 10 May 2000). Of course, the issues in this period were big and encompassing: political transition, new forms of political representation, new institutions for economic policy making (e.g., central bank autonomy), taxes, redistribution, and labor law. These issues affected all of the private sector, which made intermediation by the CPC more valuable to both business and government elites. CPC President Guzmán (1990–6) noted that the pressures within the CPC were to find "common denominators, and if they did not find one, the government would make decisions alone" (interview, 8 May 2001).

In the 1990s, in order to deliver on its electoral promise of increased spending on social welfare, the Aylwin government planned to raise taxes. Tax increases were a potentially explosive issue, and one that elsewhere is associated with business protest, both voice and exit (disinvestment). However, the Aylwin government negotiated with business and secured its agreement to temporary increases in valued added, personal income, and corporate taxes totaling a sharp 15 percent increase in total tax revenues (Weyland 1997, 42–3).[11] Yet, investment and growth remained high while the government expanded social spending and reduced poverty. The key to this smooth policy transition was encompassing organization: "sociopolitical forces have contributed to this prudent strategy only because of the existence of cohesive encompassing organizations" (Weyland 1997, 49). Given the high stakes of the transition, business leaders had strong incentives to compromise; it was better to accept some costs, such as higher taxation, if they helped secure broader support for the overall neoliberal model (interview with Manuel Feliú, 10 May 2000). Nonetheless, the CPC did serve an important function in forging consensus and overcoming the resistance of some member associations that favored more intransigence (Weyland 1997, 54). Tax rates were to revert to pre-1990 levels after several years, so the government initiated a new round of negotiations with the CPC in early 1993 (interview with Manuel Marfán,

---

[11] Critics of these negotiated agreements prefer to point out that the glass is half empty – that due to close negotiations with business, the government achieved less than it could have in redistributive measures. See, for example, Boylan (1996). The Aylwin government also proposed significant reforms to labor laws. Representatives of government and business discussed and negotiated, as in the case of tax increases, but business managed more successfully to block and stall reform (Silva 1998, 239–40), revealing more limits to the reforms possible through business–government concertation.

8 May 2001). These negotiations involved more technical personnel from the government and the CPC but ended in a compromise on more gradual and partial reductions in some tax rates.

Colombia in the late twentieth century stood out in Latin America for the infrequency of acute economic and political crises of the sort that encouraged finance ministers elsewhere to seek out business associations. Credit for the absence of crises and the unusual policy moderation is often given to better communication and cooperation between government and business associations (Thorp and Durand 1997). Despite, or perhaps because of, this overall close relation, business associations have not usually been invited to participate in designing or implementing major policy shifts such as the move to export promotion in the late 1960s or the trade liberalization of the 1990s (Juárez 1995). Overall, though, associations contributed to Colombia's remarkable tradition of policy moderation. In the 1970s, for example, when governments proposed major tax increases and an ambitious program for land reform, business associations mobilized to study the proposals, debate them in the media, and ultimately reach a compromise on less extreme policies (Hartlyn 1985; see also Urrutia 1983).

In Brazil in the 1930s and 1940s, newly formed encompassing associations for industry collaborated closely with Vargas governments in changing the overall development strategy to state-directed ISI. But since the 1950s organized business, especially more encompassing associations like FIESP and CNI, was not often closely involved in designing or implementing the major policy shifts of the late twentieth century. Government officials rarely invited business associations to discuss solutions to the debt and inflation crises of the 1980s or the neoliberal reforms of the 1990s. As noted in Chapter 4, the UBE and later Ação Empresarial, two loose and ephemeral efforts at economy-wide coordination among associations, were generally ineffectual in negotiating major reforms in the constitutional convention of 1987–8 or in subsequent periods of reform (Schneider 1997–8; Weyland 1996).

In one exception to this rule, Ação Empresarial and member business associations were central in pushing for and helping to design an overhaul of Brazilian ports. By the 1990s the situation in the ports was dire, so it was easier for diverse business interests to reach a consensus on the need to make Brazilian ports less costly and more efficient.[12] The

---

[12] In 1990 "there were 35 ports, 62 private port terminals and over 40,000 port workers handling approximately 350 million tons of cargo every year. Meanwhile, Rotterdam

trade opening of the 1990s increased the urgency of reform. Business associations overcame many of the problems that undermined effective coordination in UBE through a looser framework of Ação Empresarial. Ação Empresarial operated without an office or staff under the leadership of Jorge Gerdau, a respected steel maker from Rio Grande do Sul. This loose association helped reformers in the executive branch get the reform passed in Congress, but business demobilized too early and did not see the reform through to full implementation, something an association with greater institutional capacity might have been better able to do (Doctor 2000).

In Brazil in the 1990s state actors, business associations, and labor unions established *câmaras setoriais* (sectoral chambers) in auto and other sectors to manage stabilization policies and the competitive challenges from the trade opening.[13] In the early 1990s Dorothea Werneck, a top official in the Ministry of Economy, intended to use the *câmaras* to negotiate price stability when the government eliminated price freezes. From labor's side, the interest of CUT in tripartite negotiations was spurred by the devastating impact of the trade opening on employment in the industrial districts of São Paulo (see Arbix 1995 for the full story).[14] Alongside well-organized auto workers, assemblers (Anfavea), auto parts producers (Sindipeças), and other related businesses were very well organized and keen on finding solutions to the deep crisis in the auto sector. In March 1992 representatives of government, business, and labor signed the first sectoral accord, which committed the government to reduce taxes (6 percent in major sales taxes); business to reduce profit margins, decrease prices (by at least 22 percent), and maintain employment (for one year); and labor to wage moderation (no real increases for one year). Representatives of business, government, and labor renewed the accord for another three years in February 1993. This second accord was broader; beyond

---

alone handled this volume at one seventh the price with one fifth the number of workers" (Doctor 2000, 1).

[13] This section draws directly from Schneider (1997, 208–9). On the *câmaras* generally, see Arbix (1995), Keller (1995), Guimarães (1994), and Kingstone (1999).

[14] In 1991 Vicentinho (Vicente Paulo da Silva), then head of the metalworkers in the industrial districts around São Paulo, and after 1994 president of the entire CUT, decided to go to Detroit to try to convince Ford not to close an engine plant. The CUT delegation to Detroit was not successful in changing minds at Ford, but its members were deeply impressed and depressed by their tour of Detroit and discussions with representatives of the United Auto Workers. After this trip, Vicentinho and the metalworkers invested heavily in sectoral negotiations, so heavily that the *câmaras* became one of the key planks of the PT platform for Lula's campaign for president in 1994.

the reductions in taxes and prices, it included numerous medium- and long-term commitments to modernizing the sector (Keller 1995, 46–7).

Concertation in the auto industry appeared to have a dramatic impact. In 1993 and 1994 the auto sector set all-time records for production. In 1993 prices fell by 30 percent, domestic sales increased 43 percent, and the sector grew by 30 percent (which fueled overall growth since the sector accounted for 12 percent of GDP). The auto sector grew more than any other industrial sector in Brazil. In 1994 production grew another 14 percent. Simple measures of productivity rose over the first years from 8.8 cars per worker in 1991, to 10.2 in 1992, to an estimated 13.1 in 1993.[15] Despite the reduction in tax rates, total federal tax receipts in 1993 increased 30 percent and state tax receipts grew 22 percent (Keller 1995, 47). Critics charged that production would have increased without a *câmara*, and that therefore the accord amounted to little more than a government subsidy to wealthy consumers. Yet, econometric studies show that a substantial portion of the increase in production can be attributed to the accords.[16] Another significant and direct impact of the auto accords was on labor relations. Strikes had been widespread in the late 1980s but dropped off dramatically after the accords. Despite these various benefits, the auto *câmara* was short-lived. It broke down in 1995, and the Cardoso government did not subsequently try to revive it (Doctor 2003). Overall, the contrast between successful, even if temporary, concertation in autos and the several failed attempts at broader social pacts reveals the importance of an abiding government commitment to negotiate as well as unified representation of labor and business.

Toward the end of the Cardoso administration, government officials made clear their preference for managing crises alone. In mid-2001 the government revealed that Brazil was facing an electricity shortage. The government announced plans to reduce residential and business consumption and created the Câmara de Gestão da Crise de Energia Elétrica (CGE) to oversee the process. The label "*câmara*" harked back to the sectoral chambers, but the CGE was exclusively an interministerial chamber (formerly called "*conselhos*"). FIESP, CUT, and other groups immediately requested a place at the coordinating table (*O Globo*, 1 June 2001).

---

[15] Guimarães (1994, 12), citing data from Anfavea. Toledo (1994) notes that these data must be disaggregated because producers also began shifting a lot of production to subcontractors over these period.

[16] See Ministério da Fazenda (1994) and Toledo (1994). The Fazenda study concluded that income and interest rates had the greatest short-term effect on demand but that "over the long term the price effect dominated the others."

Reducing electricity consumption with minimal "collateral damage" to investment, production, and employment would appear to be precisely the kind of delicate task that would require flexibility, information exchange, and close coordination, all possible benefits of concertation with business. However, the government rejected requests for concertation and the inclusion of business representatives. Although not publicly cited by the government, FIESP staffers gave one reason why the government might have wanted to keep FIESP out. An advisor to FIESP President Horácio Lafer said that they wanted representation on the CGE in order to lobby for differential treatment by state ("estadualizar a crise," interview, 19 October 2001). In other words, FIESP was doing just what other business associations feared: representing Paulista industry at the potential expense of industry elsewhere, making FIESP an unreliable representative of all industry from the government's perspective.

Trade Negotiations and Regional Integration[17]

In the wake of the first wave of market-oriented reforms and macrostabilization, one of the most consequential areas of economic policy making in the 1990s was regional integration. Regional integration has complex effects across many interrelated sectors that are difficult for policy makers and negotiators to foresee. This complexity generates both informational and political problems that strong associations can help resolve. Government negotiators in Chile and Mexico relied more on business associations than could officials in Brazil and Argentina. Associations in Chile and Mexico were strong enough technically (i.e., had staff and resources to collect and analyze the data) and in terms of internal representation (they could aggregate or reconcile interests across sectors) so that they helped negotiators. How much this consultation affected the outcomes of negotiation – Nafta in the north and Mercosur (Mercado Común del Sur, known in Brazil as Mercosul) in the southern cone – is hard to measure, but the fact that government officials continually requested consultation in Mexico and Chile suggests that they found it helpful (and that they judged the associations capable of delivering the kind of information they needed). The country synopses that follow start with Mexico, the fullest case of collaboration between business and government, followed by Argentina and Brazil, two cases of state-led

---

[17] For an earlier and more extensive treatment, see Schneider (2001). Portions of this section are reprinted with permission of the Institute of Latin American Studies.

integration, and conclude with Chile, another later case of business–government cooperation.

When the Mexican government announced plans in March 1990 to pursue a free trade agreement with the United States, the CCE (with government approval) quickly created Coece (Coordinadora Empresarial de Comercio Exterior).[18] Coece and the government, in turn, created advisory committees comprised of 5 or so officials and 8–10 representatives from business to accompany negotiations in about 20 sectors. In the two years following the 1990 announcement, various groups of representatives of business and government negotiators had 1,333 meetings, or roughly a dozen a week (Puga 1994, 9). Business representatives were not allowed at the bargaining table with the United States and Canada, but they were figuratively, and often literally, "in the room next door" ("cuarto de junta").

Concertation through Coece in the Nafta negotiations helped to consolidate regional integration by building support in the private sector. Enthusiastic business endorsement of Nafta was surprising, considering that business had mobilized earlier in 1979 to block Mexico's entrance into GATT (General Agreement on Tariffs and Trade) (Kaufman et al. 1994; Story 1982). Other factors contributed to muting opposition to Nafta, but the fact that business felt consulted and included in negotiating the opening was also significant. Government leaders deemed such consensus building important enough in the early 1990s to invest heavily in campaigning in favor of Nafta by sending officials out to talk with business groups, 500–600 different presentations by one estimate (interview with Aslan Cohen, 16 November 1996). Support by big business for Nafta was nearly unanimous by 1993.[19]

Concertation increased the flow of information from business to government and vice versa. When Nafta negotiations began, many young government negotiators knew much less about North American business and trade than did Mexican exporters (interview with a Secofi negotiator, 8 November 1991). Beyond this familiarity, the government needed more systematic data, which Coece and member associations set about to collect. Initially, the government relied on the CCE's research unit to conduct a first national survey to find out what business wanted from

---

[18] The best sources on business in the Nafta negotiations are Puga (1994) and Thacker (2000).

[19] Coece was never intended to amplify the voices of, or generate support from, smaller firms. The high costs in both time and money to participate in the regular meetings of Coece, separately and with government, priced many smaller firms out of the meetings (Martínez and Schneider 2001; Shadlen 2000; Thacker 2000).

a trade agreement (Puga 1994, 7). Over time, sectoral associations began collecting more complete data on their respective sectors to use in the negotiations (Puga 1994, 15). Through these negotiations, the state also enhanced business capacity for interest intermediation within Coece. Within various advisory groups, representatives of upstream and downstream firms realized that they had to work out differences before taking joint proposals to the government; otherwise, business would lose influence (interview with Raúl Ortega, Coece, 16 November 1993).

In sum, Mexico set the standard for close collaboration between business and government in trade negotiations, a standard that would not be matched in Latin America until Chile negotiated its affiliation with Mercosur.[20] All the conditions in Mexico favored close collaboration. The government was generally predisposed to incorporate business representatives, and the minister responsible for Nafta, Jaime Serra, was especially keen on involving business. On the private side, big business in Mexico had for decades been investing in strong voluntary associations, especially CMHN and CCE. These associations took the lead in structuring, staffing, and funding Coece. CMHN, CCE, and Coece had sufficient staff and resources to provide timely, high-quality information. Moreover, they had the experience and forums necessary to talk through intersectoral differences and sometimes coerce consensus.

In the southern cone the process of integration was very different. In mid-1986 the Alfonsín and Sarney governments endorsed the Programa de Integración y Cooperación Económica (PICE). According to Cason, "from the beginning the [PICE] initiative was clearly state led. The private sector was generally not involved in the early negotiations, and only when its economic sectors were put on the agenda by trade negotiators did the private sector become involved" (Cason 2000a, 207; Manzetti 1990, 110) agrees. This pattern was later repeated in both Brazil and Argentina: presidents and their foreign ministers signed bold agreements on integration to which business later gained concessions and exemptions. The foreign ministries took the lead in implementing and administering PICE

---

[20] Business participation in Nafta negotiations was apparently the norm and was intense on all three sides of the negotiating table. This common "North American" practice may have encouraged Mexican officials to include their business representatives to balance participation by firms in the United States, and Canada. The organizers of Coece in fact directly copied the structure Canadian business had used in earlier negotiations with the United States. In the United States, major firms and associations formed the USA-Nafta Coalition to lobby in favor of the agreement. In addition, government negotiators set up a private sector advisory system (first mandated by Congress in the Trade Act of 1974) (Avery and Friman 1999).

(Manzetti 1990, 115). Historically Itamaraty, the Brazilian foreign service, was more distant and insulated from business than other ministries, in part because it recruited top officials almost exclusively from within its own ranks. By the late 1980s integration had stalled, due largely to increasing macroeconomic instability in both countries and because PICE was "not reinforced by supportive economic and social groups, which were not organized either spontaneously or by the government" (Manzetti 1990, 133). This lack of support, which would reemerge as a problem in the late 1990s when Mercosur ran into problems, contrasts sharply with the stronger business backing in Chile and Mexico. Moreover, the piecemeal approach to integration "was stymied by sectoral lobbies in both countries that made negotiations more difficult" (Jenkins 1999, 39).

After 1990 in Brazil the new Collor government, especially the foreign ministry, Itamaraty, pushed forward a bolder plan for integration but again without business input. This push culminated in the Treaty of Asunción in early 1991 that created Mercosur. Itamaraty's traditional insulation from political pressures in its design of foreign economic policy (Cason 2000a, 215; Pfeifer and Oliveira 2000) combined with Collor's public exclusion of organized business meant that Mercosur was initially designed without much consultation with business. Top economic policy makers in the Cardoso government also kept their distance from organized business. However, Brazilian business from the beginning was generally predisposed to integration with Argentina. A small survey in 1991 revealed that 82 percent of Brazilian businesses expected to gain from Mercosur (versus only 45 percent of Argentine business respondents) (Coopers and Lybrand study cited by Jenkins 1999, 42). Overall, Mercosur was less important to Brazilian business because of the smaller relative size of the economies of its trading partners. The other three countries considered here, Argentina, Mexico, and Chile, were all seeking integration into larger economies.[21]

Overall, Brazil's participation in Mercosur was state-led, with business playing a minor role (Burrell and Cason 2000; Cason 2000a, 2000b;

---

[21] Brazilian business was later incorporated into several formal forums for subsequent rounds of Mercosur negotiations. In 1994 negotiators created the Foro Consultivo Económico – Social (FCES) to bring together representatives from peak sectoral associations, unions, and consumer groups. This Foro was large, cumbersome, and met only rarely to accompany big Mercosur meetings. Mercosur negotiators also encouraged the formation of the Consejo Industrial Mercosur (CIM), composed of the peak industry associations in the four countries. Neither forum was an effective conduit for channeling private sector representation.

Manzetti 1993–4). Alfonsín and Sarney started the process for their own political and state reasons. Menem and Collor added in ideology, geopolitics, and competing regionalisms (i.e., exclusion from Nafta and the European Union). However, once states had started negotiations rolling, Brazilian businesses (especially through narrow sectoral associations) geared up to push negotiators to protect afflicted sectors or slow integration. Politically the government's strategy seems to have been less one of building a strong pro-Mercosur coalition (comparable to the pro-Nafta coalition in Mexico) and more one of undercutting the formation of an anti-Mercosur coalition by granting exceptions and concessions (see Jenkins 1999).

This model of state initiation followed by subsequent business participation also characterized the Argentine process, though perhaps with fewer concessions to business. As in Brazil, decision making in Argentina on regional integration through PICE and Mercosur was largely top-down, state-led, and dependent on presidential initiatives (Manzetti 1993–4, 117). Business participation in negotiations over integration was uneven, both over time and across sectors, but in contrast to Mexico and Chile, business participation in Argentina was not mediated by strong encompassing associations. When business did participate, it was usually through narrow sectoral associations or as individual firms or capitalists, in part because encompassing associations lacked institutional capacity and staff. Internal divisions and institutional incapacity limited the effective participation of business associations in trade negotiations.

Beyond the organizational weaknesses of UIA, the overall political and economic context also mattered, though in different ways in the 1980s and 1990s. In the Alfonsín government policy makers were generally open to business participation (see Chapter 7). In the context of the brief stability of the Austral Plan in mid-1986 Alfonsín launched the idea of integration with Brazil (PICE). Business was not in on the initial decision or on the overall framework for PICE but later had input into its implementation. Government officials decided which sectors to include in PICE and then told business associations in these sectors to work out agreements with their counterparts in Brazil. This sector-by-sector integration moved slowly in the mid-1980s but stalled by the end of the decade as the Alfonsín government unraveled, precisely because PICE was so dependent on presidential initiatives. By 1988 a protectionist lobby was arguing that Brazil was gaining an unfair advantage (Manzetti 1990, 120). Thereafter business participation in negotiations over integration was uneven; access varied over time and was generally better for top capitalists individually and particular sectoral associations than for encompassing associations like the UIA.[22]

When Menem announced Mercosur and a rapid acceleration in the timetable for integration (tariff reductions in five years instead of ten), he did not consult with business. Over the 1990s, UIA became increasingly marginalized and lacked regular institutionalized channels to consult with government negotiators. Felix Peña, one of the government's top negotiators, described two episodes that reveal the lack of capacity in UIA, both technically and in terms of reconciling conflicting interests (interview, 5 May 2000). First, Peña convened a meeting of 32 representatives from business associations to discuss coordinating macro policies with Brazil. He requested written papers before the meeting, but not one of the associations submitted anything. Second, he asked UIA to give him an opinion on a temporary change in Mercosur regulations. UIA wrote him back a week or so later, saying that UIA had no opinion because affected members could not come to an agreement. Felix Peña, after long experience as a government negotiator, concluded that business interlocutors were most effective in helping government negotiators when the business association (1) was well organized nationally, (2) had a good "technocracy" (i.e., qualified staff), (3) was concentrated and had few member firms, and (4) had high levels of "bilateral intimacy" (close contacts with counterpart associations in Brazil). A few narrow sectoral associations had these qualities, but encompassing associations like UIA did not.[23]

Overall, business in Argentina has been less enthusiastic about regional integration than business in Brazil, Mexico, and Chile. From the beginning, only 45 percent of businesses in one survey of business expected to gain from Mercosur (Jenkins 1999, 42). Thereafter the Menem government largely denied business associations access to ongoing negotiations. Worse, by 1999, Argentine business was under pressure from Brazil's devalued exports, and business was so divided over Mercosur that even the

---

[22] For example, the head of the Centro de la Industria Lechera as well as Jorge Blanco Villegas, then president of UIA, complained of inadequate consultation between business and government, and the head of a smaller dairy association claimed that there was no channel for consultation between business and government (Luján Olivera 2000, 5, and personal interview with Blanco Villegas, 3 May 2001). By comparison, Santiago Soldatti, head of one of Argentina's largest conglomerates, contrasted the failure of previous attempts at regional integration (due in part, according to Soldatti, to the lack of cooperation between business and government) to the success of Mercosur, "where business and the state participated very closely" (Luján Olivera 2000, 4–5).

[23] For example, in the auto sector, associations in both Argentina and Brazil were more active and supportive (Diaz de Landa and Sajem 2000).

"winners" would not come to an open defense of Mercosur in 1999, when the clamor of criticism was growing (interview with Felix Peña, 5 May 2000).

Chile was another case of especially close collaboration between business and government in trade negotiations, as in other major economic and social issues of the 1980s and 1990s.[24] By the 1990s policy makers became concerned about the possible exclusion of Chile from emerging trading blocs. The initial inclination of the Aylwin government was toward Nafta, but by 1995 the Frei government had shifted its attention to Mercosur. Several factors contributed to this shift. Within the Aylwin government there were advocates for both regional agreements; those favoring Nafta were strong in the Ministry of the Economy, while many in the Ministry of Foreign Relations favored Mercosur. And over the 1990s, the private sector became increasingly vocal and active in pressing for Mercosur, in part because export opportunities, especially for industry, were expanding rapidly (Burrell and Cason 2000). In 1990 trade with Mercosur countries accounted for 8 percent of Chilean exports and 16 percent of imports. By 1994 the value of exports had doubled and Mercosur accounted for 12 percent of total exports and 18 percent of imports (Meller and Donoso 1998, 25; see also Duran 1996, 193). Business perceived Mercosur as a major potential source of growth for Chilean trade.

From 1994 to 1996 associations like CPC, Sofofa, and Asexma (Asociación de Exportadores de Manufacturas) mounted a multipronged campaign to press the government to negotiate Chile's entry into Mercosur (Burrell and Cason 2000). Leaders from these and other associations wrote letters, called meetings, and made public declarations in favor of Mercosur over Nafta. Moreover, business leaders said that they wanted to be included from the start; Victor Manuel Jarpa, president of the construction association, said, "we are not going to limit ourselves to revising agreements made by the government, as we did in the past. This time, we will participate in the whole meal, including the entree, instead of just the dessert" (cited in Burrell and Cason 2000, 20). Business associations then began making specific recommendations on tariff schedules and timetables, exceptions that they pressed the government to push in negotiations. When it became clear in late 1995 that Washington was not going to accept fast-track negotiations, the pro-Nafta coalition in Chile faded, and business succeeded in pushing the government to pursue Mercosur more

---

[24] Patricio Silva writes that business was "fully integrated into negotiations" for trade agreements with Colombia, Venezuela, and Mexico (1995, 22).

aggressively. By mid-1996 negotiators had worked out an agreement for Chile's entry into Mercosur that extended protection for Chilean agriculture while reducing the initial obstacles proposed to slow manufactured exports from Chile.

The most important business connections to government came at the negotiating table. Here business was always very close to government officials in a string of trade negotiations throughout the 1990s. Just how close the association was depended on the official protocols for negotiations. In some cases, business was not allowed at the table but was in the "room next door." In other cases, business was at the table next to government negotiators. In the most extreme case, the government deputized Sofofa staffer Hugo Baierlein to negotiate, by himself, an agreement with Bolivia. The government issued Baierlein a diplomatic passport, sent him to La Paz, and rubber-stamped the trade agreement he negotiated (interview with Baierlein, 9 May 2000).[25] This kind of access gives associations very strong incentives to invest in institutional capacity, as Sofofa has in expanding the staff of its international trade department. By 2001 Sofofa had a staff of 15 working only on international trade, compared with a staff of 2 or 3 in the Argentine industry association UIA.

In sum, encompassing business associations in Chile and Mexico had access to government trade negotiators and participated actively in shaping the terms of regional integration into Mercosur and Nafta, respectively.[26] In contrast, peak industry associations in Brazil and Argentina rarely enjoyed easy access and had little influence, especially in the early 1990s, when much of Mercosur was negotiated. Government receptiveness to organized business participation was generally higher in Mexico and Chile than in Argentina and Brazil in the 1980s and 1990s. Of course, government receptiveness to collaboration with business depends

---

[25] In a similar instance of delegation, the Colombian government turned most international negotiations over sugar and cut flowers to associations representing these producers (Juárez 1996, 21).

[26] Colombia and Venezuela were less deeply involved in regional integration; however, governments in both countries liberalized trade in the 1990s and consulted closely with business during the process of liberalization (see Giacalone 1999). Consultation in Venezuela in the early 1990s resembled the intense collaboration in Mexico: "trade officials painstakingly discussed every step of the process with Conindustria [Confederación Venezolana de Industriales], explicitly identifying (rather than hiding) which sectors were likely to win or lose" (Corrales and Cisneros 1999, 2111). This consultation generated political support for liberalization, and overall, "policy transparency, rather than selective punishments and rewards, is more conducive to cooperative state-sector relations" (2117).

strongly on whether officials think associations are strong and capable (a capacity for data collection and analysis, as well as internal conflict mediation among their members, the two key dimensions of institutional strength). Over the course of the 1990s a virtuous, or at least self-reinforcing, cycle developed: when governments granted business associations a place in the negotiations, associations invested in institutional capacity for negotiating, which made associations even more valuable interlocutors for government officials. By virtue of their participation in negotiating and implementing regional agreements, associations became more specialized in trade negotiation and promotion.

Collaboration between business and government in trade negotiations generated clear political support. Business associations were publicly more supportive of regional integration in Chile and Mexico, while their counterparts in Brazil and Argentina were equivocal, lukewarm, or downright critical.[27] Chilean business in fact led the charge for Mercosur and pulled the government along with it. In contrast, as one Argentine official lamented, when the going got tough in Mercosur after the Brazilian devaluation of early 1999, even the major beneficiaries of Mercosur in Argentina did not come out to defend Mercosur against the rising chorus of critics. Had political leaders like Alfonsín, Menem, and Collor been unwilling to pay the political costs of opposition, Mercosur would likely not have gone far. Moreover, the lack of broad political support for integration in Brazil and Argentina made negotiators more vulnerable to pressures from contrary businesses, labor, or other social groups. In explaining the failure of integration between Argentina and Brazil to progress in the late 1980s, Luigi Manzetti wrote in 1990 that "governments should actively encourage the creation of a pro-integration lobby that can serve to counterbalance protectionist and isolationist groups. . . . To this end, governments should broaden the base of support for integration by promoting greater involvement of economic interests in shaping the negotiation process" (Manzetti 1990, 136). Manzetti's recommendations sound very much like the steps officials were taking at that very moment in Mexico.

These variations in business–government collaboration over regional integration depended first on government openness to, and sometimes promotion of, collaboration. Beyond idiosyncratic issues of style and personality, government openness to business participation depended on an anomalous mix of government strength and vulnerabilities. On the

---

[27] For in-depth analysis of coalition building and political support, see Thacker (2000), Pastor and Wise (1994), Kingstone (1999), and Calvo (2001).

vulnerabilities side, officials in Mexico and Chile felt that they needed the trust and support of business, though for different reasons. In Mexico, technocrats in the de la Madrid and Salinas governments were still trying to overcome deep business suspicions of government that lingered from the acrimonious 1970s and early 1980s. In Chile, Concertación governments suffered a historic deficit of trust or confidence and consulted with business on most policy changes in the 1990s (Muñoz 2000). However, this overall vulnerability (as perceived by political leaders) was coupled with the expectation of state (or bureaucratic) strength to withstand particularistic lobbying. That is, government officials had strong political backing to stand up to pressures by individual firms and sectoral associations, and they were dealing with strong encompassing associations that had incentives to discourage particularistic lobbying by member firms and associations. In contrast, presidents in Brazil and Argentina felt less need to assuage business preoccupations, or did so by appointing business executives to the cabinet rather than opening up negotiations to business associations. And, despite moments of overall political strength (Menem especially), leaders in Brazil and Argentina knew that their executive bureaucracies were weaker and more porous. They also recognized that business was more fragmented and hence more likely to infuse negotiations with intersectoral infighting.

Further Issues in Sectoral Governance

Beyond these macro-level benefits that encompassing associations can provide, narrower associations can also make more micro-level contributions to governance and coordination in particular sectors. The key questions are similar: can business associations, usually created or sustained by the state, help to organize sectoral governance in ways that generate broader benefits for the economy as a whole? Successful sectoral governance also depends on strong associations that have both technical capacity (human and material resources) and the ability to reach and enforce internal agreements among members.[28] Of course, by this measure, the number of institutionally strong associations in Latin America is small, and the number of cases of successful self-governance is correspondingly limited.

---

[28] For a broader review of governance mechanisms at a sectoral level, see Lindberg et al. (1991).

The most enduring and famous case of sectoral governance is that of Colombian coffee. As examined in Chapter 5, prior to the creation of Federacafe, Colombian coffee exporters faced debilitating market failures, due mostly to information costs and asymmetries (see Bates 1997; Junguito and Pizano 1997). Before Federacafe coffee production was dispersed among many small producers who shipped coffee of varying quality, and opportunistic growers had incentives to try to sell lower-quality coffee under high-quality labels. International buyers lacked the information to assess quality and therefore had incentives to discount all prices they paid for Colombian coffee. Federacafe's stringent quality control after the 1930s allowed Colombian coffee to expand and capture a large share of the market for high-priced, high-quality coffee. As Federacafe's resources expanded, it proceeded to eliminate other bottlenecks in transportation, access to credit, shipping, and marketing. Federacafe grew well beyond its role as a sectoral regulator into a major development agency and business conglomerate until the collapse of coffee prices in the 1990s forced a dramatic retrenchment.

State actors could also have attempted to resolve these market failures alone, as they did in other coffee-producing countries like Brazil. Without embarking on an extensive comparison of domestic governance of the coffee sector, there are signs that business associations (sometimes working with government) can outperform both pure market and exclusive state regulation of coffee. In Brazil, for example, the lack of high-quality exports or even high-quality production for the domestic market was puzzling until the 1990s, when the government closed the regulatory agency IBC (Instituto Brasileiro do Café). In the 1970s and 1980s coffee producers were alarmed to see per capita coffee consumption falling in Brazil, of all places. After the extinction of IBC several new associations formed, and one of them began a voluntary program of quality control that generated a new, lucrative, and rapidly expanding market niche for higher-quality coffees, and partly as a result, domestic consumption reversed its decline (Farina, Furquim, and Saes 1997; Saes 1997). Similarly, in Mexico in the 1990s, after Salinas dismantled national regulation of coffee, state and local elites stepped into the institutional vacuum. In Richard Snyder's comparison of four states, he finds that corporatist cooperation between coffee associations and the state government of Oaxaca in a State Coffee Council "enhanced the efficiency and quality of smallholder production" and "made small coffee farmers more competitive in global markets" (2001, 45).

A bright spot on Colombia's economic horizon in the 1990s was flower exports. By the 1980s, Colombia was already the world's second largest exporter of cut flowers (behind the Netherlands) and accounted for 8 percent of world exports (Mendez 1993, 103). The business association for flower exporters, Asocoflores, was central in promoting the growth of the flower sector. Air transportation was, of course, crucial to an export as perishable as cut flowers, and Asocoflores worked to reduce rates and attract more airlines to Colombia (Juárez 1995, 167). Asocoflores helped establish Transcold, a common handling company in Miami, to get the flowers from the airplanes through customs and into the distribution network in the United States (Mendez 1993, 110).[29] And, in a pattern often repeated in Colombia, state actors delegated policy responsibility for international negotiations to Asocoflores: as an Asocoflores official put it, "the government basically hands over negotiations to us and gives us the green light to represent Colombia in all foreign matters affecting the flower industry" (cited in Juárez 1995, 97).

Among the voluntary industry associations discussed in this book, Sofofa has taken on the widest range of responsibilities for sectoral governance. As noted in Chapter 6, Sofofa participates extensively in trade negotiations and administers the certification necessary to comply with the rules of origin stipulated in various trade treaties. Sofofa also has a significant role in vocational training through the five technical schools it took over from the government (overall, various business associations administer about 70 such technical schools; interview with Pedro Lizana, 10 May 2000, and Balze 1995, 158). The government still finances these schools, but Sofofa determines the curriculum and personnel and helps graduates find jobs.[30] In addition, Sofofa administers health insurance and housing programs for workers in industry (interview with Pedro Lizana and Sofofa 2002).

Another very different story of successful sectoral governance concerns low-tech furniture production in one of Brazil's poorest states, Ceará (Tendler 1997). Officials in the state government recognized that they were paying a high cost to import school furniture from far-off manufacturers

---

[29] Mendez (1993) argues generally that the success of flower exports is due primarily to market factors and entrepreneurship, often against policies by both the Colombian and U.S. governments, though he sometimes mentions help from Asocoflores in the category of entrepreneurship.

[30] As noted in Chapter 4, compulsory industry associations in Brazil had a huge role in training and administering a vast network of schools and training facilities that are financed out of a compulsory payroll tax.

in São Paulo, so they helped organize local furniture artisans into an association, the Aruaru Furniture Manufacturers Association, and then contracted procurement with the association. The association took on responsibility for quality control, contract enforcement, and distribution of production quotas, as well as helping with training and equipment purchases. The results were higher local production and employment for the region and lower-cost, higher-quality furniture for the schools.

Among the common themes in these and other stories of association, contributions to sectoral governance were state inducements for collective action and competitive markets, in most cases international.[31] The prevalence of export markets, of course, helped shift the attention of association leaders from rent seeking to using associations to enhance competitiveness. In addition, these sectors were characterized by many small producers, sectors prone to market failures, and obstacles to collective action. Large numbers of dispersed producers increase the likelihood that state regulation of sectoral governance alone will be ineffective and at the same time make associational effectiveness dependent on state solutions to obstacles to collective action.

The general policy implication that emerges from the examples in this chapter is not that governments should always turn to associations when confronted with policy challenges or various sorts of market and state failures. If associations are not sufficiently strong internally (in terms of technical capacity and staff and the ability to reconcile internal differences), much can be wasted, as demonstrated by the successive failures at concertation in Brazil and Argentina. Moreover, concertation is costly, sometimes visibly, as in the case of foregone tax revenues in the Brazilian *câmaras*, and sometimes less perceptibly, as in cases of surrendered policy flexibility and privileged access for business (which by definition reduces access for other groups). In many instances, governments or markets alone may be able to achieve policy goals at an acceptable cost. In other instances, acting alone and foregoing coordination through associations may be ineffectual or raise the costs of adjustment unnecessarily.

Policy decisions on whether or not to involve associations would do well to factor in historical legacies and path dependencies. The central implication of the historical analyses in previous chapters is that strength

[31] Other cases where business associations have made crucial contributions to sectoral governance are Mexican footwear (Rabellotti 1998, especially 19), Chilean wood processing (Messner 1993), Colombian rice (Urrutia 1983), Brazilian pulp and paper (Kingstone 1999, 120), and Colombian sugar (Juárez 1995). For other cases, see Traxler and Unger (1994, 16) on Europe and Doner and Schneider (2000) on developing countries.

in business organization is the result of decades of investment by business in the institutional capacity of the associations. The strong associations that joined concerted macro governance in Chile and Mexico in the 1980s and 1990s were developing strength through the 1960s and 1970s, while the ineffectual organizations in Brazil and Argentina in the 1990s were still trying to overcome weaknesses and divisions from decades earlier. These lasting differences contribute to emerging "varieties of capitalism" within Latin America.[32] Although democratization and neoliberal reform were powerful homogenizing influences at the end of the twentieth century, major differences among countries remain, especially between the more organized or coordinated market economies of Chile, Mexico, and Colombia and the disorganized governance or "uncoordinated" market economies of Argentina and Brazil.[33] Although still less institutionalized than their counterparts in developed countries, Latin American varieties of capitalism give different economies distinctive strengths and weaknesses. As such, searching for policy options that play to the strengths and sidestep the weaknesses has advantages over devising universal policy prescriptions, as in successive "Washington consensuses."

Theoretical Implications: Individuals and Organizations in the Microeconomics of Collective Action

Examples in this chapter, as well as in the empirical chapters in Part II, have revealed numerous exceptions to pessimistic expectations derived from mainstream economic theories on preference formation, collective action, free riding, and rent seeking. Many of the anomalies and theoretical lacunas derive from a neglect of the interaction of individuals and organizations on several dimensions. For one, individual-based theories require greater attention to the impact of organization – firms, associations, and states – on individual preferences and strategies. In addition, at a methodological level, greater care and discretion are advisable in

---

[32] See Hall and Soskice (2001). The range of varieties of capitalism within Latin America is not of course as great as those between Latin America and other developing regions.

[33] Carol Wise (1999) argued that post-liberalization economic performance varied in the major countries of Latin America according to whether or not governments adopted a pro-active, pro-export, competitive strategy versus a passive, laissez-faire strategy. Chile was the best example of the competitive strategy. The government used tax policy, exchange rates, training, and close business–government relations to increase investment, productivity, and exports. Argentina, in contrast, was the most "passive" case; the government has not used policy and close business–government relations to expand exports and raise productivity.

analytic efforts to transfer individual-based theories to the analysis of the behavior of organizations.

On a first issue of preference formation, assumptions of rationality and self-interest are less problematic for capitalists than for other social actors, in part because competition weeds out businesspeople who are not pre-occupied with the bottom line. However, beyond the trivial assumption that capitalists prefer higher to lower profits, more specific deductions about preferences and strategies are impractical without thick knowledge of the organizational contexts in which capitalists pursue interests.[34] One essential contextual component is the structure of ownership (as discussed in Chapter 2). For example, managers of diversified conglomerates may have quite different preferences from managers of firms with all their assets in a single sector. Another kind of organization, business associ-ations, may also provide selective incentives that alter the strategies for pursuing individual interests within collective bodies. So, for example, in the case where representatives of an association sit on the board of a development bank that offers subsidized credit, it may be more effec-tive for rational capitalists to adopt a long-term strategy of investing time and money in the association, and to translate their individual interests into more collective policy positions in order to influence association rep-resentatives on the bank's board. Once brute economic interests have been filtered through ownership and associational structures, capitalists face further decisions in trying to turn preferences into viable political strategies. Strategies (individual versus collective, open media campaigns versus closed negotiation, parties versus associations, etc.) depend on the portfolio of options available and, among those options, the ones with the greatest perceived returns. These options also delimit which types of interests capitalists can pursue. So, for example, individual networking might generate benefits for an individual firm, while active engagement in associations to influence trade negotiations encourage firms to push more collective interests.

What about the preferences and strategies of state actors, especially top officials in the economic bureaucracy who provided selective incentives to associations and influenced returns on different political investments in capitalists' portfolios? Within the state and political society, individuals and different sets of organizations – such as legislatures, bureaucracies,

---

[34] Some of the worst offenders in this regard are those who derive preferences exclusively from asset specificity, with little or no regard for who owns the assets or how those owners might already be tied into organizations with owners of other kinds of assets (see Frieden 1991 and Frieden and Martin 2002).

and independent agencies – interact to shape distinct sets of preferences. Theories that start with a primary interest in reelection are insufficient to explain the preferences of officials in the bureaucracy. Top state officials rarely ignore electoral concerns completely, but they are at least one step removed from reelection as a primary interest. For one, the concerns of appointed officials are more immediate since they can be fired at any time, even absent any change in electoral fortunes. Moreover, appointed officials serve largely at the discretion of the president, who may also, especially when barred from running again, have other interests besides reelection.

Compared to electorally driven politicians, state officials are more likely to worry about solving immediate crises and facilitating policy implementation than about screening policy options exclusively through an electoral or partisan optic. Unfortunately, the microfoundations of bureaucratic behavior are less neat than those of electorally driven politicians. It is reasonable to assume that political executives seek to survive in office and advance in their careers (Geddes 1994; Schneider 1991b). The complexity increases, though, in specifying what it takes to advance because political executives empirically follow a number of different career tracks: some continue in new positions in the executive, some go into the private sector, and a few enter electoral politics.[35] Notwithstanding this diversity in career tracks, in the short run political executives are more likely to share the encompassing political interests that presidents and party leaders have in the overall performance of government policy. In short, simple "reelection theories" will be incomplete until we incorporate as well the distinct preferences of top unelected officials into theories of state behavior.

Another preference, for free riding, informs most microeconomic studies of collective action. If nonmembers cannot be prevented from enjoying the benefits secured by the association (nonexcludability), then rational nonmembers will free ride. However, as mentioned in Chapter 2, the assumption of free riding is unwarranted under several conditions. For some encompassing business associations in Latin America, public goods

---

[35] The top officials mentioned in Chapters 3 to 7 followed very different careers after leaving government. Jaime Serra Puche was promoted to secretary of finance in 1994 and then moved into private consulting when fired shortly after taking office. Marcílio Marques Moreira returned to a career in private finance. Dorothea Werneck went into banking. Hernan Büchi, the main economics minister in Chile in the 1980s, did in fact run for president in the first elections in 1989 (though in the mid-1980s these elections were still a remote possibility and could not therefore have weighed much in the future career calculations of political executives).

were not the only or even the primary goods these associations get from government.[36] The exclusive focus on public goods seems to draw on a US-centric view of the politics of interest groups in which groups lobby Congress for nonexcludable benefits like tax exemptions or tariffs. Regardless of the questionable accuracy of this view even for the United States, it is misleading in countries of Latin America, where governments regularly make discretionary and excludable allocations of resources. If, as in the selective benefit of access to policy forums, what association members get from government are excludable, club benefits (e.g., information or material resources available collectively to members only), then free riding should not pose a major obstacle to collective action. At a minimum, then, research needs to ask first what exactly associations get from governments and why before making assumptions about free riding.[37]

More generally, in multisectoral peak organizations, whose members are themselves organizations, the logic of collective action is fundamentally different from the individual calculus at the core of microeconomics of collective action. The historical record in Latin America confirmed that encompassing associations were difficult to create and hard to hold together. However, free riding was not empirically the main problem, in part because numbers were small, monitoring was easy, and resource needs were manageable. The bigger obstacle was diversity. The most damaging conflicts came over leadership selection, which in Chile and Mexico in the 1990s led some sectoral associations to withdraw in protest from the economy-wide association. Conflicts over leadership succession, in turn, revolved largely around divisions among sectors or between large and small firms.

The other decisive factor in the fate of economy-wide associations was the variable allegiance of the largest handful of *grupos* or conglomerates. In the Mexican and Venezuelan cases, big *grupos* held the encompassing associations together, but in Colombia they undermined the fledgling peak association. Where the largest firms hold the peak association together, it

---

[36] Moreover, these assumptions on free riding lead logically to further misplaced presumptions about rent seeking. If, so the argument goes, free riding is the major obstacle to collective action, then, necessarily, only small groups with homogeneous interests will be able to act collectively, and whatever resources they extract from politics will be for some narrow purpose, that is, rents extracted at the expense of the rest of society. The rent-seeking presumption is overstated both because free riding is often not the major obstacle to collective action and because it ignores problems of aggregation and context discussed later.

[37] Thinking about degrees, or a continuum, of rivalry in consumption and excludability generates a broader range of types of goods between the pure poles of public and private goods (Noble 1998, 3).

might look like the "natural" exploitation of the large by the small, with
the small free-riding on the efforts of the large (Olson 1965, 35). However, whether big business is a decisive centripetal or centrifugal force depends largely on government. In Mexico, state officials granted CCE privileged access and thereby encouraged big business to invest in it, whereas
in Colombia state actors worked successfully to split the biggest *grupos*
away from the antigovernment position staked out by the economy-wide
Consejo Gremial. Again, the general theoretical point is that a primary
focus on free riding would only obscure the real dynamics of collective
action among large-scale organizations – both sectoral associations and
conglomerates – in an economy-wide peak association.

If business interests are aggregated artificially or politically constructed,
as in the encompassing associations considered in this book, then we have
no reason to assume that business associations form on the basis of common underlying interests in order to lobby policy makers. Much of the
work on business lobbying mistakenly starts with the assumption that
rentseeking drives business and then deduces which groups are likely to
organize the kinds of associations that are effective in securing rents.
Olson's initial *Logic* provided a first, though often forgotten, antidote
to such deductions. Olson's by-product theory was that some associations with great lobbying power were in fact formed for some reason
(typically some selective incentive) other than common lobbying interests
(1965, 132–41). The selective incentives influence who organizes and how
intensely, and the organization, in turn, shapes how preferences are aggregated and expressed. Even in Olson's original theory, there was reason to
expect divergence between the lobbying preferences promoted by the association and the objective, deducible interests of the membership base. If
states provide the selective benefits, then reasons are even stronger to expect a divergence between "natural" member interests and the "artificial"
preferences expressed by their associations.

Studies in the microeconomics of collective action devote little attention
to the longer-term effects of selective incentives on institutional development.[38] How associations collect dues and from whom, how they make
internal decisions, how members are represented, and how much power
associations have over members are all variables that profoundly affect

---

[38] The best and fullest, though still inconclusive, treatment is Schmitter and Streeck (1999).
Apart from his neglected by-product theory, Olson devoted little attention to internal
organization. Sometimes selective benefits weaken associations by drawing in nonactive
members (see Wilson 1981 on the Farm Bureau).

what associations can do for governance and politics more generally. Selective incentives like compulsory membership, or individual benefits like discounted malpractice insurance for doctors, generally strengthen association leaders and staff vis-à-vis members, while selective benefits like delegated public functions (training, marketing, etc.) as well as privileged access encourage more active participation and make the association more representative (i.e., weaken autonomy of association leaders, but also make it less vulnerable to capture by any faction of membership or staff).

In the conventional view that only small groups with common, narrow interests can act collectively, the behavior of business associations is bound to be suspect. Krueger's (1974) initial theory of rent seeking was based on *individual* firms within the same sector competing for import quotas. A crucial element of her contribution was that such rents were bad for economic performance not only because they diverted resources from their optimal market allocation but, most importantly, because firms would, theoretically, expend resources equal to the value of the rent in lobbying and competing with other rent seekers. Therefore, the net gain to the firm was zero and the cost to society was equal to double the value of the rents (excluding the welfare gains of the lobbyists). The problem of aggregation comes in transferring the same conclusions from individuals to business associations. For one, unlike an import quota for a particular product, if we take the total distribution of all sorts of subsidies, then there is no one central point of distribution (and hence focus of lobbying), nor is there a known aggregate quantity of rents distributed by all parts of the state. Therefore, associations cannot know the optimal amount to invest in lobbying, according to Krueger's criteria. An additional issue is what firms do with rents once they receive them. In Krueger's model, firms exploit rents without any productive effort in part because they have already expended on lobbying resources equal to the value of the quota. However, if a firm is in a competitive market, then it has incentives to use rents productively. For example, when firms receive rents from patents, they do not necessarily squander them. More generally, export firms have incentives not to waste rents.

Incentives for wasteful spending and socially suboptimal allocation generally seem higher in individual clientelism than in organized corporatism.[39] Individual, clientelist rent seeking is most likely to conform to

---

[39] Olson (1986, 171) makes a supporting kind of argument, though without using the terms "corporatism" and "clientelism." He argues that incentives for elected politicians to redistribute income to groups are low because they cannot be sure that all those in the

Krueger's theory of incentives and resulting waste. Individual capitalists have incentives to invest a lot in gaining a particular quota or subsidy and have fewer incentives, especially after the investment in lobbying, to use rents productively. If clientelist distribution of rents is the status quo, then corporatism, collective rent seeking, or even "distributional coalitions" can be a relative improvement. If associations and government officials can thwart individual rent seeking, or if rents are distributed to the sector as a whole, then waste and social costs can be reduced. Firms in competitive markets, even if protected by tariffs, have incentives to use rents productively. Hence, when asking "Are business associations a good thing or a bad thing for a society?", the question should first be relative: "Corporatism or associational governance compared to what?"[40]

Conceptually, the issues raised in this concluding section all touch on the difficult theoretical enterprise of factoring organization and aggregation into theories premised initially on individual motivation and behavior. What happens, in other words, to simple assumptions about firm interests, individual free riding, and rent seeking when we put individuals in organizational structures like firms and associations or when we try to transfer individual-level rationality to organizations like associations that may themselves be the units engaging in collective action or rent seeking? The answers, and resulting arguments, may not be as elegant as individual-level theories, but the analytic payoff should be worth the sacrifice.

---

group will vote for them. Clientelism is precisely the context in which politicians target only their supporters.

[40] Haggard (1997) argues that theories of rent seeking start with the assumption of preexisting rent-free markets that rent seekers then seek to distort. However, most markets are already distorted, so rent seekers may unintentionally lobby to free them up in order to gain further benefits (to the detriment, of course, of other rent seekers). See Schamis (2002) on rent seeking through market-oriented reform.

9

Democracy and Varieties of Civil Society

> An association for political, commercial, or manufacturing purposes, or even for those of science and literature, is a powerful and enlightened member of the community, which cannot be disposed of at pleasure or oppressed without remonstrance, and which, by defending its own rights against the encroachment of the Government, saves the common liberties of the country.
>
> Alexis de Tocqueville

> Where the state is the only environment in which we can live communal lives, they inevitably lose contact, become detached, and thus society disintegrates. A nation can be maintained only if, between the state and the individual, there is intercalated a whole series of secondary groups near enough to the individual to attract them strongly in their spheres of action and drag them in this way into the general torrent of social life.
>
> Emile Durkheim[1]

Business Associations and Democracy: A Checkered Past

At least since the time of Barrington Moore's (1966, 418) dictum, "no bourgeois, no democracy," contemporary social scientists have debated whether business is fundamentally a force for or against democracy (Bellin 2000; Durand and Silva 1998; Haggard and Kaufman 1995; Payne 1994; Rueschemeyer et al. 1992). My research addresses this debate but only obliquely, since it focuses more on the form of business politics, organized or not, than on the content. Nonetheless, focusing only on the dimension

---

[1] The Tocqueville quote comes from *Democracy in America* cited in Lamb and Kitelle (1956, 1). Durkheim is cited in Thomson (2001, 33).

of organization, the question can be posed: does stronger organization tend to make business more democratic? This question can be further specified in three subquestions, two historical and one contemporary. On the historical record, were strong business organizations more likely to support movements to overthrow democratic governments, and during authoritarian rule were stronger associations more likely to pressure for democratization? The contemporary question is, can associations, even those tainted by past authoritarian proclivities, contribute anything to enhancing new democracies?

On the first issue of support for coups against democracy, there is no apparent relationship with institutional capacity. Weak associations called for the end to democracy in Brazil in 1964 and in Argentina in 1966 and 1976, just as strong associations supported the military takeover in Chile in 1973. Although Colombia and Mexico were spared the wave of coups of the 1960s and 1970s, stronger associations in Colombia had endorsed the installation of the Rojas Pinilla dictatorship in the 1950s, and in Mexico the CMHN at least tacitly supported the authoritarian crackdown in 1968. Most recently and visibly, Fedecamaras, the economy-wide peak association for Venezuelan business, was deeply implicated in the bungled coup against Hugo Chávez in April 2002 (Encarnación 2002). There were some exceptions of associations opposing military coups: in Colombia in the 1960s, discussed further later on, and later in the 1980s in Argentina and in the early 1990s in Venezuela (Naim 1993, 100).[2] Overall, the degree of organization does not explain much of business endorsement or opposition to authoritarian coups. If anything, a "band wagon" pattern seems to emerge where business associations of all sorts support successful coups and oppose abortive ones, perhaps in order to ingratiate themselves with the new rulers or surviving presidents.

On the second issue of business loyalty to existing authoritarian governments, the correlation between organization and support seems slightly tighter. In the late twentieth century, strong associations like CPC in Chile, Confiep in Peru, or CMHN in Mexico sided with authoritarian governments, while Brazil's disorganized industrialists, in contrast, were pivotal in pushing the military from power.[3] However, in Colombia and Argentina, the relationship was reversed and positive. Well-organized

---

[2] In Argentina in early 1987, "fearing more radical alternatives within the military, the main business associations such as the SRA, UIA, and the CAC opposed the military uprisings and supported democracy" (Acuña 1995, 44).

[3] In the 1980s, "organized business support for continued authoritarianism in Chile was highly public and nearly unanimous" and most associations, including the CPC, endorsed

Colombian business played a pivotal role in bringing down the dictatorship in 1957, while weakly organized Argentine business was famous for supporting authoritarian rule (Freels 1970, 447). The number of cases is small, yet the wide dispersion over time and across countries is sufficient to minimize the expectation that organization alone would make business more hostile to authoritarian rule.

However, the apparent correlation between authoritarianism and organization in Chile and Mexico (and probably in Peru) is likely spurious because what best explains both high levels of organization and support for nondemocratic regimes is a third variable, namely, access.[4] That is, privileged access simultaneously encourages both collective action and support for the status quo, either democratic or authoritarian. When strong encompassing associations lost access in authoritarian regimes they shifted toward the opposition, as in Mexico in the early 1970s and again in the early 1980s, or nearly in Chile in the early 1980s before Pinochet granted associations better access. Even disorganized business in Brazil and Argentina was often supportive of military rule when they had access, though the access was not mediated by associations. In this sense, my research supports the argument that business is less likely to oppose governments, democratic or authoritarian, in which it feels well represented.[5]

Beyond the historical record, the pressing contemporary question, now that elections come and go with unprecedented regularity, is how business associations affect the quality of democracy or democratic governability. Business associations offer potential solutions to a range of maladies that afflict fledgling democracies in Latin America. Although the formal

the "yes" option in the 1988 plebiscite on maintaining Pinochet in power (Silva 1998, 235). On Peru, see Durand (2002).

[4] Strong support and good access also characterized the relationship between organized business and the post-coup Fujimori government in Peru (Durand 1998, 274).

[5] See Rueschemeyer et al. (1992), Remmer (1993), and Silva (1998, 234) on the representation or access argument, and Payne (1994), who emphasizes the fundamental pragmatism that orients business politics. In Ecuador, Bolivia, and Peru, "business interest groups played leading roles in promoting the transition to civilian rule" (Conaghan 1992, 199). In Ecuador, "procedural issues and the question of representation were pivotal to the deterioration in the relations between business and the military government. In a country with long-standing corporatist traditions, the Rodríguez Lara government suspended the Chambers' traditional voting rights in the government's Monetary Board and other public institutions" (Conaghan 1990, 76). Although not a direct test, my research did not uncover much evidence to confirm arguments that business support for authoritarian or democratic governments is contingent on economic performance (Frieden 1991; Haggard and Kaufman 1995) or on economic dependence on the state and fear of the opposition (Bellin 2000).

rules for democracy have stabilized, critics find fault with, among other things, wobbly presidential systems, perverse electoral rules, weak and fragmented parties, resurgent clientelism, feeble accountability, ineffective judiciaries, and "low-intensity citizenship."[6] Distilled, the political criticisms fault democracies in Latin America for low scores on adequate representation (the capacity for groups in society to institutionalize input into decision making), a corollary ability to check the abuse of power by elected officials (accountability and contestation), and governability (the ability of governments to formulate and implement policies). Although by no means a panacea, comparative and theoretical analysis, as well as some empirical examples from my five cases, illustrate how strong business associations can raise the scores on these three dimensions.

Representation and Interest Intermediation

Chapter 1 noted the theoretical importance scholars attach to the role of business representation in the consolidation of democracy. Beyond extending the longevity of democracy, the representation of business through associations can have several further salutary effects on democratic governance. In their comprehensive review of associations of all sorts, Joshua Cohen and Joel Rogers (1995b, 42–3) stress that the first of four "useful, democracy-enhancing functions" associations can fulfill is providing information. In their view, "good information improves citizen deliberation, facilitates the enforcement of decisions and clarifies the appropriate objects of state policy." Because associations are closer to the ground, they are better equipped than state actors to gauge preferences, and to assess the compliance with, and impact of, policies. As societies, policies, and their interactions become more complex, the value of this information increases.

Business representation through associations also has several advantages over party, electoral, or personalized representation. In contrast to the punctuated schedule of elections, associations offer continuous representation, which can be especially important in countries subject to frequent economic and political crises (see Schmitter 1995b). In cases of sudden crises, strong business associations provide government actors with immediate means to consult with businesspeople and gauge their reaction to proposed emergency measures. As noted in the country cases,

---

[6] See, for example, O'Donnell (1993), Geddes (1994), Haggard and Kaufman (1995), Haggard (1997), Domínguez (1997), and Zakaria (1997).

political leaders and economic ministers will often call on encompassing associations, or create them, in moments of crisis, most clearly in the Colombian case when López Pumarejo created ANDI in the 1940s, and again in the 1990s when then Minister Samper created the Consejo Gremial.[7]

Business associations provide clearer, specific signals on the preferences of business as distinct from the preferences of other groups. From one perspective, the advantage of business representation through the electoral system is that conservative parties and politicians must appeal to broader constituencies to get elected, and therefore business, even if it is the "core constituency," must compromise in order to build broader-based political parties (see Gibson 1996). However, from another perspective, the electoral system dilutes business representation and makes it harder for state actors to register particular business preferences from specific sectors or on individual policy measures, let alone aggregated preferences across many business sectors. In any case, business associations bypass these refractions of the electoral and party system, and offer state actors clearer and more direct signals on preferences (though, of course, the clarity and authority of the signal will depend on the association's institutional strength).

Beyond the issue of the merits of separate types of representation, parties and business associations in Latin America developed a range of different relations. As noted in Chapter 2, none of the business associations examined here developed the close, lasting linkages to political parties common between labor parties and unions, in large part because legislation prohibited business associations from partisan engagement. Even at arm's length, different kinds of relations, or divisions of labor, emerged between parties and business associations. In Chile in the 1990s, for example, business associations sometimes mediated between the government and opposition parties. The Concertación government first negotiated tax increases with associations, and these, in turn, pressured opposition parties to approve the agreement in Congress (interview with Manuel Marfán, 8 May 2000). In Colombia, associations were reported to have

---

[7] Continuous representation was valuable to these leaders, and in the absence of encompassing associations, government officials tended to seek out informal meetings with top businesspeople (often in the form of "encompassing" dinners) in order to get continuous representation, again attesting to the value of continuous, direct forms of business representation. However, strong associations have inherent advantages over informal meetings because they have mechanisms for continuously updating, aggregating, and reconciling members' preferences.

displaced parties as major channels of representation (Kline 1996, 30). In Brazil in the 1990s, more people with business backgrounds joined parties and ran successfully for election to Congress than ever before and more than is common in other countries. The scores of "business deputies" in Congress and in major political parties did not, though, have a dramatic influence on collective business representation, either through parties or by association lobbies (Schneider 1997–8).[8]

The general point is that democratic governability may be advanced through multiple channels of business representation, and that business associations – especially those with greater institutional strength – offer distinctive means of communication and intermediation not available through traditional democratic mechanisms such as parties, elections, and legislatures. Discrete and continuous representation of business through associations may be especially valuable to governability in moments of crisis and external shock.

Contestation, Accountability, and Transparency

A corollary problem to that of representation is accountability, contestation, or the exercise of power (by civil society in this case) to check the abuse of power by others. Guillermo O'Donnell (1993) characterized some new democracies in Latin America as "delegative," in the sense that voters delegated authority to elected presidents, who then ruled with few constraints until replaced by elected successors. Similarly, Fareed Zakaria (1997) called most newly competitive polities "illiberal democracies" where citizens have more political rights than civil liberties and where, as in delegative democracy, elected leaders often rule in undemocratic ways. These authors proposed institutional solutions – liberal constitutionalism (Zakaria) or horizontal accountability (O'Donnell) – as remedies for the abuse of power by heads of state. However, beyond specific political rules and institutions, others emphasize the need for a counterweight outside the state in the form of a dense civil society (Rueschemeyer et al. 1992, 6). Scholars and advocates of civil society are nearly unanimous in emphasizing its core role in contesting and constraining potentially abusive states or

---

[8] Individual businesspeople were increasingly tempted to try their fortunes in electoral politics in Chile and Mexico as well. In addition, it became more common for presidents of associations to run for elected office after finishing their terms, as in the cases of Carlos Eduardo Moreira Ferreira (FIESP), Manuel Feliú (CPC), and Eduardo Bours (CCE). These electoral activities did not, though, seem to affect relations between parties and associations and represented a further diversification of business investment in politics.

"protecting the common liberties against encroachment by government," to paraphrase Tocqueville's quote at the beginning of the chapter.[9]

Among the myriad organizations of civil society, business associations are leading candidates for the role of counterweight, as illustrated by Colombian associations. Colombia is anomalous in Latin America for its stable democratic politics, and scholars often bring in business associations to explain this "exceptionalism." The following quote from Fabio Echeverría, ex-president of the Colombian association of industrialists, ANDI, captures multiple aspects of the political role of associations, including both continuous representation and the value of contesting state power:

In Colombia the electoral victory of a certain group does not mean the economic policies this group will implement during its government have been widely and deeply debated during the electoral campaign. In our country, on the contrary, it has been the tradition that the design of the program for economic development is done later by officials and experts who often lack direct contact with economic reality. This situation makes the presence of business associations in the economic debate indispensable. If there is no sustained party analysis, maybe only business associations have the capacity to impede, or at least neutralize, the possibility that a group of technocrats convinces the government of the merits of a particular policy, even if it is not the best for the country, and gets the government to implement it. (Cited in Urrutia 1983, 77)

Colombian business associations had a great ability to contest state power (Bailey 1977, 277). Beyond Federacafe's enormous influence within the state, many other associations enjoyed excellent relations with the press and used their influence in public opinion to pressure, often successfully, the government to moderate its policies (Urrutia 1983).[10] In one remarkable feat of collective contestation, Colombian business associations organized a general strike in 1957 to topple the dictatorship of Gustavo Rojas Pinilla. As Osterling tells the story:

during the first two weeks of May 1957, Colombia's managerial class successfully organized a national strike in an effort to obtain General Rojas Pinilla's resignation. The nation's economic elite, after paying their workers, unilaterally closed all banks and factories and invited their workers to declare a strike which paralyzed

---

[9] For Robert Dahl, independent organizations, among them business associations, are "necessary to the functioning of the democratic process itself, to minimizing government coercion, to political liberty, and to human well-being" (1982, 1).

[10] See also (Osterling 1989, 204), who argues that business associations supplanted weak parties and legislatures in contesting policies adopted by the executive. Interestingly, survey data from the 1960s indicate that even the very elite so represented perceived the power of associations as excessive (Bailey 1977, 278–9).

the nation's economy and led to General Rojas Pinilla's 19 May 1957 resignation. (1989, 204–5)

Although ultimately unsuccessful, the campaign for President Samper's resignation in the 1990s was another remarkable instance of collective contestation. Contestation alone is, of course, necessary for democracy, but successful contestation by business may also create a virtuous cycle in which business develops greater allegiance to a democratic regime that is at least partially responsive to its opposition. As discussed further later on, Colombian associations have several times come to the defense of democracy in periods of crisis (Hartlyn 1985; Kline 1996; Osterling 1989, 204).[11]

In Brazil, in contrast, weaker associations were rarely conduits for contestation or opposition to governments or major policies that business opposed. FIESP, for example, was not at the forefront of business mobilization to oppose Goulart in the 1960s or later in the movement in the later 1970s to contest military rule. Instead business organized new, ad hoc, or informal movements. In another telling example, a cautious FIESP president, Mario Amato, endorsed President Sarney's quest for a five-year term, because he feared reprisals and Sarney's military backing, despite very widespread support for only a four-year term among business leaders. In a poll of 103 business leaders, 86 percent favored four years, as did a majority of FIESP directors and three quarters of CNI member federations (Payne 1990, 222–4).

Just as making the state accountable enhances democracy, so too does holding business to account for the power it wields.[12] Business, or at

---

[11] In the era of liberalized international financial markets, capital mobility gives big business greater capacity to contest economic policies, even without organization. In Hirschman's terms, the increasingly damaging consequences of exit (capital flight) may strengthen business capacity for contestation; at the same time, it intensifies the preferences of policy makers for voice (dialogue with, for example, business associations). Capital mobility may in fact make representation through parties less important and at the same time increase government interest in associations. Returning to the broad issues raised in Chapter 1, party defense of business interests used to be essential to democratic consolidation (Rueschemeyer, Stephens, et al. 1992), in large part because strong business parties ensured the defense of basic property rights and institutionalized access on essential business concerns. In the absence of such guarantees, business supported coups against democratic governments that excluded business and threatened property. Now capital mobility ensures more secure property rights and attentive government policy makers, making pro-capitalist parties potentially dispensable for the consolidation of contemporary democracies.

[12] Stallings and Peres call for closer relations between the public and private sectors but emphasize that "it is essential that [the relationship] be transparent and open to all" (2000, 220).

least some businesspeople, are powerful in all political systems (where property is mostly private) by virtue of direct influence (voice), structural power (exit), or both. Even in long-established democracies, much of the contact, communication, and influence peddling between business and government is off the record and out of public view. Campaign contributions, phone conversations, luncheons, and other points of regular and legal contact are usually invisible to the press, not to mention illicit activities like bribery and corruption. Thus, another potential benefit for democracy of associational representation, versus party representation or other informal politics, is transparency in business politics. As Tocqueville put it, "where associations are free, secret societies are unknown. In America, there are factions, but no conspiracies" (1956, 98).

For one, associations have some means of making leaders accountable to members. In terms of internal transparency, leaders regularly report on activities, sometimes in the form of detailed annual reports (e.g., CCE 1987). However, associations vary in how much internal information they make available to the general public. At one extreme, CMHN publishes no documents and has no website. Its members reveal nothing to the press after their meetings and rarely give interviews concerning CMHN deliberations or activities. At the other extreme are rare cases of publicized, polarized elections in associations during which a lot of the association's dirty laundry gets aired in the media. In the contested elections for the FIESP presidency in 1992 the contending candidates fought a very public campaign, including billboards in downtown São Paulo. The challenger, Emerson Kapaz, was openly critical of FIESP's archaic internal structure and procedures. Of course, most associations in Latin America fall between these extremes in terms of internal transparency and openness. However, they generally offer at least a partial glimpse of business politics that is not available in other forms of business–government interactions.

In addition, most encompassing business associations actively seek press exposure for their policy positions. One of the motivations of the founders of CCE in Mexico was precisely to get more exposure for general business positions and principles in the media and even in more academic debates. As noted earlier, CMHN was, in the minds of its founders, to be discreet. However, after CMHN became a voting member of CCE, its president came to occupy a much more visible position and to be cited as regularly as the presidents of other associations, though CMHN's lack of staff and offices naturally limited its visibility in the media. Business associations in Colombia were especially active in seeking exposure in the press (Urrutia 1983). As noted in Chapter 7, in Argentina the president of UIA felt that the industry association derived most of its power from media exposure. Some observers consider some associations in Colombia to be primarily think tanks, designed precisely to engage in public debate, rather than interest groups. In Brazil, FIESP leaders also sought out press coverage.[13] CEA in Argentina, like the earlier incarnation of CMHN, is not very visible and, like IEDI in Brazil, prefers to contract extensive studies to be disseminated among policy makers and political elites. Although low profile, both CEA and IEDI still contributed to making business positions more transparent. Overall, both weak and strong associations can increase transparency by voicing business preferences; however, opinions of stronger associations are likely to be more elaborated and more authoritative to the extent that they represent the results of prior interest aggregation and reconciliation. Moreover, strong institutional capacity means more resources for technical analysis and dissemination. Lastly, transparency in interest aggregation and representation by business elites at least offers some opportunities for opposition by nonelites. If, in contrast, elites operate through opaque clientelism, nonelites have fewer options for countering business influence.

Governability and Unburdening

Mancur Olson argued that strong special-interest groups made politics generally more "divisive" and policies more short-term and cyclical, rendering societies, in the extreme, "ungovernable" (1982, 47). Historically, much of Argentine politics in the twentieth century was characterized in these terms: divisiveness, intense distributional conflict, and frequent episodes of ungovernability (Manzetti 1993a; O'Donnell 1978). Cleavages within business between sectors, especially agriculture versus industry, between small and big business, and between protectionists and free traders all acquired strong organizational manifestation and contributed to polarizing policy debates. One searches in vain for instances when associations, either in ephemeral encompassing associations or in ad hoc coordinating committees, successfully hammered out compromise positions.

---

[13] In the late 1990s, FIESP President Horácio Lafer Piva reduced employment by 30 percent in FIESP (*Revista República*, 17 August 2001, p. 60) and cut 4,100 jobs from FIESP, Senai, and Sesi (*Valor* 21 August 2001). One of the departments he apparently expanded was the press department. In contrast, some associations devised ways of disguising association lobbying because the they felt they lacked legitimacy in Brazilian politics. Febraban and Ação Empresarial both attempted to maintain a low profile when they lobbied in Brasília (Doctor 2000; Schneider 1997–8).

Policy disputes were often extreme compared to debates in other countries in Latin America, and divisions among business helped make them so. Moreover, even organizational disputes burdened the political system as associations fought with each other in the press and in government forums, as in the case noted in Chapter 7, where UIA lobbied to have Congress strip its rival, CGE, of its assets.

Centrifugal, fragmented politics and distributional conflict were also common in Brazil, though these fissiparous politics were more often rent by cleavages among numerous parties, regions, and clientelistic politicians than by organized business rent seekers. Many contemporary laments over fragmentation in the Brazilian polity focus more on the party and electoral systems than on interest groups (Mainwaring 1999). Weyland (1996), though, blames the lack of progress on redistributive policies on fragmentation in both society and the state. Regardless of what share of the blame for divisiveness in Brazil and Argentina is due to the fractiousness of business representation, it is clear that there were no strong, encompassing, economy-wide associations working against fragmentation and divisiveness.

In other countries in some periods, encompassing associations worked to restrain divisive tendencies. In Colombia in early 1965, in one remarkable example, the economy was unraveling and generated a political and distributional struggle over the government's proposed tax increase. Labor threatened a general strike, and "rumors of an impending coup increased" (Hartlyn 1985, 117). Business associations, especially ANDI, organized a temporary peak association to avert collapse, while "bitterly factionalized political parties... were relying on the associations to find a way out of the impasse, or were passively watching events, having accepted the inevitability of a coup" (Hartlyn 1985, 117). Business associations successfully negotiated with labor and government, and in the end the government moderated its policies, labor called off the strike, and presumed coup conspirators were dismissed from the military.

In Chile in the 1960s and 1970s the CPC apparently restrained some of its more intransigent members, at least through the beginning of the Allende government, and again in the 1990s the CPC kept business in a unified dialogue with the new civilian government. In contrast, in the late 1990s, when the CPC could not manage the differences between agriculture and industry in negotiations over Mercosur, each respective association negotiated separately, and more divisively, with the government. In Mexico, one of the main activities of the CCE president, Agustín Legorreta, during the pacts was to negotiate, plead, and cajole with member associations to abide by the pact agreements (interview, 28 July 1998). And during the Nafta negotiations, Coece forced many intersectoral compromises and thereby spared the government the difficulties of having to reconcile conflicting, divisive claims. In these instances, CCE and Coece managed major distributional struggles internally without burdening other political arenas.

As discussed in the previous chapter, associations can enhance governability in formulating and implementing economic policy.[14] A major concern for governments in the 1990s was consolidating neoliberal reform. Haggard and Kaufman (1995, 10) claim that business support was essential for the medium-term consolidation of neoliberal reform. Their general argument is that governments need an initial moment of autonomy to enact the reforms, followed by post-reform efforts to solicit support for them. However, there are also indications that negotiating reforms, from the beginning, increasingly has advantages over the strategy of initial insulation of government reformers. This was the lesson Chilean reformers drew from failed reforms of the 1970s in Chile and later applied to the more successful consultative reforms of the "pragmatic" 1980s (Silva 1997).

To the extent that business associations regulate sectors and resolve disputes, they also depoliticize some arenas of distributional conflict and thereby unburden the political system, with potential benefits for democracy, especially young, straining democracies. For example, concerted stabilization programs reduce social costs and manage distributional negotiations directly and outside of political institutions, like parties and legislatures, that may be poorly equipped to handle antagonistic distributional questions. Furthermore, associations, encompassing and nonencompassing alike, can assist in policy implementation, which again is especially significant for states in fiscal crisis with historically low administrative capacity. Colombia is an extreme example, where Federacafe provided infrastructure, warehousing, finance, and marketing for coffee growers. Although Colombian democracy has been comparatively long-lived, it has also been fragile, and the National Front arrangements constituted a frank admission that the democratic system was not managing well open political conflict and contention. Federacafe spared this weak

---

[14] For Katzenstein, the consensual ideologies, centralized and concentrated interest groups, and continual bargaining between government, parties and interest groups make democratic corporatism a form of "a low-voltage politics" (1985, 32). See Cohen and Rogers (1995b, 44) for a more general defense of delegating governance functions to associations.

political system the potentially very divisive task of administering the coffee sector: "Perhaps one of the causes of the longevity of democracy in Colombia is the existence of sui-generis institutions like the Federación" (Urrutia 1983, 118). Bailey argues generally that the creation of decentralized economic agencies, where associations were best represented, provided "asylum from partisan conflict" (1977, 286).

Unburdening and delegation, of course, restrict the scope of authority of the government and its elected representatives, thereby circumscribing the exercise of democracy (an issue I address further at the end of the chapter). Such restrictions, especially if initially enacted through democratic procedures, may be less worrisome in the short run than more immediate and unresolved issues of effective governance. The quality of economic governance, for example, is one important yardstick by which many citizens gauge their support not only for political leaders but for democracy overall. In many countries of Latin America, opinion polls show that this instrumental support for democracy has dropped, along with other indicators of economic performance, especially since the mid-1990s.[15]

Divisive and antagonistic business associations that lack institutional means for deliberating and resolving disputes within the business community can contribute to polarizing positions and conflicts in the polity as a whole, adding tasks for the political system to process and thereby subtracting from governability. Where encompassing associations intermediate diverse member interests well, they can not only work to resolve intrabusiness disputes on their own – leaving the political system free to work on other issues – but can also participate in emergency situations to enhance the ability of policy makers to overcome crises. Lastly, though not a major issue for most encompassing organizations, business associations can also assume sectoral governance functions, as in the examples noted in Chapter 8. In these instances, associations contributed to governability both by depoliticizing policy making and implementation, and thereby removing a potential burden for politics, and by providing high-quality administration that was usually in short supply in the public sector.

Disaggregating Civil Societies and Their Effects

Among students of civil society there is apparent unanimity that business associations are part of civil society and, by extension, that the impact of

[15] See, for example, reports on Latinobarometro polls in the *Economist* on 26 July 2001 and 15 August 2002.

business associations on politics is similar to that of other groups in civil society.[16] The analysis developed in preceding sections makes this extension suspect. Lumping business associations in with the rest of civil society is theoretically unwarranted and, if anything, may impede better research on the hypothesized connections between civil society and democracy. In some cases, the interests and activities of business associations are different and opposite to those of other groups in civil society, especially on distributional issues. The assumption, usually implicit, in much of the literature is that associations of civil society empower the weak and level the political playing field. For instance, Larry Diamond cannot be thinking of elite clubs of big business like the CMHN or CEA when he writes that "only with sustained, organized pressure from below, in civil society, can political and social equality be advanced" (1996, 231).[17] Business associations may, as in Chile in the 1990s, facilitate negotiation and compromise on redistributive policies, but it is difficult to find historical instances where business associations spontaneously sought greater political and social equality. On another dimension of enhancing democracy, it makes little sense to argue that civil society promotes the rule of law, when in fact business associations may champion the rule of law only insofar as it affects property rights to the neglect of reform in other areas such as labor law or civil liberties, where progress depends more on other parts of civil society such as unions and human rights groups (Mahon 2003).

In other instances, interests might converge across a wide variety of elite and nonelite groups, but the material and political resources available to different kinds of groups in civil society vary so much that we gain more by analyzing them separately. For example, when groups across the socioeconomic spectrum oppose a government – as in the case of the Rojas Pinilla dictatorship in Colombia in the 1950s or the Collor government in the 1990s in Brazil – then business associations can be effective in shaping public opinion, investing in publicity campaigns, and bringing economic pressure to bear, but they cannot, as other groups can, bring thousands of people into the streets to demonstrate.

[16] Diamond, for example, lists seven different types of organizations, formal and informal, that comprise civil society. The list includes cultural, civic, and educational organizations but starts with economic associations, especially productive and commercial groups (1996, 229). See also Avritzer (2000). O'Connell goes so far as to include all business, not just associations but the whole private sector, in his conception of civil society (1999, 20–1).

[17] Cohen and Rogers also argue that one of the four main democracy-enhancing functions of associations is to "equalize representation" by amplifying the voices of disadvantaged groups (1995b, 43).

As a start, it makes conceptual sense to distinguish first between elite and nonelite organizations in civil society, and then to relate this distinction to the basic tensions between the principle of political equality under democracy and the reality of socioeconomic inequality under capitalism. For nonelite groups, many of the presumed contributions of civil society to democracy may come from raising these groups from the low levels they are consigned to by socioeconomic stratification so that they can participate politically on more equal terms. Civil society for elites, as in business associations, may sometimes have a leveling impact by bringing elite groups into deliberation and negotiation with nonelite groups, but the participation of economic elites in organizations of civil society may also, and more importantly, force them to articulate their power in alternative ways that are better for democratic procedure. Returning to the portfolio analogy, big business has options for exercising power, such as corruption, personal networks, and media leverage, as well as capital flight (or structural power), that all undermine political equality. To the extent that capitalists participate in politics as powerful individuals (through clientelism, for example), they weaken democracy by making political representation unequal and opaque. If associations pull business elites into civil society – drag them, as Durkheim put it in the quote at the beginning of this chapter, "into the general torrent of social life" – then elite civil society contributes to democracy as much by supplanting negative forms of business participation as by promoting alternative positive behavior through associations. Moreover, elites in encompassing associations are constrained to push for their common interests and force moderation on more radical or greedy members (who are much less constrained under clientelism).

One pro-democracy function attributed to civil society is to imbue members with citizenship skills and democratic values. Advocates of civil society – drawing on Tocqueville's dictum that "knowledge of how to combine is the mother of all other forms of knowledge" – place great hopes in associations as schools of democratic practice. Skocpol, for example, writes that "associations are . . . sites where citizens learn – and practice – the 'knowledge of how to combine' so vital to democracy" (Skocpol 1999b, 462).[18] Active engagement in an encompassing association

---

[18] One overview noted that this "socialization" function was the most common one in the recent literature on civil society. In this view, "associations of civil society are thought to play a major role, if not *the* major role, in building citizenship skills and attitudes crucial for motivating citizens to use these skills" (Edwards and Foley 2001, 5). Diamond also stresses this educating function and cites Tocqueville, who considered associations "large

might introduce businesspeople to the regular practices of compromise, consensus building, deliberation, debate, and tolerance, practices that may be rare in everyday forms of corporate management. However, there are reasons to think that these school-for-democracy effects may be weaker in the case of business associations than they would be for other social groups. For one, some business associations have called for coups to end democratic regimes, so associations in some contexts may also be effective schools for dictatorship where associations bring together like-minded coup conspirators or help convince wavering democrats to abandon their remaining scruples to help topple an elected government. Moreover, wealthy, well-educated, extensively networked capitalists are less likely to get a boost in their citizenship skills from participating in associations than are less advantaged social groups.

To summarize the chapter so far, business associations can make, and have made, a number of positive contributions to the quality of democratic governance. On the list of contributions, fine-grained, continuous representation, contestation against abuse of state power, making politics more transparent, enhancing governability (especially in economic policy), and unburdening the polity all stand out as functions that business associations are well suited for, and in many instances better suited for, than other organizations in civil society. In nearly all these functions, strong encompassing associations are likely to be more effective than weaker, fragmented associations. Where business associations encompass many diverse sectors, they can be especially helpful in contesting the state, since they can speak for large segments or all of business. For economic governance, encompassing associations are crucial for macro policy and reforms designed to affect the economy as a whole. Greater organizational capacity – material resources and effective internal interest intermediation – also enhances associational contributions, at a minimum by making the voice of business, as represented by associations, loud, clear, and authoritative. Institutional strength is especially important for representation and unburdening. As Chapters 3 to 7 showed, where associations lacked administrative capacity or authoritative representation, state actors were loath to rely on them for collaborative policy making or to delegate governance functions to them.

> free schools, where all the members of the community go to learn the general theory of association" (1996, 231). For Cohen and Rogers, "associations can function as 'schools of democracy.' Participation in them can help citizens develop competence, self-confidence and a broader set of interests than they would acquire in a more fragmented political society" (1995b, 43).

Coming to America in the early nineteenth century, Tocqueville wondered what could substitute in the new democracy for the social order of feudalism or the strong state of postrevolutionary France. Tocqueville's answer was civil society and religion, and he argued that democracy would be in serious trouble without these nonpolitical supports (Whittington 2001). A visitor to Latin America today, one sympathizing with either Tocqueville or Durkheim, would be equally, if not more, worried about the lack of social order and legitimate mechanisms binding up society. Although states in the region are far more extensive and ambitious (than the United States in the nineteenth century) in efforts to order their societies, state failures are still ubiquitous. In these contexts, Tocquevillean anxieties may be warranted, and civil societies – and even "artificial," state-promoted associations – may have many more crucial roles to play to integrate societies and nurture democracies.

States, Civil Society, and Dilemmas of Democracy

On other dimensions, strong associations pose fundamental problems for democracy, especially to the extent that they overrepresent business and displace other groups or where associations are heavily dependent on the very states they are – in democratic theory – supposed to contest. Scholars of corporatist arrangements have long wrestled with the awkward fit between corporatism and democracy. First, neocorporatist bargains allow only some portion of the citizenry to be represented at the bargaining table. Low inflation and low unemployment may be public goods that participants in tripartite concertation work for, yet the mechanisms to achieve these results are likely to favor the interests of those at the bargaining table. This exclusion violates basic rights of citizenship and equality of representation. As Andrew Shonfield remarked decades ago:

It is, however, a matter for concern when the new corporatist organizations bypass the ordinary democratic process – neither throwing their own deliberations open to the public nor subjecting the bargains struck between the centres of economic power to regular parliamentary scrutiny. After all, many of these bargains, ... will affect the life of the average person more than a lot of the legislation which parliament subjects to close and protracted scrutiny. (1965, 161)

States may mitigate some of the inherent contradictions of corporatism and democracy by encouraging democracy within associations and by assigning them a public purpose through other formal democratic and representative means (Anderson 1977; Cohen and Rogers 1995b). Moreover, internal democracy in associations ensures that members of those groups represented at the bargaining table have political rights within the associations (though internal democracy, of course, does not resolve the problem of the exclusion of nonmembers). And if a legislature delegates some policy function to associations through transparent democratic means, the "publicness" of the expected benefit of delegation can be better defended.

Apologists for associations run up against a different set of problems in the case of state-dependent associations. If states create and sustain associations, it is harder to make the case that these dependent associations will be effective counterweights to state power. Is it possible to conceive of a state-led route to a dense and vibrant civil society? Certainly the strongest common denominator in the literature on the benefits of civil society is the expectation that strong civil societies can contest and constrain the state (Levy 1999, 2). But the question of whether it matters if civil society is not independent of the state rarely comes up in this literature.

Not only has the issue of association dependence on the state not been prevalent in theorizing on civil society, but many definitions in fact make it difficult to put the issue up for discussion. By most definitions, associations must be formally independent of the state in order to qualify in the first place to be part of civil society. Such definitions help little in designing research to get at complex causal interactions between states and civil societies. In Diamond's definition,

civil society is conceived here as the *realm of organized social life that is voluntary, self-generating, (largely) self-supporting, autonomous from the state, and bound by a legal order or set of shared rules* (italics in the original). (Diamond 1996, 228)

By this strict definition, pure civil societies in Latin America may hardly exist and comprise only a fraction of organized social groups. Three years later, Diamond changed the phrase "(largely) self-supporting" to "at least partially self-supporting" (Diamond 1999, 221). Even so, an association that is only partially self-supporting is at best only "somewhat autonomous" and likely moderately dependent on external benefactors. Diamond does not delve into variations in self-support, but presumably outside support comes mostly from government (or perhaps international sources in a small number of cases), and if government support is significant, there are few grounds for presuming, in the basic definition of civil society especially, that autonomy is not somehow compromised.[19]

---

[19] Francis Fukuyama has a similarly limited definition: Civil society "is the realm of spontaneously created social structures separate from the state that underlie democratic political

In fact, the most interesting theoretical and practical political questions revolve around the usually close and dependent relations many associations have with the state. Few real-world associations are so distant from government, fully self-generating and self-supporting, or autonomous. Even in the United States, the Tocquevillean seedbed of civil society, civic organizations are heavily subsidized by federal tax law and would be greatly diminished in the absence of such subsidies. In developing countries, the hand of the state is much more visible in organizing civil society. Some observers coined the oxymoronic term GONGOs for "government-organized nongovernmental organizations." Even associations that might appear at first glance to be fully self-supporting – like many of the voluntary associations examined in this book – may in fact depend indirectly on the state for benefits like privileged access or public functions delegated to associations. A more useful definition of civil society would err on the side of inclusiveness and comprise a continuum of organizations more or less dependent on the state, from very independent groups, say choral societies, at one end to deeply controlled state-corporatist associations at the other.

An inclusive, nonrelational definition would allow us to get at the more interesting questions of how much and what types of dependence affect the range of behaviors that associations in civil society can assume.[20]

institutions. These structures take shape even more slowly than political institutions. They are less manipulable by public policy, and indeed often bear an inverse relationship to state power, growing stronger as the state recedes and vice versa" (1996, 321). For Ernest Gellner, "civil society is that set of diverse non-governmental institutions which is strong enough to counterbalance the state and, while not preventing the state from fulfilling its role of keeper of the peace and arbitrator between major interests, can nevertheless prevent it from dominating and atomizing the rest of society" (1994, 5). Both of these last two definitions are of little help in examining causal relations; they both include normative statements on relations between associations and the state, relations that are characterized by wide empirical variation.

[20] Stepan offers another good minimalist definition: "by 'civil society' I mean that arena where manifold social movements (such as neighborhood associations, women's groups, religious groupings, and intellectual currents) and civic organizations from all classes (such as lawyers, journalists, trade unions, and entrepreneurs) attempt to constitute themselves in an ensemble of arrangements so that they can express themselves and advance their interests" (2001, 100). Edward Shils's understanding of civil society is more nuanced regarding the state: civil society is "a part of society comprising a complex of autonomous institutions . . . distinguishable from the family, the clan, the locality and the state" but also "possessing a particular complex of relationships between itself and the state and a distinctive set of institutions which safeguard the separation of state and civil society and maintain effective ties between them." However, Shils goes on to include in his definition "a widespread pattern of refined or civil manners," which should be separated analytically as a possible and variable consequence of civil society (1991, 4).

For instance, Federacafe was highly dependent on government concession of tax revenues and had privileged access to policy councils. Federacafe rarely spoke out against government policies, and almost never joined with other associations to criticize the government, yet Federacafe was often effective in stopping or modifying policies within the state (Bates 1997). Other, more independent associations in Colombia did not hesitate to criticize all aspects of government, including, in several extreme instances, demanding that sitting presidents resign. In other cases, associations were such privileged interlocutors – for example, as the Chilean and Mexican peak associations in the 1980s or the Peruvian associations in the 1990s (Durand 2002) – that they almost never spoke out against the politics of their authoritarian governments, though they did sometimes venture to criticize particular economic policies. Similarly, FIESP – dependent on corporatist regulation more than access – was a regular critic of economic policies but, as noted earlier, stayed on the sidelines in larger political debates.

Determining when associations dependent on the state will be able or likely to contest different types of state actions is another project. My working hypotheses for such a project would be that the likelihood of contestation depends on variables like the kind of policy, the type of regime, the degree of organizational development within the association, the perceived threats from labor and the left, and the strategic conjunctural calculations on the part of association leaders.[21] The main point for now is that dependence and contestation are crucial theoretical and research questions that should not be assumed or defined away.

The practical challenge is to take up Madison's charge, quoted at the beginning of Chapter 1, that public policy be centrally concerned with "regulating interests."[22] In fact, state actors tend to have more narrow and immediate motives for strengthening business associations, with little concern for the long-term political consequences of the forms of collective

---

[21] For example, Korean associations, according to Kim, were subject to close control and regulation by a strong state, yet developed independent power and influence based on their control over investment and organizational capabilities (1993, 39).

[22] From a similar perspective, in the first element of Stepan's definition, the state "is the continuous administrative, legal, bureaucratic and coercive system that attempts not only to manage the state apparatus but to structure relations *between* civil society and public power and to structure many crucial relationships *within* civil and political society" (Stepan 2001, 101). The volume edited by Cohen and Rogers (1995a) offers the most sustained analysis of, and advocacy for, using public policy to shape the organization of groups in civil society (see especially the chapters by the editors (Cohen and Rogers 1995b, 1995c) and by Schmitter (1995a).

action they have strengthened. For example, state actors pursuing their own economic policy goals provide selective benefits to associations that strengthen leaders vis-a-vis members. One consequence for politics is that association leaders become less accountable to their members at the same time that they become more dependent on government. Some capitalists in Mexico aptly criticized the leaders of their associations for conceding too much autonomy and becoming "Ministers of the Private Sector." Moreover, it is not clear why state actors would want to create associations that can, in turn, constrain them, so government officials are probably poor candidates for crafting a dense civil society as a counterweight to state power. However, unintended institutional legacies matter; associations created for one purpose (by a set of state actors who are no longer in power), with selective benefits that have become acquired rights, may become less dependent over time.

In Latin America, civil society has long been subject to extensive state intervention, so incorporating such Madisonian concerns over regulating interests into policy in other areas might be less controversial. Just as the review of most development projects now incorporates environmental impact statements, so proposed economic policies might be subjected to an assessment of their "associational impact" or "associational externalities." The policy issues are: what are the optimum forms of business organization and how can states induce business to adopt these forms? Governments in Latin America have for decades closely regulated business associations, yet usually in ad hoc and sometimes unintentional fashion. The normative implication is that political leaders could make this regulation more explicit, transparent, and long-term.

Appendix A

Background Information on Major Business Associations

Basic organizational data on membership, dues, budgets, expenditures, and staff are exceedingly scarce for business associations in Latin America. Historical documents were often discarded, destroyed by fires, floods, and other natural disasters, or shipped to inaccessible warehouses. Maintaining well-staffed and organized archival centers was rarely a priority area of building institutional capacity in associations. And contemporary data on budgets, revenues, and expenditures were often treated as highly confidential. The purpose of this appendix is to summarize data I culled from unpublished sources and centralize information collected from the dispersed secondary literature. The list of associations and the basic data are still only partial The dates in parentheses after the full names of the associations are the years the associations were founded. All monetary values were converted to U.S. dollars in 2000, except where otherwise noted (see Appendix C).

Argentina

AAPIC (Asociación Argentina de la Producción, la Industria y el Comercio, 1946). AAPIC was founded by 14 industrial and commercial firms in 1946. By 1947 it had 61 affiliated organizations and 30,663 active members (Cúneo 1967, 184). AAPIC closed in 1949.

ABA (Asociación de Bancos de la Argentina, 1999). ABA was formed through the fusion of ADEBA and other associations. In 2003 ABA had 56 members, including foreign banks, that accounted for 43 percent of deposits (http://www.aba-argentina.com/index.html).

ABRA (Asociación de Bancos de la República Argentina, 1919). ABRA was founded by 21 private banks, foreign and national (Niosi 1976, 34).

Aciel (Acción Coordinadora de las Instituciones Empresariales Libres, 1958). Aciel was a peak association formed by UIA, SRA, the Stock Market Association, the Chamber of Commerce, the Grain Exchange, and the Bank Association. The anti-Peronist Aciel competed against CGE. UIA resigned from Aciel in 1972, and Aciel disbanded in 1973.

ADEBA (Asociación de Bancos Argentinos, 1972). ADEBA was an association of private Argentine banks. Members accounted for 70 percent of deposits in private national banks (Itzcovitz 1987, 228). ADEBA joined Apege in 1975.

Apege (Asamblea Permanente de Entidades Gremiales Empresarias, 1975–6). SRA, UIA, and the Chamber of Commerce (former Aciel members) created Apege. Apege coordinated the politically destabilizing lock-out of February 1976 (Cappelletti 1985, 95).

Asociación del Trabajo (1918–40s).

CAC (Cámara Argentina de Comercio, 1924). By the 1960s CAC had attracted members from all major sectors of the economy (Itzcovitz 1987, 226).

CACIP (Confederación Argentina del Comercio, la Industria y la Producción, 1916–48). CACIP members included "foreign railway and utility corporations, exporters, financiers, and agroindustrialists, in order of importance," and foreign firms dominated its leadership (Manzetti 1993, 283).

CAPIC (Confederación Argentina de la Producción, la Industria y el Comercio, 1950–2). CAPIC was a forerunner of CGE.

CARBAP (Confederación de Asociaciones Rurales de Buenos Aires y La Pampa).

CEA (*Congreso* Empresario Argentino, also known as Confederación Económica Argentina [Cúneo 1967, 186]). CEA was created by Perón in 1948. Its first president, Alfredo Rosso, was the last president of AAPIC. CEA created the Confederación Industrial Argentina in 1952.

CEA (*Consejo* Empresario Argentino, 1967). CEA consisted of about 30 members, by invitation only, of the oldest and biggest capitalists from all sectors of the economy. José Martínez de Hoz was president from 1974 to 1976. CEA had 30 members in 1967, 32 in 1982, and 31 in 1984 (Ostiguy 1990, 34, 89, 93ff.).

CEAs (Consejo Empresario *Asesor*). CEAs had almost 100 members in the late 1980s (Ostiguy 1990, 63).

CGE (Confederación General Económica, 1952). CGE was founded in 1952, outlawed at the end of 1955, legalized by President Frondizi in mid-1958, and proscribed by the military government in 1976. In other words, CGE functioned in the years 1952–5, 1958–76, and again after 1984 (though in greatly reduced form). In 1973, probably its high water mark, CGE was comprised of three confederations (Production, Industry, and Commerce), 40 regional federations, and a million businessmen (Cappelletti 1985, 79–80).

CGI (Confederación General Industrial, also know as CI). Member confederation of CGE.

CINA (Confederación Industrial Argentina, 1973).

CRA (Confederaciones Rurales Argentinas, 1942).

FAA (Federación Agraria Argentina, 1912).

Federación Argentina de Entidades Defensores del Comercio y la Industria (early 1930s–1940s) (Lindenboim 1976).

Grupo de los 9. Informal group founded in 1983 in opposition to the conservative and liberal CEA, which still supported the military government.

SRA (Sociedad Rural Argentina, 1866). Around 1900 SRA had about 2,000 members. In 1940 its membership "was just 2,300..., rising to 3,900 in 1950, 7,500 in 1960, and 12,000 in 1975" (Manzetti 1993, 246). Membership fell to 9,400 by 1985 (Palomino 1987, 150).

UIA (Unión Industrial Argentina, 1886, intervened 1946–53, outlawed 1953–5, intervened 1976–81). Around 1900, UIA members included 300 individuals and a half dozen chambers (Lindenboim 1976, 169). In 1940, UIA had 1,500 individual members, 56 member associations, and 9 affiliated associations (Schvarzer 1991, 96). By

1946 UIA had around 3,000 individual members and 91 chambers (Lindenboim 1976, 169). In 1960, UIA had 1,375 individual members and in 1970 1,127 (Schvarzer 1991, 154). In 1973 members accounted for 90 percent of industrial production and employment (Cappelletti 1985, 82). UIA had a staff of 46 in 1958, and from the late 1950s to the early 1970s its budget varied from $400,000 to $600,000 (on the order of $2–3 million 2000 dollars). UIA's budget was usually only a third to a half of SRA's budget in this period but nine times larger than the CGE's budget in 1961 (Schvarzer 1991, 179, 183).

UIA resigned from Aciel in 1972 and fused briefly with CGI in 1973. The military government intervened UIA in 1976 and nominated the president of Alpargatas, Eduardo Oxenford, to run it from 1979 to 1981. UIA was divided internally in the 1980s into MIN (Movimiento Industrial Nacional), which favored expansion of the national market, and MIA (Movimiento Industria Argentino), which was more neoliberal (see Ostiguy 1990, 881). In 1998 UIA had 24 regional and 90 sectoral members (among its affiliated members were another 9 associations and 166 companies, including many MNCs). The Consejo General and the Junta Directiva were both comprised of equal numbers of sectoral and regional representatives (http://www.uia.organization.ar, pages ei.htm, socadhe.htm, and socsecto.htm).

Brazil

State-Chartered Associations

CNA (Confederação Nacional da Agricultura, 1965; but founded as Confederação Rural Brasileira in 1951). In 1965 CNA had 237 associations and 13 state federations but income from obligatory dues (*imposto sindical*) was only $218,000 ($40,000 in 1965 dollars) (Schmitter 1971, 188, 436).

CNC (Confederação Nacional do Comércio, 1945).

CNI (Confederação Nacional da Indústria). Established in 1938, though preceded by the Confederação Industrial do Brasil (1933). Euvaldo Lodi was the president from 1938 to 1954. CNI had 244 employees in 1968 (CNI 1968).

FIESP (Federação das Indústrias do Estado de São Paulo). CIESP (Centro de Indústrias do Estado de São Paulo) was founded in 1928 and added the FIESP name in 1931, when Vargas decreed new laws governing *sindicatos* and federations (Weinstein 1990, 384). From 1934 to 1941 São Paulo had three federations. The following financial and membership data are from FIESP, *Relatórios dos trabalhos* for 1939, 1940, and 1941.

	Budget[1]	CIESP Members
1936	301,000	
1937	364,000	
1938	294,000	1,068
1939	497,000	1,350
1940	696,000	1,826
1941	684,000	2,114

In 1939, FIESP had 85 affiliated *sindicatos* with over 3,000 affiliated firms. In 1940, the 1,826 firms in CIESP represented "in capital and number of workers more than two thirds of the industrial activities in the state of São Paulo" (FIESP 1941, 11). In 1961 8,480 industrialists were affiliated with FIESP *sindicatos*, or 32 percent of the 25,521 industrial firms in the state (Schmitter 1971, 162).

FIRJ (Federação das Indústrias do Rio de Janeiro, 1931, later also known as FIERJ and Firjan). Firjan, as the representative and policy wing of industry, had about 50 employees in 2002, down from 100 in 1996. However, the whole Firjan system has 4,000 employees (interview with Luciana Sá, 28 May 2002).

Independent Sector Associations

ABDIB (Associação Brasileira para o Desenvolvimento das Indústrias de Base, 1955). ABDIB had 39 member firms in 1964, 70 in 1970, and 102 in 1975. Of the 114 member firms in 1977, 63 were Brazilian (Boschi 1979, 191, 193).

ABINEE (Associação Brasileira da Indústria Elétrica e Eletrônica). ABINEE had 281 members in the 1960s (Schmitter 1971, 199).

---

[1] In 2000 U.S. dollars. The original figures in milreis are: 1936, 282:371$900; 1937, 346:139$900; 1938, 424:037$000; 1939, 678:667$900; 1940, 939:468$000; 1941, 1.150:814$100.

Febraban (Federação Brasileira das Associações de Bancos, 1967). In 1996 154 banks, representing 90 percent of activity in the banking sector, were affiliated with Febraban (http://www.febraban.org.br/Febraban1.htm).

UDR (União Democrática Ruralista, 1985).

Voluntary Encompassing Associations

Conclap (Conferência das Classes Produtoras). III Conclap took place in 1972, IV Conclap in 1977 (Carone 1978, 154).

Forúm Informal (1987). Encompassing coordinating body for São Paulo business (Weyland 1996, 64).

IEDI (Instituto de Estudos para o Desenvolvimento Industrial, 1989).

PNBE (Pensamento Nacional das Bases Empresariais). It had 300 members in 1993 and 480 in 1995 (Schneider 1997–8).

Chile

ABIF (Asociación de Bancos e Instituciones Financieras, 1945). ABIF joined CPC in the 1980s. By 2003, 25 member banks and 13 MNC subsidiaries were members (www.abif.cl).

CChC (Cámara Chilena de Construcción, 1951 or 1953).

CNC (Cámara Nacional de Comercio, née Cámara Central Comercio, 1858). In the 1960s, membership consisted only of chambers: 30 provincial, 14 sectoral, and 11 foreign (Cusack 1972, 55). In 1966 CNC had a budget of $ 213,000 ($40,000 in 1966 dollars) and a staff of eight (Cusack 1972, 66).

Consejo Minero (1998). In 2003 the Consejo had 17 members, mostly MNCs and public firms (www.consejominero.cl)

CPC (Confederación de la Producción y del Comercio, also known as Coproco, 1933). In 1966 CPC member associations included Sofofa, SNA, CCC, Sonami, and the Construction Chamber (admitted in 1965). In 1966 CPC's budget was $164,000 ($31,000 in 1966 dollars), which supported a staff of eight (Cusack 1972, 66). ABIF joined CPC in the 1980s. The budget was around $200,000 in the early 1990s (interview with José Antonio Guzmán, 9 May 2000).

SNA (Sociedad Nacional de Agricultura, 1837). In 1960s, SNA had 5,000 individual members and 38 affiliated associations (Cusack 1972, 41). In 1966 SNA had a budget of $ 2.5 million ($467,000 in 1966 dollars) and a staff of 171 (Cusack 1972, 66).

Sofofa (Sociedad de Fomento Fabril, also known as SFF, 1883). In 1941 Sofofa represented 792 plants, or about 18 percent of all industrial plants (Cavarozzi 1975, 108–9). In the 1960s Sofofa had 19 sectoral and 8 regional association members (Cusack 1972, 44) and tried to balance representation between regional and sectoral members (Menges 1966, 346). In the 1960s, Sofofa's 2,200 members accounted for 7 percent of firms; its 32 affiliated associations accounted for 17 percent of all industrial associations; the capital of members represented 60 percent of private industry; and Sofofa claimed to represent 80 percent of industrial capacity (Cusack 1972, 46). In 1966 Sofofa had a budget of $1.1 million ($200,000 in 1966 dollars) and a staff of 40 (Cusack 1972, 66). Sofofa's annual budgets were $1.6 million in 1968, $2.2 million in 1971, $1.5 million in 1974, $1 million in 1976, $1.1 million in 1977, $1.1 million in 1978, $1.1 million in 1979, and $600,000 in 1983.[2] The budget in 2000 was about $2 million. About 20 percent of the budget came from rents paid on Sofofa properties, and another 10 percent came from income from administering certificate of origin programs (interview with Pedro Lizana, 10 May 2000). The total staff in 2000 was 60–5, including 54 employees in Sofofa itself and 6–10 in offices managing technical schools and housing programs (from the Sofofa phone directory in 2000).

Sonami (Sociedad Nacional Minería, 1883). In 1966 Sonami had a budget of $314,000 ($59,000 in 1966 dollars) and a staff of nine (Cusack 1972, 66).

Colombia

Acopi (Asociación Colombiana de Medianas y Pequeñas Industrias, 1951). In 2000 Acopi had 1,355 members (www.acopi.org.co).

[2] In original currencies the budgets were: 2.2 million escudos in 1968, 6.2 million escudos in 1971, 251 million escudos in 1974, 1.2 million pesos in 1975, 4.2 million pesos in 1976, 8 million pesos in 1977, 13 million pesos in 1978, 17 million pesos in 1979, and 27 million pesos in 1983 (Sofofa, *Memorias Anuales*, various years).

ANDI (Asociación Nacional de Industriales, 1944). ANDI had 540 members in 1963 (Mares 1993, 460), 600 firms in 1967 (Bailey 1977, 282–3), 861 members in 1981 (Urrutia 1983, 82), 691 in 1984, 685 in 1985, 715 in 1986, 734 in 1987, 759 in 1988, 796 in 1989, 781 in 1990 (ANDI 1990, 27), 608 in 1994 (ANDI 1994b, 28), over 650 in 2000 (www.andi.com.co), and 732 in 2001 (interview with Juan Carlos Beltrán, 27 August 2001). By one estimate, ANDI's members accounted for only 11 percent of industry (Osterling 1989, 209). Rettberg (2000, Chapter 3, fn 23) cites ANDI's website and interviews to support the claim that ANDI represents 65–90 percent of industry. By the 1990s, ANDI claimed that its members produced one-third of Colombia's GDP (Villegas Echeverri 1996, 3). Member firms come not only from industry but also from agribusiness, insurance, finance, and commerce (Juárez 1996, 17).

In 1981 ANDI had a budget of about $3.8 million ($2 million in 1981 dollars) (Urrutia 1983, 82). In 1990 ANDI's budget was $2.6 million (982 million 1990 pesos) (ANDI 1990, 23). In 1994 ANDI had 186 employees (65 in Medellín, 69 in Bogotá, and 52 in the other seven regional offices). One-third of these employees were professional. The budget in 1994 was $4.6 million (3.34 billion 1994 pesos, 85 percent of which came from regular dues), and average dues were $5,600 (ANDI 1994b, 28). In 2001 ANDI had 161 employees and a budget of nearly $5 million (85–90 percent of which came from dues) (interview with Beltrán, 27 August 2001).

ANIF (Asociación Nacional de Instituciones Financieras). Established in 1974 as a traditional business association, ANIF evolved, by its own definition, into more of a think tank (see www.anif.com.co and Rettberg 2000). By 2000 ANIF's main activities were research, policy papers, seminars, and publications. Representation of the financial sector, as in the Consejo Gremial, was by Asobancaria.

Asobancaria (Asociación Bancaria y de Entidades Financieras de Colombia, 1936). Asobancaria represented 90 percent of the financial sector (Rettberg 2000, Chapter 3, fn 23; www.asobancaria. com).

Asocaña (Asociación de Cultivadores de Caña de Azúcar, 1959). Asocaña represented 97 percent of sugar production (Rettberg 2000, Chapter 3, fn 23).

Asocoflores (Asociación Colombiana de Productores de Flores, 1970). Asocoflores represented 80 percent of cut flower exports (Rettberg 2000, Chapter 3, fn 23).

Consejo Gremial Nacional (CG, 1991). Sectoral associations established CG at the invitation of Secretary of Development Ernesto Samper to consult with government over trade and macroeconomic policies. CG's members were 15 major associations from agriculture, finance, industry, transportation, commerce, and construction (Rettberg 2000). Federacafe was not a member. CG had one staff person, and the presidency rotated every six months.

Federacafe (Federación Nacional de Cafeteros de Colombia, also known as FNCC, FNC, or Fedecafe, 1927). In 1928 Federacafe had a budget of $1.4 million ($139,000 in 1928 pesos), a staff of at least 10, and 2,000 members (Cortázar Toledo 1968, 54, 56). Federacafe had 4,000 members in 1930, 50,000 in 1934 (Thorp 2002, 7), and 185,000 in 1978 (Bailey 1977, 282–3). In the early 1930s, Federacafe's budget was about $4 million (it averaged $350,000 pesos from 1930 to 1934) (Ospina Pérez 1968, 27). The Fondo Nacional del Café was created in 1940. Federacafe had around 500 employees in the 1940s, 1,000 in the 1960s, 3,500 by 1978–9, 5,000 in 1990, and around 3,600 in 2001 (interview with Jorge Cárdenas, 29 August 2001).

Federalgodón. (Federación Nacional de Algodoneros, 1953).

Fedearroz (Federación Nacional de Arroceros, 1947).

Fedemetal (Federación Colombiana de Industrias Metalúrgicas, 1955).

Fenalco (Federación Nacional de Comerciantes, 1945).

SAC (Sociedad de Agricultores de Colombia, 1871).

Mexico

State-Chartered Associations

Canacintra (Cámara Nacional de la Industria de Transformación, 1941). Formally Canacintra is one of more than 60 chambers belonging to Concamin. Canacintra had 93 founding members in 1941, 5,080 in 1944 (Alcázar 1970, 47), 15,000 in the early 1960s (Vernon 1963, 167), 18,000 in 1964, 27,000 in 1971 (Shafer 1973, 277–8),

60,000 in the early 1980s (Story 1983, 354), and 82,000 by the early 1990s (Luna and Tirado 1992, 34). By 1957 Canacintra had revenues of around $1.5 million ($250,000 in 1957 dollars) and was "said to have more than 200 employees" (Shafer 1973, 95). Canacintra's budget in 1964 was $4 million (8.9 million 1964 pesos) (Alcázar 1970, 29). In the 1940s Canacintra paid over 40 percent of Concamin's budget (Shafer 1973, 282).

Concamin (Confederación de Cámaras Industriales, 1918). Concamin was founded by government initiative in 1918 and later fused briefly with Concanaco (1937–41). Concamin members were sectoral and regional chambers of industry that had to be authorized by the government. Concamin had 51 chambers in 1958 (Brandenburg 1958, 32), 64 chambers plus 14 associations in 1967 (Shafer 1973, 57), and 75 chambers and 42 associations by the 1990s (Luna and Tirado 1992, 34). Concamin had 44,000 member firms (affiliated indirectly through their sectoral chambers) in the mid-1960s (Shafer 1973, 91) and grew to 125,000 members by the 1990s (Luna and Tirado 1992, 34). Concamin had revenues in 1961 of $691,000 ($120,000 in 1961 dollars) (Shafer 1973, 94). Chambers voted in proportion to their financial contribution (and chambers set their dues independently). Ministry of Economics representatives could attend meetings of the executive organs, with a voice but not a vote (Brandenburg 1958, 35). Firms' votes in individual chambers were weighted by their financial contribution, which varied according to capitalization.

Concanaco (Confederación de Cámaras Nacionales de Comercio, 1917). Concanaco was founded by government initiative in 1917. By 1957 it had a large staff and an income of $613,000 ($100,000 in 1957 dollars) (Brandenburg 1958, 38). Concanaco had 80,812 members in 1964 (Alcázar 1970, 17), 330,000 by the early 1970s (Shafer 1973, 91), and 500,000 in 261 chambers by the 1990s (Luna and Tirado 1992, 34). The staff numbered around 30 in the early 1970s (Shafer 1973, 95).

Independent Financial Associations

ABM (Asociación de Banqueros de México, 1928). In 1957, 251 banks and investment firms (and 13 foreign banks) were affiliated with ABM (Brandenburg 1958, 41). By 1966 ABM had 296 member institutions (Shafer 1973, 58). Membership dropped to 52 banks by the late 1990s (Wood 2000, 60).

AMCB (Asociación Mexicana de Casas de Bolsa, later AMIB, Asociación Mexicana de Intermediarios Bursátiles). After the government nationalized private banks in 1982, financial firms created AMCB as a surrogate for ABM. By the 1990s AMCB had 25 members (Luna and Tirado 1992, 34).

AMIS (Asociación Mexicana de Instituciones de Seguros, 1946). In 1957, 78 insurance companies belonged to AMIS (Brandenburg 1958, 42). By the 1990s AMIS had 59 members (Luna and Tirado 1992, 34).

Other Voluntary Associations

ANIERM (Asociación de Importadores y Exportadores de la República Mexicana, Association of Importers and Exporters of the Mexican Republic, 1935).

CCE (Consejo Coordinador Empresarial, 1975). Member associations Concanaco, Concamin, Coparmex, ABM (AMCB after 1982), AMIS, CNA (agriculture), and CMHN founded CCE. Initially Canacintra was not invited to participate (Arriola 1976, 473).

CMHN (Consejo Mexicano de Hombres de Negocios, 1962). In the 1980s CMHN had around 30 members (Camp 1989, 167–8). By the early 1990s it had 37 members (Luna and Tirado 1992, 34). In 1987 CMHN's budget was $282,000 (257 million 1987 pesos)(letter from CMHN treasurer Gastón Azcarraga Tamayo, 14 January 1988).

Coece (Coordinadora de Organismos Empresariales de Comercio Exterior, 1990).

Coparmex (Confederación Patronal de la República Mexicana, 1929). Coparmex was based on voluntary membership from all sectors of the economy. Members joined regional *centros*, of which there were 18 by 1931. By 1958 "the Confederation counted more than 7,000 members, grouped into one of twenty-one . . . (*Centros Patronales*) located throughout the Republic" (Brandenburg 1958, 43). In 1966 there were 32 *centros* with 10,000 members, though some of them barely existed (Shafer 1973, 59, 71), and about the same membership base around 1970 (Alcázar 1970, 30). During the 1970s, membership rose from 13,000 to 18,000 (Camp 1989, 163). As of 1986, "Coparmex encompassed five regional federations, 51 local entrepreneurial or employers' unions with 15,000 affiliated members, and six delegations in Mexico City with 3,000 direct members" (Bravo Mena 1987, 92). By the early 1990s Coparmex had 57 *centros* and 30,000 members (Luna and Tirado 1992, 34).

Appendix B

Interviews

Several dozen interviews with prominent businesspeople and top government officials were crucial for this project. Not only did these interviews provide basic information on associations that was lacking in the published record, they also provided crucial insights into the motivations of the actors involved in building associations and in strategic exchanges between business and government elites. These data on preferences, interpretations, and motivations were crucial to arguments developed in Chapter 2 on the micro-foundations of state-led collective action.

I interviewed more business and political elites in Brazil and Mexico, often in the early 1990s, in the context of related research I was conducting on other topics. The interviews in Argentina, Colombia, and Chile were fewer and much more focused. Some respondents requested anonymity, but most were willing to talk freely, in some cases in tape-recorded interviews. Wherever possible I have attributed quotes to named individuals in an effort promote transparency.

Argentina

Business

Jorge Blanco Villegas. President of UIA (1993–7). 3 May 2000.
Eduardo Cassullo. Executive director of UIA (1993–8). 4 May 2000.
José Alfredo Martínez de Hoz. President of Acindar, president of CEA (1974–6), minister of economics (1976–81). 5 May 2000.
Murat Eurnekian. Member and director of UIA (1963–96), secretary of industry (1987–8). 4 May 2000.

Government

Felix Peña. Mercosur negotiator (1990–2) and undersecretary of trade (1998–9), 5 May 2000.

Brazil

Business

Ruy Altenfelder. Vice president of FIESP. 8 December 1996.

Mauro Arruda. Executive director of IEDI. 15 December 1993 and 23 May 1995.

Synésio Batista da Costa. Executive director (1985–) of ABRINQ (Associação Brasileira dos Fabricantes de Brinquedos, Brazilian Association of Toy Manufacturers). 23 May 1995.

Rudolf Buhler. Technical director, IBS. 27 May 2002.

Butori, Paulo. President of Sindipeças (1994–). 20 November 1997.

Pedro Camargo Neto. First coordinator of PNBE. 24 May 1995.

Eduardo Capobianco. President of Sinduscon (Sindicato da Indústria da Construção Civil do Estado de São Paulo, Syndicate for the Civil Construction Industry of the State of São Paulo). 27 January 1993.

José Augusto Coelho. Executive director of CNI. 10 December 1993; 2 September 1996.

Paulo Cunha. Grupo Ultra, founding member of IEDI. 18 November 1997.

Emerson Kapaz. Founder and president of PNBE. 27 January 1993.

Simone Lopes. Department of Economics, CNI. 29 May 2002.

Ricardo Markwald. General director of FUNCEX (Fundação Centro de Estudos do Comércio Exterior, Foundation Center for Studies of Foreign Trade). 28 May 2002.

José Mindlin. Metaleve and director of FIESP. 29 January 1993.

Paulo Guilherme Monteiro Lobato Ribeiro. President of Banco Real and director of Febraban. 22 May 1995.

Luciana de Sá. Department of Economics, FIRJAN. 28 May 2002.

Paulo Villares. President of Indústrias Villares, member of IEDI. 28 January 1993.

Government

Marcio Fortes. Ex-president of the BNDES, secretary of industry of the State of Rio de Janeiro. 27 November 1997.

Antônio Kandir. Secretary of economic policy (1990–2); federal deputy, 1994–. 24–5 May 1995.

Marcílio Marques Moreira. Minister of economics (1991–2). 26 November 1997.

Nilton Sacenco. Adjunct secretary for industrial policy, Ministry of Industry, Commerce, and Tourism. 24 May 1995.

João Sayad. Ex-minister of planning and private banker. 21 November 1997.

Chile

Business

Hugo Baierlein. Head of Department of International Trade, Sofofa. 9 May 2000.

Manuel Feliú. President of Sonami (1980–6); president of CPC (1986–90). 10 May 2000

José Antonio Guzmán. President of CPC (1990–6). 9 May 2000

Pedro Lizana. President of Sofofa (mid-1990s). 10 May 2000.

Government

Manuel Marfán. Subsecretary of the treasury (1994–9); minister of the treasury (2000). 8 May 2000.

Colombia

Business

Juan Carlos Beltrán. Administrative vice president, ANDI (1998–). 27 August 2001.

Jorge Cárdenas Gutiérrez. General director, Federacafe (1982–). 29 August 2001.

Ricardo Correa Robledo. General secretary, ANDI (1996–2001). 28 August 2001.

Diego Pizano. International and research advisor, Federacafe. 24 and 29 August 2001.

Government

Gilberto Echeverri Mejía. Minister of development (1978–80); minister of defense (1996–8). 27 August 2001.

Ernesto Samper. Minister of development (early 1990s); president of Colombia (1994–8). 24 August 2001.

Miguel Urrutia. General director, Banco de la República (1993–). 24 August 2001.

Mexico

Business

César Balsa. Member of CMHN (1962–79). 28 July 1998.

Gilberto Borja Navarette. Ex-president of ICA (Ingenieros Civiles Asociados, Associated Civil Engineers) and member of CMHN (1980s and 1990s). 24 July 1998.

Francisco Calderón. Executive director of CCE (1976–97). 12 June 1996 and 19 May 1998.

Fernando Canales Clariond. Executive vice president, IMSA (Industrias Monterrey, S.A., Monterrey Industries). 19 November 1993.

Jaime González Graf. Advisor to Concamin (1970s–90s); director of Centro de Estudios Industriales (Center for Industrial Studies), Concamin (1990–2). 10 June 1996.

Guillermo Güémez. Banamex (1974–92); director of Coece (1990–5); director of Banco de Mexico (1995–). 7–8 June 1996.

Agustín Legorreta. President of Banamex (before 1982); president of Inverlat; president of ABM (1954–5, 1973–4); president CCE (1987–9); member of CMHN (1970–96). 28 July 1998.

Luis Martínez Argüello. General coordinator of Coece. 26 February 2003.

Alejandro Martínez Gallardo. President of Concamin (1999–2001); director of Herdez (1999–). 11 May 2001 and 24 February 2003.

Frederico Müggenburg. Head of Centro de Estudios Sociales (Center for Social Studies), CCE (1976–89, 1992–). 11 June 1996.

Jorge Ocejo Moreno. President of Coparmex (1988–91), PAN deputy (1994–7). 18 March 1998.

Rómulo O'Farrill Jr. Founding member of CMHN. 27 July 1998.

Raúl Ortega. Director of COECE. 16 November 1993.

Luiz Miguel Pando. Director general of CCE (2003–); staff member of Canacintra (1974–99) and Concamin (1999–2002). 26 February 2003.

Rogelio Sada Zambrano. Ex-executive of Vitro (1974–85) and federal deputy of PAN (1997–). 6 March 1994.

Roberto Sánchez de la Vara. President of Canacintra (1990–2). 8 June 1996.

Juan Sánchez Navarro. Founder of CMHN and CCE. 10 June 1996, 30 June 1998, and 10 July 1998.

Rolando Vega Iñíquez. Ex-president of CCE (1988–90?); president of ABM (1961–2, 1969–70, 1979–80), member of CMHN (1962–). 8 November 1993.

Oscar Vera. Ex-director of CEESP. 10 June 1996.

Raymundo Winkler. Director of CEESP. 4 June 1996.

Government

Manuel Camacho. Minister and regent (mayor) of Mexico City (1987–94). 13 November 1996.

Aslan Cohen. Nafta negotiator, Secofi. 16 November 1993 and 7 June 1996.

Santiago Macias. General director, Secofi. 16 November 1993.

Jorge Montaño. Ex-ambassador to the United States (1992–5). 25 February 2003.

Norma Samaniego. Ex-subsecretary of labor and technical secretary for the pacts (1988–94). 18 March 1998.

Jaime Serra Puche. Secretary of Secofi (1988–94) and secretary of finance (1994). 15 July 1996 and 16 July 1998.

Other

David Zúñiga. Business reporter for *La Jornada*. 25–6 February 2003.

Appendix C

Conversions

Translations

All translations from Portuguese and Spanish are mine.

Currencies

To enable comparisons across countries and periods, I converted exact monetary figures to 2000 U.S. dollars. Historical and international conversions were based mostly on websites posted by the Federal Reserve Bank of Minneapolis (http://woodrow.mpls.frb.fed.us/research/data/us/calc/hist1913.cfm) and the Economic History Net (http://www.eh.net). I did not convert some dollar figures from the 1990s, when inflation was comparatively low, or from some rough estimates provided in interviews where it was sometimes unclear what dollar or year reference interviewees were using.

References

Acuña, Carlos. 1995. "Business Interests, Dictatorship, and Democracy in Argentina." In *Business and Democracy in Latin America*, ed. Ernest Bartell and Leigh Payne. Pittsburgh, PA: University of Pittsburgh Press.

Acuña, Carlos. 1998. "Political Struggle and Business Peak Associations: Theoretical Reflections on the Argentine Case." In *Organized Business, Economic Change, and Democracy in Latin America*, ed. Francisco Durand and Eduardo Silva. Miami: North-South Center Press.

Addis, Caren. 1999. *Taking the Wheel: Auto Parts Firms and the Political Economy of Industrialization in Brazil*. University Park: Pennsylvia State University Press.

Adelman, Alan. 1981. "Colombian Friendship Groups." *Journal of Developing Areas* 15 (April): 457–70.

Affonso, Rui de Britto, and Pedro Luís Baros Silva. 1995. *Federalismo no Brasil: Desigualdades regionais e desenvolvimento*. São Paulo: FUNDAP.

Alcázar, Marco. 1970. *Las agrupaciones patronales en México*. México, DF: Colegio de México.

Alcocer, Jorge, and Isidro Cisneros. 1988. "Los empresarios, entre los negocios y la política." In *México*, ed. Jorge Alcocer. México, DF: Ediciones de Cultura Popular.

Alt, James, Fredrik Carlsen, Per Heum, and Kare Johansen. 1999. "Asset specificity and the political behavior of firms." *International Organization* 53(1) (Winter): 99–116.

Alt, James, Frieden, Jeffry, Gilligan, Michael, Rodrik, Dani, and Rogowski, Ronald. 1996. "The political economy of international trade: Enduring puzzles and an agenda for inquiry." *Comparative Political Studies* 29(6) (December): 689–717.

Anderson, Charles. 1977. "Political design and the representation of interests." *Comparative Political Studies* 10(1) (April): 127–52.

ANDI. 1990. "Informe comisión de presidentes: Estados financieros 1989." Medellín: Asociación Nacional de Industriales.

ANDI. 1994a. "ANDI cinquenta años." Medellín: Asociación Nacional de Industriales.

ANDI. 1994b. "Informe anual de gestión, 1993–94." Medellín: Asociación Nacional de Industriales.

ANIF. 1975. *Legislación Cafetera*. Bogotá: Tercer Mundo y Asociación Nacional de Instituciones Financieras.

Arat, Yesim. 1991. "Politics and Big Business." In *Strong State and Economic Interest Groups: The Post-1980 Turkish Experience*, ed. Metin Heper. Berlin: Walter de Gruyter.

Arbix, Glauco. 1995. "Uma Aposta no Futuro: Os Três Primeiros Anos da Câmara Setorial da Indústria Automobilística e a Emergência do Meso-Corporatismo no Brasil." Tese de doutoramento. Universidade de São Paulo.

Arriagada, Genaro. 1970. *La oligarquía patronal chilena*. Santiago: Nueva Sociedad.

Arriagada, Genaro. 1988. "Los empresarios y la concertación social." In *Política económica y actores sociales*, ed. PREALC. Santiago: PREALC.

Arriola, Carlos. 1976. "Los grupos empresariales frente al estado (1973–1975)." *Foro Internacional* 16(4) (April–June): 449–95.

Arriola, Carlos. 1988. *Los Empresarios y el Estado, 1970–1982*. Mexico, DF: UNAM/Miguel Angel Porrúa.

Avery, William, and H. Richard Friman. 1999. "Who Got What and Why: Constructing North American Free Trade." In *Racing to Regionalize*, ed. Kenneth Thomas and Mary Ann Tétreault. Boulder, CO: Lynne Rienner.

Avritzer, Leonardo. 2000. "Democratization and changes in the pattern of association in Brazil." *Journal of Interamerican Studies and World Affairs* 42(3) (Fall): 59–76.

Ayres, Robert. 1976. "The 'social pact' as anti-inflationary policy: The Argentine experience since 1973." *World Politics* 28(4) (July): 473–501.

Baccaro, Lucio. In press. "What is dead and what is alive in the theory of corporatism." *British Journal of Industrial Relations*.

Baer, Werner. 1983. *The Brazilian Economy*. New York: Praeger.

Bailey, John. 1977. "Pluralist and Corporatist Dimensions of Interest Representation in Colombia." In *Authoritarianism and Corporatism in Latin America*, ed. James Malloy. Pittsburgh: University of Pittsburgh Press.

Balze, Felipe de la. 1995. *Remaking the Argentine Economy*. New York: Council on Foreign Relations.

Barker, Wendy. 1990. "Banks and Industry in Contemporary Brazil: Their Organization, Relationship, and Leaders." Ph.D. Dissertation, Yale University.

Barros, Alexandre. 1978. "The Brazilian Military: Professional Socialization, Political Performance and State Building." Ph.D. Dissertation. University of Chicago.

Bartell, Ernest, and Leigh Payne. 1995. *Business and Democracy in Latin America*. Pittsburgh, PA: University of Pittsburgh Press.

Bates, Robert. 1988. "Contra contractarianism: Some reflections on the new institutionalism." *Politics and Society* 16(2–3) (September): 387–401.

Bates, Robert. 1997. *Open-Economy Politics: The Political Economy of the World Coffee Trade*. Princeton, NJ: Princeton University Press.

Bejarano, Jesús Antonio. 1985. *Economía y poder. La SAC y el desarrollo agropecuario colombiano 1871–1984.* Bogotá: Sociedad de Agricultores de Colombia y Centro de Estudios de la Realidad Colombiana.

Bellin, Eva. 2000. "Contingent democrats: Industrialists, labor, and democratization in late-developing countries." *World Politics* 52(2) (January): 175–205.

Bellin, Eva. 2002. *Stalled Democracy: Capital, Labor and the Paradox of State-Sponsored Development.* Ithaca, NY: Cornell University Press.

Bianchi, Robert. 1989. *Unruly Corporatism: Associational Life in Twentieth Century Egypt.* New York: Oxford University Press.

Biddle, Jesse, Vedat Milor, Juan Manuel Ortega, and Andrew Stone. 2000. *Consultative Mechanisms in Mexico.* PSD Occasional Paper No. 39. Washington, DC: Private Sector Development Department, World Bank.

Bielschowsky, Ricardo. 1988. *Pensamento Econômico Brasileiro: O Ciclo Ideológico do Desenvolvimentismo.* Rio de Janeiro: IPEA.

Birle, Peter. 1997. *Los empresarios y la democracia en Argentina.* Buenos Aires: Belgrano.

Bisang, Roberto. 1998. "Apertura, reestructuración industrial y conglomerados económicos." *Desarrollo Económico* 38 (Fall): 143–76.

Blume, Norman. 1967–8. "Pressure groups and decision making in Brazil." *Studies in Comparative International Development* 3(11): 205–23.

Bond, Robert. 1975. "Business Associations and Interest Politics in Venezuela: The Fedecamaras and the Determination of National Economic Policies." Ph.D. Dissertation. Vanderbilt University.

Boone, Catherine. 1992. *Merchant Capital and the Roots of State Power in Senegal, 1930–1985.* New York: Cambridge University Press.

Boschi, Renato. 1979. *Elites Industriais e Democracia.* Rio de Janeiro: Graal.

Boschi, Renato. 1993. "The private sector, economic restructuring and democratization in Latin America." Unpublished paper.

Boschi, Renato. 1994. "Democratización y reestructuración del sector privado en América Latina." *Sintesis* 22 (July–December): 131–65.

Boschi, Renato, and Eli Diniz. 1978. "Empresas, burocracia e mediação de interesses." Relatório de Pesquisa. Rio de Janeiro: IUPERJ.

Bowman, John. 1989. *Capitalist Collective Action: Competition, Cooperation, and Conflict in the Coal Industry.* New York: Cambridge University Press.

Boylan, Delia. 1996. "Taxation and transition: The politics of the 1990 Chilean tax reform." *Latin American Research Review* 31(1): 7–32.

Brandenburg, Frank. 1958. "Organized business in Mexico." *Inter-American Economic Affairs* 3 (Winter): 26–50.

Brandenburg, Frank. 1962. "A contribution to the theory of enterpreneurship and economic development: The case of Mexico." *Inter-American Economic Affairs* 16(1) (Summer): 3–23.

Bravo Mena, Luis Felipe. 1987. "Coparmex and Mexican Politics." In *Government and Private Sector in Contemporary Mexico*, ed. Sylvia Maxfield, and Ricardo Anzaldúa Montoya. San Diego, CA: Center for U.S.-Mexican Studies.

Brazil. 1983. *Ministros da Fazenda, 1808–1983.* Rio de Janeiro: Museu da Fazenda Federal.

Brennan, James. 1998. "Industrialists and Bolicheros: Business and the Peronist Populist Alliance, 1943–1976." In *Peronism and Argentina*, ed. James Brennan. Wilmington, DE: Scholarly Resources.

Bresser Pereira, Luiz Carlos. 1978. *O Colapso de uma aliança de clases*. São Paulo: Brasilense.

Briz Garizurieta, Marcela. 2000. "El Consejo Mexicano de Hombres de Negocios: Surgimento y Consolidación." Tesis de maestria. México, DF: UNAM.

Buarque de Holanda Filho, Sérgio. 1983. *Estrutura industrial no Brasil: Concentração e diversificação*. Rio de Janeiro: IPEA.

Buchanan, Paul. 1995. *State, Labor, Capital*. Pittsburgh, PA: Pittsburgh University Press.

Burrell, Jennifer, and Jeffrey Cason. 2000. "Turning the Tables: State and Society in South America's Economic Integration." Unpublished paper.

Calvo, Ernesto. 2001. "Disconcerted Industrialists: The Politics of Trade Reform in Latin America." Ph.D. Dissertation, Northwestern University.

Camp, Roderic. 1987. "Attitudes and Images of the Mexican Entrepreneur: Political Consequences." In *Government and Private Sector in Contemporary Mexico*, ed. Sylvia Maxfield and Ricardo Anzaldúa Montoya. San Diego, CA: Center for U.S.-Mexican Studies.

Camp, Roderic. 1989. *Entrepreneurs and Politics in Twentieth-Century Mexico*. New York: Oxford University Press.

Camp, Roderic. 2002. *Mexico's Mandarins: Crafting a Power Elite for the Twenty-First Century*. Berkeley: University of California Press.

Campero, Guillermo. 1984. *Los gremios empresariales en el período 1970–83: comportamiento sociopolítico y orientaciones ideológicas*. Santiago: ILET.

Campero, Guillermo. 1995. "Entrepreneurs Under the Military Regime." In *The Struggle for Democracy in Chile, 1982–1990*, ed. Paul Drake and Iván Jaksic. Lincoln: University of Nebraska Press.

Campos, José, and Hilton Root. 1996. *The Key to the Asian Miracle: Making Shared Growth Credible*. Washington, DC: Brookings Institution Press.

Cappelletti, Beatriz. 1985. "La concertación económico-social en Argentina." Buenos Aires: Centro de Estudios para el Proyecto Nacional.

Cardoso, Eliana. 1991. "Deficit finance and monetary dynamics in Brazil and Mexico." *Journal of Development Economics* 37(1–2) (November): 173–97.

Cardoso, Fernando Henrique. 1972 [first edition 1964]. *Empresário industrial e desenvolvimento econômico no Brasil*. São Paulo: Difusão Européia do Livro.

Cardoso, Fernando Henrique. 1973. "Associated-Dependent Development." In *Authoritarian Brazil*, ed. Alfred Stepan. New Haven, CT: Yale University Press.

Cardoso, Fernando Henrique. 1975. *Autoritarismo e democratização*. Rio de Janeiro: Paz e Terra.

Cardoso, Fernando Henrique. 1978 [first edition 1969]. *Política e desenvolvimento em sociedades dependentes: Ideologias do empresariado industrial argentino e brasileiro*, 2nd edition. Rio de Janeiro: Zahar.

Carone, Edgard. 1978. *O Centro Industrial do Rio de Janeiro e sua importante participação na economia nacional (1827–1977)*. Rio de Janeiro: CIRJ/Cátedra.

Casar, María Amparo, et al. 1988. "Los Empresarios y el Estado en México: Un Análisis Político." In *Empresarios y Estado en América Latina*, ed. Celso Garrido N. México, DF: CIDE et al.

Cason, Jeffrey. 2000a. "Democracy Looks South: Mercosul and the Politics of Brazilian Trade Strategy." In *Democratic Brazil*, ed. Peter Kingstone and Timothy Power. Pittsburgh, PA: University of Pittsburgh Press.

Cason, Jeffrey. 2000b. "On the road to southern cone economic integration." *Journal of Interamerican Studies and World Affairs* 42(1) (Spring): 23–42.

Castañeda, Jorge. 1982. *Los últimos capitalismos*. Mexico City: Era.

Castell, Pablo. 1987. "El poder industrial: entre 'capitanes' y 'coroneles'." *Realidad Económica* 2:11–25.

Cavarozzi, Marcelo. 1975. "The Government and the Industrial Bourgeoisie in Chile: 1938–1964." Ph.D Dissertation. University of California, Berkeley.

CCE. 1987. "Informe de labores que el Ing. Claudio X. González, presidente del CCE, presenta al Consejo Directivo de dicha Institución por el Periódo 1985–87." México, DF: Consejo Coordinador Empresarial.

CEA. 1994. "Memoria." Buenos Aires: Consejo Empresario Argentino.

CEA. 1999. "Memoria." Buenos Aires: Consejo Empresario Argentino.

CEA. n.d. "Consejo Empresario Argentino." Unpublished description of the CEA written in 2000 or 2001. Buenos Aires.

Chong, Dennis. 1991. *Collective Action and the Civil Rights Movement*. Chicago: University of Chicago Press.

Cleaves, Peter. 1974. *Bureaucratic Politics and Administration in Chile*. Berkeley: University of California Press.

Cline, William. 1991. "Mexico: Economic reform and development strategy." *Exim Review* (Tokyo) (Fall): 1–44.

CNI. 1968. "Folha de pagamento." In the papers of Edmundo Macedo Soares, president of the Confederação Nacional da Indústria, rolo 11, fotos 237 and 266. CPDOC. Rio de Janeiro.

CNI. 1990. *Competitividade e estratégia industrial: A Visão de líderes industriais brasileiras*. Rio de Janeiro: Confederação Nacional da Indústria.

CNI. 1991. *Abertura comercial e estratégia tecnológica: A Visão de líderes industriais brasileiras*. Rio de Janeiro: Confederação Nacional da Indústria.

CNI. 1992. *Abertura comercial e estratégia tecnológica: A Visão de líderes industriais brasileiras em 1992*. Rio de Janeiro: Confederação Nacional da Indústria.

CNP. 1997. *El Salto Social: la sociedad pide cuentas*. Bogotá: Consejo Nacional de Planeación.

Cohen, Joshua, and Joel Rogers. 1995a. *Associations and Democracy*. London: Verso.

Cohen, Joshua, and Joel Rogers. 1995b. "Secondary Associations and Democratic Governance." In *Associations and Democracy*, ed. Joshua Cohen and Joel Rogers. London: Verso.

Cohen, Joshua, and Joel Rogers. 1995c. "Solidarity, Democracy, and Association." In *Associations and Democracy*, ed. Joshua Cohen and Joel Rogers. London: Verso.

Cohen, Youssef. 1987. "Democracy from above: The political origins of military dictatorship in Brazil." *World Politics* 40(1) (October): 30–54.

Coleman, William. 1988. *Business and Politics: A Study of Collective Action*. Kingston and Montreal: McGill-Queen's University Press.

Coleman, William. 1990. "State traditions and comprehensive business associations: A comparative structural analysis." *Political Studies* 38: 231–52.

Coleman, William. 1997. "Associational Governance in a Globalizing Era: Weathering the Storm." In *Contemporary Capitalism*, ed. J. Rogers Hollingsworth and Robert Boyer. New York: Cambridge University Press.

Collier, David, and James Mahoney. 1996. "Insights and pitfalls: Selection bias in qualitative research." *World Politics* 49 (October): 56–91.

Collier, Ruth, and David Collier. 1991. *Shaping the Political Arena: Critical Junctures, the Labor Movement, and Regime Dynamics in Latin America*. Princeton, NJ: Princeton University Press.

Collier, Ruth, and David Collier. 2002. *Shaping the Political Arena: Critical Junctures, the Labor Movement, and Regime Dynamics in Latin America*. Notre Dame, IN: University of Notre Dame Press.

Conaghan, Catherine. 1988. *Restructuring Domination: Industrialists and the State in Ecuador*. Pittsburgh, PA: University of Pittsburgh Press.

Conaghan, Catherine. 1990. "Retreat to Democracy: Business and Political Transition in Bolivia and Ecuador." In *Democratic Transition and Consolidation in Southern Europe, Latin America and Southeast Asia*, ed. Diane Ethier. Houndmills, England: Macmillan.

Conaghan, Catherine. 1992. "Capitalists, Technocrats, and Politicians: Economic Policy Making and Democracy in the Central Andes." In *Issues in Democratic Consolidation*, ed. Scott Mainwaring, Guillermo O'Donnell, and J. Samuel Valenzuela. Notre Dame, IN: University of Notre Dame Press.

Cook, María Lorena. 2002. "Labor reform and dual transitions in Brazil and the southern cone." *Latin American Politics and Society* 44(1) (Spring): 1–34.

Cordero H., Salvador, Rafael Santín, and Ricardo Tirado. 1983. *El Poder empresarial en México*. México, DF: Terra Nova.

Córdoba, José. 1991. "Diez lecciones de la reforma económica en México." *Nexos* 158 (February): 31–48.

Corrales, Javier, and Imelda Cisneros. 1999. "Corporatism, trade liberalization and sectoral responses: The case of Venezuela, 1989–99." *World Development* 27(12) (December): 2099–123.

Cortázar Toledo, Alfredo. 1968. "Breve historia de la fundación y organización de la Federación Nacional de Cafeteros, 1927 y 1928." *Revista Cafetera de Colombia* 17(143) (March–April): 48–57.

Costa, Vanda Ribeiro. 1991. "Origens do corporativismo brasileiro." In *Corporativismo e desigualdade*, ed. Renato Boschi. Rio de Janeiro: IUPERJ.

Costa, Vanda Ribeiro. 1992. "A Armadilha do Leviatã: A elite industrial paulista e o corporativismo no Brasil, 1930–45." Ph.D. Dissertation. Rio de Janeiro: IUPERJ.

Crisp, Brian. 1996. "The rigidity of democratic institutions and the current legitimacy crisis in Venezuela." *Latin American Perspectives* 23(3) (Summer): 30–49.

Cruz, Sebastião Velasco e. 1984. "Empresários e o regime no Brasil: A Campanha contra a estatização." Tese de Doutorado. Universidade de São Paulo.

Cúneo, Dardo. 1967. *Comportamiento y crisis e la clase empresaria*. Buenos Aires: Pleamar.

Cusack, David. 1972. "The Politics of Chilean Private Enterprise under Christian Democracy." Ph.D. Dissertation. University of Denver.

Dahl, Robert. 1982. *Dilemmas of Pluralist Democracy.* New Haven, CT: Yale University Press.

DANE. 1998. *Estadísticas Históricas de Colombia.* Bogotá.

Dávila, Carlos. 1986. *El empresariado Colombiano: Una perspectiva histórica.* Bogotá: Pontífica Universidad Javeriana.

Derossi, Flavia. 1971. *The Mexican Entrepreneur.* Paris: Organization for Economic Cooperation and Development.

Diamond, Larry. 1996. "Toward Democratic Consolidation." In *The Global Resurgence of Democracy,* ed. Larry Diamond and Marc Plattner. Baltimore, MD: Johns Hopkins University Press.

Diamond, Larry. 1999. *Developing Democracy: Toward Consolidation.* Baltimore, MD: Johns Hopkins University Press.

Diaz de Landa, Martha, and María Carola Sajem. 2000. "A Differential Organized Business Response to the New Regional Trading Regime in the Southern Cone: The Experience of Argentina and Brazil's Car Industries." In *Organized Business and the New Global Order,* ed. Justin Greenwood and Henry Jacek. Houndmills, England: Macmillan.

Diniz, Eli. 1978. *Empresário, Estado e capitalismo no Brasil: 1930–45.* Rio de Janeiro: Paz e Terra.

Diniz, Eli, and Renato Boschi. 1978. *Empresariado nacional e Estado no Brasil.* Rio de Janeiro: Forense Universitária.

Diniz, Eli, and Renato Boschi. 1987. "Burocracia, clientelismo e oligopólio: o Conselho Interministerial de Preços." In *As Origens da crise,* ed. Olavo Lima and Sergio Abranches. Rio de Janeiro: IUPERJ and Vertice.

Diniz, Eli, and Renato Boschi. 1988. "Empresarios y Constituyente." In *Empresarios y Estado en America Latina,* ed. Celso Garrido. México, DF: CIDE.

Diniz, Eli, and Renato Boschi. 1997. "O Legislativo como arena de interesses organizados: A atuaçao dos *lobbies* empresariais." Rio de Janeiro: Instituto Universitário de Pesquisa de Rio de Janeiro.

Dix, Robert. 1987. *The Politics of Colombia.* New York: Praeger.

Doctor, Mahrukh. 2000. "The Politics of Port Reform in Brazil: Business Lobbying and the Legacy of Corporatism (1990–98)." PhD Dissertation. University of Oxford.

Doctor, Mahrukh. 2003. "Driving for Growth: How Business–State Relations Steered Investment to the Automotive Industry in Brazil." Prepared for delivery at the 2003 meeting of the Latin American Studies Association, Dallas.

Domínguez, Jorge. 1982. "Business Nationalism: Latin American National Business Attitudes and Behavior toward Multinational Enterprises." In *Economic Issues and Political Conflict,* ed. Jorge Domínguez. Boston: Butterworth Scientific.

Domínguez, Jorge. 1997. "Latin America's Crisis of Representation." *Foreign Affairs* 76(1) (January–February): 100–13.

Doner, Richard, and Ansil Ramsay. 1997. "Competitive Clientelism and Economic Governance: The Case of Thailand." In *Business and the State in Developing Countries,* ed. Sylvia Maxfield and Ben Ross Schneider. Ithaca, NY: Cornell University Press.

Doner, Richard, and Ben Ross Schneider. 2000. "Business associations and development: Why some associations contribute more than others." *Business and Politics* 2(3) (November): 261–88.

Drake, Paul. 1978. "Corporatism and functionalism in modern Chilean politics." *Journal of Latin American Studies* 10(1) (May): 83–116.

Dreifuss, René. 1981. *1964: A Conquista do Estado*. Petrópolis: Vozes.

Dreifuss, René. 1989. *O Jogo da direita na Nova República*. Petrópolis: Vozes.

Ducatenzeiler, Graciela. 1990. "Social Concertation and Democracy in Argentina." In *Democratic Transition and Consolidation in Southern Europe, Latin America, and Southeast Asia*, ed. Diane Ethier. London: Macmillan.

Dugan, William, and Alfredo Rehren. 1990. "Impacto del régimen político en la intermediación de intereses: Instituciones públicas y grupos empresariales en Chile." *Política* 22/23 (June): 117–36.

Duran, Roberto. 1996. "Democracy and Regional Multilateralism in Chile." In *Foreign Policy and Regionalism in the Americas*, ed. Gordon Mace and Jean-Philippe Thérien. Boulder, CO: Lynne Rienner.

Durand, Francisco. 1994. "Las organizaciones empresariales latinoamericanas al final del siglo XX." In *Los Empresarios ante la globalización*, ed. Ricardo Tirado. México, DF: UNAM.

Durand, Francisco. 1998. "Collective Action and the Empowerment of Peruvian Business." In *Organized Business, Economic Change, and Democracy in Latin America*, ed. Francisco Durand and Eduardo Silva. Miami: North-South Center Press.

Durand, Francisco. 2002. "Business and the crisis of Peruvian democracy." *Business and Politics* 4(3) (November): 319–42.

Durand, Francisco, and Eduardo Silva. 1998. *Organized Business, Economic Change, and Democracy in Latin America*. Miami: North-South Center Press.

Edwards, Bob, and Michael Foley. 2001. "Civil Society and Social Capital." In *Beyond Tocqueville*, ed. Bob Edwards, Michael Foley, and Mario Diani. Hanover, NH: University Press of New England.

Encarnación, Omar. 2002. "Venezuela's 'civil society coup'." *World Policy Journal* 19(2) (Summer): 38–49.

Encarnación, Omar. 2003. *The Myth of Civil Society: Social Capital and Democratic Consolidation in Spain and Brazil*. New York: Palgrave Macmillan.

Escobar, Saúl David. 1987. "Rifts in the Mexican Power Elite, 1976–86." In *Government and Private Sector in Contemporary Mexico*, ed. Sylvia Maxfield and Ricardo Anzaldúa Montoya. San Diego, CA: Center for U.S.-Mexican Studies.

Evans, Peter. 1995. *Embedded Autonomy: States and Industrial Transformation*. Princeton, NJ: Princeton University Press.

Evans, Peter. 1996. "Government action, social capital and development: Reviewing the evidence on synergy." *World Development* 24(6) (June): 1119–32.

Evans, Peter, and Gary Gereffi. 1982. "Foreign Investment and Dependent Development." In *Brazil and Mexico*, ed. Sylvia Ann Hewlett and Richard Weinert. Philadelphia: Institute for the Study of Human Issues.

Fajnzylber, Fernando. 1990. *Unavoidable Industrial Restructuring in Latin America*. Durham, NC: Duke University Press.

Farina, Elizabeth Maria Mercier Querido, Paulo Furquim, and Maria Sylvia Saes. 1997. *Competitividade: Mercado, Estado, e Organizações*. São Paulo: Singular.

FCPS. 1994. *Organizaciones empresariales mexicanas: Banco de dados*. México: UNAM, Facultad de Ciencias Políticas y Sociales.

Federacafe. 2002. "Informe del Gerente General." Bogotá: Federación Nacional de Cafeteros de Colombia.

Feldman, Gerald, and Ulrich Nocken. 1975. "Trade associations and economic power: Interest group development in the German iron and steel and machine building industries, 1900–1933." *Business History Review* 49: 413–45.

FIEG. 1972. *Anuário industrial da Guanabara*. Rio de Janeiro: Federação das Indústrias do Estado da Guanabara.

Fields, Karl. 1997. "Creating Cooperation and Determining the Distance: Strong States and Business Organization in Korea and Taiwan." In *Business and the State in Developing Countries*, ed. Sylvia Maxfield and Ben Ross Schneider. Ithaca, NY: Cornell University Press.

FIESP. 1941. *Relatorio dos trabalhos realizados em 1940*. São Paulo: Federação da Indústria do Estado de São Paulo.

FIESP. 1990. *Livre para Crescer*. São Paulo: Federação das Indústrias do Estado de São Paulo e Cultura Editores.

Figueiredo, Rubens. 1993. "Brasil e Espanha: o papel dos empresários no processo de transiçao para a democracia." In *Empresários e Modernização Econômica*, ed. Eli Diniz. Florianópolis: UFSC.

Filgueira, Carlos. 1988. "Concertación salarial y gremios empresariales en Uruguay." In *La Política Económica y Actores Sociales*. Santiago: PREALC.

Font, Mauricio. 1990. *Coffee, Contention, and Change in the Making of Modern Brazil*. Cambridge, MA: Blackwell.

Foster, Kenneth. 2001. "Associations in the embrace of an authoritarian state: State domination of society?" *Studies in Comparative International Development* 35(4) (Winter): 84–109.

Foster, Kenneth. 2002. "Embedded within state agencies: Business associations in Yantai." *China Journal* 47 (January): 41–65.

Freels, John. 1970. "Industrialists and politics in Argentina." *Journal of Inter-American Studies and World Affairs* 12(3) (July): 439–54.

Frieden, Jeffry. 1991. *Debt, Development, and Democracy*. Princeton, NJ: Princeton University Press.

Frieden, Jeffry, and Lisa Martin. 2002. "International Political Economy: Global and Domestic Interactions." In *Political Science: The State of the Discipline*, ed. Ira Katznelson and Helen Milner. New York: Norton.

Friedman, Elizabeth Jay, and Kathryn Hochstetler. 2002. "Assessing the third transition in Latin American democratization: Representational regimes and civil society in Argentina and Brazil." *Comparative Politics* (October): 21–42.

Fukuyama, Francis. 1996. "The Primacy of Culture." In *The Global Resurgence of Democracy*, ed. Larry Diamond and Marc Plattner. Baltimore, MD: Johns Hopkins University Press.

Garcia, Patricio, ed. 1973. *Los gremios patronales*. Santiago: Nacional Quimantu.

Garrido, Celso, ed. 1988. *Empresarios y Estado en América Latina*. México DF: CIDE et al.

Gazeta Mercantil. 1992. *Balanço Anual.* São Paulo: Gazeta Mercantil.

Geddes, Barbara. 1994. *Politician's Dilemma.* Berkeley: University of California Press.

Gellner, Ernest. 1994. *Conditions of Liberty: Civil Society and Its Rivals.* New York: Penguin.

Giacalone, Rita. 1999. *Los empresarios frente al Grupo de Los Tres.* Caracas: Nueva Sociedad.

Gibson, Edward. 1996. *Class and Conservative Parties: Argentina in Comparative Perspective.* Baltimore, MD: Johns Hopkins University Press.

Goldstein, Andrea, and Ben Ross Schneider. 2003. "Big Business in Brazil: States and Markets in the Corporate Reorganization of the 1990s." In *Brazil and Korea,* ed. Edmund Amann and Ha Joon Chang. London: University of London.

Gomes, Angela Maria de Castro. 1979. *Burguesia e trabalho: política e legislação social no Brasil, 1917–1937.* Rio de Janeiro: Campus.

Guillen, Mauro. 2001. *The Limits of Convergence: Globalization and Organizational Change in Argentina, South Korea, and Spain.* Princeton, NJ: Princeton University Press.

Guimarães, Ivan Gonçalves Ribeiro. 1994. "A Experiência das Câmaras Setoriais: Democratizando a Política Econômica." Projeto PNUD/MTb/CESIT, Unicamp.

Haggard, Stephan. 1997. "Democratic Institutions, Economic Policy, and Development." In *Institutions and Economic Development,* ed. Christopher Clague. Baltimore, MD: Johns Hopkins University Press.

Haggard, Stephan, and Robert Kaufman. 1995. *The Political Economy of Democratic Transitions.* Princeton, NJ: Princeton University Press.

Hall, Peter, and David Soskice, eds. 2001a. *Varieties of Capitalism: The Institutional Foundations of Comparative Advantage.* New York: Oxford University Press.

Hall, Peter, and David Soskice. 2001b. "An Introduction to Varieties of Capitalism." In *Varieties of Capitalism,* ed. Peter Hall and David Soskice. New York: Oxford University Press.

Hardin, Russell. 1982. *Collective Action.* Baltimore, MD: Johns Hopkins University Press.

Hardin, Russell. 1995. *One for All: The Logic of Group Conflict.* Princeton, NJ: Princeton University Press.

Hartlyn, Jonathan. 1985. "Producer associations, the political regime, and policy processes in contemporary Colombia." *Latin American Research Review* 20(3): 111–38.

Hartlyn, Jonathan. 1988. *The Politics of Coalition Rule in Colombia.* Cambridge: Cambridge University Press.

Hollingsworth, J. Rogers, and Boyer Robert. 1997. "Coordination of Economic Actors and Social Systems of Production." In *Contemporary Capitalism,* ed. J. Rogers Hollingsworth and Robert Boyer. Cambridge: Cambridge University Press.

Huneeus, Carlos. 1998. "Technocrats and Politicians in the Democratic Politics of Argentina (1983–95)." In *The Politics of Expertise in Latin America,* ed. Miguel Centeno and Patricio Silva. London: Macmillan.

IDB. 1992. *Economic and Social Progress in Latin America: 1992 Report*. Washington, DC: Inter-American Development Bank.

IEA. 1988. *Estadísticas Historicas Argentinas – Compendio 1873–1973*. Buenos Aires: Instituto de Economia Aplicada.

Imaz, José. 1964. *Los que mandan*. Buenos Aires: EUDEBA.

INEGI. 1994. *Cuentas Nacionales*. México, DF: Instituto Nacional de Estadística, Geografía e Informática.

Itzcovitz, Victoria. 1987. "La Cámara Argentina de Comercio y la Asociación de Bancos Argentinos." In *Ensayos sobre la transición democrática en la Argentina*, ed. José Nun and Juan Carlos Portantiero. Buenos Aires: Puntosur.

Jenkins, Barbara. 1999. "Assessing the 'New' Integration: The Mercosur Trade Agreement." In *Racing to Regionalize*, ed. Kenneth Thomas and Mary Ann Tétreault. Boulder, CO: Lynne Riener.

Johnson, Dale. 1967. "Industry and Industrialists in Chile." Ph.D. dissertation. Stanford University.

Johnson, Dale. 1968–9. "The national and progressive bourgeoisie in Chile." *Studies in Comparative International Development* 14(4): 63–86.

Juárez, Carlos. 1995. "The Political Economy of Economic Policy Reform in Colombia: Technocratic Bureaucracy and Business–Government Relations, 1966–92." Ph.D. Dissertation. University of California, Los Angeles.

Juárez, Carlos. 1996. "Politics and economic policy in colombia." Paper presented at the meeting of the American Political Science Association, San Francisco, September.

Junguito, Roberto, and Diego Pizano. 1997. *Instituciones e instrumentos de política cafetera en Colombia (1927–97)*. Bogotá: Fedesarrollo y Fondo Cultural Cafetero.

Kalmanovitz, Salomón. 1990. "Los gremios industriales ante la crisis." In *Al filo del caos*, ed. Francisco Leal and León Zamosc. Bogotá: Tercer Mundo Editores – Universidad Nacional de Colombia.

Kang, David. 2002. *Crony Capitalism: Corruption and Development in South Korea and the Philippines*. New York: Cambridge University Press.

Katzenstein, Peter. 1985. *Small States in World Markets: Industrial Policy in Europe*. Ithaca, NY: Cornell University Press.

Kaufman, Robert, Carlos Bazdresch, and Blanca Heredia. 1994. "Mexico: Radical Reform in a Dominant Party System." In *Voting for Reform*, ed. Stephan Haggard and Steven Webb. New York: Oxford University Press.

Keller, Wilma. 1995. *Neocorporativismo e relações de trabalho*. Textos para Discussão. São Paulo: Instituto de Estudos do Setor Público.

Key, V. O. 1952. *Politics, Parties, and Pressure Groups*. New York: Crowell.

Khanna, Tarun, and Krishna Palepu. 2000. "Is group affiliation profitable in emerging markets? An analysis of diversified Indian business groups." *Journal of Finance* 55(2) (April): 867–91.

Kim, Eui-Young. 1993. "The developmental state and the politics of business interest associations: The case of the textile industry in South Korea." *Pacific Focus* 8(2) (Fall): 31–60.

Kim, Euiyoung. 1999. "The state's authority in the organizing of the world of business: Corporatist business interest representation in South Korea." *Asian Perspective* 23(2): 285–309.

Kingstone, Peter. 1998. "Corporatism, neoliberalism, and the failed revolt of big business: Lessons from the case of IEDI." *Journal of Interamerican Studies and World Affairs* 40(4) (Winter): 73–96.

Kingstone, Peter. 1999. *Crafting Coalitions for Reform: Business Preferences, Political Institutions, and Neoliberal Reform in Brazil.* University Park; Pennsylvania State University Press.

Klein, Lúcia. 1987. "Bens de capital e estado no Brasil: A implementação do programa de eletricidade." *Revista Brasileira de Ciências Sociais* 1(3) (February): 83–101.

Kline, Harvey. 1974. "Interest groups in the Colombian Congress." *Journal of Interamerican Studies and World Affairs* 16(3) (August): 274–300.

Kline, Harvey. 1996. "Colombia." In *Constructing Democratic Governance*, ed. Jorge Domínguez and Abraham Lowenthal. Baltimore, MD: Johns Hopkins University Press.

Knoke, David. 1990. *Organizing for Collective Action: The Political Economies of Associations.* New York: Aldine de Gruyter.

Koffman, Bennett. 1969. "The National Federation of Coffee Growers of Colombia." Ph.D. Dissertation. University of Virginia.

Krasner, Stephen. 1984. "Approaches to the state." *Comparative Politics* 16(2) (January): 223–46.

Krueger, Anne. 1974. "The political economy of the rent-seeking society." *American Economic Review* 64(3) (June): 291–303.

Kuo, Cheng-Tian. 1995. *Global Competitiveness and Industrial Growth in Taiwan and the Philippines.* Pittsburgh, PA: University of Pittsburgh Press.

Lagos, Ricardo. 1961. *La concentración del poder económico: Su teoría, realidad chilena.* Santiago: Editorial del Pacífico.

Lamb, George, and Sumner Kittelle. 1956. *Trade Association Law and Practice.* Boston: Little, Brown.

Lamounier, Bolívar. 1992. "Empresários, partidos e democratização no Brasil (1974–90)." Unpublished paper. São Paulo: IDESP.

Laothamatas, Anek. 1992. *Business Associations and the New Political Economy of Thailand.* Boulder, CO: Westview Press.

La Porta, Rafael, Florencio López-de-Silanes, and Andrei Shleifer. 1999. "Corporate ownership around the world." *Journal of Finance* 54(2) (April): 471–517.

Lauterbach, Albert. 1965. "Government and development: Managerial attitudes in Latin America." *Journal of Inter-American Studies* 7(2) (April): 201–25.

Leff, Nathaniel. 1968. *Economic Policy-Making and Development in Brazil 1947–1964.* New York: Wiley.

Leff, Nathaniel. 1978. "Industrial organization and entrepreneurship in the developing countries: The economic groups." *Economic Development and Cultural Change* 26(4) (July): 661–75.

Leopoldi, M. Antonieta. 1984. "Industrial Associations and Politics in Contemporary Brazil." Ph.D. Dissertation. St. Anthony's College.

Levine, Robert. 1970. *The Vargas Regime: The Critical Years, 1934–1938.* New York: Columbia University Press.

Levy, Jonah. 1999. *Tocqueville's Revenge: State, Society, and Economy in Contemporary France.* Cambridge, MA: Harvard University Press.

Ley de Cámaras y Confederaciones Empresariales 1997. México, DF:

Lichbach, Mark. 1996. *The Cooperator's Dilemma*. Ann Arbor: University of Michigan Press.

Lindberg, Leon, John Campbell, and J. Rogers Hollingsworth. 1991. "Economic Governance and the Analysis of Structural Change in the American Economy." In *Governance of the American Economy*, ed. John Campbell, J. Rogers Hollingsworth, and Leon Lindberg. New York: Cambridge University Press.

Lindenboim, Javier. 1976. "El empresariado industrial argentino y sus organizaciones gremiales entre 1930 y 1946." *Desarrollo Económico* 26(62) (July–September): 163–201.

López Maya, Margarita, Luis Gómez Calcaño, and Thaís Maingón. 1989. *De Punto Fijo al Pacto Social: Desarrollo y hegemonía en Venezuela (1958–1985)*. Caracas: Acta Científica Venezolana.

Losada Lora, Rodrigo. 2000. *Los gremios empresariales en Colombia en los inicios del siglo XXI*. Bogotá: Pontificia Universidad Javeriana.

Lowi, Theodore. 1964. "American business, public policy, case studies, and political theory." *World Politics* 16(4) (July): 677–715.

Luján Olivera, Noemí. 2000. "La participación de las organizaciones empresariales en las negociaciones del Mercosur." Paper presented at the 50th Congress of Americanists. Warsaw, July.

Luna, Matilde. 1992. *Los empresarios y el cambio político, México 1970–1987*. México, DF: Era.

Luna, Matilde, and Ricardo Tirado. 1992. *El Consejo Coordinador Empresarial: Una Radiografía*. México, DF: UNAM.

Luna, Matilde, Ricardo Tirado, and Francisco Valdés. 1987. "Businessmen and Politics in Mexico, 1982–1986." In *Government and Private Sector in Contemporary Mexico*, ed. Sylvia Maxfield and Ricardo Anzaldúa Montoya. San Diego, CA: Center for U.S.-Mexican Studies.

Lustig, Nora. 1992. *Mexico: The Remaking of an Economy*. Washington, DC: Brookings Institution Press.

MacIntyre, Andrew. 1994. *Business and Government in Industrialising Asia*. Ithaca, NY: Cornell University Press.

Mahon, James. 2003. "Reforms in the Administration of Justice in Latin America: Comparative Overview and Emerging Trends." In *Reinventing Leviathan*, ed. Ben Ross Schneider and Blanca Heredia. Miami: North-South Center Press.

Mainwaring, Scott. 1986. "The state and the industrial bourgeoisie in Perón's Argentina, 1945–1955." *Studies in Comparative International Development* 21(3) (Fall): 3–31.

Mainwaring, Scott. 1999. *Rethinking Party Systems in the Third Wave of Democratization: The Case of Brazil*. Stanford, CA: Stanford University Press.

Mallon, Richard, and Juan Sourrille. 1975. *Economic Policy Making in a Conflict Society: The Argentine Case*. Cambridge, MA: Harvard University Press.

Mamalakis, Markos. 1969. "An analysis of the financial and investment activities of the Chilean development corporation, 1939–1964." *Journal of Development Studies* 5(2) (January): 118–37.

Manzetti, Luigi. 1990. "Argentine–Brazilian economic integration." *Latin American Research Review* 25(3): 109–40.

Manzetti, Luigi. 1993–4. "The political economy of Mercosur." *Journal of Interamerican Studies and World Affairs* 35 (Winter): 101–41.

Manzetti, Luigi. 1993. *Institutions, Parties, and Coalitions in Argentine Politics*. Pittsburgh, PA: University of Pittsburgh Press.

Mares, David. 1993. "State leadership in economic policy: A collective action framework with a Colombian case." *Comparative Politics* 25(4) (July): 455–73.

Martin, Cathie Jo. 1991. *Shifting the Burden: The Struggle over Growth and Corporate Taxation*. Chicago: University of Chicago Press.

Martínez, Leonardo, and Ben Ross Schneider. 2001. "Gatekeeper of influence: The Mexican state and agroindustry in the NAFTA negotiations." *Canadian Journal of Latin American and Caribbean Studies* 26(51) 83–119.

Maxfield, Sylvia. 1987. "Introduction." In *Government and Private Sector in Contemporary Mexico*, ed. Sylvia Maxfield and Ricardo Anzaldúa Montoya. San Diego, CA: Center for U.S.-Mexican Studies.

Maxfield, Sylvia. 1990. *Governing Capital: International Finance and Mexican Politics*. Ithaca, NY: Cornell University Press.

McCleary, Rachel. 1999. *Dictating Democracy: Guatemala and the End of Violent Revolution*. Gainesville: University Press of Florida.

Meller, Patricio, and Rodrigo Donoso. 1998. *La industria chilena y Mercosur*. Santiago: Dolmen.

Mendez, José. 1993. "The Development of the Colombian Cut Flower Industry." In *Antidumping*, ed. J. Michael Finger. Ann Arbor: University of Michigan Press.

Menges, Constantine. 1966. "Public policy and organized business in Chile." *Journal of International Affairs* 20(2): 343–65.

Messner, Dirk. 1993. "Shaping Industrial Competitiveness in Chile: The Case of the Chilean Wood-processing Industry." In *International Competitiveness in Latin America and East Asia*, ed. Klaus Esser, Wolfgang Hillebrand, Dirk Messner, and Jörg Meyer-Stamer. London: Frank Cass.

Middlebrook, Kevin. 2000. "Introduction." In *Conservative Parties, the Right, and Democracy in Latin America*, ed. Kevin Middlebrook. Baltimore, MD: Johns Hopkins University Press.

Miller, Gary. 1997. "The impact of economics on contemporary political science." *Journal of Economic Literature* 35 (September): 1173–204.

Minella, Ary. 1988. *Banqueiros: Organização e poder político no Brasil*. Rio de Janeiro: Espaço e Tempo/ANPOCS.

Ministério da Fazenda. 1994. "Avaliação das câmaras setoriais." Unpublished report. Brasília, DF.

Mizrahi, Yemile. 1994. "A New Conservative Opposition in Mexico: The Politics of Entrepreneurs in Chihuahua, 1983–92." Ph.D. Dissertation. University of California, Berkeley.

Monteiro, Jorge Vianna, and Luiz Azevedo Cunha. 1974. "Alguns aspectos da evolução do planejamento econômico no Brasil, 1934–63." *Pesquisa e Planejamento Econômico* 4(1) (February): 1–24.

Montero, Alfred. 2001. "Making and remaking 'good government' in Brazil: subnational industrial policy in Minas Gerais." *Latin American Politics and Society* 43(2) (Summer): 49–80.

Moore, Barrington. 1966. *Social Origins of Dictatorship and Democracy*. Boston: Beacon Press.

Moore, Pete. 2002. "Rentier fiscal crisis and regime stability in the Middle East: Business and the state in the Gulf." *Studies in Comparative International Development* 37(1) (Spring): 34–57.

Mosk, Sanford. 1950. *Industrial Revolution in Mexico*. Berkeley: University of California Press.

Motta, Fernando. 1979. *Empresários e hegemonia política*. São Paulo: Brasilense.

Moulian, Tomás, and Isabel Torres. 1986. "La derecha en Chile: Evolución histórica y proyecciones a futuro." *Estudios Sociales* 47 63–118.

Muñoz, Oscar. 1986. "El papel de los empresarios en el desarrollo." *Estudios Cieplan* 20 (December): 95–120.

Muñoz, Oscar, ed. 2000. *El Estado y el Sector Privado*. Santiago: Dolmen.

Naim, Moisés. 1993. *Paper Tigers and Minotaurs: The Politics of Venezuela's Economic Reforms*. Washington, DC: Carnegie Endowment.

Naím, Moisés, and Antonio Francés. 1995. "The Venezuelan Private Sector: From Courting the State to Courting the Market." In *Lessons of the Venezuelan Experience*, ed. Louis Goodman. Baltimore, MD: Johns Hopkins University Press.

Niosi, Jorge. 1974. *Los empresarios y el Estado argentino (1955–1969)*. Buenos Aires: Siglo Veintiuno.

Niosi, Jorge. 1976. *Les entrepreneurs dans la politique Argentine, 1955–73*. Montréal: Les Presses de l'Université du Québec.

Noble, Gregory. 1998. *Collective Action in East Asia: How Ruling Parties Shape Industrial Policy*. Ithaca, NY: Cornell University Press.

O'Connell, Brian. 1999. *Civil Society: The Underpinnings of American Democracy*. Hanover, NH: University Press of New England.

O'Donnell, Guillermo. 1978. "State and alliances in Argentina, 1956–1976." *Journal of Development Studies* 15(1) (October): 3–33.

O'Donnell, Guillermo. 1988. *Bureaucratic Authoritarianism: Argentina, 1966–1973, in Comparative Perspective*. Berkeley: University of California Press.

O'Donnell, Guillermo. 1993. "On the state, democratization and some conceptual problems." *World Development* 21(8): 1355–69.

Offe, Claus. 1995. "Some Skeptical Considerations on the Malleability of Representative Institutions." In *Associations and Democracy*, ed. Joshua Cohen and Joel Rogers. London: Verso.

Olsen, Johan. 1981. "Integrated Organizational Participation in Government." In *Handbook of Organizational Design*, ed. Paul Nystrom and William Starbuck. Oxford: Oxford University Press.

Olson, Mancur. 1965. *The Logic of Collective Action*. Cambridge, MA: Harvard University Press.

Olson, Mancur. 1982. *The Rise and Decline of Nations*. New Haven, CT: Yale University Press.

Olson, Mancur. 1986. "A theory of the incentives facing political organizations: Neo-corporatism and the hegemonic state." *International Political Science Review* 7(2) (April): 165–89.

Ortega, Juan Manuel. 2002. "Institutions and Economic Reform in Mexico: The Case of Economic Pacts, 1987–1997." Ph.D. Dissertation. Boston University.

Ortega, Juan Manuel. 2003. "Instituciones, inercias y el 'error' de diciembre." Unpublished paper.

Ortiz Rivera, Alicia. 1997. *Juan Sánchez Navarro*. México, DF: Grijalbo.

Ortiz Rivera, Alicia. 1998. "Consejo Mexicano de Hombres de Negocios." Masters thesis. Mexico City: Instituto Mora.

Ospina Pérez, Mariano. 1968. "La Federación, su origen y su desarrollo." *Revista Cafetera de Colombia* 17(143) (March–April): 23–31.

Osterling, Jorge. 1989. *Democracy in Colombia: Clientelist Politics and Guerilla Warfare*. New Brunswick, NJ: Transaction.

Ostiguy, Pierre. 1990. *Los capitanes de la industria: Grandes empresarios, política y economía en la Argentina de los años 80*. Buenos Aires: Legasa.

Palacios, Marco. 1980. *Coffee in Colombia, 1850–1970*. Cambridge: Cambridge University Press.

Palomino, Mirta de. 1987. "Tradición y poder: La Sociedad Rural Argentina, 1955–83." Buenos Aires: CISEA.

Pastor, Manuel, and Carol Wise. 1994. "The Origins and Sustainability of Mexico's Free Trade Policy." *International Organization* 48(3) (Summer): 459–89.

Payne, Leigh. 1990. "Pragmatic Actors: The Political Attitudes and Behavior of Brazilian Industrial Elites." Ph.D. Dissertation. Yale University.

Payne, Leigh. 1994. *Brazilian Industrialists and Democratic Change*. Baltimore, MD: Johns Hopkins University Press.

Pécaut, Daniel. 1979. "La constitution des *gremios* en instance quasi-gouvernementale: l'exemple colombien dans les années 1945–1950." *Revue Française d'Histoire d'Outre-Mer* 66(244–5): 331–41.

Petras, James, and Thomas Cook. 1972. "Componentes de la acción política: El ejecutivo industrial argentino." *Desarrollo Económico* 12 (July–September): 387–96.

Pfeifer, Alberto, and Amâncio Jorge de Oliveira. 2000. "Third Generation Private Sector: The Latin American Business Council (CEAL) and Its Role in Promoting Regional Integration in Latin America." Paper presented at the meetings of the International Political Science Association. Quebec, August.

Picciotto, Robert. 1995. *Putting Institutional Economics to Work: From Participation to Governance*. World Bank Discussion Papers 304. Washington, DC.

Pinto, Anibal. 1985. "Estado y gran empresa: De la precrisis hasta el gobierno de Jorge Alessandri." *Colección Estudios CIEPLAN* 16 (June): 5–40.

Polit, Gustavo. 1968. "The Industrialists of Argentina." In *Latin America*, ed. James Petras and Maurice Zeitlin. New York: Fawcett.

Porras Martínez, José Ignacio. 2000. "Reformas estructurales, institucionalidad y dilemas en la acción colectiva del empresariado agrícola en Brasil." Unpublished manuscript. Santiago de Chile.

Poveda Ramos, Gabriel. 1984. *Andi y la industria en Colombia, 1944–1984*. Medellín: Andi.

Puga, Cristina. 1994. "Las organizaciones empresariales en la negociación del Tratado de Libre Comercio." In *Los Empresarios ante la Globalización*, ed. Ricardo Tirado. Mexico, DF: UNAM.

Putnam, Robert. 1993. *Making Democracy Work: Civic Traditions in Modern Italy*. Princeton, NJ: Princeton University Press.

Rabellotti, Roberta. 1998. *Recovery of a Mexican Cluster: Devaluation Bonanza or Collective Efficiency?* Working Paper 71. University of Sussex: Institute of Development Studies, Brighton.

Rehren, Alfredo. 1995. "Empresarios, transición y consolidación democrática en Chile." *Revista de Ciencia Política* 27(1–2): 5–61.

Remmer, Karen. 1993. "Democratization in Latin America." In *Global Transformation and the Third World*, ed. Robert Slater, Barry Schutz and Steven Dorr. Boulder, CO: Lynne Rienner.

Rettberg, Beatriz Angelika. 2000. "Corporate Organization and the Failure of Collective Action: Colombian Business during the Presidency of Ernesto Samper (1994–1998)." Ph.D. Dissertation. Boston University.

Revéiz Roldán, Edgar. 1981. "La concertación: Experiencias y posibilidades en Colombia." In *Controversia sobre el Plan de Integración Nacional*, ed. Edgar Revéiz, Fernando Cepeda Ulloa, and Juan Martín Caicedo Ferré. Bogotá: Universidad de los Andes.

Rock, David. 1985. *Argentina 1516–1982.* Berkeley: University of California Press.

Rodríguez Vargas, Francisco. 1997a. "Las organizaciones del sector cafetero colombiano." In *Lecturas críticas de administración*, ed. Eduardo Sáenz Rovner. Bogotá: Siglo del Hombre.

Rodríguez Vargas, Francisco. 1997b. "Relaciones de poder y estructura de decisiones del gremio cafetero colombiano." *Innovar* 10 (July–December): 66–92.

Roxborough, Ian. 1992. "Inflation and social pacts in Brazil and Mexico." *Journal of Latin American Studies* 24(3) (October): 639–64.

Rueschemeyer, Dietrich, Evelyne Huber Stephens, and John Stephens. 1992. *Capitalist Development and Democracy.* Cambridge: Polity.

Sáenz Rovner, Eduardo. 1992. *La ofensiva empresarial: Industriales, políticos y violencia en los años 40 en Colombia.* Bogotá: Tercer Mundo.

Sáenz Rovner, Eduardo. 2002. *Colombia años 50: industriales, política y diplomacia.* Bogotá: Universidad Nacional de Colombia.

Saes, Maria Sylvia. 1997. *A racionalização econômica da regulamentação no mercardo brasileiro de café.* São Paulo: Annablume.

Sánchez Navarro, Juan. 1996. "El empresario mexicano en transformación." Presentation to the Unión Social de Empresarios de México.

Sandler, Todd. 1992. *Collective Action.* Ann Arbor: University of Michigan Press.

Santos, Wanderley dos. 1986. *Sessenta e quatro: Anatomia da crise.* São Paulo: Vértice.

Sargent, John. 2001. "Getting to know the Neighbors: Grupos in Mexico." *Business Horizons* 44(6) (November–December): 16–25.

Schamis, Hector. 2002. *Re-Forming the State: The Politics of Privatization in Latin America and Europe.* Ann Arbor: University of Michigan Press.

Schmitter, Philippe. 1971. *Interest Conflict and Political Change in Brazil.* Stanford, CA: Stanford University Press.

Schmitter, Philippe. 1974. "Still the century of corporatism?" *Review of Politics* 36(1) (January): 85–121.

Schmitter, Philippe. 1985. "Neo-corporatism and the State." In *The Political Economy of Corporatism*, ed. Wyn Grant. New York: St. Martin's Press.

Schmitter, Philippe. 1992. "The consolidation of democracy and the representation of social groups." *American Behavioral Scientist* 35(4/5) (March–June): 422–49.

Schmitter, Philippe. 1995a. "The Irony of Modern Democracy and the Viability of Efforts to Reform its Practice." In *Associations and Democracy*, ed. Joshua Cohen and Joel Rogers. London: Verso.

Schmitter, Philippe. 1995b. "Organized Interests and Democratic Consolidation in Southern Europe." In *The Politics of Democratic Consolidation*, ed. Richard Gunther, Nikiforos Diamandouros, and Hans-Jürgen Puhle. Baltimore, MD: Johns Hopkins University Press.

Schmitter, Philippe, and Jurgen Grote. 1997. "Der korporatistische Sisyphus: Vergangenheit, Gegenwart und Zukunft." *Politische Vierteljahresschrift* 38(3): 530–54.

Schmitter, Philippe, and Wolfgang Streeck. 1999. [originally distributed in 1981]. "The Organization of Business Interests: Studying the Associative Action of Business in Advanced Industrial Societies." Cologne: MPIfG Discussion Paper 99/1.

Schneider, Ben Ross. 1991a. "Brazil under Collor: Anatomy of a crisis." *World Policy Journal* 8(2) (Spring): 321–47.

Schneider, Ben Ross. 1991b. *Politics within the State: Elite Bureaucrats and Industrial Policy in Authoritarian Brazil*. Pittsburgh, PA: University of Pittsburgh Press.

Schneider, Ben Ross. 1997–8. "Organized business politics in democratic Brazil." *Journal of Interamerican Studies and World Affairs* 39(4) (Winter): 95–127.

Schneider, Ben Ross. 1997. "Big Business and the Politics of Economic Reform: Confidence and Concertation in Brazil and Mexico." In *Business and the State in Developing Countries*, ed. Sylvia Maxfield and Ben Ross Schneider. Ithaca, NY: Cornell University Press.

Schneider, Ben Ross. 1998a. "Elusive synergy: Business–government relations and development." *Comparative Politics* 31(1) (October): 101–22.

Schneider, Ben Ross. 1998b. "The Material Bases of Technocracy: Investor Confidence and Neoliberalism in Latin America." In *The Politics of Expertise in Latin America*, ed. Miguel Centeno and Patricio Silva. London: Macmillan.

Schneider, Ben Ross. 1999. "The Desarrollista State in Brazil and Mexico." In *The Developmental State*, ed. Meredith Woo-Cumings. Ithaca, NY: Cornell University Press.

Schneider, Ben Ross. 2001. "Business Politics and Regional Integration: The Advantages of Organization in NAFTA and MERCOSUR." In *Regional Integration in Latin America and the Caribbean: The Political Economy of Open Regionalism*, ed. Victor Bulmer-Thomas. London: Institute for Latin American Studies.

Schneider, Ben Ross. 2002. "Why is Mexican business so organized?" *Latin American Research Review* 37(1): 77–118.

Schvarzer, Jorge. 1991. *Empresarios del pasado: La Unión Industrial Argentina*. Buenos Aires: Cisea/Imago Munid.

Schvarzer, Jorge, and Ricardo Sidicaro. 1988. "Empresarios y Estado en la reconstrucción de la democracia en Argentina." In *Empresarios y Estado en America Latina*, ed. Celso Garrido. México: CIDE.

Schwartz, Frank. 1992. "Of Fairy Cloaks and Familiar Talks: The Politics of Consultation." In *Political Dynamics in Contemporary Japan*, ed. Gary Allinson and Yasunori Sone. Ithaca, NY: Cornell University Press.

Seoane, María. 1998. *El burgués maldito: La historia secreta de José Ber Gelbard*. Buenos Aires: Planeta.

Sguiglia, Eduardo. 1988. *Los grandes grupos industriales en la Argentina actual*. Buenos Aires: Centro Editor de America Latina.

Shadlen, Kenneth. 2000. "Neoliberalism, corporatism, and small business political activism in contemporary Mexico." *Latin American Research Review* 35(2): 73–106.

Shadlen, Kenneth. In press. *Democratization Without Representation: The Politics of Small Industry in Mexico*. College Park, PA: Pennsylvania State University Press.

Shafer, D. Michael. 1994. *Winners and Losers: How Sectors Shape the Developmental Prospects of States*. Ithaca, NY: Cornell University Press.

Shafer, Robert. 1973. *Mexican Business Organizations*. Syracuse, NY: Syracuse University Press.

Shils, Edward. 1991. "The virtue of civil society." *Government and Opposition* 26(1) (Winter): 3–20.

Shonfield, Andrew. 1965. *Modern Capitalism*. London: Oxford University Press.

Sikkink, Kathryn. 1991. *Ideas and Institutions: Developmentalism in Brazil and Argentina*. Ithaca, NY: Cornell University Press.

Silva, Eduardo. 1996. *The State and Capital in Chile: Business Elites, Technocrats, and Market Economics*. Boulder CO: Westview.

Silva, Eduardo. 1997. "Business Elites, the State, and Economic Change in Chile." In *Business and the State in Developing Countries*, ed. Sylvia Maxfield and Ben Ross Schneider. Ithaca, NY: Cornell University Press.

Silva, Eduardo. 1998. "Business Associations, Neoliberal Economic Restructuring, and Redemocratization in Chile." In *Organized Business, Economic Change, and Democracy in Latin America*, ed. Francisco Durand and Eduardo Silva. Miami: North-South Center Press.

Silva, Eduardo. 2002. "State–Business Relations in Latin America." In *Emerging Market Democracies*, ed. Laurence Whitehead. Baltimore, MD: Johns Hopkins University Press.

Silva, Patricio. 1995. "Empresarios, neoliberalismo y transición democrática en Chile." *Revista Mexicana de Sociología* 57(4) (October–December): 3–25.

Skidmore, Thomas. 1967. *Politics in Brazil, 1930–1964*. New York: Oxford University Press.

Skidmore, Thomas. 1988. *The Politics of Military Rule in Brazil, 1964–85*. New York: Oxford University Press.

Skocpol, Theda. 1985. "Bringing the State Back In: Strategies of Analysis in Current Research." In *Bringing the State Back In*, ed. Peter Evans, Dietrich Rueschemeyer, and Theda Skocpol. New York: Cambridge University Press.

Skocpol, Theda. 1999a. "How Americans Became Civic." In *Civic Engagement in American Democracy*, ed. Theda Skocpol and Moris Fiorina. Washington, DC: Brookings Institution Press.

Skocpol, Theda. 1999b. "Advocates without Members: The Recent Transformation of American Civic Life." In *Civic Engagement in American Democracy*, ed. Theda Skocpol and Moris Fiorina. Washington, DC: Brookings Institution Press.

Smith, Peter. 1969. *Politics and Beef in Argentina*. New York: Columbia University Press.

Smith, Peter. 1974. *Argentina and the Failure of Democracy: Conflict Among Political Elites 1904–1955*. Madison: University of Wisconsin Press.

Snyder, Richard. 2001. *Politics after Neoliberalism: Reregulation in Mexico*. New York: Cambridge University Press.

Soares, Gláucio Ary Dillon. 1975. "O Novo Estado na América Latina." *Estudos CEBRAP* 13 (July–September): 55–77.

Sofofa. 2002. *Memoria anual 2001–2002*. Santiago: Sociedad de Fomento Fabril.

Spalding, Rose. 1998. "Revolution and the Hyperpoliticized Business Peak Association: Nicaragua and el Consejo Superior de la Empresa Privada." In *Organized Business, Economic Change, and Democracy in Latin America*, ed. Francisco Durand and Eduardo Silva. Miami: North-South Center Press.

SRA. 1999. *Anales*. Buenos Aires: Sociedad Rural Argentina.

Stallings, Barbara. 1978. *Class Conflict and Economic Development in Chile, 1958–1973*. Stanford, CA: Stanford University Press.

Stallings, Barbara, and Wilson Peres. 2000. *Growth, Employment, and Equity: The Impact of the Economic Reforms in Latin America and the Caribbean*. Washington, DC: Brookings Institution Press.

Stepan, Alfred. 1971. *The Military in Politics: Changing Patterns in Brazil*. Princeton, NJ: Princeton University Press.

Stepan, Alfred. 1978. "Political Leadership and Regime Breakdown: Brazil." In *The Breakdown of Democratic Regimes*, ed. Juan Linz and Alfred Stepan. Baltimore, MD: Johns Hopkins University Press.

Stepan, Alfred. 2001. *Arguing Comparative Politics*. New York: Oxford University Press.

Story, Dale. 1982. "Trade politics in the third world: A case study of the Mexican GATT decision." *International Organization* 36(4) (Autumn): 767–94.

Story, Dale. 1983. "Industrial elites in Mexico: Political ideology and influence." *Journal of Interamerican Studies and World Affairs* 25(3) (August): 351–76.

Story, Dale. 1986. *Industry, the State and Public Policy in Mexico*. Austin: University of Texas Press.

Story, Dale. 1987. "The PAN, the Private Sector, and the Future of the Mexican Opposition." In *Mexican Politics in Transition*, ed. Judith Gentleman. Boulder, CO: Westview Press.

Teichman, Judith. 1981. "Interest conflict and entrepreneurial support for Perón." *Latin American Research Review* 16(1): 144–55.

Tendler, Judith. 1997. *Good Government in the Tropics*. Baltimore, MD: Johns Hopkins University Press.

Thacker, Strom. 2000. *Big Business, the State, and Free Trade: Constructing Coalitions in Mexico*. Cambridge: Cambridge University Press.

Thelen, Kathleen. 2002. "How Institutions Evolve: Insights from Comparative-Historical Analysis." In *Comparative Historical Analysis in the Social Sciences*, ed.

James Mahoney and Dietrich Rueschemeyer. New York: Cambridge University Press.

Thelen, Kathleen, and Sven Steinmo. 1992. "Historical Institutionalism in Comparative Politics." In *Historical Institutionalism in Comparative Politics*, ed. Kathleen Thelen, Sven Steinmo, and Frank Longstreth. Cambridge: Cambridge University Press.

Thomson, Ken. 2001. *From Neighborhood to Nation: The Democratic Foundations of Civil Society*. Hanover, NH: University Press of New England.

Thorp, Rosemary. 1991. *Economic Management and Economic Development in Peru and Colombia*. Pittsburgh, PA: University of Pittsburgh Press.

Thorp, Rosemary. 2002. "Has the Coffee Federation become Redundant? Collective Action and the Market in Colombian Development." In *Group Behavior and Economic Development*, ed. Judith Heyer, Frances Stewart, and Rosemary Thorp. Oxford: Oxford University Press.

Thorp, Rosemary, and Francisco Durand. 1997. "A Historical View of Business–State Relations: Colombia, Peru, and Venezuela Compared." In *Business and the State in Developing Countries*, ed. Sylvia Maxfield and Ben Ross Schneider. Ithaca, NY: Cornell University Press.

Tirado, Ricardo, ed. 1994. *Los Empresarios ante la Globalización*. México, DF: UNAM.

Tirado, Ricardo. 1998. "Mexico." In *Organized Business, Economic Change, and Democracy in Latin America*, ed. Francisco Durand and Silva Eduardo. Miami: North-South Center Press.

Tocqueville, Alexis de. 1956. *Democracy in America*. New York: New American Library.

Toledo, Celso de Campos. 1994. "Avaliação dos acordos setoriais automobilísticos." Masters thesis, Fundação Getúlio Vargas, São Paulo.

Toledo, Roberto. 1992. "A pirâmide e o vazio." *Veja*, 29 July.

Traxler, Franz, and Brigritte Unger. 1994. "Governance, economic restructuring, and international competitiveness." *Journal of Economic Issues* 28(1) (March): 1–23.

Trevisan, Maria José. 1986. *50 Anos em 5: A Fiesp e o desenvolvimentismo*. Petrópolis: Vozes.

UNCTAD. 2002. *Handbook of Statistics*. New York: United Nations.

Urrutia, Miguel. 1983. *Gremios, política económica y democracia*. Bogotá: Fondo Cultural Cafetero.

Valdés Ugalde, Francisco. 1996. "The Private Sector and Political Regime Change in Mexico." In *Neoliberalism Revisited*, ed. Gerardo Otero. Boulder, CO: Westview.

Valdés Ugalde, Francisco. 1998. *Autonomia y legitimidad: Los empresarios, la política y el Estado en México*. México, DF: Siglo XXI.

Vera Azargado, Héctor. 1998. "Duelo minero." *Qué Pasa* (online version www.quepasa.cl/revista/1424/22.html).

Vernon, Raymond. 1963. *The Dilemma of Mexico's Development: The Roles of the Private and Public Sectors*. Cambridge, MA: Harvard University Press.

Vianna, Maria Lúcia Teixeira. 1987. *A Administração do milagre: O Conselho Monetário Nacional, 1964–1974*. Petrópolis: Vozes.

Villegas Echeverri, Luis Carlos. 1996. "La Andi al servicio del país." *Revista ANDI* 142 (September–October): 3–19.

Waarden, Franz van. 1991. "Two Logics of Collective Action?" In *Employers' Associations in Europe*, ed. Dieter Sadowski and Otto Jacobi. Baden-Baden: Nomos.

Waisman, Carlos. 1987. *Reversal of Development in Argentina*. Princeton, NJ: Princeton University Press.

Wallerstein, Michael. 1989. "Union organization in advanced industrial democracies." *American Political Science Review* 83(2) (June): 481–501.

Weinstein, Barbara. 1990. "The industrialists, the state, and the issues of worker training and social services in Brazil, 1930–50." *Hispanic American Historical Review* 70(3): 379–404.

Weinstein, Barbara. 1995. "Industrialists, the State, and the Limits of Democratization in Brazil, 1930–1964." In *The Social Construction of Democracy, 1870–1990*, ed. George Reid Andrews and Herrick Chapman. New York: New York University Press.

Weinstein, Barbara. 1996. *For Social Peace in Brazil: Industrialists and the Remaking of the Working Class in São Paulo, 1920–1964*. Chapel Hill: University of North Carolina Press.

Weyland, Kurt. 1996. *Democracy without Equity: Failures of Reform in Brazil*. Pittsburgh, PA: University of Pittsburgh Press.

Weyland, Kurt. 1997. "'Growth with equity' in Chile's new democracy?" *Latin American Research Review* 32(1): 37–68.

Whittington, Keith. 2001. "Revisting Tocqueville's America: Society, Politics, and Association in the Nineteenth Century." In *Beyond Tocqueville*, ed. Bob Edwards, Michael Foley, and Mario Diani. Hanover, NH: University Press of New England.

Wilson, Frank. 1983. "French interest group politics: Pluralist or neocorporatist?" *American Political Science Review* 77(4) (December): 895–910.

Wilson, Graham. 1981. *Interest Groups in the United States*. Oxford: Clarendon Press.

Wirth, John. 1970. *The Politics of Brazilian Development, 1930–54*. Stanford, CA: Stanford University Press.

Wise, Carol. 1999. "Latin American trade strategy at century's end." *Business and Politics* 1(2) (August): 117–54.

Wood, Duncan. 2000. "Business Associations, Regional Integration and Systemic Shocks: The Case of the ABM in Mexico." In *Organized Business and the New Global Order*, ed. Justin Greenwood and Henry Jacek. Houndmills, England: Macmillan.

World Bank. 1991. *Colombia: Industrial Competition and Performance*. Washington, DC: World Bank.

World Bank. 1997. *World Development Report: The State in a Changing World*. New York: Oxford University Press.

World Bank. 2002. *World Development Report 2002: Building Institutions for Markets*. New York: Oxford University Press.

Wright, Thomas. 1982. *Landowners and Reform in Chile: The Sociedad Nacional de Agricultura 1919–40*. Urbana: University of Illinois Press.

Zakaria, Fareed. 1997. "The rise of illiberal democracy." *Foreign Affairs* 76(6) (November–December): 22–43.

Zeitlin, Maurice, and Richard Ratcliff. 1988. *Landlords and Capitalists: The Dominant Class of Chile*. Princeton, NJ: Princeton University Press.

Zuckerman, Leo. 1990. "Inflation Stabilization in Mexico: The Economic Solidarity Pact." M.Sc. Thesis. Oxford University.

Index